A

STATISTICAL VIEW

OF THE

COMMERCE

OF THE

UNITED STATES

BY

TIMOTHY PITKIN

[1816]

REPRINTS OF ECONOMIC CLASSICS

AUGUSTUS M. KELLEY · PUBLISHERS
NEW YORK · 1967

FIRST EDITION 1816

(Hartford: Charles Hosmer, 1816)

Reprinted 1967 by

Augustus M. Kelley · Publishers

Library of Congress Catalogue Card Number

65-26374

PRINTED IN THE UNITED STATES OF AMERICA

by SENTRY PRESS, NEW YORK, N. Y. 10019

A

STATISTICAL VIEW

OF THE

COMMERCE

OF THE

UNITED STATES OF AMERICA:

ITS CONNECTION WITH

AGRICULTURE AND MANUFACTURES:

AND AN ACCOUNT OF THE

PUBLIC DEBT, REVENUES, AND EXPENDITURES

OF THE

UNITED STATES.

WITH A BRIEF REVIEW OF THE TRADE, AGRICULTURE, AND
MANUFACTURES OF THE COLONIES, PREVIOUS TO
THEIR INDEPENDENCE.

*ACCOMPANIED WITH TABLES, ILLUSTRATIVE OF THE
PRINCIPLES AND OBJECTS OF THE WORK.*

===

BY TIMOTHY PITKIN,

A MEMBER OF THE HOUSE OF REPRESENTATIVES OF THE UNITED STATES,
FROM THE STATE OF CONNECTICUT.

===

HARTFORD:

PRINTED BY CHARLES HOSMER.

....

1816.

ADVERTISEMENT.

THE greater part of the following collection of tables and facts was made without any view to publication. Being shewn to some of our friends, they thought it would be useful, that additions should be made to it, of other important tables, relative to the same subject, scattered through a mass of public documents, which few possessed, or were able to procure, without great expense; and that the whole, in a condensed form, should be presented to the public.

Influenced, in no small degree, by their wishes and opinions, we consented to the undertaking. The original plan was enlarged, by adding a brief review of the state of the Colonies, relative to commerce, agriculture, and manufactures, previous to their independence.

Statistical enquiries have been less the subject of attention in America, than in Europe. During the last fifty years, many statistical works have appeared, giving particular accounts of the power, wealth and resources of most of the European nations.

As the United States have been considered, and justly so, as the second commercial nation in the world, it cannot be uninteresting to every American citizen, to become acquainted with the facts, tending to shew, that they are entitled to this rank.

That enquiries of this nature are useful and important, in many respects, is acknowledged by all, who have attended to them. They are particularly so, to merchants, and to all, who are concerned, in the management of national affairs: and every individual must feel an interest, in obtaining a knowledge of the wealth and resources of his own country.

As necessarily connected with the subject of our enquiry, we have given a view of the public debt, revenues, and expenditures, from the commencement of the government, to as late a period as we were able, from official documents, to which we had access.   The public debt is brought down to the 20th of February, A. D. 1815, when it was ascertained to be, about one hundred and eight millions of dollars.   From late official documents, it appears, that up to the 1st of October following, it had increased, to about one hundred and twenty millions.

The following collection, therefore, may be resorted to, by all, who may wish to be acquainted with the exports and imports of the United States, and the *quantity* and *value* of the various articles exported and imported, with the general commerce of the United States, and the amount of their trade with particular nations, with the amount of their tonnage, public debt, revenues, and expenditures, at different periods, since the establishment of the present government.

We have added, by way of appendix, an account of the coinage of the extensive kingdom of New-Spain, which adjoins the U. States on the West, and an authentic sketch of its commerce, in 1810, particularly that part carried on from the port of La Vera Cruz, on the Gulph of Mexico ; also a statistical view of the finances, trade, and commerce of Great-Britain and Ireland, from 1804 to 1813, which was laid before Parliament, in July, 1813, in the form of resolutions, by the Chancellor of the Exchequer.

Many of the tables, in this collection, were obtained directly from the Treasury books, and have never been published ; and great pains have been taken, that the tables and calculations should be correct.   In such a number of figures and calculations, however, some errors will, probably, be found.   It is hoped, they will be few and unimportant.

In making the collection, we have aimed at fidelity and impartiality ; and in presenting it to the public, our object is, to give, as far as the subject admits, a condensed and connected view of the wealth and resources of the American nation at different periods.   Should it meet the approbation of the public, and serve, in some degree, to lay the foundation of more extensive and useful enquiries on the subject, in future, we shall be satisfied.   JANUARY, 1816.

CONTENTS.

———

CHAPTER I.

CHAPTER II.

CHAPTER III.

CHAPTER IV.

CHAPTER V.

EXPORTS OF FOREIGN PRODUCE.

CONTENTS

OF THE TABLES ANNEXED TO THE CHAPTERS.

CHAPTER I.

CHAPTER III.

CHAPTER IV.

CHAPTER I.

A SPIRIT of commercial enterprise led to the discovery and settlement of America—Policy of the European nations with respect to their American Colonies—Trade of the Colonies restricted at different periods—Report of the Board of Trade, concerning the trade and manufactures of the Colonists, in the year 1731-2—Colonies restricted in some manufactures—Bounties given on the importation of certain articles into England, the produce of the Colonies—Population, exports, and imports at different periods—Plan of union agreed upon, by Commissioners from several Colonies—Tonnage and vessels built in the Colonies about the year 1770.

A SPIRIT of commercial enterprise, which prevailed in the 14th century, and a desire to find a new route, to the wealth of India, led to the important discovery of the western Continent. The new race of beings which inhabited the new world, as it was called, excited the curiosity of all Europe ; and the valuable productions found there, particularly the vast quantities of the precious metals, soon interested most of the commercial nations in that quarter of the old world. Individuals, as well as governments, were solicitous to share in the advantages of this discovery ; and numerous adventures, both public and private, were set on foot, some for the purpose of further discoveries and conquest, and others for the purpose of trade and commerce. The Spaniards, the English, the French, the Portuguese, the Dutch, and the Danes and Swedes, at different periods, in consequence of prior discoveries or settlements, had claims, more or less extensive, to different parts of the western Continent. The avarice of Henry VII. of England, prompted him to employ the Cabots, in the discovery of the northern part of the Continent, which was afterwards called North-America.

In consequence of the discoveries made by these bold navigators, almost the whole of North-America was claimed by him, and at subsequent periods, was by his successors granted, from the 48th to the 29th degree of north latitude, and in extent, from the Atlantic to the South-Sea.

Under these various grants, at different periods, the North-American Colonies were settled, and principally from the enterprise of individuals.

The Colonies, thus settled by emigrations from Europe, were considered as a part, or rather an appendage of the nation, from which they originated, and under whose patronage they were settled. But a new kind of policy, which has been called a colonial policy, was adopted respecting them, by all the European nations; a policy, which had for its object, the particular interest and prosperity of the parent country, without much regard to the interest and prosperity of the Colonies themselves. The trade and commerce of the Colonies was generally confined to the parent country. The right of trading with their Colonies was, by some of the European nations, granted exclusively to particular companies. By others, the colonial trade was limited to particular ports, and afterwards to particular ships, called registered ships. The policy of Great-Britan, though generally more liberal than any other European nation, has always been, to secure to herself the carriage of the produce of her Colonies, to monopolize their raw materials, and to furnish the Colonists, with all the manufactures or other imported articles they consume. Lord Sheffield, in his " Observations or American commerce" says, " the only use and advantage of American Colonies, or West-India islands, is the monopoly of their consumption, and the carriage of their produce." In pursuance of this policy, as early as 1660, in the celebrated act of Parliament, entitled " An Act for the encouraging and increasing of shipping and navigation," it is enacted (Chap. 18,) " That from and after the 1st day of April 1661, no " sugars, tobacco, cotton-wool, indigo, ginger, fustick, or other dying woods, of the growth, produce, or manufacture of any English Plantations in America, Asia, or Africa, shall be shipped, carried, conveyed, or transported from any of the said English Plantations, to any land, island, territory, dominion, port or place whatsoever, other than to such other English Plantations as do belong to his Majesty, his heirs and successors, or to the Kingdom of England or Ireland, or Principality of Wales, or town of Berwick upon Tweed, there to be laid on shore, under the penalty of the forfeiture of the said goods, or the full value thereof, as also of the ship, with all her guns, tackle, apparel." &c.— And all vessels sailing to the Plantations, are to give bonds, to bring said commodities to England.

In 1663, another act of Parliament prohibited the importation, into any of the English Colonies, in Asia, Africa, or America, of any commodities of the growth, production, or manufacture of Europe, except they were laden or shipped in England, Wales, or the town of Berwick upon Tweed, and in English built shipping, or which were bought before the first day of October, 1662, &c. and which were to be carried directly to the said Colonies, &c. with an exception of " salt for the fisheries, wines from Madeira and Azores, and all sorts of victuals from Scotland and Ireland."*—The British Colonies, therefore, by this act could obtain no European goods, but through the ports in England. A drawback of the duties, however, was generally allowed on the exportation of those goods to the Colonies.

Before the Independence of the United States, and subsequent to the year 1766, the trade of the British Colonies, as to their exports, was limited to the parent country, to that part of Europe, which lies south of Cape Finisterre, to certain parts of Africa, and to the West-Indies. Many of the most valuable articles of colonial produce were confined to the market of the parent country.—To those enumerated in the act of navigation before recited, many others were, afterwards, at different

---

* The preamble to this act (15 Charles II.) shews the policy which then prevailed in Europe, respecting distant Colonies. It is in the following words.—" And in regard his Majesty's Plantations beyond the seas, are inhabited and peopled by his subjects of this his Kingdom of England, for the maintaining a greater correspondence and kindness between them, and keeping them in a firmer dependence upon it, and rendering them yet more beneficial and advantageous unto it, in the further employment and increase of English shipping and seamen, vent of English woolens, and other manufactures and commodities, rendering the navigation to and from the same more safe and cheap, and making this Kingdom a staple, not only of the commodities of these plantations, but also of the commodities of other countries and places for the supplying of them, and it being the usage of other nations, to keep their plantation trade to themselves, Be it Enacted," &c.

periods, added, such as molasses, tar, pitch, turpentine, hemp, masts, yards, copper ore, pig and bar iron, pot and pearl ashes, beaver skins, whale fins, hides, &c. Rice and lumber were once among the *enumerated commodities*, as those were called, which could only be shipped to Great-Britain. They were afterwards however permitted to be carried to that part of Europe, lying south of Cape Finisterre. The *non enumerated commodities*, as those were called, which were not confined to the market of Great-Britain, could originally be shipped to any part of the world; but by the 6th of George III. (1766) were limited, in the same manner as rice and lumber, to the part of Europe south of Cape Finisterre.

The Colonies sent to Africa, New-England rum, and such articles as were necessary for the purchase of slaves. The trade of the Colonies, and particularly the northern Colonies, to the West-India islands, was, from their first settlement, of great importance. They sent their fish, grain, and other provisions, lumber, &c. to the foreign West-India islands, as well as to the British; and received, in return, rum, sugar, coffee, salt, molasses, and such other articles as were permitted to be brought from them. This trade with the foreign West-India islands was always considered, by the Colonists, as highly advantageous, but was viewed by the British merchants, and the West-India planters, with no small degree of jealousy. As the population of the Colonies increased, this trade also increased; and the superior fertility of some of the foreign West-India islands gave them great advantages over the British planter. With the increase of wealth and population, the Colonists began also to introduce sundry manufactures, for their own consumption, such as woolen and linen cloths, iron, hats, paper, &c. This excited the jealousy of the British manufacturer, and various complaints were made to the Lords Commissioners of trade and Plantations, and to Parliament, by the merchants, Planters, and manufacturers, that the Colonists were carrying on trades, and setting up manufactures injurious to them, and to the interest of the parent country. In consequence of these complaints, the British house of Commons, in 1731, directed the Board of trade and Plantations, to make a report " with respect to laws made, manufactures set up, or trade carried on in the Colonies, detrimental to the trade, navigation, or manufactures of Great-Britain."

In pursuance of this order, the Board of trade, on the 15th of Feb. 1731-2 made a report, which, as it contains a statement relative to the trade and manufactures of the Colonies, at that period, is here inserted.—They say " The following complaints have been lately made to this Board, against some plantation laws, viz. in Massachusetts Bay, an act was made to encourage the manufacture of paper, which law interferes with the profit made by the British merchants on foreign paper sent thither.

" In New-England, New-York, Connecticut, Rhode-Island, Pennsylvania, and in the county of Somerset in Maryland, they have fallen into the manufacture of woolen cloth and linen cloth, for the use of their own families only ; for the product of these Colonies being chiefly cattle and grain, the estates of the inhabitants depended wholly on farming, which could not be managed, without a certain quantity of sheep ; and their wool would be entirely lost, were not their servants employed during winter, in manufacturing it, for the use of their families.

" Flax and hemp being likewise easily raised, the inhabitants manufactured them into coarse sort of cloth, bags, traces, and halters for their horses, which they found did more service, than those they had from any part of Europe.

" However, the high price of labour in general in America, rendered it impracticable for people there to manufacture their linen cloth at less than 20 per cent. more than the rate in England, or woolen cloth at less than 50 per cent. dearer, than that, which is exported from home for sale. It were to be wished, that some expedient might be fallen upon, to direct their thoughts from undertakings of this nature ; so much the rather, because these manufactures, in process of time, may be carried on, in a greater degree, unless an early stop be put to their progress by employing them in naval stores. Wherefore, we take leave to renew our repeated proposals, that reasonable encouragement be given to the same. Moreover, we find that certain trades carried on, and manufactures set up there, are detrimental to the trade, navigation, and manufactures of Great-Britain. For the state of these Plantations varying almost every year, more or less, in their trade and manufactures, as well as in other particulars, we thought it necessary .for his Majesty's service, and for the discharge of our trust, from time to time, to send general queries to the several Governours in America, that we might be the more exactly informed of the condition of the Plantations, among which there were several, that related to their trade and manufactures, to which we received the following returns viz. : The Governour of New-Hampshire, in his answer said, that there were no settled manufactures in that Province, and that their trade principally consisted in lumber and fish.

" The Governour of Massachusetts Bay informed us, that in some parts of this Province, the inhabitants worked up their wool and flax into an ordinary coarse cloth for their own use, but did not export any. That the greatest part of the woolen and linen clothing, worn in this Province, was imported from Great-Britain, and sometimes from Ireland ; but considering the excessive price of labor in New-England, the merchants could afford what was imported cheaper, than what was made in that country. That there was also a few hat makers in the maritime towns, and that the greater part of the leather used in that country, was manufactured among themselves. That there had been for many years, some iron works in that Province, which had afforded the people iron for some of their necessary occasions ; but that the iron imported from Great-Britain was esteemed much the best, and wholly used by the shipping ; and that the iron works of the Province were not able to supply the twentieth part of what was necessary for the use of the country.

" They had no manufactures in the Province of New-York, that deserve mentioning. Their trade consisted chiefly in furs, whale-bone, oil, pitch, tar, and provisions. No manufactures in New-Jersey, that deserve mentioning, their trade being chiefly in provisions shipped from New-York and Pennsylvania. The chief trade of Pennsylvania lay in their exportation of provisions and lumber ; no manufactures being established, and their clothing and utensils for their houses being all imported from Great-Britain. By further advices from New-Hampshire, the woolen manufacture appears to have decreased, the common lands, on which the sheep used to feed, being now appropriated, and the people almost wholly clothed with woolen from Great-Britain. The manufactures of flax, into linens, some coarse, some fine, daily increased, by the great resort of people from Ireland thither, who are well skilled in that business. By late accounts from

Massachusetts Bay, in New-England, the Assembly have voted a bounty of thirty shillings for every piece of duck or canvass made in the Province. Some other manufactures are carried on there, as brown holland, for women's wear, which lessens the importation of calicoes, and some other sorts of East-India goods.

" They also make some small quantities of cloth, made of linen and cotton for ordinary sheeting. By a paper mill set up three years ago, they make to the value of £200 sterling yearly. There are also several forges for making bar iron, and some furnaces for cast iron or hollow ware, and one slitting mill, and a manufacture for nails. The Governour writes concerning the woolen manufacture, that the country people, who used formerly to make most of their clothing out of their own wool, do not now make a third part of what they wear, but are mostly clothed with British manufacture. The surveyor general of his Majesty's woods writes, that they have in New-England, six furnaces and nineteen forges, for making iron, and that in this Province many ships are built for the French and Spaniards, in return for rum, molasses, wines, and silks, which they truck there by connivance. Great quantities of hats are made in New-England, of which the company of hatters in London have complained to us, that great quantities of these hats are exported to Spain, Portugal, and our West-India Islands. They also make all sorts of iron work for shipping. There are several still houses and sugar bakers established in New-England. By late advices from New-York, there are no manufactures there, that can affect Great-Britain. There is yearly imported into New-York, a very large quantity of the woolen manufactures of this Kingdom, for their clothing, which they would be rendered incapable to pay for, and would be reduced to the necessity of making for themselves, if they were prohibited from receiving from the foreign sugar Colonies, the money, rum, molasses, cocoa, indigo, cotton-wool, &c. which they at present take in return for provisions, horses, and lumber, the produce of that Province and of New-Jersey, of which he affirms the British Colonies do not take off above one half. But the company of hatters of London have since informed us, that hats are manufactured in great quantities in this Province.

" By the last letters from the Deputy Governour of Pennsylvania, he does not know of any trade carried on, in that Province, that can be injurious to this Kingdom. They do not export any woolen or linen manufactures; all that they make, which are of a coarse sort, being for their own use. We are farther informed, that in this Province are built many brigantines and small sloops, which they sell to the West-Indies. The Governour of Rhode-Island informs us, in answer to our queries, that there are iron mines there, but not a fourth part iron enough to serve their own use; but he takes no notice of any manufactures there. No return from the Governour of Connecticut. But we find, by some accounts, that the produce of this Colony is timber, boards, all sorts of English grain, hemp, flax, sheep, black cattle, swine, horses, goats, and tobacco. That they export horses and lumber to the West-Indies, and receive, in return, sugar, salt, molasses, and rum. We likewise find, that their manufactures are very inconsiderable; the people there being generally employed in tillage, some few in tanning, shoemaking, and other handicrafts; others in building, and in joiner's, taylor's and smith's work, without which they could not subsist. No report is made from Carolina, the Bahama, nor the Bermuda isles."

The Commissioners then proceed to say—" From the foregoing state, it is observable, that there are more trades carried on, and manufactures set up, in the Provinces on the Continent of America, to the northward of Virginia, prejudicial to the trade and manufactures of Great-Britain, particularly in New-England, than in any other of the British Colonies; which is not to be wondered at, for their soil, climate, and produce, being pretty nearly the same with ours, they have no staple commodities of their own growth to exchange for our manufactures, which puts them under greater necessity, as well as under greater temptations, for providing for themselves at home; to which may be added, in the charter governments, the little dependence they have upon the mother country, and consequently the small restraint they are under, in any matters detrimental to her interests. And, therefore, we humbly beg leave to repeat and submit to the wisdom of this honourable house, the substance of what we formerly proposed in our report, on the silk, linen, and woolen manufactures herein before recited, namely, whether it might not be expedient to give these Colonies proper encouragements for turning their industry to such manufactures and products, as might be of service to Great-

Britain, and more particularly to the production of all kinds of naval stores."*

* Macpherson's Annals of Commerce, vol. 3.

NOTE. The British merchants and manufacturers were always jealous of the trade and manufactures of the northern Colonies and particularly of New-England. Sir Josiah Child, in his discourse on trade, written about the year 1680, says "That New-England is the most prejudicial Plantation to this Kingdom." In attempting to prove this he says " I am now to write of a people, whose frugality, industry, and temperance, and the happiness of whose laws and institutions, promise to them long life, with a wonderful increase of people, riches, and power ; and although no men ought to envy that virtue and wisdom in others, which themselves either can or will not practise, but rather to commend and admire it ; yet I think it is the duty of every good man primarily to respect the welfare of his native country ; and therefore, though I may offend some, whom I would not willingly displease, I cannot omit, in the progress of this discourse, to take notice of some particulars, wherein old England suffers diminution by the growth of these Colonies settled in New-England, and how that Plantation differs from those more southerly, with respect to the gain or loss of this Kingdom, viz.

" 1. All our American Plantations, except that of New-England, produce commodities of different natures from those of this Kingdom, as sugar, tobacco, cocoa, wool, ginger, sundry sorts of dying woods, &c. Whereas New-England produces generally the same we have here, viz. corn and cattle ; some quantity of fish they do likewise kill, but that is taken and saved altogether by their own inhabitants, which prejudices our Newfoundland trade, where, as has been said, very few are, or ought according to prudence, to be employed in those fisheries, but the inhabitants of old England. The other commodities we have from them, are some few great masts, furs, and train oil, of which the yearly value amounts to very little, the much greater value of returns from them being made in sugar, cotton, wool, tobacco, and such like commodities, which they first receive from some other of his Majesty's Plantations, in barter for dry cod fish, salt mackerel, beef, pork, bread, beans, flour, peas, &c. which they supply Barbadoes, Jamaica, &c. with, to the diminution of the vent of those commodities from this Kingdom ; the great experience of which in our West-India Plantations, would soon be found in the advantage of the value of our lands in England, were it not for the vast and almost incredible supplies these Colonies have from New-England. 2. The people of New-England, by virtue of their primitive charter, being not so strictly tied to the observation of the laws of this Kingdom, do sometimes assume the liberty of trading, contrary to the act of na-

This report exhibits a view, although a very imperfect one, of the state of the trade and manufactures of the Colonies, about the year 1731—2.

The Governours of the several Provinces and Colonies, especially those who were independent of the crown, aware of the object of the queries put to them by the Lords Commissioners, returned answers as favourable as possible to the Colonists, and which would least excite the jealousy of the British merchant and manufacturer.

The disputes, however, between the British West-India sugar Colonies and the northern Colonies, concerning the trade of the latter with the foreign West-India islands, still continued with great warmth, and in 1733, in order to settle this dispute, and to encourage their own sugar Colonies, Parliament passed an act (6 George II. c. 13) "For the better securing and encouraging the trade of his Majesty's sugar Colonies in America."

This act imposed a duty of nine pence sterling on every gallon of rum, six pence on every gallon of molasses, and five shillings on every hundred weight of sugar, imported into any of the British Plantations in America from foreign sugar Colonies. This duty was afterwards reduced to six pence on rum, and three pence on molasses. The duty was always very odious to the northern Colonists. It was justly considered by them as sacrificing their interest to the interest of the sugar planter. And it is well known that although this duty was attempted to be collected in the Colonies, by officers appointed by the crown, and by severe legal penalties, yet,

vigation, by reason of which, many of our American commodities, especially tobacco and sugar, are transported in New-English shipping, directly into Spain, and other foreign countries, without being landed in England, or paying any duty to his Majesty; which is not only a loss to the King, and a prejudice to the navigation of old England, &c.

"3. Of all the American Plantations, his Majesty has none so apt for the building of shipping as New-England, nor none comparably so qualified for the breeding of seamen, not only by reason of the natural industry of that people, but principally by reason of their cod and mackerel fisheries; and in my poor opinion, there is nothing more prejudicial, and in prospect more dangerous to any mother Kingdom, than the increase of shipping in her Colonies, Plantations, or Provinces."

by smuggling or some other way, the payment of it was generally evaded. In consequence of the statements in this report, relative
to the manufacture and exportation of hats from the Colonies, and undoubtedly at the instigation of the manufacturers of that article in
Great-Britain, Parliament passed an act (5 George II. 1732) " to
prevent the exportation of hats out of any of his Majesty's Colonies or
Plantations in America, and to restrain the number of apprentices
taken by the hat-makers in the said Colonies or Plantations, and for
the better encouraging the making of hats in Great-Britain." By
this act, not only was the exportation of hats prohibited to a foreign
port, but their transportation from one British Plantation to another British Plantation, was also prohibited, under severe penalties ;
nor could they " be loaden upon any horse, cart, or other carriage,
to the intent or purpose to be exported, transported, shipped off," &c.
By the same act no person could make hats, unless he had serv-
ed an apprenticeship for seven years, nor could he employ more
than two apprentices at any one time.

The making of pig and bar iron had become an object of some
consequence in the Colonies. The British government were willing
to encourage the importation of it into England, in its raw and unmanufactured state, but were opposed to the manufacture of it in the
Colonies. In the year 1750, therefore, an act was passed (23
George II.) " to encourage the importation of pig and bar iron from
his Majesty's Colonies in America, and to prevent the erection of any
mill, or other engine for slitting or rolling of iron, or any plating
forge to work with a tilt hammer, or any furnace for making steel, in
any of said Colonies." By this act, pig iron is admitted into England duty free, and bar iron is admitted duty free, into the port
of London. But the erection of any slitting mill, plating forge, or
furnace for making steel, is prohibited under severe penalties.
While the British government were thus jealous of the trade and manufactures of the Colonies, which were supposed to interfere with the
particular interests of the mother country, they were disposed to encourage the production of such raw materials as were necessary for
their manufactures, and such other articles as could not be raised in
England, but for which they were entirely, or in a great measure,
dependent upon other countries. At different periods, therefore,

Parliament offered liberal bounties on the importation of various articles into Great-Britain, which were the growth and production of the Colonies. By the 3 and 4 Ann, c. 10, (1706) a large bounty was given on the importation of tar, pitch, rosin, turpentine, masts, yards, and bowsprits, from the Colonies; and at subsequent periods, a bounty was given upon indigo, hemp, and flax, and timber of different kinds, raw silk, and on pipe, hogshead, and barrel staves. The society also instituted at London, in 1753, " for the encouragement of arts, manufactures, and commerce," offered liberal premiums for the production and culture of certain articles in the British Colonies.

In 1762, this society gave premiums on the importation of the following articles from the Colonies, viz. cochineal, sturgeon, raw silk, scammony, opium, pesiman gum, silk grass, safflower, pot and pearl ashes; and on the culture of logwood, olive trees, vines for raisins, vines for wines, cinnamon, aloes, hemp, silk, and sarsaparilla.

POPULATION, EXPORTS, AND IMPORTS OF THE COLONIES.

In 1749, the whole white population of the North American Colonies, now the United States, was estimated at 1,046,000. The number in each Colony, was estimated as follows, viz,

New-Hampshire	30,000
Massachusetts Bay	220,000
Rhode-Island	35,000
Connecticut	100,000
New-York	100,000
Jersies	60,000
Pennsylvania and Delaware	250,000
Maryland	85,000
Virginia	85,000
North-Carolina	45,000
South-Carolina	30,000
Georgia	6,000

At this period, the annual value of the imports into these Colonies from England, was about £900,000 sterling. Dr. Franklin* states the value of the imports from Great-Britain, (exclusive of Scotland)

* Fourth volume Franklin's Works, page 69.

into the northern Colonies, at two different periods, viz. from 1744 to 1748, and from 1754 to 1758, taken, as is supposed, from the English custom-house books, as follows, viz.

1744	- - -	£640,114 12	4
1745	- - - -	534,316 2	5
1746	- - -	754,945 4	3
1747	- - - -	726,648 5	5
1748	- - -	830,243 16	9
	Total - -	£3,486,268 1	2
1754	- - - -	£1,246,615 1	11
1755	- - -	1,177,848 6	10
1756	- - - -	1,428,720 18	10
1757	- - -	1,727,924 2	10
1758	- - - -	1,832,948 13	10
	Total - -	£7,414,057 4	3

The great increase of imports during the last period of five years was owing, undoubtedly, in no small degree, to the war then existing between England and France, and which occasioned greater shipments than usual to the Colonies, in order to supply the troops during those years. This war, which has generally been called the French war of 1755, was occasioned, in a great measure, by a contest for boundaries and limits in North America, between the English and French. In all the former wars between these powers, the Colonists had been warmly engaged, and several attempts had been made by them to take possession of Canada and other parts of North America then in possession of the French. In consequence of these attempts, and in defending themselves against the attacks of the French from Canada, great expenses had been incurred by the Colonies ; and having few resources, most of the colonial governments, at different periods, for the purpose of defraying these and other expenses, had issued paper money, but which in most if not in all instances depreciated.

The Colonies felt themselves more than ever interested in the result of the contest, as to the boundaries between them and the French Canadian settlements. The French were making such encroachments on the western and northern frontiers, as, if acquiesced in, would leave them but a small strip of territory along the Atlantic. They now, more than ever, felt the necessity of union and concert among themselves, for their mutual protection and defence, against those encroachments, and also of a general treasury, from which, the expense of such protection and defence might be defrayed. For the purpose of forming such an union, Commissioners from New-Hampshire, Massachusetts, Rhode-Island, Connecticut, New-Jersey, Maryland, and Pennsylvania, met at Albany, in July, 1754. Commissioners from the other Colonies were expected, but were not present.

A plan of union was agreed upon by the Commissioners present. This plan was submitted to the King and Parliament for their approbation, and to the Assemblies of the several Colonies, but was rejected by the former, as vesting too much power in the Colonies, and was disapproved by the latter as giving too much power to the crown. By this plan, " the general government was to be administered by a president general to be appointed and supported by the crown, and a general council to be chosen by the representatives of the several Colonies met in their respective Assemblies." So far as respects the defence of the Colonies, the regulation of trade, and the collection of the taxes, this general government was authorized " to raise and pay soldiers, build forts for the defence of any of the Colonies, and equip vessels of force, to guard the coasts and protect the trade on the ocean, lakes, or great rivers ; but they were not to impress men in any Colony, without the consent of the legislature. That for these purposes, they had power to make laws, and levy such general duties, imposts, and taxes, as to them should appear most equal and just (considering the abilities, and other circumstances of the inhabitants in the several Colonies) and such as may be collected with the least inconvenience to the people ; rather discouraging luxury, than loading industry with unnecessary burdens."

Had this plan been adopted, the separation of the Colonies from the parent country, might have been postponed for many years.

The importation and consumption of foreign articles into the Colonies increased with the increase of wealth and population. The following is an account of the value of imports from Great-Britain, into Pennsylvania, at different periods.*

In 1723 the imports amounted only to	£15,993	19	4
1730 they were - - -	48,592	7	5
1737 - - -	56,690	4	7
1742 - - -	75,295	3	4
1747 - - -	82,404	17	7
1752 - - -	201,666	19	11
1757 - - - -	248,426	6	6

In 1766 Doctor Franklin, in his examination before the House of Commons, stated, that the value of imports at that time into Pennsylvania, was computed by the merchants, to be above £500,000. The tables of Lord Sheffield, in his " Observations on American Commerce," taken undoubtedly from the custom-house books, shew the value of the trade between Great-Britian, and that part of America now the United States, from 1700 to 1780, to be as follows :

	IMPORTS FROM	EXPORTS TO
	THE COLONIES, NOW UNITED STATES.	
Average from 1700 to 1710	£265,783 0 10	£267,205 3 4
from 1710 to 1720	392,653 17 1½	365,645 6 11¾
from 1720 to 1730	578,830 16 4	471,342 12 10½
from 1730 to 1740	670,128 16 0½	660,136 11 1¼
from 1740 to 1750	708,943 9 6¼	812,647 13 0¼
from 1750 to 1760	802,691 6 10	1,577,419 14 2½
from 1760 to 1770	1,044,591 17 0	1,763,409 10 3
from 1770 to 1780	743,560 10 10	1,331,206 1 5

It is difficult to ascertain with accuracy, the value of the trade of the Colonies, previous to the year 1776. A smuggling trade was carried

* Fourth volume of Franklin's Works.

on to a considerable extent, not only with the foreign West-India islands, but some parts of Europe. The custom-house books, therefore, do not furnish a true account of the whole trade of the Colonies. They must, however, be resorted to, as the best source of information. We have before stated, that for some years previous to the American revolution, the trade of the Colonies was limited to Great-Britain, to that part of Europe lying south of Cape Finisterre, to the West-Indies and to Africa. Table No. I. at the end of this chapter contains the official value in sterling money of the exports and imports from each of these countries, for the year 1769. From this it appears, that the exports from the several Colonies, now the United States, during that year, to Great-Britain amounted to

		£1,531,516	8	6
*To the South of Europe	-	552,736	11	2
To the West-Indies	- -	747,910	3	7
To Africa	- - - -	20,278	5	1
Total		£2,852,441	8	4

or about thirteen millions of dollars.

And that the imports from Great-Britain, amounted to

		£1,604,975	11	11
From the South of Europe	-	76,684	9	11
From the West-Indies	-	789,754	4	5
From Africa	- - -	151,998	0	0
Total		£2,623,412	6	3

or about twelve millions of dollars.

Those who are anxious to see the quantity, as well as the value of the various articles exported from the Colonies prior to the revolution, and the countries to which they were sent, so far as the custom-house books will shew, may consult table No. II. annexed to this chapter, which contains an account of the principal articles exported from the North American Colonies, including the islands of Newfoundland, Bahama, and Bermuda, with their official value, and places of destination, for the year 1770.†

* Taken from Macpherson's Annals of Commerce, vol. 3, page 571.
† Macpherson's Annals of Commerce, and Lord Sheffield.

The total value of the articles exported, as American produce, during the year 1770, from the Colonies now the United States, including those exported from other Provinces, and from New-Foundland, Bahama, and Bermuda, was £3,356,159 10 2

As little was exported from the other Provinces and the islands, except fish from New-Foundland, the value of the exports from the Colonies, now the United States, in that year, must have been, at least, three millions sterling, or about thirteen and a half millions of dollars.

The value of the imports from Great-Britain into the Colonies, for several years previous to a final rupture between them, in 1775, was different in different years, in consequence of those disputes, which led to a separation, and of the non-importation agreement entered into among the Colonists. The average value for the years 1771, 2, and 3, is stated by some, at more than three millions.* It is allowed, however, that the imports for those years were beyond example great.

It is difficult also to ascertain the amount of tonnage employed in the trade of the Colonies, and particularly the amount owned by the Colonists themselves.

The amount of tonnage entered from January 5th, 1770, to January 5th, 1771, was three hundred thirty-one thousand six hundred and forty-four, and the amount cleared, three hundred fifty-one thousand six hundred and eighty-six.† It will be observed, that the amount is taken from the custom-house books, and includes the entry of the same vessel, two or three times, or as often as the voyages were in the course of the year, and repeated although the tonnage as registered is generally less than the real amount, yet the tonnage as entered and cleared is probably much above its real amount. The tonnage of vessels built in the Colonies in the years 1769, 1770, and 1771,‡ was as follows, viz.

				Tonnage.
In 1769	-	-	-	20,001
1770	-	-		20,610
1771	-	-	-	24,068

---

* See Lord Sheffield. † Chalmer's Estimate.
‡ See Macpherson's Annals of Commerce, vol. 3, p. 570.

Of this amount, a little more than one half was built in Massachusetts and New-Hampshire. The trade of the Colonies was no doubt highly beneficial to Great-Britain, and was made more so, as she conceived, by her system of colonial policy ; and while she confined herself to the regulation of the external trade of the Colonies, the Colonists acquiesced, though many of those regulations were considered by them, as injurious and oppressive. But when Parliament not only imposed internal taxes upon the Colonies, without their consent, but declared, that they had a right to bind them in all cases whatsover, this led to a resistance on their part, which finally ended in a separation. Some account of the footing on which the trade of the United States was placed with Great-Britain, and her dependencies, subsequent to the peace of 1783, will be given hereafter.

TABLE No. I.

An account of the value in sterling money, of the imports of the several Provinces under-mentioned in the year 1769.*

	From Great-Britain.	From the South of Europe.	From the West-Indies.	From Africa.	TOTAL.
New-Hampshire,	} 223,695 11 6	652 7 6	48,528 18 7	} 180 0 0	} 564,034 3 8
Massachusetts,		21,908 5 6	155,387 1 4		
Rhode-Island,		2,580 19 6	56,839 17 3		
Connecticut,		267 5 3	53,993 17 3		
New-York,	} 75,930 19 7	14,927 7 8	97,420 4 0	} 697 10 0	188,976 1 3
New-Jersey,		326 18 2	1,663 19 9		1,990 17 11
Pennsylvania,	204,979 17 4	14,249 8 4	180,591 12 4		399,820 18 0
Maryland,	} 714,943 15 8	4,683 2 3	32,197 13 9	5,400 0 0	} 851,140 6 6
Virginia,		9,442 2 4	77,453 12 6	7,020 0 0	
North-Carolina,		932 19 9	10,603 13 3	1,080 0 0	
South-Carolina,	327,084 8 6	6,166 6 1	65,666 4 8	124,180 10 0	535,714 2 3
Georgia,	58,340 19 4	547 7 7	9,407 9 9	13,440 0 0	81,735 16 8
TOTAL,	1,604,975 11 11	76,684 9 11	789,754 4 5	151,998 0 0	2,623,412 6 3

* The above account of imports and exports is taken from Macpherson's Annals of Commerce, Vol. 3d, pages 571-2.

TABLE NO. I.—CONTINUED.

An account of the value, in sterling money of the exports of the several Provinces under-mentioned in the year 1769.

	To Great-Britain.	To the South of Europe.	To the West-Indies.	To Africa.	TOTAL.
New-Hampshire,		464 0 5	40,431 8 4	96 11 3	550,089 19 2
Massachusetts, .	142,775 12 9	76,702 0 4	123,394 0 6	9,801 9 10	
Rhode-Island, .		1,440 11 0	65,206 13 2	7,814 19 8	
Connecticut, .		2,567 4 5	79,395 7 6		
New-York, . .	113,382 8 8	50,885 13 0	66,324 17 5	1,313 2 6	231,906 1 7
New-Jersey, . .			2,531 16 5		2,531 16 5
Pennsylvania, .	28,112 6 9	203,752 11 11	178,331 7 8	560 9 9	410,756 16 1
Maryland, . .	759,961 5 0	66,555 11 11	22,303 9 2		991,401 18 6
Virginia, . .		73,635 3 4	68,946 9 1		
North-Carolina,	405,014 13 1	3,238 3 7	27,944 7 9	71 15 4	569,584 17 3
South-Carolina,	72,881 9 3		59,814 11 6	619 16 9	
Georgia, . . .	82,270 2 3	614 2 0	13,285 15 1		96,169 19 4
TOTAL,	1,531,516 8 6	552,736 11 2	747,910 3 7	20,278 5 1	2,852,441 8 4

TABLE No. II.

An account of the principal articles exported from all the British Continental Colonies, including the islands of New-Foundland, Bahama, and Bermuda, with the places to which they were sent, and their official value, at the ports of exportation, during the year 1770.*

Species of Mer'dize	To G. Britain	To Ireland	To the S. of Europe	To the West Indies	To Africa	TOTALS. Quantity	TOTALS. Value in sterling money
Pot ashes, tons	1,173					1,173	£35,191 18 7
Pearl do. "	737					737	29,468 10 7
Sperm. candles, lb.	4,865	450	14,167	351,625	7,905	379,012	23,688 4 6
Tallow do. "			1,630	57,550	240	59,420	1,237 18 4
Coals, chaldron,				20		20	25 0 0
Castorium, lb.	7,465					7,465	1,679 12 6
Fish dried, quint'ls	22,086	450	431,386	206,081		660,003	375,393 17 0
Fish, pickled, bbls.	123	25	307	29,582	31	30,068	22,551 7 6
Flax-seed, bushels	6,780	305,083	749			312,612	31,168 18 1
Indian Corn, "		150	175,221	402,958	20	578,349	43,376 4 2
Oats, "			3,421	21,438		24,859	1,242 19 0
Wheat, "	11,739	149,985	588,561	955		851,240	131,467 0 0
Peas & beans, "			1,046	49,337		50,383	10,076 12 0
Ginseng, lb.	74,604					74,604	1,243 8 3
Hemp, tons	86					86	129 11 0
Iron, pig, "	5,747	267		3		6,017	30,088 10 3
Do. bar, "	2,102	85	273			24,064	36,960 17 11
Do. cast, "				2		2	32 13 1
Do. wrought, "				8		8	167 7 1
Indigo, lb.	584,593			83		584,672	151,552 2 9
Whale oil, tons	5,202	22	175	268		5,667	83,012 15 6
Do. fins, lb.	112,971					112,971	19,121 7 3
Linseed Oil, tons	161			7		168	487 18 3
Copper ore, "	41					41	853 13 0
Lead, do. "	6					6	82 10 0

It is to be remembered, that in the account I have given of the trade of all the Colonies, who have since withdrawn their allegiance from Great-Britain, as also in the subsequent one of the exports of the whole Colonies, the prices are rated by the official valuation, and consequently are considerably under the real amount.

* *In this account I have omitted the fractional parts of the quantities, which are of no use in a general view, but their value is retained in the totals. The attentive reader may find some disagreements between the totals and the particular numbers, owing partly to the omission of the fractional parts, and partly to errors which I saw, but had no means of correcting.*

TABLE No. II.—CONTINUED.

Species of Merchandize.		To Great-Britain.	To Ireland.	To the south of Europe.	To the West Indies.	To Africa.	TOTALS.	
							Quantity.	Value in sterling money.
Bread & flour,	tons	263	3,583	18,501	23,449	72	45,868	£504,553 6 1
Meal,	bushels				4,430		4,430	443 0 0
Potatoes,	"				3,382		3,382	126 16 6
Beef and pork,	barrels			244	2,870 tons	300		66,035 1 10
Butter,	lb.				167,313		167,613	3,491 18 9
Cheese,	"				55,997			933 5 8
New England rum,	gallons	600	7,931	45,310	2,574	292,966	349,281	21,836 0 0
Rice,	barrels	74,073		36,296	40,033	117	150,529	340,692 15 0
Rough rice,	bushels				8,200			615 9 0
American loaf sugar,	lb.			600	8,548	1,500	10,648	332 15 3
Raw silk,	"	541					541	541 11 6
Soap,	"			550	85,035	1,000	86,585	2,164 12 6
Shoes,	pairs				3,149		3,149	393 12 0
Ship stuff,	barrels				640			9,958 15 5
Onions,	value			7,327	£6,378 16 1		7,964	6,495 9 0
Pitch,	barrels	8,265			822	57	9,114	3,200 8 0
Tar, common,	"	78,115			3,173	134	81,422	24,426 12 0
Do. green,	"	653					653	261 4 0
Turpentine,	"	15,125			1,807	82	17,014	6,805 12 0
Rosin,	"	195			28		223	278 15 0
Oil of Turpentine,	"	11			30			102 10 0
Masts, yards, &c.	tons	3,043			2		41	16,630 0 0
Walnut wood,	value	£105 15 1½	9 0 0	£116,13 4			3,045	114 15 11
Pine, oak, cedar, boards, feet		6,013,519	329,741	486,078	35,922,168	4,800	42,756,306	58,617 15 10

TABLE No. II.—CONTINUED.

Species of Merchandize.	To Great-Britain.	To Ireland.	To the south of Europe.	To the West-Indies.	To Africa.	TOTALS. Quantity.	TOTALS. Value in sterling money.
Pine timber, - tons	10,582	50	64	315		11,011	4,404 14 5
Oak timber, - "	3,710	10	10	144		3,874	3,487 8 2
Houses, framed, - No.				163		163	3,260 0 0
Staves and heading, "	4,921,020	2,828,762	1,680,403	11,116,141		20,546,326	61,618 19 5
Hoops, - - "	18,912		7,072	3,817,899	8,500	3,852,383	8,667 16 8
Shook hogsheads, - "			549	62,099	30	62,678	7,834 15 0
Cattle, - - "				3,184		3,184	14,328 0 0
Horses, - - "				6,692			60,228 0 0
Sheep and hogs, - "				12,797			4,478 19 0
Poultry, - dozens				2,615		2,615	1,177 1 9
Furs, - - value	£91,485 14 9						91,485 14 9
Deer skins, - lb.	799,652	185				799,652	57,738 19 7
Tobacco, - value	£904,981 14 0			1,569 0 4	87 3 9		906,637 18 1
Tallow and lard, - lb.	800			183,893	450	185,143	3,857 2 11
Bees-wax, - - "	62,794	10,980	50,529	1,820	2,400	128,523	6,426 3 0
Total value of articles shipped as American produce, -	£1,686,654 4 6	£114,078 13 6	685,920 6 4	844,178 14 9	21,381 16 6		3,356,159 10 2
Foreign merchandize mostly from the West-Indies, -	£65,860 6 9	4,698 5 10	5,991 17 1	4,754 16 0	296 12 0		81,554 17 0
Total exports,	£1,752,514 11 3	118,776 19 4	691,912 3 5	848,933 10 5	21,678 8 6		3,437,714 7 2

CHAPTER II.

COMMERCE interrupted, during the American revolutionary war—Old Congress no power to regulate commerce, or to levy duties on imports—Amount of the public debt in 1783—Requisitions upon the states for the payment of it not complied with—Power to levy certain duties on imports not granted to the old Congress by the states—Depreciation of the public debt—Exports from the United States to Great-Britain, and imports from Great-Britain, from 1784, to 1790—Distressed state of the country—Meeting of Commissioners at Annapolis in 1786—Adoption of the new Constitution, and the organization of the government under it in 1789.

DURING the war of the revolution, the commerce of the United States was interrupted, not only with Great-Britain, but in a great measure with the rest of the world. They were then compelled, to depend almost entirely upon themselves for supplies, not only of arms and munitions of war, but of those articles of common consumption, which they had previously imported from Great-Britain and elsewhere. Those articles, which their soil would not produce, or which they were unable to make, they were obliged to obtain, at great risque and expense, from other countries, or to be content without them. Encouragement was given to all the necessary manufactures, and the zeal, ingenuity, and industry of the people, supplied the place of a foreign market.

At the close of the war, when we became an independent nation, our commercial as well as our political situation was new, and we had many difficulties to encounter. During a contest of more than seven years, our commerce was annihilated, our shipping nearly destroyed, public credit impaired, a vast debt accumulated upon our hands, and the general government was illy calculated to repair those losses, and to bring into active operation the energies and resources of the nation. The whole expense of the war, was more than one hundred and thirty-five millions of dollars.* About one half of this

* The whole expense of the revolutionary war cannot be ascertained,

expense was paid by taxes, levied and collected during the war, and the residue remained a debt due from the United States, or from the individual states, on the return of peace. In April, 1783, the debt

with certainty. The following are estimates of this expense, made out by the Register of the Treasury in the year 1790, and furnished a committee of the house of representatives of Congress.

" General abstract of the annual estimates, and abstract statements of the total amount of the expenditures and advances at the Treasury of the United States.

" The estimated amount of the expenditures of	Dolls.	90ths.
1775 and 1776 is in specie - - -	20,064,666	66
1777 - - - - - -	24,986,646	85
1778 - - - - - -	24,289,438	26
1779 - - - - - -	10,794,620	65
1780 - - - - - -	3,000,000	00
1781 - - - - - -	1,942,465	30
1782 - - - - - -	3,632,745	85
1783 - - - - - -	3,226,583	45
To Nov. 1st, 1784, as pr. schedule D. and subordinate accounts, - - - - - -	548,525	63
Forming an amount total of - - - -	$92,485,693	15

" The foregoing estimates being confined to actual Treasury payments, are exclusive of the debts of the United States, which were incurred at various periods, for the support of the late war, and should be taken into a general view of the expense thereof, viz. :—

	Dolls.	90ths.
Army debt, upon commissioners' certificates,	11,080,576	1
For supplies furnished by the citizens of the several states, and for which certificates were issued by the commissioners, - - - - -	3,723,625	20
For supplies furnished in the quarter-master, commissary, hospital, clothing, and marine departments, exclusive of the forageing, - - -	1,159,170	5
For supplies, on accounts settled at the Treasury, and for which certificates were issued by the Register, - - - - - -	744,638	49
	16,708,009	75

" NOTE. The loan office debt formed a part of the Treasury expenditures.

" The foreign expenditures, civil, military, naval,

of the United States (inclusive of the state debts) was estimated at
$42,009,375, and the annual interest at $2,415,956. No funds had,
at this time, been provided for the payment either of the interest or
principal of this debt. As the war was now brought to a close, it became necessary for Congress to provide permanent funds for this purpose. It had been foreseen by many, that this could not be done,
unless Congress had the power to regulate the commerce of the country, or at least, were vested with a power to levy duties on imports.
By the articles of confederation, this power was not delegated to
them, but remained in the respective states, who had the right of laying and collecting such duties on imports, as they judged proper for
their own benefit. Congress could only recommend to the states, the
propriety and necessity of delegating to them this power for the ben-

and contingences, amount, by computation to
the sum of - - - - - - -   5,000,000 00
" The expenditures, of the several states, from the
commencement of the war, to the establishment
of peace, cannot be stated with any degree of
certainty, because the accounts thereof remain
to be settled. But as the United States have
granted certain sums for the relief of the several
states, to be funded by the general government,
therefore, estimate the total amount of said
assumption, - - - - - -   21,000,000 00

" Estimated expense of the late war, specie dolls,   135,193,703 00
The advances made from the Treasury, were principally in a paper medium, which was called continental money, and which in a short time depreciated ; the specie value of it is given in the foregoing estimate. The advances made at the Treasury of the United States, in continental money in old
and new emissions, are estimated as follows, viz. :—

	OLD EMISSION.		NEW EMISSION.	
	Dolls.	90ths.	Dolls.	90ths.
In 1776 - - - -	20,064,666	66		
1777 - - -	26,426,333	1		
1778 - - - -	66,965,269	34		
1779 - - -	149,703,856	77		
1780 - - - -	82,908,320	47	891,236	80
1781 - - -	11,408,095	00	1,179,249	00
	$357,476,541	45	$2,070,485	80

efit of all. Accordingly, as early as the 3d day of July, 1781, they passed a resolution, recommending it to the several states " as indispensably necessary, that they vest a power in Congress, to levy, for the use of the United States, a duty of five per cent. ad valorem, at the time and place of importation, upon all goods, wares, and merchandize of foreign growth and manufacture, which may be imported into any of the said states, from any foreign Port, Island, or Plantation, after the first day of May, 1781," with the exception of certain articles. They also, at the same time, resolved, " that the monies, arising from the said duties, be appropriated to the discharge of the principal and interest of the debts already contracted, or which may be contracted, on the faith of the United State, for supporting the war, and that the said duties be continued until the said debts be fully and finally discharged." The journals of the old Congress shew, that this resolution, in the opinion of some of the members of that body was not sufficiently extensive ; but that Congress ought to have the general power of regulating the whole commerce of the states, and the exclusive right of laying duties on imported articles. A substitute was, therefore, proposed, couched in more general terms, declaring it to be " indispensably necessary, that the United States in Congress assembled, should be vested with a right of superintending the *commercial regulations* of every state, that none may take place, that shall be partial or contrary to the common interest ; and that they should be vested, with the *exclusive* right of laying duties upon all imported articles." This substitute was negatived, and the resolution which passed was not accepted by the states. On the 18th of April, 1783, Congress again urged the several states to establish some permanent funds for the payment of the debts of the United States. For this purpose, by a resolution of that date, they recommended to the states, " as indisensably necessary to the restoration of public credit, and to the punctual discharge of the public debts, to invest the United States in Congress assembled, with a power to levy, for the use of the United States, the following duties upon goods imported into the said states, from any foreign Port, Island, or Plantation.

" Upon all rum, of Jamaica proof, per gall. 4-90ths of a dollar.

— all other spiritous liquors, - 3 " do.
— Madeira wine, - - - 12 " do.

— all other wines,	-	-	6-90ths of a dollar.
— common Bohea tea, per lb.		-	6 "	do.
— all other teas,	-	-	24 "	do.
— pepper,	-	-	-	-	3 "	do.
— brown sugar,	-	-	-	$\frac{1}{2}$ "	do.
— loaf sugar	-	-	-	2 "	do.
— all other sugars	-	-	-	1 "	do.
— molasses, per gallon,	-	-	1 "	do.
— cocoa and coffee,	-	-	-	1 "	do.

and upon all other goods, a duty of five per cent. ad valorem, at time and place of importation ; with a proviso that none of the said duties should be applied to any other purpose, than the discharge of the interest and principal of the debts contracted on the faith of the United States, for supporting the war, agreeably to the resolution of the 16th of December last, nor be continued for a longer term, than twenty-five years," &c. It was calculated, that the proposed duties would raise an annual sum of 915,956 dollars. This would fall short of paying the annual interest of the debt, about one million and a half of dollars, Congress, therefore, at the same time, recommended to the states " to establish for a time limited to 25 years, and to appropriate to the discharge of the interest and principal of the debt, substantial and effectual revenues, of such nature, as they may judge convenient, for supplying their respective proportions of 1,500,000 dollars, annually, exclusive of the aforementioned duties."

This system was not to take effect, until acceded to, by all the states, but when adopted by all, was to be a mutual compact, irrevocable by one or more, without the concurence of the whole, or a majority of the United States in Congress assembled. To induce its adoption, an appeal was made to the states, by Congress in an able address, in which they urged the propriety and justice of making some permanent provision, for the payment, at least, of the interest of a debt, which was the price of their independence. These propositions, however, were not agreed to by all the states, in such a manner, as to take effect. Congress, therefore, had no means of paying either the principal or interest of the debt, but by requisitions upon the states. Had this plan been adopted, the produce of the duties recommended by Congress would, no doubt, have exceeded the estimate. Before the adoption of the present constitution, and the regular establishment of custom-houses, under the present government, there were no data from which any accurate calculation could be made, of the amount of exports and imports of the United States, or of the value of their trade with particular countries. The English custom-house books shew the imports from and exports to the United States, and furnish the best account of the amount of our trade with Great-Britain from the peace of 1783, to the establishment of the present general government.

The following is an account of the imports into England from the United States, and exports to the United-States from that country in sterling money, from 1784 to 1790, taken from the English custom-house books—viz.

Years.	Imports.	Exports.
1784 - - - -	£749,345	- - - £3,679,467
1785 - - - -	893,594	- - - - 2,308,023
1786 - - - - -	843,119	- - - - 1,603,465
1787 - - - -	893,637	- - - - 2,009,111
1788 - - - -	1,023,789	- - - - 1,886,142
1789 - - - -	1,050,198	- - - - 2,525,298
1790 - - - -	1,191,071	- - - - 3,431,778

During the first two years after the war, goods imported from England alone, amounted to nearly six millions sterling. As the value here stated is the official value, which is considerably less than the real, the amount of goods imported from England into the United States in the year 1784 must have been about eighteen millions of dollars, and in 1785, about twelve millions, making, in those two years, thirty millions of dollars;—while the exports from the United States to England during that time, were only between eight and nine millions. This vast influx of goods soon drained the United States of a great part of the specie they had, at the close of the war. Congress in vain therefore made requisitions upon the states, for money to fill the public treasury. The impoverished state of the country, in consequence of the war, the want of regular markets for its produce, the burden of the states, in providing for the payment of their own particular debts, incurred during the war, and a jealousy which began to exist among the states, all combined to retard a compliance with these requisitions.* The interest of the debt was, therefore, unpaid, public credit was gone, the debt itself was considered of little value, and was sold at last by many of the original holders for about one-tenth of its nominal value. In addition to this, private credit was much impaired. During the war, the collection of debts was, in a great measure, suspended, and on the return of peace, goods were imported to a larger amount, than we had the means of paying for; many, therefore, contracted debts beyond their abilities to pay. The courts of justice were filled with suits against delinquent debtors. The importing states took advantage of their situation, and levied a duty on imports, for their own benefit, at the expense of the other states.

Thus burdened with public and private debts, and called upon for the payment of heavy taxes, and with a scarcity of money, the people, in some of the states, to remedy those evils, had recourse to paper money, and in one state, there was an open insurrection, which threatened not only the peace and existence of that state, but the peace and existence of the union.

In this situation, all became sensible of the inefficiency of the general government, and of the necessity of vesting Congress, with the power of regulating trade and commerce, and of bringing into operation, the energies and resources of the country, for the general benefit.

In September, 1786, in consequence of a proposition from the state of Virginia, Commissioners from that state, and from the states of Pennsylvania, New-York, New-Jersey, and Delaware, met at Annapolis, in Maryland, " to take into consideration the *trade and commerce* of the United States, to consider how far an uniform system, in

---

* In a report made to Congress, by the board of Treasury, dated September 20th, 1787, it is stated, that the requisitions upon the states, for the payment of the interest of the domestic debt, in the years 1782, 1784-5 & 6, amounted to the sum of $6,279,376 27, and the Board say, " It is with regret we are constrained to observe, that to the 31st of March last, the aggregate payments, on account of these requisitions, do not appear, from any documents in the Treasury office, to exceed the sum
of   -   -   -   -   -   -   -   -   -   - $1,003,725 57
Leaving a balance due of no less, than   -   -   -   -   5,275,650 60
                                                              _____
                                                              $6,279,376 27

their commercial intercourse and regulations, might be necessary to their common interest and permanent harmony, and to report to the several states, such an act, relative to this great object, as, when unanimously ratified by them, would enable the United States in Congress assembled, effectually to provide for the same." Commissioners were appointed also from the states of New-Hampshire, Massachusetts, Rhode-Island, and North-Carolina, but did not attend. In consequence of the partial representation of the states and their limited powers, the Commissioners present did not think proper to proceed on the business of their appointment. They, however, drew up an address and report, to their respective state Legislatures, in which, after stating the reasons of their not proceeding, they say, " deeply impressed, however, with the magnitude and importance of the object confided to them on this occasion, your Commissioners cannot forbear to indulge an expression of their earnest and unanimous wish, that speedy measures may be taken to effect a general meeting of the states in a future convention, for the same and such other purposes, as the situation of public affairs may be found to require." They, therefore, suggest the propriety of a meeting of Commissioners from all the states, to be held at Philadelphia, on the second Monday in May, 1787, " to take into consideration the situation of the United States, to devise such further provision as shall to them appear necessary to render the constitution of the federal government adequate to the exigences of the union." &c. This report and address, was sent to Congress, and to the Executives of the several states, not represented at Annapolis. In consequence of the recommendation contained in this address and a resolution of Congress, of February 21st, 1787, a general convention of the states was held at Philadelphia, in May, 1787, and on the 17th of September following, a new constitution was agreed upon, and went into operation on the 4th day of March, 1789. By this constitution the general government, among other important powers, are vested with power " *to regulate commerce, and to levy duties, imposts,*" &c. Under this new form of government, with the father of his country at its head, trade and commerce soon revived, public and private credit was restored, a new spring was given to agriculture and manufactures, and new security afforded to the various pursuits of honest industry. Since the establishment of the present government, the progress of national, as well as individual, wealth has kept pace with the increase of population ; and until the commencement of commercial restrictions in December, 1807, and the declaration of war against Great-Britain, in 1812, no nation, it is believed, had ever increased so rapidly in wealth as the United States. This will appear, from an attention to the increase in the quantity and value of their exports and imports, and the great increase of duties on imports ; from the vast increase of their shipping, and of their trade and intercourse with different parts of the world ; from the various monied institutions, which have been established ; from the great sum expended in making roads and canals, and in other internal improvements ; from the rapid growth of cities and towns ; and from the rise in the value of lands, in every part of the union. A view of this increase of the wealth and resources of the United States, together with some of the principal causes of it, from the commencement of the present government, until the year 1814, a period of about twenty-four years, is one principal object, and will be the subject of the following chapters.

CHAPTER III.

EXPORTS—Divided into those of domestic, and those of foreign origin—Exports of domestic produce, distinguished into those, which are 1st, the produce of the sea—2d, the produce of the forest—3d, the produce of agriculture—and 4th, manufactures—Products of the sea, derived from the cod and whale fisheries—State of the cod fishery previous to the American revolution, and to the time of the establishment of the present government—Number of vessels employed in this fishery from 1791 to 1813, and quantity of fish exported during the same period—Whale fishery originated at Nantucket in 1690—Amount of tonnage and number of seamen employed in it at different periods—Value of exports, the produce of the fisheries from 1803 to 1814—Products of the forest—viz. lumber, naval stores, pot and pearl ashes, skins and furs, ginseng, and oak bark, and other dyes—Value and quantity of each exported at different periods.

WE shall begin with the exports—these consist of articles of the growth, produce, and manufacture of the United States, and of those which are of foreign growth and produce. Provision was made at the Treasury, at an early period of the present government, to ascertain the quantity and value of all the exports of the country ; but in the general accounts no discrimination was made between the value of domestic or foreign articles, until 1802. In order to ascertain the value of the exports, directions are given, from the Treasury department, to the several collectors of the customs, to add, in their quarterly returns of duties the quantity of the various articles exported, and also their prices at the places of exportation. The quantity of the articles exported is furnished the collectors, by the exporters, and may sometimes fall short, and sometimes exceed the real quantity. At the Treasury, an average is made of the prices returned by the collectors, from the principal ports, and the value of the articles exported is calculated from the average price thus ascertained. Table No. I. annexed to this chapter, contains a statement of the value of all the exports from each state and territory, annually, from the

1st of October, 1790,* to the 30th of September, 1810. Table No. II. exhibits a statement of the value of the exports of domestic growth, produce, and manufacture, from each state and territory from October, 1802, to September 30th, 1810, and Table No. III. a statement of the value of the exports of foreign growth and produce, during the same period. The articles exported both domestic and foreign are various, and are contained in Table No. IV. in each year, from 1791 to 1814—taken from the Treasury books.

The whole value of exports in each year, from 1790 to 1814, and the value of those of domestic and foreign origin, since 1803, was as follows :—

to Sept. 30.	Total value of exports. Dolls.	Value of exports of domestic origin. Dolls.	Value of exports of foreign origin. Dolls.
1791	- 19,012,041		
1792	- 20,753,098		
1793	- 26,109,572		
1794	- 33,026,233		
1795	- 47,989,472		
1796	- 67,064,097		
1797	- 56,850,206		
1798	- 61,527,097		
1799	- 78,665,522		
1800	- 70,971,780		
1801	- 94,115,925		
1802	- 72,483,160		
1803	- 55,800,033	- 42,205,961	- 13,594,072
1804	- 77,699,074	- ` 41,467,477	- 36,231,597
1805	- 95,566,021	- 42,387,002	- 53,179,019
1806	- 101,536,963	- 41,253,727	- 60,283,236
1807	- 108,343,150	- 48,699,592	- 59,643,558
1808	- 22,430,960	- 9,433,546	- 12,997,414
1809	- 52,203,283	- 31,405,702	- 20,797,531

* No annual return of exports had been made at the Treasury, prior to October, 1790.

		Total value of exports. Dolls.		Value of exports of domestic origin. Dolls.		Value of exports of foreign origin. Dolls.
to Sept. 30.						
1810	-	66,757,970	-	42,366,675	-	24,391,295
1811	-	61,316,833	-	45,294,043	-	16,022,790
1812	-	38,527,236	-	30,032,109	-	8,495,127
1813	-	27,855,997	-	25,008,152	-	2,847,845
1814	-	6,927,441	-	6,782,272	-	145,169

The exports of domestic growth, produce, and manufacture, have been distinguished, at the Treasury, into those which are—

    1st. The produce of the Sea.
    2d. The produce of the Forest.
    3d. The produce of Agriculture.
    4th. Manufactures and those which are uncertain.

This division of the exports of domestic produce has been made, and the value of the articles exported, under each division, has been ascertained at the Treasury, and exhibited in the annual account of exports, since the year 1802. It presents a useful and important view of the different pursuits and employments of the citizens of the United States, inhabiting, as they do, an extensive country, differing in climate, as well as soil ; and indicates the various sources of the wealth of the nation.

Each of these will be considered in their order :—

1st. THE PRODUCTS OF THE SEA.

These are derived from the cod and whale fisheries, and from the river fisheries, such as herring, shad, salmon, mackarel, &c. The cod fishery has been an object of the first importance to the states of Massachusetts and New-Hampshire, from their first settlement. It has furnished a lucrative employment to the inhabitants of these states, situated as they are, in the neighbourhood of the fishery. It has given employment to the ship-builder, and has always been considered, as the best nursery for seamen.

The vast quantities of fish, which, after the discovery of North-America, were found along the banks of New-Foundland, soon attracted the attention of the Europeans. The inhabitants of Biscay in Spain, and of Britanny in France, are said to have first engaged in this fishery. The English and French afterwards claimed the exclusive right to it, in consequence of their possessing the adjacent coasts. While we were Colonies, we had the right of fishing there, as being a part of the British empire; and by the 3d article of the treaty of peace, between Great-Britain and the United States, in 1783, " It is agreed that the people of the United States shall continue to enjoy unmolested the right to take fish of every kind, on the grand bank, and on all other banks of New-Foundland; also, in the gulph of St. Lawrence, and at all other places in the sea, where the inhabitants of both countries used at any time to fish; that the inhabitants of the United States shall have liberty to take fish of every kind on such part of the coast of New Foundland, as British fishermen shall use (but not to dry or cure the same on the island;) and also on the coasts, bays, and creeks of all other his Britannic Majesty's dominions in America; and that the American fishermen shall have liberty to dry and cure fish in any of the unsettled bays, harbours, and creeks of Nova-Scotia, Magdalen islands, and Labrador, so long as the same shall remain unsettled; but so soon as the same or either of them shall be settled, it shall not be lawful for the said fishermen to dry or cure fish at such settlement, without a previous agreement for that purpose with the inhabitants, proprietors, or possessors of the ground." The cod fishery previous to the American revolution, in Massachusetts alone, gave employment annually to about four thousand seamen, and about twenty-eight thousand tons of shipping, and produced about three hundred and fifty thousand quintals of fish, which, at the place of exportation, were valued at more than one million of dollars. Tables Nos. V. and VI. shew the state of the fishery in Massachusetts, from 1765 to 1775; and also from 1786 to 1790*, containing an average of the number of vessels annually employed, their tonnage, number of seamen, and also the quantity of fish exported during those two

* See the representation of the Legislature of Massachusetts to Congress in 1790, on the subject of their fisheries, and report of the secretary of state on the subject of their fisheries in 1791.

periods, from August 20th, 1789, to September 30th, 1790, and the countries to which exported. From this it will be seen, that up to the year 1790, the cod fishery had not recovered from the effects of the revolutionary war. From 1765 to 1775, the average number of vessels annually employed was six hundred and sixty-five, their tonnage twenty-five thousand six hundred and thirty, seamen four thousand four hundred and five, and fish exported amounted to three hundred and fifty-one thousand three hundred quintals ; and from 1786 to 1790, the average number of vessels annually employed was only five hundred and thirty-nine, tonnage nineteen thousand one hundred and eighty-five, seamen three thousand two hundred and eighty-seven, and fish exported only two hundred and fifty thousand six hundred and fifty quintals.

In consequence of a representation made to Congress, by the Legislature of Massachusetts, in the year 1790, of the low and embarrassed state of the fisheries, and a report made thereon by the secretary of state, a bounty was given, on the exportation of salted fish, by way of draw-back of the duty on imported salt, and afterwards an allowance in money was made to vessels employed for a certain number of months in the cod fishery. In consequence of this encouragement, and the happy effects upon trade and commerce, produced by the establishment of the general government, the cod fishery increased until the commencement of the embargo and restrictive system. The quantity of dried or smoked fish, and of pickled fish, exported from 1791 to 1814, was as follows, viz. :—

	Dried Fish. Quintals.	Bbls. of pickled fish.	Kegs of pickled fish.
1791	383,237	57,424	
1792	364,898	48,277	
1793	372,825	45,440	
1794	436,907	36,929	
1795	400,818	55,999	
1796	377,713	84,558	5,256
1797	406,016	69,782	7,351
1798	411,175	66,827	6,220
1799	428,495	63,542	15,993

	Dried Fish. Quintals.	Bbls. of pickled fish.	Kegs of pickled fish.
1800 - - -	392,726 - - -	50,388 - - -	12,403
1801 - - -	410,948 - - -	85,935 - - -	10,424
1802 - - -	440,925 - - -	75,819 - - -	13,229
1803 - - -	461,870 - - -	76,831 - - -	11,565
1804 - - -	567,828 - - -	89,482 - - -	13,045
1805 - - -	514,549 - - -	56,670 - - -	7,207
1806 - - -	537,457 - - -	64,615 - - -	10,155
1807 - - -	473,924 - - -	57,621 - - -	13,743
1808 - - -	155,808 - - -	18,957 - - -	3,036
1809 - - -	345,648 - - -	54,777 - - -	9,380
1810 - - -	280,804 - - -	34,674 - - -	5,964
1811 - - -	214,387 - - -	44,716 - - -	9,393
1812 - - -	169,019 - - -	23,636 - - -	3,143
1813 . - -	63,616 - - -	13,833 - - -	568
1814 - - -	31,310 - - -	8,436 - - -	87

The amount of tonnage employed in the cod fishery, from 1795 to 1813, was as follows, viz. :—

	Enrolled Tonnage. Tons. 95-100.	Tonnage of Vessels, Licensed under 20 tons. Tons. 95-100
1795 - -	24,887 6 - -	6,046 5
1796 - -	28,509 39 - -	6,453 41
1797 - -	33,406 67 - -	7,222 31
1798 - -	35,476 81 - -	7,269 37
1799 - -	23,932 26 - -	6,046 17
1800 - -	22,306 94 - -	7,120 6
1801 - -	31,279 57 - -	8,101 85
1802 - -	32,987 42 - -	8,533 56
1803 - -	43,416 20 - -	8,394 24
1804 - -	43,088 08 - -	8,925 73
1805 - -	48,479 30 - -	8,986 37
1806 - -	50,353 20 - -	8,820 57
1807 - -	60,689 88 - -	9,616 20

	Enrolled Tonnage. Tons. 95-100.	Tonnage of Vessels, licensed under 20 tons. Tons. 95-100
1808 - -	43,597 40	- - 8,400 22
1809 - -	26,109 67	- - 8,376 93
1810 - -	26,250 91	- - 8,577 28
1811 both enrolled & licensed under 20 tons was		37,588 7
1812 do. do.	do.	27,841 17
1813 do. do.	do.	18,522 81

The vessels employed in the cod fishery are owned in the states of New-Hampshire, Massachusetts, Rhode-Island, Connecticut and New-York, except sixty-six tons in Virginia in 1796, and forty-eight tons in New-Jersey, in 1803, but principally in Massachusetts. The greatest amount of tonnage ever employed from the United States in the cod fishery was in the year 1807, being seventy thousand three hundred and six tons. Of this, Massachusetts owned sixty-two thousand two hundred and thirteen tons. The number of seamen employed in this fishery, on an average of ten years, from 1791 to 1800, has been estimated at five thousand, and the average tonnage, for the same period, at thirty-three thousand.*

From 1801 to 1807, the annual average amount of tonnage employed, was about forty-four thousand, and the number of seamen, according to the above proportion, about seven thousand annually.

The value of the dried fish, and pickled fish, exported since the year 1802, has been as follows :—

	Cod or dried fish.	Pickled fish.
1803 -	- $1,620,000	- - $560,000
1804 -	- 2,400,000	- - 640,000
1805 -	- 2,058,000	- - 348,000
1806 -	- 2,150,000	- - 366,000
1807 -	- 1,896,000	- - 302,000
1808 -	- 623,000	- - 98,000
1809 -	- 1,123,000	- - 282,000
1810 -	- 913,000	- - 214,000

* See letter from the Secretary of the Treasury, to the House of Representatives, July 29th, 1803.

	Cod or dried fish.	Pickled fish.
1811	$757,000	$305,000
1812	592,000	146,000
1813	210,000	81,000
1814	128,000	50,000

The French had formerly the greatest share in the cod fishery. In 1745, the Governour of the province of Massachusetts, Shirley, transmitted to the British government, an estimate of the French fishery in the preceding year, from the gut of Canso to Lewisburgh, and thence to the north-east part of Cape Breton. According to this estimate, the French employed, in 1744, four hundred and fourteen large ships in taking and carrying the fish to market, and about twenty-four thousand five hundred and twenty men, and the quantity of fish taken was one million one hundred and forty-nine thousand quintals. The French fishery was afterwards reduced, and for many years past has been annihilated.

For many years previous the late war, between the United States and Great-Britain, this fishery has been carried on, principally, by the British and Americans. The usual markets for American fish are the West-Indies and the southern parts of Europe. (See Table VII.)

The late treaty of peace between the United States and Great-Britain is silent on the subject of the cod fishery. Our right to take fish in the open sea cannot be questioned ; what will hereafter be the state of the coast fishery, which we enjoyed under the treaty of 1783, is yet uncertain.

THE WHALE FISHERY.

The whale fishery first attracted the attention of the Americans in 1690, and originated at the island of Nantucket, in boats from the shore. In 1715, six sloops, of thirty-eight tons burden each, were employed in this fishery, from that island. For many years their adventures were confined to the American coast, but as whales grew scarce here, they were extended to the Western Islands, and to the Brazils, and at length to the North and South Seas.* For a long time, the Dutch seemed

* See Collections of the Massachusetts Historical Society.

to monopolize the whale fishery, which they followed, with success, in the Greenland or Northern Seas.

As early as 1663, they had two hundred and two ships employed in this fishery, and in 1721, as many as two hundred and sixty ; in 1788, the number was reduced to sixty-nine, and for many years past, not only has this branch of their commerce, but almost every other, been completely annihilated. In 1731, the Americans had about thirteen hundred tons of shipping employed in this fishery along their coast. About the year 1750, the whale left the American coast. The hardy enterprise and activity of the American sailor, however, soon followed him in every part of the Northern and Southern Seas.

From 1771 to 1775, Massachusetts employed, annually, one hundred and eighty-three vessels, of thirteen thousand eight hundred and twenty tons, in the northern whale fishery, and one hundred and twenty-one vessels, of fourteen thousand and twenty-six tons, in the southern, navigated by four thousand and fifty-nine seamen. The peculiar mode of paying the seamen, in these hazardous voyages, has contributed not a little to the success of the voyages themselves. Each has a share in the profits of the voyage, and is dependent on his own exertions for the reward of his toils. Whether he shall be rich or poor, depends on his activity in managing the boat, in pursuit of the whale, and his dexterity, in directing the harpoon. This has led to a spirit of enterprise and hardihood, never surpassed, if ever equalled, by the seamen of any nation in the world.*

* The celebrated Burke, in his speech, in the House of Commons, about the year 1774, on the subject of American affairs, has done ample justice to the industrious and enterprising spirit of this class of American seamen. "As to the wealth (said he) which the Colonists have drawn from the sea, by their fisheries, you had all that matter fully opened at your bar. You surely thought these acquisitions of value, for they seemed to excite your envy, and yet the spirit by which that enterprising employment has been exercised, ought rather, in my opinion, to have raised esteem and admiration. And pray, sir, what in the world is equal to it ? Pass by the other parts, and look at the manner, in which the New-England people of late carried on the whale fishery. While we follow them among the tumbling mountains of ice, and behold them penetrating into the deepest frozen recesses of Hudson's and Davis' Straits ; while we are looking for them beneath the arctic circle, we hear, that they have pierced into the opposite re

During the war of the American revolution, this fishery was destroyed; on the return of peace, it recovered, by degrees, and from 1787 to 1789, ninety-one vessels, of five thousand eight hundred and twenty tons, were annually employed in the northern fishery, and thirty-one vessels, of four thousand three hundred and ninety tons, in the southern, with one thousand six hundred and eleven seamen. The quantity of spermaceti oil taken annually, from 1771 to 1775, was thirty-nine thousand three hundred and ninety barrels, and of whale oil eight thousand six hundred and fifty. From 1787 to 1789, the quantity of spermaceti oil taken annually was seven thousand nine hundred and eighty barrels, and whale oil thirteen thousand one hundred and thirty. In the representation made to Congress in the year 1790, by the legislature of Massachusetts, it is stated that, before the late war, about four thousand seamen, and twenty-four thousand tons of shipping were annually employed from that state in the whale fishery, and that the produce thereof was about £350,000 lawful money, or about $1,160,000.* A great part of this fishery has been

* In the papers which accompanied this representation it is stated, that "about one quarter of the spermaceti is head matter, one quarter of which was exported to Great-Britain, the remainder manufactured into candles. The spermaceti oil, previous to the revolution, was mostly exported to Great-Britain. The average price in that market, for five years, previous to the war, was about £40 sterling for the spermaceti oil and £50 for head. The whale oil was formerly about one half exported to the French and English West-India Islands; the other half sold in the United States. The ave-

gion of polar cold; that they are at the antipodes, and engaged under the frozen serpent of the south. Faulkland Island, which seemed too remote and romantic an object for the grasp of national ambition, is but a stage and resting place for their victorious industry. Nor is the equinoctial heat more discouraging to them than the accumulated winter of both poles. We know, that while some of them draw the line or strike the harpoon on the coast of Africa, others run the longitude and pursue their gigantic game along the coast of Brazil. No sea, but what is vexed with their fisheries. No climate, that is not witness of their toils. Neither the perseverance of Holland, nor the activity of France, nor the dexterous and firm sagacity of English enterprise, ever carried their most perilous mode of hardy industry to the extent to which it has been pursued by this recent people; a people who are still in the gristle, and not hardened into manhood."

carried on from Nantucket, where it originated, a small island about fifteen miles in length, and two or three miles in breadth, situated about thirty miles from the coast. Before the revolutionary war, this small island had sixty-five ships, of four thousand eight hundred and seventy-five tons, annually employed in the northern, and eighty-five ships, of ten thousand two hundred tons, in the southern fishery. From 1787 to 1789, it had only eighteen ships, of one thousand three hundred and fifty tons, in the northern, and eighteen ships, of two thousand seven hundred tons, in the southern fishery.* For many years past, this fishery has been carried on from this island and from New-Bedford, a large commercial and flourishing town on the coast, in its neighbourhood, and has employed from fifteen thousand to eighteen thousand tons of shipping, principally in the Southern Seas. Although Great-Britain has, at various times, given large bounties to her ships employed in this fishery, yet the whalemen of Nantucket and New-Bedford, unprotected and unsupported by any thing but their own industry and enterprise, have generally been able to meet their competitors in a foreign market. The quantity of spermaceti and common whale oil, whale bone, and spermaceti candles exported from 1791 to 1814 appears from table No. IV. Their value since 1802, has been as follows :—

	Whale (common) oil and bone. Dolls.	Spermaceti oil and candles. Dolls.
1803	280,000	175,000
1804	310,000	70,000

* See Tables No. VIII and IX.

rage price of this oil, about $70 per ton. A whale, producing one hundred and twenty barrels of whale oil, will generally produce two thousand pounds of bone, which was chiefly exported to Great-Britain, the price about half a dollar per pound. A whale, producing fifty to sixty barrels, will generally produce nearest ten pounds of bone to a barrel of oil. The average price of oil for three years past, (viz. 1787, 1788, and 1789) :—

Spermaceti $100 per ton
Whale oil - - - 50 do.
Head matter - 150 do.
Bone, about 15 cts. per pound."

		Whale (common) oil and bone. Dolls.		Spermaceti oil and candles. Dolls.
1805	- -	315,000	- -	163,000
1806	- -	418,000	- -	182,000
1807	- -	476,000	- -	130,000
1808	- -	88,000	- -	33,000
1809	- -	169,000	- -	136,000
1810	- -	222,000	- -	132,000
1811	- -	78,000	- -	273,000
1812	- -	56,000	- -	141,000
1813	- -	2,500	- -	10,500
1814	- -	1,000	- -	9,000

The following is the total value of exports, consisting of the produce of the sea, from 1803 to 1814, viz.

		Dolls.
1803	- - - - - -	2,635,000
1804	- - - - - -	3,420,000
1805	- - - - - -	2,884,000
1806	- - - - - -	3,116,000
1807	- - - - - -	2,804,000
1808	- - - - - -	832,000
1809	- - - - - -	1,710,000
1810	- - - - - -	1,481,000
1811	- - - - - -	1,413,000
1812	- - - - - -	935,000
1813	- - - - - -	304,000
1814	- - - - - -	188,000

The common whale oil finds a market in the West-Indies, Great-Britain, France, Spain, and Portugal. The greatest part of the spermaceti oil, is carried to Great-Britain. (See Table No. X.) The late war between the United States and Great-Britain has again almost annihilated the cod and whale fisheries.* While in the years previous to the restrictive system and the war, the fisheries furnished

* Twenty-four whalemen were taken by the British in the late war.

articles for exportation to an amount of more than three millions of dollars, in 1814, the exports of the produce of the fisheries is reduced to the sum of $188,000.

2d. THE PRODUCTS OF THE FOREST.

The products of the forest consist of lumber of all kinds, naval stores (such as tar, pitch, turpentine and rosin) pot and pearl ashes, skins and furs, ginseng, and oak bark and other dyes.

The exportation of lumber has always been an object of no inconsiderable importance to this country. The first settlers found here immense forests of wood and timber, and as they cleared these lands the timber was of little value except for exportation. The lumber exported consists of staves and heading, shingles, hoops and poles, boards, plank, scantling and timber of various sorts for masts, spars, buildings, &c. The official value of lumber of all kinds exported in the year 1770, was about £154,637 sterling, or $686,588. From 1803 to 1807, the value of lumber exported, on an average, exceeded two millions and a half of dollars. Naval stores, such as tar, pitch, turpentine, and rosin, have long been an object of importance, not only for home consumption, but for exportation. Great-Britain has always been dependent upon foreign countries for these articles, which to her are of the first necessity. Before they were produced in her North-American Colonies, she obtained them from the north of Europe, and particularly from the pitch and tar company of Sweden. About the year 1703, this company attempted to raise their price upon these articles, by prohibiting the exportation of them, except in their own ships. This induced the British government to encourage the production of them in their Colonies. By the 3 and 4 of Ann, a bounty of £4 per ton was given on the importation of tar and pitch, and £3 per ton on rosin and turpentine from the American Colonies. These articles are produced principally in North-Carolina, and this bounty, no doubt, had its effect in increasing the production of them in that Province. In the year 1770, the quantity of tar exported was eighty-two thousand and seventy-five barrels, of pitch, nine thousand one hundred and fourteen barrels, and of turpentine, seventeen thousand and fourteen, and their official value was £34,693 sterling, or about $144,000.

Since the year 1791, the quantity of these articles has varied almost every year; in 1795, ninety thousand and sixty-six barrels of tar were exported. During the years 1805–6 and 7, the average quantity of tar exported was sixty-four thousand nine hundred and seventeen barrels—of turpentine, seventy-four thousand six hundred and seven barrels, and of pitch, nine thousand and eight barrels, and their average value was about $500,000. Before the American Revolution, Great-Britain also encouraged the production of pot and pearl ashes in her North-American Colonies, as being necessary for her manufac· tures. In 1761, the society instituted at London for the encouragement of arts, manufactures, and commerce, offered large premiums to those who should import from the American Colonies the greatest quantity of pot and pearl ashes. Treatises, describing the method of making these articles, were, about the same time, sent over, and circulated among the Colonists. In the year 1770, one thousand one hundred and seventy-three tons of pot ashes, and seven hundred thirty-seven tons of pearl ashes were exported from the North-American Colonies; the value of these was then estimated at £64,660 9 2 sterling, or about $290,000. The exportation of these articles has since greatly increased; the value of pot and pearl ashes exported in 1807, amounted to $1,490,000.

As the American forests abounded in wild animals, whose skins and furs were valuable, furs and peltry have always constituted a part of American exports. In the year 1770, the official value of these articles exported, from all the North-American Colonies, which included Canada, was £149,224 14 4 sterling, or about $670,000. The average value of these articles, exported from the United States from 1791 to 1803, was about $300,000; from 1804 to 1807 inclusive, the annual average value was about $900,000. It is believed, that during these years, a large proportion of the furs exported were brought from Canada, and shipped at the Atlantic ports.

Ginseng, a root so highly valued in China, has been long known in North-America, and has become an article of export. In 1770, the quantity exported was seventy-four thousand six hundred and four pounds, and was valued at about $5,000. The greatest quantity exported since 1791, was in 1806, being four hundred forty-eight thousand three hundred and ninety-four pounds, and valued at $139,000. Oak and other bark and wood for tanning and dying, have also become articles of exportation of some value. In 1803, they amounted to $225,000.

The following is the value of all the exports, which are the produce of the forest, from 1803 to 1814, viz.—

1803	$4,850,000
1804	4,630,000
1805	5,261,000
1806	4,861,000
1807	5,476,000
1808	1,399,000
1809	4,583,000
1810	4,978,000
1811	5,286,000
1812	2,701,000
1813	1,107,000
1814	570,000

The value of each of the articles exported during the same periods, is as follows, viz.—

	Lumber of all kinds. Dolls.	Naval stores. Dolls.	Pot & pearl ashes. Dolls.	Furs & skins. Dolls.	Ginseng. Dolls.	Oak bark & other dyes. Dolls.
1803	2,800,000	460,000	735,000	500,000	100,000	225,000
1804	2,540,000	322,000	640,000	956,000	84,000	88,000
1805	2,607,000	702,000	776,000	967,000	148,000	61,000
1806	2,495,000	409,000	935,000	841,000	139,000	42,000
1807	2,637,000	335,000	1,490,000	852,000	143,000	19,000
1808	723,000	102,000	408,000	161,000		5,000
1809	1,843,000	737,000	1,506,000	332,000	136,000	29,090
1810	2,537,000	473,000	1,579,000	177,000	140,000	72,000
1811	3,195,000	834,000	752,000	314,000	79,000	112,000
1812	1,638,000	490,000	333,000	123,000	10,000	107,000
1813	636,000	91,000	204,000	58,000		118,000
1814	258,000	31,000	217,000	22,000	39,900	3,000

The articles of lumber are carried, principally, to the West-Indies, except staves and heading, many of which go to Great-Britain and Portugal. Nearly all the naval stores, and pot and pearl ashes, go to Great-Britain. For the destination of these articles from 1800 to 1811, see Tables No. XI, XII, XIII, XIV, XV, XVI. and XVII annexed to this chapter.

TABLE No. I.

A summary statement of the value of the exports of the sev[..] al States and Territories, annually, from the 1st of October, 1790, t[..] the 30th of September, 1810.

States & Territories.	1791.	1792.	1793.	1794.	1795.	1796.	1797.
New-Hampshire, -	142,859	181,413	198,204	153,860	229,427	378,161	275,840
Vermont, - -	-	-	-	-	-	-	-
Massachusetts, -	2,519,651	2,888,104	3,755,347	5,292,441	7,117,907	9,949,345	7,502,047
Rhode-Island, -	470,131	698,109	616,432	954,599	1,222,917	1,589,872	975,530
Connecticut, -	710,353	879,753	770,255	812,765	819,465	1,452,793	814,506
New-York, - -	2,505,465	2,535,790	2,932,370	5,442,183	10,304,581	12,208,027	13,308,064
New-Jersey, -	26,988	23,406	54,179	58,154	130,814	59,227	18,161
Pennsylvania, -	3,436,093	3,820,662	6,958,836	6,643,092	11,518,260	17,513,866	11,446,291
Delaware, - -	119,879	133,972	93,559	207,985	158,041	201,142	98,929
Maryland, - -	2,239,691	2,623,808	3,665,056	5,686,191	5,811,380	9,201,315	9,811,799
Dist. of Columbia,	-	-	-	-	-	-	-
Virginia, -	3,131,865	3,552,825	2,987,098	3,321,636	3,490,041	5,268,655	4,908,713
North-Carolina, -	524,548	527,900	365,414	321,587	492,161	671,487	540,901
South-Carolina, -	2,693,268	2,428,250	3,191,867	3,867,908	5,998,492	7,620,049	6,505,118
Georgia, -	491,250	459,106	520,955	263,832	695,986	950,158	644,307
Kentucky, -	-	-	-	-	-	-	-
Tennessee, -	-	-	-	-	-	-	-
Ohio, -	-	-	-	-	-	-	-
Indiana Territory,	-	-	-	-	-	-	-
Michigan do. -	-	-	-	-	-	-	-
Mississippi do. -	-	-	-	-	-	-	-
Orleans do. -	-	-	-	-	-	-	-
Total,	19,012,041	20,753,098	26,109,572	33,026,233	47,989,472	67,064,097	56,850,206

52

TABLE NO. I.—CONTINUED.

States and Territories.	1798.	1799.	1800.	1801.	1802.	1803.	1804.
New-Hampshire,	361,453	361,789	431,836	555,055	565,394	494,620	716,091
Vermont,	-	20,480	57,041	57,267	31,479	117,450	191,725
Massachusetts,	8,639,252	11,421,591	11,326,876	14,870,556	13,492,632	8,768,566	16,894,378
Rhode-Island,	947,827	1,055,273	1,322,945	1,832,773	2,433,363	1,275,596	1,735,671
Connecticut,	763,128	1,143,818	1,114,743	1,446,216	1,606,809	1,248,571	1,516,110
New-York,	14,300,892	18,719,527	14,045,079	19,351,136	13,792,276	10,818,387	16,081,281
New-Jersey,	61,877	9,722	2,289	25,406	26,227	21,311	24,829
Pennsylvania,	8,915,463	12,431,967	11,949,679	17,438,193	12,677,475	7,525,710	11,030,157
Delaware,	183,727	297,065	418,695	662,042	440,504	428,153	697,396
Maryland,	12,746,190	16,299,609	12,264,331	12,767,530	7,914,225	5,078,062	9,151,939
District of Columbia,	-	-	-	894,467	774,063	1,444,994	1,452,198
Virginia,	6,113,451	6,292,986	4,430,689	5,655,574	3,978,363	6,100,708	5,790,001
North-Carolina,	537,810	485,921	769,799	874,884	659,390	952,614	928,687
South-Carolina,	6,994,179	8,729,015	10,663,510	14,304,045	10,639,365	7,811,108	7,451,616
Georgia,	961,848	1,396,759	2,174,268	1,755,939	1,854,951	2,370,875	2,077,572
Kentucky,	-	-	-	-	626,673	-	-
Tennessee,	-	-	-	29,430	-	-	-
Ohio,	-	-	-	-	-	-	-
Indiana Territory,	-	-	-	-	443,955	33,214	17,320
Michigan do.	-	-	-	-	-	210,392	276,964
Mississippi do.	-	-	-	1,095,412	526,016	1,099,702	64,777
Orleans do.	-	-	-	-	-	-	1,600,362
Total,	61,527,097	78,665,522	70,971,780	94,115,925	72,483,160	55,800,033	77,699,074

TABLE No. I.—CONTINUED.

States and Territories.	1805.	1806.	1807.	1808.	1809.	1810.
New-Hampshire,	608,408	795,263	680,022	125,059	286,595	234,650
Vermont,	169,402	193,775	204,285	108,772	175,782	432,631
Massachusetts,	19,435,657	21,199,243	20,112,125	5,128,322	12,142,293	13,013,048
Rhode-Island,	2,572,049	2,091,835	1,657,564	242,034	1,284,532	1,331,576
Connecticut,	1,443,727	1,715,828	1,624,727	413,691	666,513	768,643
New-York,	23,482,943	21,762,845	26,357,963	5,606,058	12,581,562	17,242,330
New-Jersey,	20,743	33,867	41,186	20,799	319,175	430,267
Pennsylvania,	13,762,252	17,574,702	16,864,744	4,013,330	9,049,241	10,993,398
Delaware,	358,383	500,106	229,275	108,735	138,036	120,342
Maryland,	10,859,480	14,580,905	14,298,984	2,721,106	6,627,326	6,489,018
District of Columbia,	1,320,215	1,246,146	1,446,378	285,317	703,415	1,038,103
Virginia,	5,606,620	5,055,396	4,761,234	526,473	2,894,125	4,822,611
North-Carolina,	779,903	789,605	745,162	117,129	322,994	403,949
South-Carolina,	9,066,625	9,743,782	10,912,564	1,664,445	3,247,341	5,290,614
Georgia,	2,394,846	82,764	3,744,845	24,626	1,082,108	2,238,686
Kentucky,	-	-	-	-	-	-
Tennessee,	-	-	-	-	-	-
Ohio,	-	62,318	28,889	13,115	3,850	10,583
Indiana Territory,	-	-	-	-	-	-
Michigan do.	313,223	221,260	311,947	50,848	136,114	3,615
Mississippi do.	-	-	701	-	305	2,958
Orleans do.	3,371,545	3,887,323	4,320,555	1,261,101	541,926	1,890,948
Total,	95,566,021	101,536,963	108,343,150	22,430,960	52,203,233	66,757,970

TABLE No. II.

Statement shewing the value of the exports, the growth, produce and manufacture, of the United States, from each State and Territory, annually, from the 1st of October, 1802, to the 30th of September, 1810.

States and Territories.	1803.	1804.	1805.	1806.	1807.	1808.	1809.	1810.
New-Hampshire	443,527	453,394	389,595	411,379	365,950	122,294	201,063	225,623
Vermont	89,510	135,930	101,997	91,732	148,469	83,103	125,881	406,138
Massachusetts	5,399,020	6,303,122	5,697,051	6,621,696	6,185,748	1,508,632	6,022,729	5,761,771
Rhode-Island	664,230	917,736	1,065,579	949,336	741,988	139,684	658,397	874,870
Connecticut	1,238,388	1,486,882	1,353,537	1,522,750	1,519,083	397,781	655,258	762,785
New-York	7,626,831	7,501,096	8,098,060	8,053,076	9,957,416	2,362,438	8,348,764	10,928,573
New-Jersey	21,311	24,829	20,633	26,504	36,063	12,511	269,104	392,798
Pennsylvania	4,021,214	4,178,713	4,365,240	3,765,313	4,809,616	1,066,527	4,238,358	4,751,634
Delaware	187,687	180,081	77,827	125,787	77,695	38,052	96,495	79,988
Maryland	3,707,040	3,938,840	3,408,543	3,661,131	4,016,699	764,992	2,570,957	3,275,904
District of Columbia	1,412,056	1,157,895	1,135,350	1,091,760	1,363,352	281,936	681,650	984,463
Virginia	5,949,267	5,394,903	4,945,635	4,626,687	4,393,521	508,124	2,786,161	4,632,829
North-Carolina	926,318	919,545	767,434	786,029	740,933	117,129	322,834	401,465
South-Carolina	6,863,343	5,142,100	5,957,646	6,797,064	7,129,365	1,404,043	2,861,369	4,881,840
Georgia	2,345,387	2,003,227	2,351,169	*82,764	3,710,776	24,626	1,082,108	2,234,912
Ohio	-	-	-	62,318	28,889	13,115	3,850	10,583
Indiana Territory	738	-	-	-	-	-	-	-
Michigan do.	210,392	276,964	313,223	221,260	311,947	50,848	136,114	3,571
Mississippi do.	1,099,702	60,127	-	-	701	-	305	2,958
Orleans	-	1,392,098	2,338,483	2,357,141	3,161,581	537,711	344,305	1,753,970
Total,	42,205,961	41,467,477	42,387,002	41,253,727	48,699,592	9,433,546	31,405,702	42,366,675

* The exports from the port of Savannah, in Georgia, are not included, those were about two million two hundred and fifty thousand dollars, which would make the domestic exports for 1806, about forty-three million and a half.

TABLE No. III.

Statement shewing the value of the exports, the growth, produce and manufacture, of Foreign Countries, from each State and Territory, annually, from the 1st of October, 1802, to the 30th of September, 1810.

States and Territories.	1803.	1804.	1805.	1806.	1807.	1808.	1809.	1810.
New-Hampshire,	51,093	262,697	218,813	383,884	314,072	2,765	85,532	9,027
Vermont,	27,940	55,795	67,405	102,043	55,816	25,669	49,901	26,493
Massachusetts,	3,369,546	10,591,256	13,738,606	14,577,547	13,926,377	3,619,690	6,119,564	7,251,277
Rhode-Island,	611,366	817,935	1,506,470	1,142,499	915,576	102,350	626,135	456,706
Connecticut,	10,183	29,228	90,190	193,078	'105,644	15,910	11,255	5,858
New-York,	3,191,556	8,580,185	15,384,883	13,709,769	16,400,547	3,243,620	4,232,798	6,313,757
New-Jersey,	- -	- -	110	7,363	5,123	8,288	50,071	37,469
Pennsylvania,	3,504,496	6,851,444	9,397,012	13,809,389	12,055,128	2,946,803	4,810,883	6,241,764
Delaware,	240,466	517,315	280,556	374,319	151,580	70,683	41,541	40,354
Maryland,	1,371,022	5,213,099	7,450,937	10,919,774	10,282,285	1,956,114	4,056,369	3,213,114
District of Columbia,	32,938	294,303	184,865	154,386	83,026	3,381	21,765	53,640
Virginia,	151,441	395,098	660,985	428,709	367,713	18,349	107,964	189,782
North-Carolina,	26,296	9,142	12,469	3,576	4,229	- -	160	2,484
South-Carolina,	947,765	2,309,516	3,108,979	2,946,718	3,783,199	260,402	385,972	408,774
Georgia,	25,488	74,345	43,677	- -	34,069	- -	- -	3,774
Indiana Territory,	32,476	17,320	- -	- -	- -	- -	- -	- -
Michigan do.	- -	- -	- -	- -	- -	- -	- -	- -
Mississippi do.	- -	4,650	- -	- -	- -	- -	- -	44
Orleans do.	- -	208,269	1,033,062	1,530,182	1,159,174	723,390	197,621	136,978
Total,	13,594,072	36,231,597	53,179,019	60,283,236	59,643,558	12,997,414	20,797,531	24,391,295

TABLE No. IV.

Aggregate of articles exported from the United States, for each year, from the year 1791, to the year 1814.

Species of Merchandize.	1791.	1792.	1793.	1794.	1795.	1796.	1797.	1798.
Ashes, pot, . . tons	3,083	4,474	4,359	4,854	3,145	3,661	2,191	5,855
do. pearl, . . do.	3,270	3,350	1,807	2,337	1,835	1,423	2,045	3,796
Apples, . . . bbls.	12,352	6,582	8,994	5,634	6,875	5,502	5,118	4,231
Beer & porter in casks, gls	95,526	93,386	137,631	83,871	224,075	328,883	48,664	76,991
do. in bottles, doz.	1,919	1,063	776	569	1,179	14,002	12,794	7,200
Beef, . . . bbls.	62,771	74,638	75,106	100,866	96,149	92,521	51,812	89,000
Biscuit or ship bread, do.	100,279	80,986	76,653	69,907	71,331	181,065	84,679	52,793
do. . . . kegs	15,346	37,645	43,306	42,922	37,462	26,102	21,139	25,807
Buck-Wheat, bushels	14,499	1,961	330	346	678	32	136	27
Barley, . . do.	35	-	30	26	-	345	479	4,066
Beans, . . do.	55,091	64,023	13,540	65,959	62,256	51,762	19,312	23,003
Bran and shorts, do.	-	108	-	-	-	80	228	150
Butter, . . lbs.	666,300	470,440	367,600	1,550,880	1,135,560	2,554,885	1,255,435	1,313,563
Boots, . . pairs	499	513	1,167	6,111	4,660	7,950	6,477	3,554
Bark essence of, galls.	-	-	208	-	-	-	-	12
Bricks, . . numb.	737,764	743,900	683,070	493,480	421,600	602,700	487,160	599,800
Corn Indian, . bushels	1,713,241	1,964,973	1,233,768	505,977	1,935,345	1,173,552	804,922	1,218,231
Cotton, . . . lbs.	189,316	138,328	487,600	1,601,760	6,276,300	6,106,729	3,788,429	9,360,005
Coffee, . . do.	962,977	2,136,742	17,580,049	33,720,983	47,443,179	62,385,117	44,521,887	49,580,927
Chocolate, . . do.	14,370	6,692	7,432	12,544	87,050	29,698	9,610	277,625
Cocoa, . . . do.	8,32?	6,000	234,875	1,188,302	525,432	928,107	875,334	3,146,445
Cheese, . . . do.	120,901	125,925	146,269	601,954	2,343,093	1,794,536	1,256,109	1,183,234

TABLE No. IV.—CONTINUED.

Species of Merchandize.		1799.	1800.	1801.	1802.	1803.	1804.	1805.	1806.
Ashes, pot,	tons	4,667	6,760	7,228	3,395	3,270	3,411	3,557	4,616
do. pearl,	do.	2,495	1,261	1,297	1,785	2,194	1,138	1,575	1,512
Apples,	bbls.	12,781	16,593	9,022	5,825	9,593	6,801	5,654	2,500
Beer & porter in casks, gls		110,340	74,763	128,588	60,595	41,110	38,772	140,996	176,916
do. in bottles, - doz.		12,622	1,721	8,307	5,499	468	4,804	7,070	9,831
Beef,	bbls.	91,321	75,045	75,331	61,520	77,934	134,896	115,532	117,419
Biscuit or ship bread, do.		47,340	81,199	105,983	94,872	108,272	85,512	90,737	88,086
do.	kegs	32,534	38,482	44,079	36,167	38,085	50,390	23,962	38,229
Buck-Wheat, - bushels		-	851	154	1,999	74	2	90	25
Barley,	do.	552	432	8,796	485	2,745	5,318	7,185	156
Beans, "	do.	19,998	7,621	12,144	13,314	41,677	156	22,700	21,660
Bran and shorts, - do.		220	195	335	616	1,221	36,614	105	472
Butter,	lbs.	1,314,502	1,822,341	2,830,016	2,361,576	2,289,954	2,476,550	1,656,724	1,898,690
Boots,	pairs	10,599	6,473	4,437	5,298	1,826	6,213	10,128	8,958
Bark, essence of, galls.		384	291	622	75	1,336	1,031	-	49
Bricks,	numb.	789,366	332,222	666,817	1,546,375	736	941	1,043	1,060
Corn, Indian, - bushels		1,200,492	1,694,327	1,768,162	1,633,283	2,079,608	1,944,873	861,501	1,064,263
Cotton,	lbs.	9,532,263	17,789,803	20,911,201	27,501,075	41,105,623	38,118,041	40,383,491	37,491,282
Coffee,	do.	31,987,088	38,597,479	45,106,494	36,501,998	10,294,693	48,312,713	46,760,294	47,001,662
Chocolate,	do.	9,011	6,304	48,723	20,117	12,414	9,489	5,008	9,959
Cocoa,	do.	5,970,590	4,925,518	7,012,155	3,878,526	367,177	695,135	2,425,680	6,846,758
Cheese,	do.	1,164,590	913,843	1,674,834	1,332,224	1,268,321	1,378,438	843,005	683,163

TABLE No. IV.—CONTINUED.

Species of Merchandize.	1807.	1808.	1809.	1810.	1811.	1812.	1813.	1814.
Ashes, pot, - tons	5,852	1,464	5,998	7,083	4,289	2,477	1,670	1,225
do. pearl, - do.	2,773	867	2,732	3,227	1,557	626	285	227
Apples, - - bbls.	9,327	3,880	603	6,465	16,321	2,212	1,621	2,150
Beer & porter in casks, gls	211,135	19,275	95,082	91,000	18,421	35,116	4,008	3,504
do. in bottles, doz.	10,794	2,524	10,319	15,863	33,875	7,155	20	30
Beef, - - bbls.	84,209	20,101	28,555	47,699	76,743	42,757	43,741	20,297
Biscuit or ship bread, do.	102,431	21,579	69,699	62,418	103,901	46,344	28,626	14,044
do. - - kegs	37,157	6,628	24,518	39,842	47,536	12,526	4,073	1,717
Buck-Wheat, bushels	66	-	60	73	150	-	-	-
Barley, - do.	4,893	173	200	6,942	29,716	49,707	-	2,300
Beans, - do.	22,226	11,312	41,401	25,578	47,867	34,656	4,201	1,416
Bran and shorts, do.	-	-	-	-	-	-	-	-
Butter, - - lbs.	1,963,480	894,152	1,366,374	1,620,538	1,878,789	1,614,112	419,395	185,100
Boots, - pairs	8,053	914	7,012	5,169	7,667	2,097	55	51
Bark, essence of, galls.	25	-	103	150	55	-	-	-
Bricks, - numb.	837	892	286	265	225	114	20	47
Corn, Indian, - bushels	1,018,721	249,533	522,047	1,054,252	2,790,850	2,039,999	1,486,970	61,284
Cotton, - lbs.	66,612,737	12,064,366	53,210,225	93,874,201	62,186,081	28,952,544	19,399,911	117,806,479
Coffee, - do.	42,122,573	7,325,448	24,364,099	31,423,477	10,261,136	10,073,722	6,568,527	220,594
Chocolate, - do.	12,125	6,000	3,930	13,333	16,203	4,900	5,000	-
Cocoa, - - do.	8,540,524	1,896,990	2,029,336	1,286,010	2,221,442	752,148	108,188	27,386
Cheese, - - do.	879,697	316,876	588,907	741,878	944,116	707,787	276,552	184,827

TABLE No. IV.—CONTINUED.

Species of Merchandize.		1791.	1792.	1793.	1794.	1795.	1796.	1797.	1798.
Candles wax,	lbs.	7,400	7,960	1,920	3,040	30,480	9,978	3,481	21,179
do. spermaceti,	do.	182,400	157,520	235,600	214,960	240,720	221,903	130,438	144,149
do. tallow,	do.	174,700	246,000	591,420	1,357,620	1,721,700	1,997,398	763,744	982,728
Canvass or sail cloth,	pieces	683	1,592	2,630	609	3,031	4,683	1,739	2,335
Cables and cordage,	cwt.	3,533	4,518	9,400	1,790	2,680	8,707	7,872	9,434
Cards, wool and cotton,	doz.	25	6	34	113	397	85	1,824	103
do. playing,	packs	-	1,000	-	-	-	200	-	3,230
Coal,	bushels	3,788	13,023	14,719	2,397	3,749	9,536	11,432	512
Copper or Brass, and } Copper manufactured,}	dolls.	8,300	4,600	5,300	3,958	4,500	3,272	17,676	20,532
Coaches and other carriages,	do.	3,000	5,950	10,800	9,500	5,200	13,999	9,024	11,533
Flour,	bbls.	619,681	824,464	1,074,639	846,010	687,369	725,194	515,633	567,558
Fish, dried or smoaked,	quintals	383,237	364,898	372,825	436,907	400,818	377,713	406,016	411,175
do. pickled,	bbls.	57,424	48,277	45,440	36,929	55,999	84,558	69,782	66,827
do. do.	kegs	-	-	-	-	-	5,256	7,351	6,220
Furniture, household,	dolls.	13,208	6,111	8,867	6,500	8,300	9,483	22,091	32,065
Flax-seed,	bushels	292,460	261,905	258,540	270,340	411,264	256,200	222,269	224,473
Flax,	lbs.	18,600	10,400	1,474	8,665	90,460	16,594	4,274	-
Gun-powder,	do.	25,854	27,920	32,152	6,700	20,525	2,519	7,500	6,875
Ginseng,	do.	29,208	42,310	90,350	23,232	20,460	10,713	4,004	59,165
Hats,	dolls.	2,175	17,200	13,885	66,175	156,900	57,416	44,617	63,262
Hams and Bacon,	lbs.	296,247	585,353	521,483	1,147,262	1,778,564	2,096,877	1,084,008	1,105,584

60

TABLE No. IV.—CONTINUED.

Species of Merchandize.		1799.	1800.	1801.	1802.	1803.	1804.	1805.	1806.
Candles, wax, -	lbs.	49,275	13,818	24,893	6,438	1,705	- -	5,980	3,737
do. spermaceti, -	do.	240,301	181,321	290,666	135,627	238,034	127,602	180,535	294,789
do. tallow, -	do.	1,060,391	752,402	1,318,199	1,077,908	1,260,997	2,266,084	1,019,642	2,125,976
Canvass or sail cloth, -	pieces	1,835	58	1,543	20	6	54	100	100
Cables and cordage, -	cwt.	5,766	12,406	10,089	10,375	4,854	6,721	5,519	8,874
Cards, wool and cotton, -	doz.	59	1,017	368	1,090	298	258	112	398
do. playing, -	packs	377	- -	3,828	3,410	8,994	4,032	480	13,501
Coal, -	bushels	18,587	8,406	16,334	13,422	1,886	2,982	1,493	18,987
Copper or Brass, and Copper manufactured, }	dolls.	56,655	50,608	69,474	107,030	6,233	31,979	12,977	25,340
Coaches and other carriages, do.		42,470	16,678	13,468	23,285	9,890	14,755	20,279	30,293
Flour, -	bbls.	519,265	653,052	1,102,444	1,156,248	1,311,853	810,008	777,513	782,724
Fish, dried or smoaked,	quin.	428,495	392,726	410,948	440,925	461,870	567,828	514,549	537,457
do. pickled, -	bbls.	63,542	50,388	35,935	75,819	76,831	89,482	56,670	64,615
do. do. -	kegs	15,993	12,403	10,424	13,229	11,565	13,045	7,207	10,155
Furniture, household, -	dolls.	95,181	81,421	90,133	92,342	53,776	78,558	141,008	172,900
Flax-seed, -	bushels	350,857	289,684	461,266	155,358	311,459	281,757	179,788	352,280
Flax, -	lbs.	6,304	2,488	28,960	7,482	2,829	986	340	5,532
Gun-powder, -	do.	650	19,565	88,532	212,918	67,367	510,520	492,699	225,708
Ginseng, -	do.	147,192	268,371	286,458	201,910	384,979	301,499	370,932	448,394
Hats, -	dolls.	101,366	42,076	57,366	31,163	27,158	76,174	95,098	105,051
Hams and Bacon, -	lbs.	1,412,005	1,173,244	2,034,630	1,588,267	1,686,546	1,901,884	903,924	1,347,018

TABLE No. IV.—CONTINUED.

Species of Merchandize.		1807.	1808.	1809.	1810.	1811.	1812.	1813.	1814.
Candles, wax,	lbs.	746	1,648	3,584	7,636	4,337	433	3,446	198
do. spermaceti,	do.	172,132	45,130	214,444	187,190	257,094	157,596	26,522	21,154
do. tallow,	do.	1,864,317	381,629	881,847	618,039	1,026,633	542,406	270,050	308,895
Canvass or sail-cloth,	pieces	100	-	-	134	14	12	-	-
Cables and cordage,	cwt.	8,705	2,521	8,366	8,253	13,971	25,104	946	344
Cards, wool and cotton,	doz.	167	23	12	207	204	-	240	251
do. playing,	packs	4,889	1,728	728	9,036	4,256	-	1,728	-
Coal,	bushels	8,974	411	648	-	1,976	-	-	-
Copper or Brass, and Copper manufactured,	dolls.	12,742	4,031	3,095	17,426	9,282	2,644	-	-
Coaches, and other carriages,	do.	25,390	4,243	7,167	10,762	21,252	2,210	200	-
Flour,	bbls.	1,249,819	263,813	846,247	798,431	1,445,012	1,443,492	1,260,943	193,274
Fish, dried or smoaked,	quintals	473,924	155,808	345,648	280,804	216,387	169,019	63,616	31,310
do. pickled,	bbls.	57,621	18,957	54,777	34,674	44,716	23,636	13,333	8,436
do. do.	kegs	13,743	3,036	9,380	5,964	9,393	3,143	568	87
Furniture, household,	dolls.	113,571	342,231	71,232	131,448	148,758	43,248	2,230	2,526
Flax-seed,	bushels	301,242	102,930	184,311	240,579	304,114	325,022	189,538	14,800
Flax,	lbs.	-	187	8,797	73,803	32,200	19,522	-	-
Gun-powder,	do.	173,490	32,225	58,236	116,863	64,525	92,875	13,650	20,770
Ginseng,	do.	368,207	-	271,693	279,246	314,131	33,129	-	58,720
Hats,	dolls.	89,653	9,399	57,826	45,065	55,182	27,572	8,143	132
Hams and Bacon,	lbs.	1,311,246	258,418	1,082,610	1,218,855	1,268,809	729,398	607,196	138,556

TABLE No. IV.—CONTINUED.

Species of Merchandize.		1791.	1792.	1793.	1794.	1795.	1796.	1797.	1798.
Hair powder,	lbs.	1,276	2,540	12,810	19,984	78,400	30,561	58,694	93,256
Hops,	do.	650	2,250	7,300	98,712	84,965	76,634	1,000	5,848
Hemp,	cwt.	14	10	-	-	2,200	2,090	-	-
Hides, raw,	number	704	1,602	9,278	35,531	27,865	40,363	108,862	11,838
Horned Cattle,	do.	4,627	4,551	3,728	3,495	2,510	4,625	3,827	4,283
Horses,	do.	6,975	5,656	3,728	3,495	2,626	4,283	1,177	2,132
Hogs,	do.	16,803	21,291	9,934	5,705	4,922	6,753	3,484	4,237
Iron, pig,	tons	4,179	3,268	2,089	2,037	1,046	502	597	128
Do. bar,	do.	350	360	763	843	2,444	843	204	793
Do. castings,	dolls.	2,598	3,202	12,200	2,681	3,500	453	22,001	29,861
Do. manufactured,	do.	3,500	8,000	10,250	24,304	25,600	160,094	135,594	173,074
Indigo,	lbs.	497,720	858,996	875,789	1,528,928	1,296,026	915,635	269,639	311,457
Lard,	do.	522,715	515,245	597,297	1,100,780	1,490,554	1,124,971	731,511	876,773
Leather,	do.	5,424	19,536	17,501	749,903	1,819,224	127,044	61,169	118,748
Lead, & Shot manufactured, do.		41,960	28,756	75,252	20,302	32,911	1,199,439	306,189	24,662
Meal, rye,	*bushels	120,310	70,630	63,475	20,170	24,410	152,784	36,570	48,444
Do. Indian,	do.	351,695	263,405	189,715	241,570	512,645	540,286	254,799	211,694
Do. buck-wheat,	do.	2,110	1,325	730	1,805	-	1,076	216	84
Do. oat,	do.	30	-	-	-	-	-	3,880	2,000
Mustard,	lbs.	780	1,120	-	-	1,500	5,240	1,666	2,077
Molasses,	galls.	12,721	11,338	28,733	7,216	20,124	112,257	48,559	32,350
Mules,	number	444	1,101	1,105	1,617	1,426	1,718	1,064	993
Medicinal drugs,	dolls.	1,500	10,900	11,200	10,250	11,300	53,949	23,110	10,149

* Barrels from 1805 to 1814 inclusive.

TABLE No. IV.—CONTINUED.

Species of Merchandize.		1799.	1800.	1801.	1802.	1803.	1804.	1805.	1806.
Hair powder,	lbs.	42,141	33,887	25,021	12,542	293	5,587	18,894	12,319
Hops,	do.	18,336	100	70,784	60,866	915,473	385,886	181,606	946,827
Hemp,	cwt.	34	1,540	561	4,310	313	-	-	-
Hides, raw,	number	72,650	33,003	3,691	953	4,814	4,635	5,692	1,819
Horned Cattle,	do.	5,304	9,826	8,486	9,039	7,563	6,290	5,822	7,107
Horses,	do.	6,290	4,406	5,085	6,607	5,569	5,126	4,046	5,193
Hogs,	do.	3,786	14,294	7,312	5,501	6,859	5,599	2,808	1,747
Iron, pig,	tons	140	190	223	535	877	454	365	79
Do. bar,	do.	614	531	70	100	177	379	927	307
Do. castings,	dolls.	16,573	11,174	22,798	21,106	5,923	9,168	25,821	47,014
Do. manufactured,	do.	271,575	372,261	300,316	317,825	237,979	341,396	40,559	29,700
Indigo,	lbs.	312,133	572,999	411,140	493,220	21,203	175,838	455,698	457,836
Lard,	do.	1,451,657	1,633,562	2,376,500	1,958,400	2,052,302	2,565,719	1,308,287	1,542,500
Leather,	do.	164,513	171,103	210,316	123,215	95,923	214,299	203,231	388,223
Lead, & Shot manuf. of,	do.	6,985	420,020	538,972	241,978	62,018	146,782	356,342	326,984
Meal, rye,	*bushels	49,269	79,6./	392,276	32,292	28,273	21,779	23,455	18,090
Do. Indian,	do.	231,226	338,108	919,355	266,816	133,606	111,327	116,131	108,342
Do. buck-wheat,	do.	754	93	1,907	3,260	229	48	98	124
Do. oat,	do.	200	1,637	347	-	-	1	-	-
Mustard,	lbs.	1,808	3,130	2,093	2,012	1,585	5,023	6,540	2,612
Molasses,	galls.	61,911	39,122	421,628	56,959	38,552	55,259	48,474	53,798
Mules,	number	707	151	483	1,003	344	605	481	1,341
Medicinal drugs,	dolls.	15,025	23,477	11,900	15,037	18,042	154,834	13,644	53,074

* Barrels from 1805 to 1814 inclusive.

TABLE No. IV.—CONTINUED.

Species of Merchandize.		1807.	1808.	1809.	1810.	1811.	1812.	1813.	1814.
Hair powder,	lbs.	2,915	1,996	1,198	-	-	-	-	-
Hops,	do.	20,492	20,697	5,963	4,460	-	55,313	-	-
Hemp,	cwt.	469	60	1,000	15	1	11,695	-	-
Hides, raw,	number	4,301	-	-	2,500	800	-	277	68
Horned Cattle,	do.	3,148	2,050	3,981	5,212	8,622	4,713	469	227
Horses,	do.	4,750	1,800	2,072	2,899	2,853	2,115	95	8
Hogs,	do.	1,831	1,956	537	250	4,454	2,380	485	160
Iron, pig,	tons	114	9	70	93	21	-	-	-
Do. bar,	do.	132	67	277	429	217	63	-	-
Do. castings,	dolls.	55,394	4,165	5,595	9,410	8,143	1,750	19,621	6,581
Do. manufactured,	do.	41,239	5,899	30,461	39,293	31,454	36,316	812	3,010
Indigo,	lbs.	882,242	140,592	354,168	844,011	574,120	237,057	11,520	513,928
Lard,	do.	1,815,998	585,173	1,371,089	1,365,333	1,927,451	1,616,417	1,084,565	1,560
Leather,	do.	336,414	87,316	199,766	279,043	363,945	233,811	76,259	53,680
Lead, & Shot manufactured of,	do.	321,987	60,026	359,582	292,135	125,525	80,327	276,940	2,716
Meal, rye,	barrels	29,067	6,167	1,306	5,078	29,378	69,839	65,680	26,438
Do. Indian,	do.	136,460	30,818	57,260	86,744	147,425	90,810	58,521	-
Do. buck-wheat,	do.	30	56	-	1	189	-	1	-
Do. oat,	do.	-	-	-	-	4	-	-	-
Mustard,	lbs.	3,817	55	1,945	985	112	12	-	-
Molasses,	galls.	40,947	7,337	33,943	40,245	18,837	8,001	1,309	-
Mules,	number	704	173	220	218	198	6	-	-
Medicinal drugs,	dolls.	16,724	4,328	16,777	19,524	18,767	11,604	5,264	83

TABLE No. IV.—CONTINUED.

Species of Merchandize.		1791.	1792.	1793.	1794.	1795.	1796.	1797.	1798.
Merchandize and other articles not enumerated,	dolls.	2,840,310	3,560,119	4,110,240	4,976,120	5,670,260	6,794,346	7,835,456	8,967,828
Oil, linseed,	gls.	90	199	1,183	6,997	48,995	34,721	19,759	17,016
Do. spermaceti,	do.	134,595	63,383	140,056	82,493	80,856	164,045	27,556	128,758
Do. whale,	do.	447,323	436,423	512,780	1,000,208	810,524	1,176,650	582,425	700,040
Oats,	bushels	116,634	119,733	78,524	55,053	64,335	59,797	38,221	46,475
Pork,	bbls.	27,781	38,098	38,563	49,442	88,193	73,881	40,125	33,115
Pitch,	do.	3,818	9,145	8,338	8,303	9,200	18,083	7,979	5,192
Poultry,	dozens	10,217	7,316	6,428	5,131	4,461	5,084	2,502	3,897
Peas,	bushels	110,182	128,048	27,080	131,918	124,514	103,525	52,403	128,228
Potatoes,	do.	22,263	19,634	20,367	37,815	48,208	48,767	41,333	69,805
Rice,	tierces	94,980	141,762	134,611	116,486	138,526	131,039	60,111	125,243
Rye,	bushels	36,737	12,727	1,305	696	703	4,319	1,331	2,721
Rosin,	bbls.	228	1,337	1,715	2,480	3,200	14,183	7,015	8,364
Spices, pepper,	lbs.	492	5,040	14,361	23,386	301,692	491,330	1,901,130	501,982
Do. pimento,	do.	141,701	310,635	114,255	37,573	1,158,274	498,028	263,305	18,320
Do. all other,	dolls.	9,200	2,200	5,300	3,250	4,300	6,235	156,643	110,283
Spirits, foreign,	gls.	27,319	84,273	256,897	142,258	466,364	667,606	398,777	557,062
Do. domestic from foreign produce,	do.	513,234	948,115	665,522	276,137	685,167	963,325	373,328	305,010
Do. domestic from domestic produce,	do.	753	-	-	-	-	-	43,692	6,233

TABLE No. IV.—CONTINUED.

Species of Merchandize.		1799.	1800.	1801.	1802.	1803.	1804.	1805.	1806.
Merchandize & other art. not enumerated,	dls.	18,718,477	16,076,868	17,159,016	14,906,081	15,351,524	9,377,805	15,201,483	19,016,909
Oil, linseed, -	gls.	24,227	18,857	31,564	9,099	3,816	19,047	9,690	20,967
Do. spermaceti, -	do.	114,264	221,762	91,684	28,470	46,984	5,550	72,624	42,785
Do. whale, -	do.	420,949	204,468	215,522	379,976	550,535	646,505	626,089	826,233
Oats, -	bushels	57,359	57,306	100,544	70,778	84,497	73,726	55,400	69,993
Pork, -	bbls.	52,268	55,467	70,779	78,239	96,602	111,532	57,925	36,277
Pitch, -	do.	2,592	1,881	2,682	3,091	4,808	6,225	13,977	7,948
Poultry, -	dozens	5,577	6,300	6,457	6,683	7,694	6,044	3,302	2,931
Peas, -	bushels	47,603	27,851	53,791	90,825	48,650	42,213	56,086	100,647
Potatoes, -	do.	40,353	56,253	104,186	80,798	79,217	96,427	62,995	52,885
Rice, -	tierces	110,599	112,056	94,866	79,822	81,838	78,385	56,830	102,627
Rye, -	bushels	1,595	8,227	31,110	2,492	50,753	11,715	1,474	614
Rosin, -	bbls.	16,396	3,075	2,397	3,189	5,861	4,675	9,057	7,486
Spices, pepper, -	lbs.	441,312	635,849	3,153,139	5,422,144	2,991,430	5,703,646	7,559,224	4,111,983
Do. pimento, -	do.	416,464	324,458	320,447	52,724	335,906	463,539	148,844	61,007
Do. all other, -	*lbs.	55,175	28,241	80,426	120,021	132,264	115,047]	461,114	213,959
Spirits, foreign,	gls.	903,522	604,361	520,205	507,256	299,182	1,119,059	1,812,216	1,366,560
Do. domestic from foreign produce,	do.	494,365	481,569	320,649	747,939	802,965	409,521	929,658	1,259,360
Do. domestic from domestic produce,	do.	16,979	27,801	16,920	58,533	18,126	41,976	77,092	43,016

* Value in dollars to 30th September, 1804.

TABLE No. IV.—CONTINUED.

Species of Merchandize.		1807.	1808.	1809.	1810.	1811.	1812.	1813.	1814.
Merchandize and other articles not enumerated,	dolls.	18,971,539	4,765,737	5,889,669	8,438,349	8,815,294	8,591,755	368,603	206,285
Oil, linseed,	gallons	5,037	279	13,371	23,502	35,579	9,603	4,178	8,132
Do. spermaceti,	do.	44,339	612	51,071	63,910	136,249	63,216	-	-
Do. whale,	do.	932,797	198,019	421,282	544,734	186,661	106,369	4,979	837
Oats,	bushels	65,277	23,698	20,361	44,425	211,894	48,469	14,105	6,046
Pork,	bbls.	89,247	15,478	42,652	37,209	37,270	22,746	17,337	4,040
Pitch,	do.	5,099	624	5,433	7,563	11,375	9,615	3,270	511
Poultry,	dozens	2,951	737	1,352	1,752	1,713	1,305	152	211
Peas,	bushels	25,891	14,335	57,691	22,209	38,784	43,210	18,080	2,211
Potatoes,	do.	97,694	36,316	19,690	59,443	76,755	50,838	25,728	42,156
Rice,	tierces	94,692	9,228	116,907	131,341	119,356	77,190	120,843	11,476
Rye,	bushels	6,650	530	1,185	448	14,818	82,705	140,136	-
Rosin,	bbls.	3,802	800	8,998	7,483	13,412	8,564	2,097	465
Spices, pepper,	lbs.	4,207,166	1,709,978	4,722,098	5,946,336	3,057,456	2,521,003	99,660	-
Do. pimento,	do.	674,889	31,333	33,161	29,967	12,389	68,964	5,160	-
Do. all other,	do.	330,773	34,047	197,589	326,707	453,685	310,193	7,359	-
Spirits, foreign,	gls.	1,622,127	229,992	266,423	122,900	116,788	37,895	29,338	5,598
Do. domestic, from foreign produce,	do.	765,916	31,120	241,359	474,990	344,455	208,985	495	1,866
Do. domestic, from domestic produce,	do.	32,767	6,696	97,282	133,853	500,918	294,230	60,053	8,132

TABLE No. IV.—CONTINUED.

Species of Merchandize.		1791.	1792.	1793.	1794.	1795.	1796.	1797.	1798.
Shoes and slippers,	pairs	7,046	8,738	15,102	102,498	165,000	212,774	106,074	155,534
Skins and furs,	dolls.	280,000	295,000	290,000	295,000	280,250	273,201	288,591	355,487
Saddlery,	do.	3,228	6,554	6,967	1,698	2,500	4,823	2,105	748
Silk, raw,	lbs.	153	250	104	-	-	-	33	47
Starch,	do.	160	4,920	5,440	23,920	16,953	51,816	24,469	26,102
Soap,	do.	41,460	61,200	397,200	1,087,560	2,625,180	2,713,729	1,223,619	999,856
Sugar, brown, and other clayed,	do.	74,504	1,176,156	4,539,809	20,721,761	21,377,747	34,848,644	38,366,262	51,703,963
Do. refined,	do.	1,157	21,760	43,954	27,155	739,520	984,146	203,789	36,754
Sheep,	numbers	10,880	12,213	12,064	9,577	6,494	6,140	3,291	4,808
Ship stuffs,	cwt.	12,968	12,200	7,742	1,106	1,560	8,706	2,840	2,591
Salt,	bushels	4,208	1,955	1,107	16,329	36,915	52,163	65,703	101,214
Snuff,	lbs.	15,689	10,042	35,559	37,415	129,436	267,046	73,257	114,151
Tobacco, manufactured,	do.	81,122	117,874	137,784	23,650	20,263	29,181	12,805	142,269
Do. unmanufactured,	hhds.	101,272	112,428	59,947	76,826	61,050	69,018	58,167	68,567
Tallow,	lbs.	317,195	152,622	309,366	187,212	49,515	187,403	26,012	16,610
Tar,	bbls.	51,044	69,279	67,961	46,650	90,066	64,600	47,397	33,898
Turpentine,	do.	58,107	67,148	36,957	20,598	30,200	41,490	53,291	40,188
Do. spirits of,	gls.	1,172	1,028	3,720	3,000	920	28,628	54,151	31,603
Tea, bohea,	lbs.	5,712	17,600	21,521	49,786	43,800	74,547	73,009	70,397
Do. souchong,	do.	41,328	23,100	3,020	7,718	24,450	9,327	8,668	50,236
Do. hyson,	do.	187,824	67,088	17,672	48,238	33,550	30,531	45,393	41,396

TABLE No. IV.—CONTINUED.

Species of Merchandize.	1799.	1800.	1801.	1802.	1803.	1804.	1805.	1806.
Shoes & slippers, pairs	137,879	68,722	133,545	59,432	26,911	134,347	103,164	163,430
Skins and furs, dolls.	493,724	308,262	281,639	316,030	532,367	958,609	967,534	840,347
Saddlery, - do.	3,141	5,128	1,976	14,130	7,574	7,827	23,516	18,237
Silk, raw, - lbs.	-	92	-	-	-	-	-	-
Starch, - do.	26,329	90,445	203,360	7,735	7,166	30,401	5,683	2,243
Soap, - do.	1,686,721	2,284,553	2,668,536	1,789,302	1,465,806	3,538,997	3,141,001	4,014,197
Sugar, brown & other clayed, do.	78,821,751	56,432,516	97,565,732	61,061,820	23,223,849	74,964,366	123,031,272	145,837,320
Do. refined, do.	232,469	124,939	168,479	118,468	99,633	132,035	108,236	304,099
Sheep, - numbers	9,733	9,445	11,621	12,157	13,677	12,456	6,091	6,544
Ship stuffs, - cwt.	15,599	432	1,986	1,121	2,642	2,466	1,301	207
Salt, - bushels	99,991	38,703	70,067	42,832	25,548	28,427	15,065	63,925
Snuff, - lbs.	109,682	41,453	52,297	43,161	17,928	20,678	33,127	42,212
Tobacco, manuf. do.	416,076	457,713	472,282	233,591	152,415	278,071	532,311	385,727
Do. unmanuf. hhds.	96,070	78,680	103,758	77,721	86,291	83,343	71,252	83,186
Tallow, - lbs.	19,926	15,079	37,142	32,863	59,217	35,440	22,647	449,305
Tar, - bbls.	58,254	59,410	67,487	37,497	78,989	58,181	72,745	62,723
Turpentine, - do.	40,382	33,129	35,413	38,764	61,178	77,825	95,640	74,731
Do. spirits of, - gls.	33,899	4,900	4,783	8,990	11,336	19,526	26,247	29,514
Tea, bohea, - lbs.	30,135	938,376	669,208	389,263	1,853,035	231,842	98,959	10,993
Do. souchong, - do.	18,989	42,905	211,920	613,312	531,885	760,064	926,758	1,210,306
Do. hyson, - do.	10,176	152,093	488,848	613,583	95,208	101,785	332,168	276,441

TABLE No. IV.—CONTINUED.

Species of Merchandize.		1807.	1808.	1809.	1810.	1811.	1812.	1813.	1814.
Shoes and slippers,	pairs	163,360	32,819	110,549	56,285	45,002	21,398	5,716	7,025
Skins and furs, -	dolls.	851,609	161,216	331,513	177,081	313,915	122,638	58,355	-
Saddlery, -	do.	14,252	1,328	14,854	13,361	14,677	3,794	167	-
Silk, raw, -	lbs.	-	-	-	-	-	-	-	-
Starch, -	do.	25,040	8,916	1,846	11,654	1,812	30	-	-
Soap, -	do.	3,740,763	724,794	2,365,100	1,616,542	1,006,356	1,638,969	813,338	561,055
Sugar, brown, and other clayed,	do.	143,136,905	28,974,927	45,248,128	47,038,125	18,383,673	13,927,277	7,347,038	762
Do. refined, -	do.	122,586	7,942	301,306	748,198	72,916	10,769	2,570	-
Sheep, -	numbers	5,698	1,531	3,221	4,613	5,801	3,572	934	1,669
Ship stuffs, -	cwt.	2,580	-	-	675	12	415	67	-
Salt, -	bushels	90,195	16,326	597	7,657	898	1	-	-
Snuff, -	lbs.	59,768	25,845	35,955	46,040	19,904	3,360	-	-
Tobacco, manufactured,	do.	236,004	26,656	314,880	495,427	732,713	583,258	283,512	79,377
Do. unmanufactured,	hhds.	62,232	9,576	53,921	84,134	35,828	26,094	5,314	3,125
Tallow, -	lbs.	169,582	31,922	215,255	181,299	44,775	46,403	300	2,360
Tar, -	bbls.	59,282	18,764	128,090	87,310	149,796	87,937	10,065	5,222
Turpentine, -	do.	53,451	17,061	77,398	62,912	100,242	57,266	16,123	3,507
Do. spirits of,	gls.	8,146	1,530	7,923	12,708	43,133	21,960	3,589	404
Tea, bohea,	lbs.	114,915	4,013	64,452	155,383	353,618	25,328	-	-
Do. souchong,	do.	926,069	99,544	1,093,179	536,310	304,602	395,507	-	-
Do. hyson, -	do.	609,319	56,173	344,871	349,014	221,440	57,825	129	-

TABLE No. IV.—CONTINUED.

Species of Merchandize.		1791.	1792.	1793.	1794.	1795.	1796.	1797.	1798.
Tea, green, -	lbs.	14,952	7,738	7,725	3,253	19,320	20,923	5,280	16,608
Wheat, -	bushels	1,018,339	853,790	1,450,575	696,797	141,273	31,226	15,655	15,021
Whalebone -	lbs.	124,829	154,407	202,620	354,617	410,664	308,314	452,127	62,805
Wax, -	do.	226,810	299,558	273,800	347,171	312,845	317,831	188,727	149,774
Wines, Madeira,	galls.	76,466	22,145	49,180	10,718	157,181	198,645	46,562	164,874
Do. other, -	do.	32,336	33,262	180,929	850,336	1,517,427	1,505,427	1,519,255	1,162,883
Do. bottled, -	dozen	6	500	1,330	12,463	23,303	30,108	77,097	55,878
WOOD.									
Staves & heading,	num.	29,861,590	30,197,309	30,630,994	28,342,860	31,883,039	34,588,904	33,073,521	28,073,279
Shingles, -	do.	74,205,976	71,637,863	80,813,357	28,869,117	38,938,814	47,307,112	51,604,896	50,915,427
Hoops and poles, -	do.	1,425,605	2,563,393	2,304,853	2,654,845	3,423,609	3,711,062	3,956,340	2,328,027
Boards, planks, scantling, &c.	feet	50,134,056	60,646,861	65,844,024	35,154,444	40,735,561	53,871,476	43,220,969	52,404,392
Timber, -	tons	13,780	20,391	25,838	6,100	10,043	8,585	13,664	5,574
All other lumber,	dolls.	101,676	103,210	109,320	112,460	110,340	120,197	109,877	116,772
Oak bark and other dyes,	dolls.	114,900	118,640	140,410	160,319	170,410	188,453	168,531	75,612
All manufactures,	do.	108,600	110,900	112,210	118,219	114,810	111,848	158,576	82,586

TABLE No. IV.—CONTINUED.

Species of Merch'dize.	1799.	1800.	1801.	1802.	1803.	1804.	1805.	1806.
Tea, other green, lbs.	7,561	47,258	39,277	278,380	666,364	125,542	431,003	504,465
Wheat, - bushels	10,056	26,353	239,929	280,281	686,415	127,024	18,041	86,784
Whalebone, - lbs.	89,552	32,636	23,106	80,334	96,802	134,006	21,335	50,594
Wax, - do.	172,982	203,703	177,358	223,912	197,148	217,889	248,394	346,974
Wines, Madeira, gls.	34,431	17,597	29,401	35,911	22,832	22,399	53,873	40,750
Do. other,* - do.	1,689,350	1,465,234	1,447,358	1,248,315	268,940	1,521,826	72,763	23,162
Do. bottled,† - doz.	62,182	43,804	54,993	42,883	14,245	41,167	[‡3,393,144]	3,506,297
wood.								
Staves & heading, nos.	34,008,285	19,375,625	37,189,498	29,808,430	35,290,000	34,614,000	42,062,000	44,624,000
Shingles, - do.	58,510,460	76,027,827	81,044,316	82,110,413	78,926,000	75,156,000	74,854,000	82,146,000
Hoops and poles, do.	2,914,089	2,121,189	3,730,086	3,831,809	3,501,000	4,228,000	5,523,000	6,239,000
Boards, plank, scantling, &c. feet	56,647,098	68,825,280	71,629,831	80,877,657	79,225,000	76,000,000	94,939,000	85,948,000
Timber, - tons	6,038	9,195	9,657	10,222	20,172	19,826	18,063	25,878
All other and lumber, dolls.	72,902	73,344	61,070	102,751	67,102	55,924	53,380	68,531
Oak bark and other dyes, do.	80,997	15,774	31,043	100,601	225,732	88,470	61,512	41,971
All manufactures, do.	166,041	117,651	170,027	164,837	145,500	203,175	§278,688	231,430

* Including all other wines to 30th September, 1804.

† Including all other wines after 30th September, 1804.

‡ All other wines, gallons.

§ "Manufactures of wood," include masts and spars.

TABLE No. IV.—CONTINUED.

Species of Merchandize.		1807.	1808.	1809.	1810.	1811.	1812.	1813.	1814.
Tea, green, -	lbs.	1,012,758	78,153	268,114	297,025	146,302	40,602	-	-
Wheat, -	bushels	766,814	87,330	393,889	325,924	216,833	53,832	288,535	-
Whalebone -	lbs.	104,635	8,660	8,825	42,843	30,346	8,128	-	-
Wax, -	do.	318,636	93,770	376,523	294,007	230,350	68,212	39,714	22,757
Wines, Madeira,	galls.	46,381	9,118	6,248	32,594	24,146	6,110	982	103
Do. other, bottled,	dozen	33,551	3,769	14,029	11,097	9,653	9,289	53	15,394
Do. do. -	galls.	3,100,543	1,174,194	601,426	195,232	310,722	288,295	100,408	1,907
WOOD.									
Staves & heading,	num.	37,701,000	10,003,000	26,991,000	27,137,000	30,284,000	18,285,000	7,179,000 m.	2,671
Shingles, -	do.	76,890,000	17,512,000	34,047,000	43,122,000	69,097,000	30,327,000	10,750,000 do.	4,196
Hoops and poles, -	do.	3,621,000	2,186,000	3,419,000	3,250,000	2,240,000	2,392,000	1,888,000 do.	1,064
Boards, planks, scantling, &c.	feet	79,424,000	25,845,000	64,725,000	63,042,000	85,340,000	56,565,000	20,699,000 do.	11,646
Timber, -	tons	48,855	7,412	29,342	103,294	116,428	42,442	1,671	127
All other & lumber,	dolls.	90,469	21,740	55,081	86,505	125,330	115,003	6,979	2,673
Oak bark and other dyes,	dolls.	19,064	5,136	28,750	72,049	111,825	106,688	118,416	3,270
All manufactures,	do.	212,876	46,399	142,461	298,113	298,655	120,306	62,659	49,462

TABLE No. V.

State of the Cod Fishery of Massachusetts, from 1765 to 1775. — From 1786 to 1790 inclusive.

	Vessels annually.	Tonnage.	Seamen	Quintals to Europe a 3. 5 dolls.	Quintals to West-Indies a 2. 6 dolls.	Vessels annually.	Tonnage.	Seamen	Quintals to Europe, a 3 dolls.	Quintals to West-Indies a 2 dolls.
Marblehead,	150	7,500	1,200	80,000	40,000	90	5,400	720	50,000	25,000
Gloucester,	146	5,530	888	35,000	42,500	160	3,600	680	19,500	28,500
Manchester,	25	1,500	200	10,000	10,000	15	900	120	3,000	7,500
Beverly,	15	750	120	6,000	6,000	19	1,235	157	5,200	10,000
Salem,	30	1,500	240	12,000	12,000	20	1,300	160	6,000	10,000
Newburyport,	10	400	60	2,000	2,000	10	460	80	1,000	5,000
Ipswich,	50	900	190	8,000	5,500	56	860	248	3,000	6,000
Plymouth,	60	2,400	420	8,000	16,000	36	1,440	252	6,000	12,000
Cohasset,	6	240	42	800	1,600	5	200	35	1,000	1,500
Hingham,	6	240	42	800	1,600	4	180	32	800	1,200
Scituate,	10	400	70	1,000	3,000	2	90	16	400	600
Duxborough,	4	160	28	400	1,200	9	360	72	1,500	3,000
Kingston,	6	240	42	800	1,600	4	160	28	700	1,300
Yarmouth,	30	900	180	3,000	6,000	30	900	180	2,000	10,000
Wellfleet,	3	90	21	300	600	-	-	-	-	-
Truro,	10	400	80	1,000	3,000	-	-	-	-	-
Provincetown,	4	160	32	500	1,100	11	550	88	3,000	5,200
Chatham,	30	900	240	4,000	8,000	30	900	240	3,000	9,000
Nantucket,	8	320	64	1,000	2,200	5	200	40	500	1,500
Maine,	60	1,000	230	4,000	8,000	30	300	120	1,000	3,500
Weymouth,	2	100	16	200	600	3	150	24	1,000	1,250
Total,	665	25,630	4,405	178,800	172,500	539	19,185	3,278	108,600	142,050

TABLE No. VI.

Abstract of the produce of the Fisheries, exported from the United States, from about Aug. 20th, 1789, to Sept. 30th, 1790.

	FISH DRIED		FISH PICKLED.		OIL WHALE.		OIL SPERMACETI		WHALE-BONE.		CANDLES, SPERM.		Total val.
	Quant. Quin's.	Value Dollars.	Quant. Barrels	Value Dollars.	Quant. Barrels	Value Dollars.	Quant. Barrels	Value Dollars	Quant. Pounds	Value Dollars	Quant. Pounds	Value Dollars.	Dollars.
France, - - - -	543	1,086	12	20	9,914	73,767	1,403	17,523	108,807	17,917	1,200	480	749,497
French West-Indies,	251,116	518,288	29,294	90,818	1,756	13,685	80	1,029	-	-	38,754	14,884	
Amount of 1st. Class,	251,659	519,374	29,306	90,838	11,670	87,452	1,483	18,552	108,807	17,917	39,954	15,364	749,497
Spain, - - -	72,300	194,457	280	813	593	4,147	-	-	-	-	2,896	1,256	203,276
Spanish W. Indies and Florida,	824	978	300	886	5	38	-	-	-	-	1,685	674	
Great-Britain, -	5	10	-	-	1,738	21,048	3,940	60,000	1,075	215	-	-	89,859
British West-Indies,	1,970	4,114	795	3,075	15	124	-	-	-	-	756	353	
Nova-Scotia, -	-	-	13	40	1	10	100	870	-	-	-	-	
Holland, - -	-	-	15	45	807	5,683	-	-	5,220	1,050	-	-	79,404
Dutch West-Indies,	23,822	48,631	4,778	13,404	179	1,317	-	-	-	-	23,162	9,274	
Portugal, - -	18,594	41,306	69	242	4	60	8	120	-	-	-	-	55,137
Portuguese Islands,	5,432	11,307	292	801	139	1,243	-	-	-	-	148	58	
Germany, - - -	-	-	-	-	470	2,990	-	-	6,150	1,230	-	-	4,220
Danish West-Indies,	1,180	2,386	803	2,421	3	27	-	-	-	-	-	-	4,834
African Isl. & C.Afri.	613	1,324	147	564	6	42	-	-	-	-	165	66	1,996
Mediterranean, -	2,314	4,628	6	36	135	700	-	-	29	5	238	150	5,519
Sweden, - -	8	16	-	-	-	-	-	-	-	-	-	-	16
East-Indies, -	-	-	-	-	-	-	-	-	-	-	1,285	529	529
Amount of 2d. Class,	127,060	309,157	7,498	22,327	4,095	37,456	3,948	60,990	12,474	2,500	30,425	12,360	444,790
Am't. of both Classes,	378,721	828,531	36,804	113,165	15,765	124,908	5,431	79,542	121,281	20,417	70,379	27,724	1,194,287

TABLE No. VII.

Statement shewing the destination of the principal articles of domestic produce exported from the United States in each year from October 1st, 1779, to September 30th, 1811.

FISH, DRIED OR SMOKED—Quintals.

Whither exported.	1800.	1801.	1802.	1803.	1804.	1805.	1806.	1807.	1808.	1809.	1810.	1811.
Swedish West-Indies,	7,115	2,852	1,009	983	3,533	1,339	1,381	6,560	1,227	103,081	20,854	17,142
Danish West-Indies,	9,003	7,128	2,187	3,195	6,355	8,758	11,567	11,436	1,120	610	2,087	4,865
Dutch West-Indies,	20,218	30,163	23,060	62,988	69,028	35,727	30,670	29,258	7,793	-	2,363	-
British West-Indies,	141,420	111,030	92,679	71,495	76,822	55,676	59,471	48,911	26,998	66,566	55,456	33,242
British American Colonies,	-	-	-	-	-	-	6,906	6,331	-	-	-	-
France,	-	1,687	27,067	3,491	37,656	73,004	19,347	87,654	16,144	-	2,150	28,622
French West-Indies,	36,703	66,166	46,157	84,291	49,333	66,022	96,929	103,351	30,044	-	-	4,238
Spain,	110,184	114,376	124,945	96,942	150,615	127,951	175,366	84,109	29,654	69,757	95,748	3,023
Spanish West-Indies,	17,388	19,851	29,495	3,090	6,471	15,715	18,246	13,816	-	57,176	23,632	33,389
Portugal,	3,670	7,104	26,053	19,094	10,595	9,100	8,077	-	1,658	10,349	6,384	2,517
Madeira,	6,147	2,564	3,069	1,226	2,895	6,795	4,132	2,961	2,422	3,619	6,048	2,475
West-Indies, (generally)	12,516	16,444	43,386	97,527	106,993	71,500	61,308	55,000	27,399	2,801	14,652	35,595
Europe, do.	-	-	6,184	10,537	5,098	21,561	18,310	4,420	-	5,995	2,920	13,405
Africa, do.	76	36	35	-	72	133	308	780	-	70	71	239
Italy,	24,492	27,886	11,239	2,694	9,417	13,272	18,458	13,837	6,463	2,103	11,501	12,005
Average price,							$ 4	4	4	3 25	3 25	3 50

77

TABLE No. VII.—CONTINUED.

FISH, PICKLED—Barrels.

Whither exported.	1800.	1801.	1802.	1803.	1804.	1805.	1806.	1807.	1808.	1809.	1810.	1811.
Swedish West-Indies,	1,586	506	387	1,617	1,511	1,108	2,090	7,694	2,120	18,976	4,742	9,231
Danish West-Indies,	3,108	1,301	2,018	3,312	3,737	4,027	4,239	6,916	1,187	-	-	-
Dutch West-Indies,	4,179	2,338	5,399	12,732	9,613	1,161	2,377	2,135	497	-	-	-
British West-Indies,	21,745	39,235	29,462	28,523	36,095	18,556	35,035	23,782	9,304	11,985	12,208	10,323
French West-Indies,	14,674	31,920	24,673	16,399	15,859	16,769	10,422	6,412	2,034	-	423	5,200
Spain,	1,135	1,109	232	-	1,455	384	-	-	-	-	-	-
Spanish West-Indies,	2,766	3,471	2,377	-	4,230	4,888	4,999	1,783	363	11,187	8,340	5,804
West-Indies, (generally)	-	2,819	9,082	12,039	13,442	4,507	3,898	5,001	2,698	1,199	3,412	8,566
Average price,							$5 50	5	5	5	6	6 50

TABLE No. VIII.

State of the Whale Fishery in Massachusetts, from 1771 to 1775, inclusive.

Ports from which the equipments were made.	The number of vessels fitted out annually for the northern fishery.	Their tonnage.	The number of vessels fitted out annually for the southern fishery.	Their tonnage	The number of Seamen employed	Barrels of Spermaceti Oil, taken annually.	Barrels of Whale Oil taken annually.
Nantucket,	65	4,8	85	10,200	2,025	26,000	4,000
Wellfleet,	20	1,600	10	1,000	420	2,250	2,250
Dartmouth,	60	4,500	20	2,000	1,040	7,200	1,400
Lynn,	1	75	1	120	28	200	100
Martha's Vineyard,	12	720	-	-	156	900	300
Barnstable,	2	150	-	-	26	240	-
Boston,	15	1,300	5	700	260	1,800	600
Falmouth, county of Barnstable,	4	300	-	-	52	400	-
Swanzey,	4	300	-	-	52	400	-
Total,	183	13,820	121	14,020	4,059	39,390	8,650

TABLE No. IX.

State of the Whale Fishery, from 1787 to 1789, both inclusive.

Ports from which the equipments were made.	The number of vessels fitted out annually for the northern fishery.	Their tonnage.	The number of vessels fitted out annually for the southern fishery.	Their tonnage.	The number of Seamen employed.	Barrels of Spermaceti Oil, taken annually.	Barrels of Whale Oil taken annually.
Nantucket, - - -	18	1,350	18	2,700	487	3,800	8,260
Wellfleet, and other ports } at Cape Cod, - - -	12	720	4	400	212	-	1,920
Dartmouth, - - -	45	2,700	5	750	650	2,700	1,750
Cape Ann, - - -	-	-	2	350	28	-	1,200
Plymouth, - - -	1	60	-	-	13	100	-
Martha's Vineyard, -	2	120	1	100	39	220	-
Boston, - - -	6	450	-	-	78	360	-
Dorchester and Wareham,	7	420	1	90	104	800	-
Total,	91	5,820	31	4,390	1,611	7,980	13,130

TABLE No. X.

WHALE OIL—gallons.

Whither exported.	1800.	1801.	1802.	1803.	1804.	1805.	1806.	1807.	1808.	1809.	1810.	1811.
Russia,	-	-	-	-	-	24,072	-	-	-	22,535	6,797	-
Prussia,	-	-	-	-	14,320	-	-	-	-	-	-	-
Sweden,	-	-	-	-	-	-	-	6,805	-	31,563	77,958	11,123
Swedish West-Indies,	-	-	871	399	507	1,034	1,819	31,610	-	71,999	15,102	7,358
Denmark and Norway,	-	-	-	-	4,885	-	-	10,082	-	44,440	80,156	-
Danish West-Indies,	2,021	236	1,546	9,131	3,330	6,185	13,692	-	-	-	1,080	-
Holland,	16,733	12,315	2,138	18,080	79,673	55,595	37,553	185,121	-	10,435	-	-
Dutch West-Indies,	19,706	19,642	21,856	37,288	56,597	4,510	14,949	12,430	4,115	10,947	7,205	-
Great-Britain,	10,927	17,907	18,843	60,907	12,390	-	2,000	-	-	6,760	6,760	-
British West-Indies,	-	-	40,075	22,759	26,248	22,187	49,245	30,879	12,065	26,637	17,130	15,822
Hamburg, Bremen, &c.	18,349	13,685	18,223	17,850	48,986	-	4,440	32,440	-	-	-	-
France,	84,413	46,609	127,128	175,715	288,837	325,568	342,837	290,959	37,793	8,816	57,609	46,099
French West-Indies,	20,287	70,257	20,777	54,006	16,176	30,331	34,248	15,992	15,122	26,636	26,284	2,315
Spain,	-	17,541	54,681	66,551	38,348	83,230	195,393	161,331	97,306	56,466	170,468	4,810
Spanish West-Indies,	-	-	8,480	12,597	6,567	25,512	33,273	17,695	2,896	36,058	-	23,536
Portugal,	-	-	14,282	2,380	4,184	2,056	19,120	16,400	-	22,319	23,650	34,799
Madeira,	2,749	4,785	4,528	5,812	8,525	6,332	-	21,842	8,712	-	2,617	5,978
West-Indies, (generally)	-	5,474	15,082	29,889	22,033	31,931	32,824	17,533	3,202	-	-	4,602
Europe,	-	-	1,700	870	597	30,240	31,875	-	-	-	-	5,204
Average price,	-	-	-	-	-	50 cts.	50 cts.	50 cts.	44 cts.	40 cts.	40 cts.	40 cts.

TABLE No. X.—CONTINUED.

SPERMACETI OIL—gallons.

Whither exported.	1800.	1801.	1802.	1803.	1804.	1805.	1806.	1807.	1808.	1809.	1810.	1811.
Denmark and Norway,	-	-	252	-	-	235	-	676	-	-	-	-
Danish West-Indies,	367	720	475	-	-	-	395	386	220	-	-	-
Dutch West-Indies,	2,100	731	-	245	2,445	-	-	1,582	-	-	-	-
Great-Britain,	204,717	66,869	-	42,540	540	56,733	12,827	7,426	-	50,652	62,367	135,773
British West-Indies,	2,443	6,102	1,349	253	2,080	648	2,402	1,114	336	-	-	-
France,	-	7,294	13,226	-	-	5,652	10,798	9,190	-	-	-	-
French West-Indies,	2,120	4,354	591	1,416	-	609	9,662	3,603	-	-	-	-
Spain,	3,819	-	7,980	2,530	-	-	-	-	-	-	-	-
Spanish West-Indies,	6,196	4,384	-	-	-	2,801	4,831	2,910	-	-	-	-
Portugal,	-	-	1,667	-	-	-	-	-	-	-	1,507	-
Madeira,	-	-	1,225	-	-	-	-	-	-	-	-	-
West-Indies, (generally)	-	1,148	594	-	338	5,401	-	1,983	-	-	-	-
Average price,						80 cts.	80 cts.	$1.	80 cts.	60 cts.	75 cts.	$1 25.

TABLE No. XI.

STAVES and HEADING—thousands of.

Whither exported.	1800.	1801.	1802.	1803.	1804.	1805.	1806.	1807.	1808.	1809.	1810.	1811.
Sweden,	333	-	-	-	-	-	-	-	-	1,749	207	-
Swedish West-Indies,	196	121	-	163	260	127	218	116	-	4,366	3,461	1,667
Denmark and Norway,	120	-	-	-	-	-	-	-	-	143	289	-
Danish West-Indies,	861	924	1,587	883	883	2,084	1,267	1,739	165	320	149	-
Holland,	73	62	180	173	524	454	1,404	590	-	-	-	-
Dutch West-Indies,	207	351	435	646	747	179	473	492	147	-	-	-
Great-Britain,	11,776	9,337	4,177	8,303	9,145	9,234	10,522	10,499	3,221	3,658	6,138	8,090
British West-Indies,	1,677	16,551	16,402	16,555	14,392	15,408	20,645	16,800	4,422	3,583	6,353	11,991
British American Colonies,	262	147	-	105	347	458	235	177	-	900	914	350
Hamburg, Bremen, &c.	150	-	-	-	-	-	-	-	-	129	260	-
France,	-	6,349	-	357	328	466	716	614	105	-	-	-
French West-Indies,	347	672	2,134	2,275	1,220	1,597	1,617	2,329	423	-	-	-
Spain,	1,263	-	1,685	1,152	1,801	2,100	2,383	813	394	1,047	1,120	1,566
Spanish West-Indies,	312	379	217	99	369	409	202	-	-	5,056	1,082	1,544
Portugal,	594	389	523	517	667	1,063	1,220	243	141	977	706	445
Madeira,	319	237	464	362	536	381	791	424	-	1,887	1,225	467
West-Indies, (generally)	-	193	765	1,714	1,583	7,095	1,460	1,564	763	-	672	1,877
Average price,							$20.	25.	23.	25.	30.	30.

TABLE No. XII.

SHINGLES—thousands of.

Whither exported.	1800.	1801.	1802.	1803.	1804.	1805.	1806.	1807.	1808.	1809.	1810.	1811.
Swedish West-Indies,	1,626	1,067	765	1,448	1,855	1,133	789	980	157	13,368	9,541	12,667
Danish West-Indies,	5,871	3,899	1,636	2,059	5,608	7,512	7,371	7,319	475	312	372	195
Dutch West-Indies,	2,415	3,094	1,741	3,156	2,760	1,185	1,328	1,574	-	-	-	-
British West-Indies,	60,048	61,329	50,283	47,231	44,340	41,784	52,506	43,501	11,962	11,969	22,745	42,004
British American Colonies,	345	122	-	136	746	599	297	540	-	476	322	210
French West-Indies,	2,381	9,239	20,477	12,970	9,155	14,774	13,103	13,614	1,846	-	287	476
Spanish West-Indies,	2,345	1,250	1,622	342	241	916	638	360	143	7,403	6,233	5,512
Madeira,	-	-	-	250	-	-	-	-	-	-	-	-
West-Indies, (generally)	539	794	5,426	10,798	9,810	6,711	5,164	8,471	2,780	-	2,197	6,916
Average price,							$3.	3.	3.	3.	3 50.	4.

84

TABLE No. XIII.

BOARDS and PLANK—thousand feet.

Whither exported.	1800.	1801.	1802.	1803.	1804.	1805.	1806.	1807.	1808.	1809.	1810.	1811.
Swedish West-Indies,	1,322	755	778	576	1,502	691	692	833	149	13,581	10,421	9,849
Danish West-Indies,	4,155	3,007	2,609	2,015	2,993	7,334	6,701	6,845	516	1,135	515	255
Dutch West-Indies,	4,167	5,002	3,406	6,644	9,204	4,182	4,416	5,075	1,310	122	412	-
Great-Britain,	1,288	1,865	1,350	2,659	3,086	2,203	4,207	4,112	1,206	1,165	2,879	3,055
British West-Indies,	47,704	43,729	42,832	43,206	35,499	36,975	42,096	36,205	14,314	16,412	17,361	27,363
British American Colonies,	737	203	168	1,004	3,008	1,958	1,913	2,079	183	1,388	3,359	2,030
French West-Indies,	1,813	5,484	16,592	8,725	4,767	20,550	9,598	12,436	1,583	-	102	472
Spanish West-Indies,	6,146	9,448	4,842	3,496	5,062	11,152	7,346	933	2,600	26,021	17,061	17,960
Madeira,	232	144	985	871	388	301	1,001	457	319	1,202	1,815	1,579
West-Indies, (generally)	178	854	5,436	7,960	8,228	7,372	5,478	8,317	3,368	-	2,818	13,282
Average price,							$12.	13.	13.	12.	12.	12.

TABLE No. XIV.

TAR—barrels.

Whither exported.	1800.	1801.	1802.	1803.	1804.	1805.	1806.	1807.	1808.	1809.	1810.	1811.
Sweden,	-	-	-	-	-	-	-	-	-	7,721	939	-
Swedish West-Indies,	-	-	-	-	-	-	-	-	-	3,053	1,103	-
Danish West-Indies,	511	-	679	-	839	3,039	1,013	837	-	-	-	-
Dutch West-Indies,	536	-	1,911	615	512	-	-	-	-	-	-	-
Great-Britain,	43,438	49,224	42,756	68,850	35,630	53,759	43,252	41,656	15,505	28,725	46,127	117,589
British West-Indies,	2,937	7,248	5,527	3,560	6,110	3,338	5,007	4,119	845	1,215	1,759	3,619
British American Colonies,	2,418	6,160	3,047	2,885	3,476	2,342	2,404	5,445	360	3,132	2,139	1,826
France,	1,094	-	797	-	-	-	-	-	-	-	-	-
French West-Indies,	-	-	4,286	-	395	349	404	-	-	-	-	-
Spain,	1,354	-	-	-	-	-	-	-	-	-	-	1,834
Spanish West-Indies,	-	-	2,784	-	953	1,183	487	1,173	-	6,801	1,033	3,199
Portugal,	-	-	-	-	584	1,649	1,345	871	-	8,225	6,617	6,397
Madeira,	-	-	-	-	-	-	-	-	-	6,418	8,767	-
West-Indies (generally)	-	-	846	313	333	-	-	-	-	14,734	1,742	-
do.	-	-	-	574	851	-	-	-	-	571	-	1,352
Europe	-	-	-	-	-	-	-	-	-	-	-	-
Average price,							$2 50	2 50	2 50	3.	2.	3.

TABLE No. XV.

TURPENTINE—barrels.

Whither exported.	1800.	1801.	1802.	1803.	1804.	1805.	1806.	1807.	1808.	1809.	1810.	1811.
Great-Britain, - -	31,504	33,921	36,327	60,403	76,234	93,607	70,279	50,564	16,729	22,448	36,397	95,415
British West-Indies, -	586	842	201	123	282	237	587	524	-	-	-	375
British American Colonies,	490	380	241	206	344	484	1,000	1,019	280	437	608	1,470
French West-Indies, -	-	-	426	-	-	-	-	-	-	-	-	-
Spain, - - -	-	-	-	-	-	-	-	-	-	-	2,854	-
Spanish West-Indies, -	-	-	367	-	-	-	-	-	-	3,742	1,099	-
Portugal, - - -	-	-	238	-	-	-	-	-	-	2,505	7,826	998
Madeira, - - -	-	-	-	-	-	-	-	-	-	4,437	2,385	-
West-Indies, (generally) do. -	-	-	-	-	115	-	-	-	-	9,219	-	-
Europe, do. -	-	-	214	100	-	-	-	-	-	-	-	-
Average price,							$2 75	3.	3.	4.	4.	3.

TABLE No. XVI.

POT ASHES—tons.

Whither exported.	1800.	1801.	1802.	1803.	1804.	1805.	1806.	1807.	1808.	1809.	1810.	1811.
Sweden,	-	-	-	-	-	-	-	-	-	574	87	-
Swedish West-Indies,	-	-	-	-	-	-	-	-	-	57	45	-
Denmark and Norway,	-	-	-	-	-	-	-	-	-	364	620	-
Danish West-Indies,	-	-	-	-	-	1	-	-	-	-	-	-
Holland,	154	806	530	131	30	83	642	1,006	4	232	-	-
Great-Britain,	5,993	5,221	1,828	2,711	2,549	2,277	2,713	2,782	962	1,132	3,661	2,519
British West-Indies,	-	2	13	-	-	-	-	-	-	-	7	-
British American Colonies,	272	520	163	220	342	511	597	643	178	950	1,018	1,660
Hamburg, Bremen, &c.	292	120	39	38	-	-	-	-	-	177	8	-
France,	-	514	819	169	458	685	664	1,421	320	-	8	104
French West-Indies,	-	15	3	1	-	-	-	-	-	-	-	-
Spain,	39	30	3	-	-	-	-	-	-	44	555	-
Spanish West-Indies,	-	-	-	-	-	-	-	-	-	6	6	-
Portugal,	10	-	-	-	-	-	-	-	-	515	359	-
Madeira,	-	-	-	-	-	-	-	-	-	249	130	-
Europe, (generally)	-	-	-	-	32	-	-	-	-	-	46	6
Average price,							$150.	160.	160.	160.	150.	130.

TABLE No. XVII.

PEARL ASHES—tons.

Whither exported.	1800.	1801.	1802.	1803.	1804.	1805.	1806.	1807.	1808.	1809.	1810.	1811.
Prussia,	5	-	-	-	-	-	-	-	-	-	-	-
Sweden,	-	-	-	-	-	-	-	-	-	330	12	-
Swedish West-Indies,	-	-	-	-	-	-	-	-	-	90	19	-
Denmark and Norway,	-	-	-	-	-	-	-	-	-	220	398	-
Holland,	337	154	218	62	44	64	283	545	130	84	-	-
Great-Britain,	884	1,094	1,496	2,071	975	1,336	1,162	2,024	592	804	1,900	1,411
British West-Indies,	-	-	-	-	-	-	1	-	-	-	-	-
British American Colonies,	-	-	-	-	-	-	-	-	-	-	-	-
Hamburg, Bremen, &c.	35	6	14	16	-	-	-	-	36	-	115	96
France,	-	39	57	31	119	175	67	202	109	166	-	-
French West-Indies,	-	4	-	14	-	-	1	1	-	-	-	47
Spain,	-	-	-	-	-	-	-	-	-	44	222	-
Portugal,	-	-	-	-	-	-	-	-	-	173	232	-
Madeira,	-	-	-	-	-	-	-	-	-	110	101	-
Europe, (generally)	-	-	-	-	-	-	-	-	-	25	3	3
Average price,						$160.	200.	200.	200.	200.	160.	125.

CHAPTER IV.

THE produce of agriculture divided into that, 1st, which constitutes vegetable food, as wheat, flour, rice, indian corn, rye, &c.—2d, the products of animals, as beef, pork, butter, lard, cheese, and cattle, horses, &c.—3d, tobacco,
—4th, cotton, and 5th, others of less importance, as flax-seed, indigo, wax,
&c.—The quantity and value of each of these exported at different periods—
Value of manufactures exported—A comparative view of the value of the
products of the sea, of the forest, of agriculture, and manufactures exported
in each year from 1803 to 1814.

THE principal employment of the inhabitants of North-America,
from its first settlement, has been that of agriculture. The first emigrants soon found, that nothing promised such important advantages,
and furnished such easy means of subsistence, as the cultivation of
new lands. The labour bestowed in clearing them, not only furnished the surest means of subsistence, but also added to the permanent
value of the lands themselves. The immense tracts of vacant, uncleared
lands in the United States, has always rendered it easy, for those who
possessed an ordinary share of industry, to obtain more than sufficient
for cultivation. The ease with which families can be supported, by
this mode of employment, has induced early marriages; population
has increased with the means of subsistence; and wealth and happiness
have generally attended the independent cultivator of the soil.

The surplus produce of the agriculture of the United States has
been exchanged for those articles, either of necessity, convenience, or
luxury, which they did not manufacture, or which could only be procured from foreign nations; and the productions of agriculture, both
before and since the American revolution, have constituted much
the greatest portion of their domestic exports. These productions
have been classed into those—

1st, which constitute vegetable food, such as wheat, flour, rice, indian corn, rye, peas, beans, potatoes, &c.

2d, the product of animals, as beef, tallow, hides, butter and cheese, pork and lard, or the animals themselves, as live cattle, horses, mules, sheep, &c.

3d, tobacco.

4th, cotton.

5th, others of minor importance, as indigo, flax-seed, wax, &c.

Wheat, the most valuable of all vegetables, was brought into America by the first settlers, and has been cultivated with success, from the first settlement of the country. For a long time, it has been the staple of the middle states, and was formerly produced in great abundance, in the eastern states. For some years past, however, the growth of wheat in New-England has, in a great degree, failed. The states of Maryland and Virginia, have, long since, exchanged part of their tobacco lands, for wheat; and lately, in the more southern states, the cultivation of wheat has been substituted for cotton. Wheat and flour have always constituted a large proportion of the exports of this country.

In the year 1770, the quantity of wheat exported from the North-American Colonies, now United States, was seven hundred and fifty-one thousand two hundred and forty bushels; of this eleven thousand seven hundred and thirty-nine went to England; one hundred and forty-nine thousand nine hundred and eighty-five, to Ireland; five hundred and eighty-eight thousand five hundred and sixty-one, to the south of Europe, and nine hundred and fifty-five, to the West-Indies. During the same year, forty-five thousand eight hundred and sixty-eight tons of flour and bread were also exported, of which two hundred and sixty-three tons went to England; three thousand five hundred and eighty-three, to Ireland; eighteen thousand five hundred and one, to the south of Europe; twenty-three thousand four hundred and forty-nine, to the West-Indies; and seventy-two, to Africa. The official value of the wheat, was estimated at £131,467 0 10 sterling, and the flour and bread at £504,553 6 1 making £636,020 6 11 or about $2,862,190. The amount exported from the United States, from the peace of 1783, to the commencement of the present government, cannot be ascertained with any degree of precision.

The quantity exported from 1791, to 1814, with the value since 1803, was as follows:—

	Wheat. Bushels.		Flour. Barrels.		Value of both. Dolls.
1791	-	1,018,339	-	619,681	
1792	-	853,790	-	824,464	
1793	-	1,450,575	-	1,074,639	
1794	-	6 6,797	-	846,010	
1795	-	141,273	-	687,369	
1796	-	31,226	-	725,194	
1797	-	15,655	-	515,633	
1798	-	15,021	-	567,558	
1799	-	10,056	-	519,265	
1800	-	26,853	-	653,052	
1801	-	239,929	-	1,102,444	
1802	-	280,281	-	1,156,248	
1803	-	686,415	-	1,311,853	- 9,310,000
1804	-	127,024	-	810,008	- 7,100,000
1805	-	18,041	-	777,513	- 8,325,000
1806	-	86,784	-	782,724	- 6,867,000
1807	-	766,814	-	1,249,819	- 10,753,000
1808	-	87,330	-	263,813	- 1,936,000
1809	-	393,889	-	846,247	- 5,944,000
1810	-	325,924	-	798,431	- 6,846,000
1811	-	216,833	-	1,445,012	- 14,662,000
1812	-	53,832	-	1,443,492	- 13,687,000
1813	-	288,535	-	1,260,943	- 13,591,000
1814	-	- -	-	193,274	- 1,734,000

The years of greatest exportation of these articles, since 1791, were 1793, 1801-2 and 3, 1807, and 1811, in the last of which, the value of wheat and flour exported amounted to the sum of $14,662,000, exceeding, by nearly four millions, that of any former year. This great increase, however, was owing, principally, to the enhanced price of those articles, during that year. In 1807, the average price of wheat, at the principal places of exportation, was $1 25 per bushel, and of flour, $7 per barrel; in 1811, the price of wheat was $1 75, and of flour, $9 50.*

Tables No. I. and II. annexed to this chapter, shew the different countries and places, to which these articles have been exported from 1800, to 1811. The West-Indies, Spain, Portugal, and Great-Britain have been the principal consumers of our wheat and flour. The West-India Islands have always furnished a market for a large proportion of them, and in times of scarcity in Great-Britain, and in the southern parts of Europe, the United States have come in competition with the grain countries of the north of Europe. In 1801, in a time of scarcity in Great-Britain, the United States exported to that kingdom two hundred and sixteen thousand nine hundred and seventy-seven bushels of wheat, and four hundred and seventy-nine thousand seven hundred and twenty barrels of flour. In 1807, six hundred and sixty-nine thousand nine hundred and fifty bushels of wheat, and three hundred twenty-three thousand nine hundred and sixty-eight barrels of flour were also exported to Great-Britain. The late unfortunate and distressed situation of Spain and Portugal, has called for a large proportion of our grain, not only for the ordinary supply for the inhabitants, but for the support of the allied armies, in those countries. In 1811, no less than five hundred twenty-nine thousand one hundred and five barrels of flour, and fifty-five thousand and thirty-three bushels of wheat were shipped to Portugal, and three hundred six thousand and seventy-four barrels of flour and twenty-one thousand one hundred and

* The prices, by which the value of wheat and flour exported has been calculated at the Treasury Department, since the year 1806 (being the average prices at the principal places of exportation,) were as follows :—

	Wheat price per bushel.	Flour price per barrel
1806	$1 33	$8
1807	1 25	7
1808	1 25	6 50
1809	1 25	6
1810	1 50	7 50
1811	1 75	9 50
1812	1 94	10 00
1813	1 75	11 00
1814		9 50

ninety-nine bushels of wheat, to Spain, making in the whole, to the Peninsula, during that year, eight hundred thirty-five thousand one hundred and seventy-nine barrels of flour, and seventy-six thousand two hundred and thirty-two bushels of wheat, the value of which at the places of exportation exceeded eight millions of dollars. If to this is added the enhanced price, in the foreign market, the value cannot fall much short of twelve millions. The following quantities of wheat and flour were shipped to Spain and Portugal, during the years 1812 and 1813, viz.—

	To Spain.		To Portugal.	
	Wheat. bushels.	Flour. barrels.	Wheat. bushels.	Flour. barrels.
1812	8,865	381,726	33,591	557,218
1813	74,409	431,101	214,126	542,399

Making nine hundred seventy-three thousand and five hundred barrels of flour to Spain and Portugal, for the year 1813. The value of wheat and flour, therefore, which went to those countries in that year was $11,213,447, at the places of exportation. In a foreign market their value could not be less than fifteen millions.

In Great-Britain, various regulations, at different times, have been made, relative to the exportation and importation of grain. The limited extent of that country, in proportion to its population, and the employment of so many of its inhabitants, in commerce and manufactures, have, for many years past, rendered a foreign supply of grain necessary, in case of any considerable failure of their crops. To encourage the production of domestic grain, and to remedy the evils, arising from a scarcity in consequence of bad crops, the British government have given a bounty on the exportation of grain, when its price was below a certain sum, and have allowed its importation, with a very small duty, when it has risen in price to a sum which is fixed by law ; and for many years past, in times of great scarcity, a large bounty has been given, on the importation of foreign grain. In 1773, when the price of middling wheat in Great-Britain, was under 44s. rye 28s. barley 22s. oats 14s. a bounty of 5s. per quarter on wheat, 3s. on rye, 2s. 6d. on barley, and 2s. on oats was given on its exportation. When the price of middling wheat was 44s. or more, its exportation was prohibited, under a forfeiture of 20s. per bushel; and when the price of wheat was at, or above 48s. rye, peas or beans 32s. barley 24s. oats 16s., the high duties on importation ceased, and wheat was allowed to be imported, on paying the trifling duty of 6d. per quarter, 2d. per cwt. on flour, 3d. per quarter on rye, peas or beans, 2d. on barley and 2d. on oats. These prices were altered at subsequent periods. In consequence of a scarcity in 1795, a bounty was granted of 16 to 20s. per quarter, according to the quality, on wheat, and 6s. per cwt. on flour, from the South of Europe, till the quantity imported should amount to four hundred thousand quarters, and from America, till it should amount to five hundred thousand quarters; and 12s. to 15s. from any other part of Europe, till it should amount to five hundred thousand quarters, and 8s. to 10s. after it exceeded that quantity, to continue till the 30th of September, 1796. In 1800, in consequence of a deficiency in the harvest of the preceding year, the British government, by an act passed the beginning of April, granted to the importer, the difference between the average price of English wheat, the second week after importation, and 90s. on wheat from the South of Europe, Africa, and America; 85s. from the Baltic, and Germany; and 90s. from Archangel, if imported before the 1st of October of that year. In December of the same year, the prices still continuing high, by another act, the difference between the average price of foreign wheat, the third week after entry, and 100s. was guaranteed to the importers of all wheat weighing fifty-three pounds per bushel, or four hundred and twenty-four pounds per quarter imported after the 1st of December of that year,—two hundred and eighty pounds of wheaten flour, except American, to be equal to a quarter. American flour was to be sold by auction, and to receive the difference between the price at which it sold and 90s. per each barrel of one hundred and ninety-six pounds. In consequence of these acts, the bounty paid, on the importation of grain, in 1796, amounted to £599,834 sterling; and in 1801, it amounted to the sum of £1,420,355 sterling, or about $6,381,000. The quantity of grain of all sorts, imported into Great-Britain in 1801, was two million twenty-seven thousand five hundred and fifteen quarters, or more than sixteen millions of bushels, and the quantity of meal was one million one hundred and twenty-five thousand seven hundred and four cwt. The average price of wheat in England in 1795 was 74s. 2d. per quarter, and in 1796 was 77s. 1d. ; in 1800, the average price per quarter was 113s. 7d. and in 1801, 118s. 3d. In 1803, the price was reduced to 56s. per quarter, and the growers complained of the inadequacy of this price, and in 1804, a law was passed, granting a bounty of 5s. per quarter on the exportation of wheat, when the average price of it was at 48s. per quarter, and when above 54s. not to be exported. By this act, also, wheat, if imported from Quebec, or other British Colonies, when the average price is under 53s. pays the high duty of 24s. 3d. above 53s. and under 56s. pays 2s. 6d., and above 56s. 6d. ; when imported from any foreign country, the average price being under 63s. pays the high duty of 24s. 3d. per quarter ; above 63s. and under 66s., 2s. 6d., above 66s. 6d.* By the report of a committee of the house of Commons, made in July, 1814, on petitions relating to the corn laws of Great-Britain, it appears that, in consequence of the advanced price of rent and labour, and the increase of taxes, particularly the property tax, 80s. per quarter, or 10s. sterling, ($2 25) per bushel, is the lowest prices which would afford the British grower of wheat, an adequate remuneration. This report is founded on information, obtained from every part of the kingdom. In consequence of this report, the British Parliament have lately passed a law, prohibiting the importation of foreign wheat, unless the price of English wheat is 10s. sterling or more per bushel. The law, however, was not popular in London, and its passage occasioned serious riots in that city. This brief sketch of the corn laws of Great-Britain, about which a diversity of opinion has prevailed among the political economists of that country, cannot be uninteresting to the American farmer, merchant, or statesman. It is difficult to ascertain what price will remunerate the grower of wheat in the United States. In 1806 and 1807, when great quantities of wheat and flour were exported, the average price of wheat was only $1 27 per bushel, and the average price of flour $7 50 per barrel.

The population of England and Wales in 1801, according to an

---

* See Comber's Enquiry, 1808, and Oddy's European Commerce.

enumeration then made, was about nine millions three hundred and thirty thousand, and Mr. George Chalmers estimated the consumption of grain of all sorts, at that time, in England and Wales, to be as follows, viz.—

	Quarters.			Bushels.
Bread corn, one qr. each,	9,330,000	eight bush. per qr.		74,640,000
Corn made into drink,	4,665,000	do.	do.	37,320,000
Corn for cattle, poultry,&c.	4,665,000	do.	do.	37,320,000
	18,660,000	or		149,280,000

How far the United States have come in competition, with the grain countries situated around the Baltic, in the articles of wheat and flour, will appear on comparing the exports of those articles, from those countries respectively.

The whole quantity of wheat, exported from all the ports of the Baltic in the years 1801 and 1802, being years of great exportation, was, for

1801 . . . . 994,609 quarters*
1802 . . . . 1,032,941 do. being, on an average of these two years, about one million of quarters, or eight millions of Winchester bushels. The average quantity exported from the United States, during the same years, (allowing five bushels of wheat to a barrel of flour,) was about five millions nine hundred thousand bushels, falling about two millions short of the quantity exported from all the extensive grain countries situated around the Baltic. The value of grain of all kinds annually exported from the Baltic, in common years, amounts to about two millions sterling, or about nine millions of dollars. In some years, however, it has amounted to eight millions sterling.† The value of grain, including rice, shipped from the United States, on an average of the years 1805-6, and 7, was about twelve and a half millions of dollars, and in the years 1811–12, and 13, was as follows, viz.—

						Dolls.
1811	.	.	.	.	.	20,391,000
1812	.	.	.	.	.	17,797,000
1813	.	.	.	.	.	19,041,000

* 2 Vol. of Oddy.   † 2 Vol. of Oddy.

This increase, it is well known, was occasioned by the great demand for grain and provisions of all kinds in Spain and Portugal during these years, and the enhanced prices of the articles themselves. In 1811, the year of the greatest exportation, the value

of wheat, flour, and biscuit, was	$14,662,000
of Indian corn and meal,	2,896,000
of rice,	2,387,000
of all other, rye, oats, pulse, potatoes, &c.	446,000

Making $20,391,000*

RICE.

The culture of rice was introduced into South-Carolina about the year 1694. Different accounts have been given as to the manner of its first introduction. The account, however, given by Dr. Ramsay, in his valuable history of South-Carolina, published in 1809, is probably the most correct, and which we shall give in his own words:

" Landgrave Thomas Smith, who was governour of the Province in 1693, had been at Madagascar, before he settled in Carolina. There he observed, that rice was planted and grew in low and moist ground. Having such ground, at the western extremity of his garden attached to his dwelling-house in East Bay street, he was persuaded that rice would grow therein, if seed could be obtained. About this time a

* The value of grain exported from the empire of Russia, in 1802, was as follows :‡

							Rubles.
Wheat	-	-	-	-	-	-	4,055,907
Rye	-	-	-	-	-	-	5,604,422
Barley	-	-	-	-	-	-	1,004,144
Oats	-	-	-	-	-	-	206,056
Other corn	-	-	-	-	-	-	99,754
Wheat and rye flour		-	-	-	-	157,809
In spirits made from native corn			-	-	368,153

11,496,245

‡ Oddy's European Commerce.

vessel from Madagascar, being in distress, came to anchor near Sulli-
van's Island. The master of this vessel inquired for Mr. Smith as an
old acquaintance. An interview took place. In the course of con-
versation Mr. Smith expressed a wish to obtain some seed rice to plant
in his garden, by way of experiment. The cook being called said
he had a small bag of rice suitable for that purpose. This was presented to Mr. Smith, who sowed it in a low spot of his garden, which
now forms a part of Longitude lane. It grew luxuriantly. The little
crop was distributed by Mr. Smith, among his planting friends. From
this small beginning, the first staple commodity of Carolina took its
rise. It soon after became the chief support of the Colony."*

Its introduction was an object of great importance to that country.
It was valuable, not only for the consumption of the inhabitants of
that Province, but it soon became the staple of the country, as an article of exportation. By an act of Parliament of the 3 and 4 of Ann,
(1706) rice was placed among the enumerated commodities, and could
only be shipped directly to Great-Britain; but afterwards, in the
year 1730, it was permitted, under certain limitations and restrictions, to be shipped and carried directly from Carolina, to any part
of Europe south of Cape Finisterre. In the year 1724, eighteen
thousand barrels of rice were exported, and in the year 1733, thirty-
six thousand five hundred and eighty-four barrels from South-Carolina,
and in 1739, seventy-one thousand four hundred and eighty-four barrels, and in 1740, no less than ninety-one thousand one hundred and
ten barrels. From November 1760 to September 1761, one hundred
thousand barrels were exported.† From the table of exports of the
North-American Colonies, for the year 1770, it appears, that during
that year, one hundred fifty thousand five hundred and twenty-nine
barrels of rice were exported, and that seventy-four thousand and seventy-three were shipped to Great-Britain, thirty-six thousand two
hundred and ninety-six to the South of Europe, forty thousand and
thirty-three to the West-Indies, and one hundred and seventeen to
Africa, the value of this, as estimated in the custom-house books, was
£340,692 15 0 sterling, or about $1,530,000.

* Doct. Ramsay's History of South-Carolina.

† Macpherson's Annals of Commerce and Ramsay's History.

The quantity exported from the United States, from 1791 to 1804, and its value since 1803, was as follows, viz.—

	Tierces.	Value. Dolls.
1791 - -	96,980	
1792 - -	141,762	
1793 - -	134,611	
1794 - -	116,486	
1795 - -	138,526	
1796 - -	131,039	
1797 - -	60,111	
1798 - -	125,243	
1799 - -	110,599	
1800 - -	112,056	
1801 - -	94,866	
1802 - -	79,822	
1803 - -	81,838 - -	2,455,000
1804 - -	78,385 - -	2,350,000
1805 - -	56,830 - -	1,705,000
1806 - -	102,627 - -	2,617,000
1807 - -	94,692 - -	2,367,000
1808 - -	9,228 - -	221,000
1809 - -	116,907 - -	2,104,000
1810 - -	131,341 - -	2,626,000
1811 - -	119,356 - -	2,387,000
1812 - -	77,190 - -	1,544,000
1813 - -	120,843 - -	3,021,000
1814 - -	11,476 - -	230,000

INDIAN CORN AND MEAL, RYE, &c.

Indian corn, or maize, was found among the natives on the first discovery of this country, and from them, has received its usual name; and has always been considered indigenous in America. It was cultivated by the Indians, for food, both in North and South-America. It seems adapted to the climate of all the states, except in the extreme parts of the north, where the summers are sometimes too short and cold, to bring it to maturity ; and where it is also liable to be injured by early frosts. It is exported in large quantities, in a raw state, or when manufactured into meal.

When manufactured, it is, principally, shipped to the West-Indies, though in times of scarcity, it has, occasionally, gone to Europe. In 1770, five hundred seventy-eight thousand three hundred and forty-nine bushels, were exported from the North-American Colonies ; of this, one hundred fifty went to Ireland, one hundred seventy-five thousand two hundred and twenty-one to the south of Europe, four hundred two thousand nine hundred and fifty-eight to the West-Indies, twenty to Africa ; and in the custom-house books, it was valued at £43,376 4 2 sterling, or about $194,000.

Of late years, before the corn is manufactured into meal, it is dried by a fire, in a kiln prepared for that purpose. By this process, the meal is much less liable to become sour on the voyage, and can be preserved much longer in a warm climate.

The following is the quantity of Indian corn and meal exported, annually, from 1791 to 1814—viz.

	Corn.	Meal.	Value.
	Bushels.	Bushels.	Dolls.
1791	1,713,241	351,695	
1792	1,964,973	263,405	
1793	1,233,768	189,715	
1794	1,505,977	241,570	
1795	1,935,345	512,445	
1796	1,173,552	540,286	
1797	804,922	254,799	
1798	1,218,231	211,694	
1799	1,200,492	231,226	
1800	1,694,327	338,108	
1801	1,768,162	919,355	
1802	1,633,283	266,816	
1803	2,079,608	133,606	2,025,000
1804	1,944,873	111,327	2,500,000

	Corn. Bushels.	Meal. Barrels.	Value. Dolls.
1805	861,501	116,131	1,442,000
1806	1,064,263	108,342	1,286,000
1807	1,018,721	136,460	987,000
1808	249,533	30,818	298,000
1809	522,047	57,260	547,000
1810	1,054,252	86,744	1,138,000
1811	2,790,850	147,426	2,896,000
1812	2,039,999	90,810	1,939,000
1813	1,486,970	58,521	1,838,000
1814	61,284	26,438	170,000

The West-Indies, Spain, and Portugal, are the principal markets for Indian corn and meal.

The other articles of vegetable food, exported from the United States, are rye, oats, peas, beans, potatoes, &c. These, however, constitute but a small part of the value of their exports. Most of the rye in the United States is used for bread, or is made into spirits, at home. The distillation of grain has, within a few years, increased very rapidly in this country. In 1801, the quantity of spirits, distilled from grain and fruit, was estimated at ten millions of gallons. By the returns of the marshals, giving an account of the manufactures of the several states, in 1810, it appears that the quantity distilled during that year, from grain and fruit, exceeded twenty millions of gallons. Much the greatest part of this, probably more than three quarters, was from grain. It is calculated, that a bushel of rye, or corn, will produce from two and a half to three gallons of spirits. In 1810, therefore, between five and six millions of bushels of rye and corn must have been made into spirits. In Pennsylvania alone, in that year, there were three thousand three hundred and thirty-four distilleries, producing no less than six million five hundred fifty-two thousand two hundred and eighty-four gallons of spirits, principally from grain. The whole, or nearly the whole, of this is consumed in the United States. When we add to this the quantity distilled in this country from molasses, and that which is imported and consumed here, we find the annual consumption of spirits in the United States amounting to thirty-one million seven hundred twenty-five thousand four hundred and seventeen gallons, as the following calculation will shew :—

	Galls.
Spirits distilled in the United States in 1810, from foreign and domestic materials, as by the returns of the marshals, (about five millions from molasses) - - - -	25,499,382

Exported during that year, spirits from foreign materials - -	474,990	
do. do. from domestic materials	133,853	
		608,843

Leaving to be consumed - -	24,890,539
The average quantity of spirits imported and consumed from 1801 to 1812 inclusive	6,834,878

Making - - - -	31,725,417

about four and a half gallons for every person. Very little rye is exported from this country. In 1801, the year of scarcity in Great-Britain, three hundred ninety-two thousand two hundred and seventy-six bushels of rye meal were exported, which was more than three times the quantity exported in any one year since 1791; and the average number of bushels of rye exported, annually from 1791 to 1811, has not exceeded six or eight thousand. Much greater quantities were exported in the years 1812 and 1813; in the former of which, eighty-two thousand seven hundred and five, and in the latter, one hundred forty thousand one hundred and thirty-six bushels were exported.

Vast quantities of rye are produced in Europe, and particularly in the northern parts. The bread of the common people, in the northern Kingdoms of Europe, is made of rye meal, and great quantities are also exported from the Baltic. In France, one of the best wheat countries, rye is also common. It is said, that more of it is gathered there than of wheat, and that half of the people in France use rye bread.*

* See Peccohet's Statistics of France, digested and abridged by James N. Taylor, Esq. printed in 1815.

The average quantity of oats exported, for twenty years, has been about seventy thousand bushels, annually ; of peas, about ninety thousand, and of beans, between thirty and forty thousand. Potatoes, which constitute such a valuable part of our agricultural productions, especially in our domestic economy, are also exported, but the average quantity will not exceed about sixty thousand bushels a year.

The following is the aggregate value of all the exports, the produce of agriculture, constituting vegetable food, from 1802, to 1814 :—

					Dolls.
1802	-	-	-	-	12,790,000
1803	-	-	-	-	14,080,000
1804	-	-	-	-	12,250,000
1805	-	-	-	-	11,752,000
1806	-	-	-	-	11,850,000
1807	-	-	-	-	14,432,000
1808	-	-	-	-	2,550,000
1809	-	-	-	-	8,751,000
1810	-	-	-	-	10,750,000
1811	-	-	-	-	20,391,000
1812	-	-	-	-	17,797,000
1813	-	-	-	-	19,041,000
1814	-	-	-	-	2,179,000

PRODUCE OF ANIMALS.

Beef, pork, tallow, hams, butter and cheese, lard, live cattle and horses, have long been articles of export, of no inconsiderable value. They have generally been shipped to the West-Indies.

The colonial custom-house books shew that in the year 1770, there was shipped to the South of Europe, two hundred and forty-four barrels, and to the West-Indies two thousand eight hundred and seventy tons of beef and pork, making about twenty-eight thousand nine hundred and forty-four barrels, and which was then valued at £66,035 1 10 sterling, or about $277,000. Beef and pork, with live cattle, have been among the most considerable articles of domes-

tic export from some of the Northern states, where the lands are better for grazing than for grain.

The following quantities of beef and pork have been exported annually from 1791 to 1814, viz.—

	Beef. Bbls.	Pork. Bbls.
1791	62,771	27,781
1792	74,638	38,098
1793	75,106	38,563
1794	100,866	49,442
1795	96,149	88,193
1796	92,521	73,881
1797	51,812	40,125
1798	89,000	33,115
1799	91,321	52,268
1800	75,045	55,467
1801	75,331	70,779
1802	61,520	78,239
1803	77,934	96,602
1804	134,896	111,532
1805	115,532	57,925
1806	117,419	36,277
1807	84,209	39,247
1808	20,101	15,478
1809	28,555	42,652
1810	47,699	37,209
1811	76,743	37,270
1812	42,757	22,746
1813	43,741	17,337
1814	20,297	4,040

In the year 1770, one hundred sixty-seven thousand six hundred
and thirteen pounds of butter, fifty-five thousand nine hundred and
ninety-seven pounds of cheese, and one hundred eighty-five thousand
one hundred and forty-three pounds of tallow and lard were exported.

Large quantities of these articles have been exported, averaging between one and two millions of pounds annually, and in some years exceeding two millions. In 1804, two millions eight hundred and thirty thousand and sixteen pounds of butter, and two millions five hundred sixty-five thousand seven hundred and nineteen pounds of lard, were shipped from the United States. Tables No. IV. and V. annexed to this chapter, shew the countries and places to which our beef and pork have been carried, from 1800 to 1811. Beef and pork, butter and lard, as well as live stock, have generally found a market in the West-India Islands. During the late war in Europe, the British West-Indies, for certain periods, have been open for our beef and pork, and large quantities have been shipped directly to British West-India ports. In 1804, no less than forty-five thousand six hundred and fifty-six barrels of beef, and forty-seven thousand nine hundred and twenty-six barrels of pork went to those parts. In the year 1811, ten thousand four hundred and thirty-two barrels of beef were shipped to Spain, and fourteen thousand three hundred and eighty-one to Portugal.

The value of the exports, the produce of animals, since 1803, as ascertained at the Treasury department, has been as follows, viz.—

	Beef, tallow, hides, and live cattle.	Butter and cheese.	Pork, bacon, lard, and live hogs.	Horses and mules.	Sheep.
	Dolls.	Dolls.	Dolls.	Dolls.	Dolls.
1803	1,145,000	585,000	1,890,000	460,000	55,000
1804	1,520,000	490,000	1,990,000	270,000	30,000
1805	1,545,000	415,000	1,960,000	220,000	1,500
1806	1,360,000	481,000	1,096,000	321,000	16,000
1807	1,108,000	490,000	1,157,000	317,000	14,000
1808	265,000	196,000	398,000	105,000	4,000
1809	425,000	264,000	1,001,000	113,000	8,000
1810	747,000	318,000	907,000	185,000	12,000
1811	1,195,000	395,000	1,002,000	254,000	20,000
1812	524,000	329,000	604,000	191,000	9,000
1813	539,000	95,000	457,000	8,000	2,000
1814	241,000	59,000	176,000	1,000	5,000

The following is the aggregate value of these articles :—

							Dolls.
1803	-	-	-	-	-	-	4,135,000
1804	-	-	-	-	-	-	4,300,000
1805	-	-	-	-	-	-	4,141,500
1806	-	-	-	-	-	-	3,274,000
1807	-	-	-	-	-	-	3,086,000
1808	-	-	-	-	-	-	968,000
1809	-	-	-	-	-	-	1,811,000
1810	-	-	-	-	-	-	2,169,000
1811	-	-	-	-	-	-	2,866,000
1812	-	-	-	-	-	-	1,657,000
1813	-	-	-	-	-	-	1,101,000
1814	-	-	-	-	-	-	482,000

The national legislature have heretofore encouraged the exportation of salted beef and pork, by allowing a bounty on each barrel exported, by way of draw-back of the duty on imported salt. This bounty was supposed to be equal to the amount of the duty on the salt used in a barrel of beef or pork. It was discontinued on the repeal of the duty in 1807. It was not again allowed by Congress on salted beef and pork on the renewal of the duty on imported salt, in July, 1813, although allowed on pickled fish. The policy of the measure, however, is too obvious to admit a doubt, that, on the return of regular commerce, this bounty on salted provisions exported, will be again allowed, as well as on the exportation of pickled fish. It is obvious, that unless it is allowed, the merchant or exporter of this country cannot be on an equal footing with others in a foreign market. The amount of the duty on imported salt will be charged in the price of the provisions, either at home or abroad. If other nations allow a drawback, on the exportation of salted provisions equal to the amount of the duty on salt, and the United States do not make the same allowance, they can undersell us in a foreign market.

In that case, our salted provisions must either remain at home, or the price of the provisions themselves must lessen in proportion to the amount of the duty on salt. This loss will fall on the farmer.

TOBACCO.

Tobacco has been the great staple of Virginia and Maryland, from their first settlement. This plant is a native of America, and was found here on the first discovery of the country. It was introduced into England, by Sir Walter Raleigh, about the year 1584. It soon got into general use, and became the subject of regulation, by royal proclamations and by acts of Parliament. King James I. was violently opposed to its introduction, and issued proclamations against the use of it, and against planting it in England. About the year 1624 it became a royal monopoly, and afterwards, in order to encourage its growth in the Colonies, and thereby derive a revenue to the crown, an act of Parliament prohibited the planting of it in Great-Britain.

The average quantity imported from the North-American Colonies into England, for ten years preceding the year 1709, was twenty-eight millions eight hundred fifty-eight thousand six hundred and sixty-six pounds.*

From 1761 to 1775, the quantity imported annually into England and Scotland, and the amount exported during the same period, was as follows :—

	ENGLAND.		SCOTLAND.	
	Imported.	Exported.	Imported.	Exported.
	Pounds.	Pounds.	Pounds.	Pounds.
1761	47,065,787	36,788,944	24,048,380	23,525,326
1762	44,102,491	36,445,951	27,339,433	26,694,999
1763	65,173,752	40,940,312	31,613,170	30,613,738
1764	54,433,318	54,058,336	26,310,219	25,902,170
1765	48,306,593	39,121,423	33,889,565	33,379,201
1766	43,307,453	32,986,790	32,175,223	31,723,205
1767	39,140,639	36,400,398	29,385,343	28,871,522
1768	35,545,708	30,864,536	33,261,427	32,488,543
1769	33,784,208	23,793,272	35,920,685	34,714,630
1770	39,187,037	33,238,437	39,226,354	38,498,522

Macpherson's Annals of Commerce.

	ENGLAND.		SCOTLAND.	
	Imported.	Exported.	Imported.	Exported.
	Pounds.	Pounds.	Pounds.	Pounds.
1771	58,079,183	41,439,386	49,312,146	48,488,681
1772	51,493,522	49,784,009	43,748,415	42,806,548
1773	55,928,957	50,349,967	44,485,194	43,595,102
1774	56,048,393	44,829,835	40,157,589	39,533,552
1775	55,965,463	43,880,864	55,927,542	

In 1770, eighty-four thousand nine hundred and ninety-seven hogs-heads of tobacco were exported from the North-American Provinces, which were valued in the custom-house books at £906,637 18 1 sterling, or about $4,050,000. This article constituted about one third in value of all the exports in that year, and exceeded the value of wheat and flour exported during the same year, more than one million of dollars.

The following is an account of the quantity exported from the United States, from 1791 to 1814, in its raw, and manufactured state, and its value since 1802 :—

	No, of hhds.		Manufactured. Pounds.		Snuff. Pounds.		Value. Dolls.
1791	-	101,272	-	81,122	-	15,689	
1792	-	112,428	-	117,874	-	10,042	
1793	-	59,947	-	137,784	-	35,559	
1794	-	76,826	-	23,650	-	37,415	
1795	-	61,050	-	20,263	-	129,436	
1796	-	69,018	-	29,181	-	267,046	
1797	-	58,167	-	12,801	-	73,257	
1798	-	68,567	-	142,269	-	114,151	
1799	-	96,070	-	416,076	-	109,682	
1800	-	78,680	-	457,713	-	41,453	
1801	-	103,758	-	472,282	-	52,297	
1802	-	77,721	-	233,591	-	43,161	-	6,220,000
1803	-	86,291	-	152,415	-	17,928	-	6,209,000
1804	-	83,343	-	278,071	-	20,678	-	6,000,000

		No. of hhds.		Manufactured. Pounds.		Snuff. Pounds.		Value. Dolls.
1805	-	71,252	-	532,311	-	33,127	-	6,341,000
1806	-	83,186	-	385,727	-	42,212	-	6,572,000
1807	-	62,186	-	236,004	-	59,768	-	5,476,000
1808	-	9,576	-	26,656	-	25,845	-	833,000
1809	-	53,921	-	314,880	-	35,955	-	3,774,000
1810	-	84,134	-	495,427	-	46,640	-	5,048,000
1811	-	35,828	-	732,713	-	19,904	-	2,150,000
1812	-	26,094	-	583,258	-	3,360	-	1,514,000
1813	-	5,314	-	283,512	-	- -	-	319,000
1814	-	3,125	-	79,377	-	- -	-	232,000

The above value only includes that exported in its raw state.

Tobacco has been one of the greatest articles of export from North-America from its first settlement. Previous to the American revolution, it constituted in value, between a quarter and one third of all the exports of the American Colonies, now the United States. The quantity exported since 1791 has not exceeded, if it has equalled, the quantity exported from 1761 to 1775; although, with other articles, it has increased in price. From 1802 to 1807, the average annual value was about six millions of dollars, and from 1808 to 1813, in consequence of commercial restrictions, and the war between the United States and Great-Britain, the average annual value has not exceeded $2,300,000.*

* The average price of tobacco, at the places of exportation, since 1806, has been as follows, viz.—

						Per hhd. Dolls.
1806	-	-	-	-	-	79
1807	-	-	-	-	-	88
1808	-	-	-	-	-	87
1809	-	-	-	-	-	70
1810	-	-	-	-	-	60
1811	-	-	-	-	-	60
1812	-	-	-	-	-	70
1813	-	-	-	-	-	67
1814	-	-	-	-	-	74

The principal markets for tobacco are Great-Britain, France, Holland, and the North of Europe. (See Table No. VI.) A great part of that shipped to Great-Britain is sent to the Continent of Europe.

COTTON.

Cotton is a native of the tropical regions, in every quarter of the world. It is mentioned by Herodotus as growing in India, at the time he wrote his history. It was found among the Mexicans and Peruvians, on the first discovery of America; and among the latter, the manufacture of it was carried to no inconsiderable extent. Previous to the American revolution, it was cultivated in the southern states for domestic use.

Soon after the peace of 1783, small quantities were exported from Georgia.* It was not, however, cultivated to much extent, for exportation, in the United States, until about the year 1791 or 1792. Since that period, it has become the great staple of the states of South-Carolina and Georgia, and next to grain, the most valuable of all the exports of the United States.

American cotton has been generally known by the names of sea-island and upland cotton. The former grows along the sea coast, has a black seed, is of a long staple, and is easily cleaned or separated from the seed; the latter grows on the upland, at a distance from the coast, has a green seed, is of a short staple, and until the invention of a machine for the purpose, was so difficult to be cleaned, or separated from the seed, as to be scarcely worth the trouble and expense of cultivation. This machine was invented by Mr. Eli Whitney, a native of Massachusetts, who was accidentally in Georgia, in the year 1795; a gentleman of education, and distinguished for his mechanical genius. This machine has enriched the southern planter by enabling him to cultivate, to the greatest advantage, one of the most valuable staples in the world.

Before its invention, very little upland cotton was cultivated, and scarcely a single pound was exported from the United States; afterterwards, the culture of this species of cotton became the principal

* Ramsay's History of South-Carolina

object of the planter in South-Carolina and Georgia; and in the year 1807, more than fifty-five millions of pounds of upland cotton was exported, and which was valued at more than eleven and a half millions of dollars. It has rarely occurred, that the invention of a single machine has, at once, changed the employment of so many thousand people, and has added so much to the wealth and resources of a nation. In the year 1792, the value of the exports of the United States, was only $20,753,098, (upland cotton, the growth of the United States, constituted very little, if any part of these exports,) and in the short period of fifteen years, a new article of export is produced, amounting in value to more than one half of that sum.*

The rapid increase of the culture of cotton in the United States will appear, from the following account of the quantity exported from 1791 to 1814, and the value of that of domestic growth since 1802 :—

			Cotton of all kinds exported from 1791 to 1804. Pounds.	Value of cotton of domestic growth. Dolls.
1791	-	-	189,316	
1792	-	-	138,328	
1793	-	-	487,600	

* Mr. Whitney obtained a patent for this invention, at an early period, under the laws of the United States; and has been liberally rewarded for the right of using it, by all the cotton planting states, except the state of Georgia. South-Carolina gave him, and Mr. Miller, who was concerned with him, the sum of $50,000, for the right of using the machine in that state. In the state of Georgia, his right to the invention was disputed, and his machine was used, with the exception of a few individuals, without making him any compensation. He was compelled therefore, in that state, to have recourse to the judicial tribunals for redress. Owing, however, to a defect in the first patent law, and to the powerful interest opposed to him, he was unable to obtain a decision in his favor, until thirteen years of his patent had expired. This decision was had, before the Circuit Court of the United States, in which Judge Johnson, of South-Carolina, presided. In his charge to the jury, on the trial of the case, the Judge did ample justice to Mr. Whitney, as the original inventor, as well as to the importance and utility of the invention itself.

	Cotton of all kinds exported from 1791 to 1804. Pounds.		Value of cotton of domestic growth. Dolls.
1794	-	1,601,760	
1795	-	6,276,300	
1796	-	6,106,729	
1797	-	3,788,429	
1798	-	9,360,005	
1799	-	9,532,263	
1800	-	17,789,803	
1801	-	20,911,201	
1802	-	27,501,075	- - 5,250,000
1803	-	41,105,623	- - 7,920,000
1804	-	38,118,041	- - 7,650,000

Cotton of domestic growth exported from 1804 to 1814 :—

	Sea-island. Pounds.		Upland. Pounds.		Value. Dolls.
1805	-	8,787,659	-	29,602,428	- 9,445,000
1806	-	6,096,082	-	29,561,383	- 8,332,000
1807	-	8,926,011	-	55,018,448	- 14,232,000
1808	-	949,051	-	9,681,394	- 2,221,000
1809	-	8,654,213	-	42,326,042	- 8,515,000
1810	-	8,604,078	-	84,657,384	- 15,108,000
1811	-	8,029,576	-	54,028,660	- 9,652,000
1812	-	4,367,806	-	24,519,571	- 3,080,000
1813	-	4,134,849	-	14,975,167	- 2,324,000
1814	-	2,520,338	-	15,208,669	- 2,683,000*

* The price of cotton at the places of exportation, according to which the value has been ascertained at the Treasury, since 1804, has been as follows, viz.—

	Sea-island. lb.				Upland. lb.
1806	-	-	-	30 cents.	- - - 22 cents.
1807	-	-	-	30 do.	- - - 21 do.
1808	-	-	-	30 do.	- - - 20 do.
1809	-	-	-	25 do.	- - - 15 do.

Tables No. VII. and VIII. shew the countries to which cotton has been exported, from 1800 to 1811. Great-Britain has been the principal market for this article. In 1807, before the commencement of our commercial restrictions, more than fifty-three millions of pounds were shipped directly to that country, leaving about thirteen millions for all other parts of the world.

During the continuance of those restrictions, the greatest part reached Great-Britain, by the way of the Floridas, the Azores, Madeira, Spain, Portugal, and Sweden.

The value of cotton shipped to Great-Britain, in 1807, according to the American custom-house books, was $11,953,378. According to the English custom-house books, and a valuation made by the inspector-general of imports and exports, the *real* value of cotton, imported from the United States into Great-Britain, (exclusive of Scotland) in the year ending the 10th of October, 1807, was £3,036,392 sterling, or $13,481,580. If we add to this, the quantity imported into Scotland, the value cannot be less than about fifteen millions of dollars. The increase, in the culture and manufacture of cotton, of late years, has been astonishingly great, and to trace its rapid progress is not a matter of idle or useless curiosity. From 1768 to 1779, the average quantity of cotton annually imported into England, from all parts of the world, did not exceed about five millions of pounds. From 1784 to 1787, the quantity imported into Great-Britain was as follows, viz.—

							Pounds.
1784	-	-	-	-	-	-	11,280,338
1785	-	-	-	-	-	-	17,992,888
1786	-	-	-	-	-	-	19,151,867
1787	-	-	-	-	-	*	22,600,000

				Sea-island. lbs.					Upland. lbs.	
1810	-	-	-	28	cents.	-	-	-	15	cents.
1811	-	-	-	26	do.	-	-	-	14	do.
1812	-	-	-	20	do.	-	-	-	9	do.
1813	-	-	-	20	do.	-	-	-	10	do.
1814	-	-	-	28	do.	-	-	-	13	do.

The cotton imported in 1787, is supposed to have come from the following places :—

	Pounds.
British West-Indies, - - - -	6,600,000
French and Spanish Colonies, - - -	6,000,000
Dutch, - - do. - - -	1,700,000
Portuguese, - - - - - -	2,500,000
East-Indies, procured from Ostend, - -	100,000
Smyrna and Turkey, - - - -	5,700,000
	22,600,000

In 1800, the quantity imported into England,	
was - - - - - -	42,806,507
Into Scotland - - - - -	13,204,225
Making	56,010,732*

In the year 1807, the following quantity was imported into the ports of London, Liverpool, and Glasgow, from different parts of the world :†—

	Bags.
From the United States, - - - -	171,267
The British West-Indies, - - -	28,969
The Colonies conquered from the Dutch,	43,651
Portugal, - - - - -	18,981
East-Indies, - - - - -	11,409
All other parts, - - - -	8,390
	282,667

* Macpherson's Annals of Commerce.

† Sir Alexander Baring's inquiry relative to the British orders in council, &c.—1808.

The number of bales imported into Great-Britain, and the countries from where imported in 1810 and 1811, were as follows, viz.—

	1810.	1811.
From America - -	240,516	128,482
Portugal and Colonies -	142,946	118,514
Spain and do. -	14,589	7,881
East-Indies - - -	79,382	14,646
Demarara, Berbice, Surinam, and Cayenne, - -	40,291	34,838
West-India Islands, -	33,571	19,295
Mediterranean, - -	3,592	974
Ireland, - - -	6,082	1,300
Heligoland, - -	182	274
Africa, - - - -	22	37
Baltic, - - - - -		40
	561,173	326,281

In the year 1810, the number of bales from the United States, was two hundred forty thousand five hundred and sixteen. As these bales would average three hundred pounds each, they contained seventy-two million one hundred fifty-four thousand and eight hundred pounds of cotton. The bales from Portugal are said not to average more than one hundred pounds, making fourteen million two hundred ninety-four thousand and six hundred. During this year, therefore, from one half to two thirds of all the cotton imported into Great-Britain, was from the United States, notwithstanding seventy-nine thousand three hundred and eighty-two bales were, during that year, imported from the East-Indies. The foregoing was taken from British accounts.

The following is the quantity of cotton exported from the United States to Great-Britain, as appears by the American custom-house books, from 1800 to 1811 :*—

		Number of pounds.
1800	- - - - - -	16,179,513
1801	- - - - - -	18,953,065

* See Tables No. VII. and VIII annexed to this chapter.

	Number of pounds.
1802 - - - - - -	23,473,925
1803 - - - - - -	27,757,307
1804 - - - - - -	25,770,748
1805 - - - - - -	32,571,073
1806 - - - - - -	24,256,457
1807 - - - - - -	53,180,211
1808 - - - - - -	7,992,593
1809 - - - - - -	13,365,987
1810 - - - - - -	36,171,915
1811 - - - - - -	46,872,452

As the direct intercourse between the United States and Great-Britain, was open but a part of the year 1810, only about thirty-six millions of pounds was shipped *directly* to that country. During that year, however, more than five millions was shipped to Sweden; more than fourteen millions to Denmark and Norway; about nine millions to Spain, Portugal, and Madeira; four millions, to the Azores, and ten millions to the Floridas; the greatest part of which undoubtedly went to Great-Britain.

Europe is, and always must be, dependent upon other quarters of the world, for a supply of cotton. The climate is, for the most part, too cold for the production of this valuable plant. Some small quantities have been raised in the southern parts of Spain and Italy. The French government, under Bonaparte, attempted to introduce the culture of it in France. In 1807, a distinguished agriculturalist, Monsieur Lasteyric, was employed by the French government to give instructions, relative to the culture of the cotton plant. He accordingly published a treatise on the subject, entitled " Du Cotonnier, et de sa culture," in which he gives an account of the various kinds of cotton, in different parts of the world, and the modes of cultivating it. The Minister of the Interior also, at the same time, sent a circular letter to the Prefects of all the Departments, requesting their particular attention, to the cultivation of cotton, and informing them that he had sent for cotton seed, to Spain, Italy, and North-America, to be distributed to the different departments, and offering a premium of one franc* for every killogramme (two pounds English) of cotton raised and cleaned ready for spinning. It is understood that the experiment, if ever made, did not succeed. France has received a great part of her cotton fabrics, particularly those of the finer kind, from Great-Britain. Monsieur Lasteyric himself states that the value of cotton goods imported into France from England in 1806, amounted to 65,000,000 francs, or about $13,000,000.

He also states the quantity of cotton imported into France, from the year 5 of the republic, (1796) to 1806, to be as follows, viz.—

Year	5	-	-	-	-	9,000,000	killogrammes.
	6	-	-	-	-	5,145,000	- do.
	7	-	-	-	-	3,363,000	- do.
	8	-	-	-	-	5,504,000	- do.
	9	-	-	-	-	7,560,000	- do.
	10	-	-	-	-	7,890,000	- do.
	11	-	-	-	-	8,600,000	- do.
	12	-	-	-	-	9,205,000	- do.
	13	-	-	-	-	10,857,000	- do.

Three months and ten days of the year 14, and the whole of 1806, making 15 months and 10 days ⎱ 11,850,000 ⎰ Four millions of which came from Portugal.

Total of ten years	-	78,974,000	killogrammes.
Annual average	- -	7,897,400	- do.

The annual average of cotton, therefore, imported into France from 1796 to 1806, was only fifteen million seven hundred ninety-four thousand and eight hundred pounds. The whole quantity imported into France during this period, did not exceed the quantity exported from the United States in the years 1810 and 1811.

* A franc is about twenty cents, making a premium of about ten cents for a pound of cotton.

The following is the quantity exported from the United States to France, from 1800 to 1811.

							Pounds.
1800	-	-	-	-	-	-	
1801	-	-	-	-	-	-	844,728
1802	-	-	-	-	-	-	1,907,849
1803	-	-	-	-	-	-	3,821,840
1804	-	-	-	-	-	-	5,946,848
1805	-	-	-	-	-	-	4,504,329
1806	-	-	-	-	-	-	7,082,118
1807	-	-	-	-	-	-	6,114,358
1808	-	-	-	-	-	-	2,087,450
1809	-	-	-	-	-	-	none direct.
1810	-	-	-	-	-	-	do.
1811	-	-	-	-	-	-	do.

The manufacture of cotton has increased, and is still increasing very rapidly, in the United States. The quantity consumed in this country, on the average of the years 1811, 1812, and 1813, cannot be less than twenty millions of pounds.

FLAX-SEED, INDIGO, &c. &c.

The other articles of export, the produce of agriculture, are flax-seed, indigo, wax, flax, poultry, &c. The principal of these are flax-seed and indigo. In the year 1770, three hundred twelve thousand six hundred and twelve bushels of flax-seed were exported from the North-American Colonies, of which six thousand seven hundred and eighty went to England, three hundred five thousand and eighty-three to Ireland, and seven hundred forty-nine to the South of Europe. The custom-house value of it was then £31,168 18 1 sterling, or about $139,000.

The following is an account of the quantity exported from the United States from 1791 to 1814, with its value since 1803, viz.—

			Bushels.			Value. Dolls.
1791	-	-	292,460			
1792	-	-	261,905			
1793	-	-	258,540			
1794	-	-	270,340			
1795	-	-	411,264			
1796	•	-	256,200			
1797	-	-	222,269			
1798	-	-	224,473			
1799	-	-	350,857			
1800	-	-	289,684			
1801	-	-	461,266			
1802	-	-	155,358			
1803	-	-	311,459	-	-	465,000
1804	-	-	281,757	-	-	420,000
1805	-	-	179,788	-	-	360,000
1806	-	-	352,280	-	-	529,000
1807	-	-	301,242	-	-	452,000
1808	-	-	102,930	-	-	131,000
1809	-	-	184,311	-	-	230,000
1810	-	-	240,579	-	-	301,000
1811	-	-	304,114	-	-	380,000
1812	-	-	325,022	-	-	455,000
1813	-	-	189,538	-	-	265,000
1814	-	-	14,800	-	-	31,000

Flax-seed has been generally shipped to Ireland.

INDIGO.

Indigo was one of the principal articles of produce and export from South-Carolina and Georgia, before the planting of cotton in those states became an object of so much importance.

The culture of it was introduced into South-Carolina about the year 1741 or 1742, and that state is indebted to a lady for the introduction of this valuable plant. An account of the manner of its introduction is given by Doct. Ramsay in his history of South-Carolina, and serves to shew, among other instances, how much a nation oftentimes is indebted for its wealth to the exertions and perseverance of a single individual.

" The second great staple of Carolina (says the Doctor) was Indigo. Its original native country was Hindostan ; but it had been naturalized in the West-India Islands, from which it was introduced into Carolina by Miss Eliza Lucas the mother of Major General Charles Cotesworth Pinckney.

" Her father, George Lucas, Governour of Antigua, observing her fondness for the vegetable world, frequently sent to her tropical seeds and fruits, to be planted for her amusement on his plantation at Wappoo.   Among others he sent her some indigo seed as a subject of experiment.

" She planted it in March 1741 or 1742. It was destroyed by frost. She repeated the experiment in April ; this was cut down by a worm. Notwithstanding these discouragements she persevered, and her third attempt was successful. Governour Lucas, on hearing that the plant had seeded and ripened, sent from Montserrat a man, by the name of Cromwell, who had been accustomed to the making of indigo, and engaged him at high wages to come to Carolina, and let his daughter see the whole process for extracting the dye from the weed. This professed indigo maker built vats on Wappoo creek, and there made the first indigo that was formed in Carolina. It was but indifferent.

" Cromwell repented of his engagement, as being likely to injure his own country ; made a mystery of the business, and, with the hope of deceiving, injured the process by throwing in too much lime. Miss Lucas watched him carefully, and also engaged Mr. Deveaux to superintend his operations. Notwithstanding the duplicity of Cromwell, a knowledge of the process was obtained. Soon after Miss Lucas had completely succeeded in this useful project, she married Charles Pinckney ; and her father made a present of all the indigo on his plantation, the fruit of her industry, to her husband. The whole was saved for seed. Part was planted by the proprietor next year at Ashapoo, and the remainder given away to his friends in small quantities for the same purpose. They all succeeded. From that time the culture of indigo was common, and in a year or two it became an article of export."

In the year 1748, (21 of George II.) a bounty of six pence on the pound, on Plantation indigo, when it was worth three fourths of the price of the best French indigo, was granted by the British Parliament. This increased its culture in South-Carolina, and in 1754, two hundred sixteen thousand nine hundred and twenty-four pounds of indigo were exported from that Province. From November 1760 to September 1761, three hundred ninety-nine thousand three hundred and sixty-six pounds were exported; and shortly before the American Revolution, the export amounted to one million one hundred and seven thousand six hundred and sixty pounds.*

In the year 1794, one million five hundred fifty thousand eight hundred and eighty pounds were exported from the United States, being the greatest quantity exported in any one year. Probably a considerable part of this was foreign indigo.

Since the planting of cotton has become general in South-Carolina and Georgia, the culture of indigo has been in a great measure neglected.

MANUFACTURES.

Manufactured articles constitute a part of the domestic exports of the United States. The manufactures exported are :—

1st. from domestic materials.
2d. from foreign materials.

The value of both these kinds of manufactures, exported from 1803 to 1814, was as follows, viz.—

	From domestic materials. Dolls.	From foreign materials. Dolls.	Total of both. Dolls.
1803	- 790,000	- 565,000	- 1,355,000
1804	- 1,650,000	- 450,000	- 2,100,000

* See Ramsay's History and Macpherson's Annals of Commerce.

		From domestic materials. Dolls.		From foreign materials. Dolls.		Total of both. Dolls.
1805	-	1,579,000	-	721,000	-	2,300,000
1806	-	1,889,000	-	818,000	-	2,707,000
1807	-	1,652,000	-	468,000	-	2,120,000
1808	-	309,000	-	35,000	-	344,000
1809	-	1,266,000	-	240,000	-	1,506,000
1810	-	1,359,000	-	558,000	-	1,917,000
1811	-	2,062,000	-	314,000	-	2,376,000
1812	-	1,135,000	-	220,000	-	1,355,000
1813	-	372,000	-	18,000	-	390,000
1814	-	233,200	-	13,100	-	246,300

The manufactures from domestic materials are soap, tallow candles, leather, boots, shoes, saddlery, hats, of grain (as spirits, beer, starch, &c.) of wood, (including furniture, coaches, &c.) cordage, canvass, linseed oil, iron, and various other articles, such as snuff, silk shoes, wax candles, tobacco, lead, bricks, turpentine, spirits, wool and cotton cards, &c.

The manufactures from foreign materials, are spirits from molasses, refined sugar, chocolate, gun powder, brass and copper, and medicines.

The value of each of these for the years 1806 and 1811 was as follows, viz.—

DOMESTIC MATERIALS.	1806. Value—dls.		1811. Value—dls
Soap, and tallow candles, - -	652,000	-	371,000
Leather, boots, shoes, and saddlery, -	276,000	-	176,000
Hats, - - - -	105,000	-	55,000
Wood (including furniture, coaches, &c.)	418,000	-	361,000
Cordage, canvass, linseed oil, -	118,000	-	274,000
Grain, (spirits, beer, starch, &c.) -	94,000	-	506,000
Iron, - - - -	132,000	-	101,000
Other articles, (snuff, silk shoes, &c.) -	94,000	-	218,000
	1.889,000		2,062,000

FOREIGN MATERIALS.				1806.		1811.
				Value—dls.		Value—dls.
Spirits from molasses,	-	-		630,000	-	241,000
Sugar refined,	-	-	-	66,000	-	13,000
Chocolate,	-	-	-	2,000	-	4,000
Gun-powder,	-	-	-	42,000	-	29,000
Brass and copper,	-	-	-	25,000	-	9,000
Medicines,	-	-	-	53,000	-	18,000
				$818,000		$314,000

Many small articles exported are not ascertained, although their value is returned to the treasury department.

Some of these are manufactured, and others are in a raw state. We have now completed our view of the domestic exports of the United States ; we add the following table, exhibiting the value of the produce of the sea, of the forest, of agriculture and of manufactures exported, for each year, from 1803 to 1814, by which the proportion of each can be, at once, seen, during that period.

	Of the sea.	Of the forest.	Of agriculture.	Of manufactures.
	Dolls.	Dolls.	Dolls.	Dolls.
1803	2,635,000	4,850,000	32,995,000	1,355,000
1804	3,420,000	4,630,000	30,890,000	2,100,000
1805	2,884,000	5,261,000	31,562,000	2,300,000
1806	3,116,000	4,861,000	30,125,000	2,707,000
1807	2,804,000	5,476,000	37,832,000	2,120,000
1808	832,000	1,399,000	6,746,000	344,000
1809	1,710,000	4,583,000	23,234,000	1,506,000
1810	1,481,000	4,978,000	33,502,000	1,917,000
1811	1,413,000	5,286,000	35,556,000	2,376,000
1812	935,000	2,701,000	24,555,000	1,355,000
1813	304,000	1,107,000	23,119,000	390,000
1814	188,000	570,000	5,613,000	246,300

From this, it appears, that on an average of eight years, from 1803 to 1811, the produce of agriculture, constituted about three quarters, in value, of all the domestic exports of the United States, the produce of the forest about one ninth, of the sea, about one fifteenth, and manufactures, about one twentieth. For the year 1812, the whole value of the domestic exports, was $30,032,109, of this, the value of the produce of agriculture, was $24,555,000, leaving but five and a half millions for the rest; and in the year ending October 1st, 1813, about sixteen months from the commencement of the late war with Great-Britain, the whole value of the domestic exports was $25,008,152; of this, the value of the produce of agriculture, was $23,119,000, consisting, principally, of flour and provisions, sent to the Peninsula; in the year 1814, in consequence of the blockade of our coast, the whole exports of the United States amounted only to $6,927,441, of which $6,782,272 was of domestic produce, which found its way, through certain ports, which, for a time, were not subject to the blockade.

TABLE No. I.

WHEAT—bushels.

Whither exported.	1800.	1801.	1802.	1803.	1804.	1805.	1806.	1807.	1808.	1809.	1810.	1811.
Sweden,	-	-	-	-	1,166	-	-	-	-	-	-	-
Swedish West-Indies,	-	-	-	-	-	-	-	-	-	45,634	-	-
Holland,	-	-	-	-	-	-	-	9,992	-	-	-	-
Great-Britain,	21,001	216,977	201,250	234,386	-	-	76,707	669,950	67,024	152,144	179,751	136,204
British American Colonies,	4,550	17,679	19,554	10,931	6,692	120	1,577	7,009	-	1,450	4,381	4,397
Hamburg, Bremen, &c.	-	-	1,574	9,830	-	-	-	-	-	-	-	-
France,	702	3,000	3,127	107,750	56,946	-	-	-	-	-	-	-
Spain,	-	-	-	-	-	-	-	3,108	-	-	13,125	21,199
Spanish West-Indies,	-	832	-	-	-	-	8,348	-	-	-	-	-
Portugal,	1,440	-	31,667	214,148	33,068	11,234	-	68,102	18,048	43,214	45,588	55,033
Madeira,	600	-	7,805	13,948	7,591	4,714	-	8,647	2,200	15,605	23,169	-
West-Indies, (generally)	-	-	-	-	-	-	-	-	-	7,150	-	-
Average price,							$1 33	1 25	1 25	1 25	1 50	1 75

TABLE No. II.

FLOUR—barrels.

Whither exported.	1800.	1801.	1802.	1803.	1804.	1805.	1806.	1807.	1808.	1809.	1810.	1811.
Sweden,	-	-	-	-	-	-	-	-	-	59,008	-	-
Swedish West-Indies,	9,228	4,769	11,227	12,482	14,887	6,580	7,912	15,159	2,494	105,767	73,673	23,922
Denmark and Norway,	-	-	-	-	-	-	-	4,857	-	2,765	5,068	-
Danish West-Indies,	52,554	23,872	32,267	40,161	31,425	50,558	34,923	67,909	6,157	-	-	-
Holland,	-	-	-	-	-	-	1,877	-	-	-	-	-
Dutch West-Indies,	23,070	10,019	26,334	42,711	34,773	5,612	15,061	9,137	1,317	1,186	-	-
Great-Britain,	172,815	479,730	208,744	203,127	7,140	36,752	127,619	323,968	2,922	159,741	92,136	38,183
British West-Indies,	165,739	252,851	245,708	260,555	220,586	181,816	148,439	251,706	59,648	53,793	80,944	205,538
British American Colonies,	26,472	25,452	30,434	38,324	30,789	17,608	32,000	44,244	10,514	17,288	18,397	31,813
Hamburg, Bremen, &c.	-	-	-	4,805	-	-	21,340	15,398	-	-	-	-
France,	-	-	14,628	18,645	1,074	-	-	-	-	-	-	2,966
French West-Indies,	59,633	103,870	151,788	167,886	66,244	107,948	82,252	112,137	36,929	-	2,232	8,909
Spain,	2,550	11,079	59,409	144,935	109,906	103,646	19,196	39,842	30,449	40,047	144,436	306,074
Spanish West-Indies,	97,919	94,579	70,238	36,314	93,071	131,028	113,178	166,170	44,778	143,857	138,892	124,735
Portugal,	5,333	43,612	85,784	122,410	54,648	22,633	91,273	76,352	41,761	65,149	88,696	529,105
Madeira,	13,178	19,491	28,205	24,599	41,253	23,127	26,230	40,902	8,124	87,082	49,801	45,487
West-Indies, (generally)	3,468	7,061	20,754	32,379	50,964	44,588	8,436	18,540	3,139	2,531	8,230	41,360
Europe, do.	-	-	10,055	3,890	3,041	4,395	-	-	-	-	3,211	-
Average price,							$ 8.	7.	6.50.	6.	7.50	9.50

126

TABLE No. III.

RICE—tierces.

Whither exported.	1800.	1801.	1802.	1803.	1804.	1805.	1806.	1807.	1808.	1809.	1810.	1811.
Russia,	-	-	-	-	-	-	-	499	-	776	5,270	1,205
Prussia,	-	-	-	5,550	8,576	2,213	-	822	-	-	-	1,283
Sweden,	-	-	-	-	-	-	-	-	-	20,648	3,879	1,446
Swedish West-Indies,	646	102	137	-	403	-	-	-	-	3,888	5,582	-
Denmark and Norway,	2,226	909	4,141	4,528	10,987	3,774	1,954	12,103	-	1,988	8,305	-
Danish West-Indies,	1,822	617	598	580	1,857	852	615	1,294	-	-	-	-
Holland,	682	1,936	4,159	6,942	6,753	3,605	17,137	21,163	841	2,413	-	-
Dutch West-Indies,	447	309	740	457	1,572	312	-	-	-	-	-	-
Great-Britain,	58,117	50,547	29,385	26,675	14,409	19,931	32,222	26,723	2,032	28,634	23,726	25,634
British West-Indies,	19,430	14,475	8,008	6,525	10,566	4,275	6,248	10,069	2,266	2,796	6,585	14,411
British American Colonies,	-	-	-	-	-	531	828	625	-	708	807	734
Hamburg, Bremen, &c.	6,551	6,932	10,054	17,633	3,666	3,183	24,849	5,130	-	1,333	509	-
France,	-	2,724	7,186	3,116	6,014	1,601	3,392	3,006	1,082	-	-	-
French West-Indies,	1,046	2,108	2,767	3,929	1,365	2,062	2,237	2,624	971	-	-	-
Spain,	4,276	856	2,582	1,828	3,475	4,684	2,860	2,317	1,008	6,493	20,787	10,991
Spanish West-Indies,	9,086	7,329	3,616	659	2,014	5,833	4,650	3,508	-	9,076	7,586	14,312
Portugal,	2,341	532	694	204	627	-	536	452	-	12,173	19,796	34,080
Madeira,	2,427	2,249	977	1,164	1,604	731	1,662	1,521	-	6,989	5,426	4,620
West-Indies, (generally) do.	-	-	445	247	1,374	915	343	411	-	-	810	2,515
Europe,	1,002	1,524	2,729	837	261	-	-	-	-	1,011	568	956
Average price,							$251.	25.	24.	18.	20.	20.

TABLE No. IV.

BEEF—barrels.

Whither exported.	1800.	1801.	1802.	1803.	1804.	1805.	1806.	1807.	1808.	1809.	1810.	1811.
Russia,										12	437	197
Prussia,												10
Sweden,										26	33	78
Swedish West-Indies,	4,132	2,138	606	979	4,267	1,651	1,650	1,839	242	7,642	4,247	3,370
Denmark and Norway,				10	176		26	19		16	123	440
Danish West-Indies,	5,789	4,657	1,768	2,885	5,609	5,057	6,513	5,866	767		339	243
Holland,	36	48	195	24	60	46	12	64		5		
Dutch West-Indies,	5,440	4,916	4,608	11,872	14,375	4,658	4,952	2,705	963	34	310	
Great-Britain,	143	3,027	13	939	3,347	307	75	24		18		320
British West-Indies,	30,944	37,526	21,695	21,098	45,656	30,378	31,176	20,561	5,129	1,858	3,264	6,261
British American Colonies,	1,243	1,265	532	1,044	1,088	1,225	1,194	1,470	55	60	951	2,436
Hamburg, Bremen, &c.	72	23				14				23		
France,		4	207	3,136	357	715	257	295				184
French West-Indies,	7,876	7,024	11,646	15,905	10,102	16,112	20,337	23,144	6,307	150	194	1,172
Spain,	1,231	171	922	2,183	3,234	1,622	874	401	516	3,150	8,495	10,432
Spanish West-Indies,	10,472	9,047	5,949	950	3,896	16,797	24,108	7,043	1,385	6,037	10,793	7,939
Portugal,	340	265	1,120	958	872	1,059	903	492	236	1,110	5,098	14,381
Madeira,	1,006	396	379	578	2,355	1,999	1,850	1,864	393	2,510	2,772	4,533
West-Indies, (generally)	369	2,074	6,934	12,636	28,902	20,941	15,891	11,785	2,524	286	806	5,645
Europe, do.			302	104	84	391		24		137	100	194
Africa, do.	950	471	281	51	592	1,687	1,187	1,283	26	148	316	425
Average price,							$10.	10.	10.	10.	11.	11.

TABLE No. V.

PORK—barrels.

Whither exported.	1800.	1801.	1802.	1803.	1804.	1805.	1806.	1807.	1808.	1809.	1810.	1811.
Russia,	-	-	-	-	46	5	-	-	-	8	30	61
Sweden,	-	-	-	-	-	-	-	-	-	161	63	-
Swedish West-Indies,	1,725	577	483	1,011	2,438	746	885	2,767	669	12,188	4,940	2,770
Denmark and Norway,	-	-	-	5	310	-	16	8	-	5	63	47
Danish West-Indies,	5,493	2,604	1,955	4,145	6,290	3,822	4,378	5,746	949	2	32	80
Holland,	24	21	81	15	29	126	8	50	-	-	-	-
Dutch West-Indies,	3,193	1,205	2,896	6,719	6,700	1,109	998	578	263	46	23	-
Great-Britain,	619	14,162	2,549	7,683	6,081	56	21	8	-	14	25	19
British West-Indies,	19,282	27,883	29,393	30,989	47,926	17,046	10,221	8,624	2,517	3,633	2,048	5,363
British American Colonies,	2,155	4,473	5,329	10,098	3,939	1,235	1,927	1,377	1,989	404	3,231	4,813
Hamburg, Bremen, &c.	9	21	21	-	-	6	-	-	-	19	-	-
France,	-	4	69	793	214	241	8	113	1	-	-	552
French West-Indies,	12,700	12,905	16,700	17,830	11,525	11,578	7,807	5,730	2,521	100	4871	1,480
Spain,	696	440	573	1,915	2,723	553	168	1,159	1,442	4,097	4,512	4,027
Spanish West-Indies,	4,081	2,972	4,978	1,016	6,982	6,609	4,236	3,693	1,932	9,220	10,123	6,058
Portugal,	365	117	619	1,468	465	229	338	288	361	3,152	2,735	1,899
Madeira,	476	323	469	296	1,749	590	505	825	422	3,093	1,862	2,480
West-Indies, (generally)	123	648	2,622	6,278	14,918	6,632	1,240	1,552	715	421	698	-
Europe, do.	-	-	596	120	144	98	-	12	-	67	121	333
Africa, do.	378	237	124	27	380	738	661	486	15	228	83	-
Average price,						$18.	$18.	18.	17.	16.	16.	16.

TABLE No. VI.

TOBACCO—hogsheads.

Whither exported.	1800.	1801.	1802.	1803.	1804.	1805.	1806.	1807.	1808.	1809.	1810.	1811.
Russia,	-	-	-	-	-	-	-	-	-	131	1,462	1,241
Prussia,	129	575	1,147	-	1,728	1,156	-	-	-	-	464	-
Sweden,	674	424	-	-	346	293	-	-	-	10,103	6,897	1,716
Swedish West-Indies,	223	-	-	-	-	138	-	165	-	1,664	965	500
Denmark and Norway,	850	535	624	380	1,559	2,233	794	1,687	191	5,950	18,797	1,027
Danish West-Indies,	767	272	636	406	548	435	765	419	-	-	-	-
Holland,	6,087	15,300	9,670	12,721	17,948	16,745	29,851	20,444	3,683	2,316	654	-
Dutch West-Indies,	308	523	453	617	863	131	245	313	-	-	-	-
Great-Britain,	37,798	55,256	29,938	47,829	24,700	18,169	26,273	23,047	2,526	8,965	24,067	20,342
British West-Indies,	1,774	1,457	1,398	1,335	1,378	950	1,233	1,150	315	656	562	1,103
British American Colonies,	558	-	-	-	-	-	-	173	-	175	-	271
Hamburg, Bremen, &c.	16,756	18,625	10,696	7,348	8,787	9,421	7,526	4,911	-	6,700	10,905	-
France,	143	5,006	16,216	9,815	14,623	12,135	9,182	2,876	566	-	-	569
French West-Indies,	476	969	1,340	972	507	984	933	504	390	-	-	195
Spain,	7,555	2,486	871	449	2,858	2,942	1,263	964	1,144	3,836	6,183	3,556
Spanish West-Indies,	719	130	-	187	2,086	468	237	427	-	1,549	1,243	721
Portugal,	110	-	101	-	-	142	100	-	-	2,908	4,464	127
Madeira,	-	-	-	-	-	-	-	-	-	2,012	1,579	-
West-Indies, (generally)	-	-	136	202	541	709	227	205	-	-	116	232
Europe, - do.	-	-	330	-	-	-	-	-	-	152	148	184
Africa, - do.	789	389	162	-	483	1,422	2,053	894	-	834	151	173
Average price,							$79.	88.	87.	70.	60.	60.

TABLE No. VII.

COTTON, SEA-ISLAND—pounds.

Whither exported.	1800	1801	1802	1803	1804	1805	1806	1807	1808	1809	1810	1811.
Russia, -	-	-	-	-	-	-	-	-	-	67,188	-	113,435
Sweden, -	-	-	-	-	-	-	-	-	-	3,023,226	202,771	19,368
Swedish West-Indies,	-	-	-	-	-	-	-	-	-	173,257	-	-
Denmark and Norway	-	-	-	-	-	-	-	-	-	30,000	109,202	-
Holland, -	-	-	-	-	-	64,628	-	-	-	-	47,871	-
Great-Britain, -	-	-	-	-	-	8,563,274	6,002,617	8,728,162	941,001	2,266,505	4,758,783	7,788,865
France, -	-	-	-	-	-	156,442	75,451	188,572	-	-	-	-
Spain, -	-	-	-	-	-	-	-	-	-	-	50,710	-
Spanish West-Indies,	-	-	-	-	-	-	-	-	-	397,159	-	-
Portugal, -	-	-	-	-	-	-	-	-	-	110,444	734,739	-
Madeira, -	-	-	-	-	-	-	-	-	-	1,002,788	-	-
Europe, (generally)	-	-	-	-	-	-	-	-	-	168,000	138,020	-
Floridas, -	-	-	-	-	-	-	-	-	-	852,461	2,510,475	-
Fayal and the other } Azores,	-	-	-	-	-	-	-	-	-	372,769	120,512	-
Average price,						30 cts.	30 cts.	30 cts.	39 cts.	25 cts.	28 cts.	26 cts.

TABLE No. VIII.

COTTON—pounds.

Whither exported.	1800.	1801.	1802.	1803.	1804.
Russia,	-	-	-	-	-
Prussia,	-	-	-	-	203,866
Sweden,	-	-	-	-	57,065
Swedish West-Indies,	-	-	-	-	-
Denmark and Norway,	-	-	-	184,193	288,540
Holland,	79,694	338,563	877,491	1,339,122	1,475,979
Great-Britain,	16,179,513	18,953,065	23,473,925	27,757,307	25,770,748
Hamburg, Bremen, &c.	997,581	475,922	438,521	760,871	314,126
France,	-	844,728	1,907,869	3,821,840	5,946,848
Spain,	493,280	89,375	97,172	31,915	250,486
Spanish West-Indies,	-	-	-	-	237,100
Portugal,	-	-	-	-	-
Madeira,	-	-	-	-	-
Floridas,	-	-	-	-	-
Europe, (generally)	-	-	-	-	104,037
Fayal and the other Azores,	-	-	-	-	-

NOTE.—There was not any distinction made between the *Sea-Island* and *other* Cotton, until the year 1805—both are included in the above statement, from 1800 to 1804, inclusive.

TABLE No. VIII.—CONTINUED.

COTTON—OTHER THAN SEA-ISLAND—pounds.

Whither exported.	1805.	1806.	1807.	1808.	1809.	1810.	1811.
Russia,	-	-	-	-	557,924	3,769,137	9,255,404
Prussia,	-	-	-	-	-	936,579	231,679
Sweden,	-	-	-	-	9,939,934	5,234,293	252,310
Swedish West-Indies,	-	-	-	-	-	168,500	-
Denmark and Norway,	-	-	272,134	-	2,268,827	14,484,922	722,448
Holland,	881,584	3,129,146	3,146,209	491,814	1,068,096	100,869	-
Great-Britain,	24,007,799	18,253,840	44,452,049	7,051,592	11,099,482	31,413,132	39,083,587
Hamburg, Bremen, &c.	122,003	955,400	993,342	14,860	1,067,013	976,762	1,836,288
France,	4,427,887	7,006,667	5,925,786	2,087,450	-	-	-
Spain,	-	-	-	-	796,496	4,292,055	228,880
Spanish West-Indies,	-	-	-	-	534,766	55,740	-
Portugal,	-	-	-	-	1,733,081	2,870,142	-
Madeira,	-	-	-	-	3,722,280	2,936,738	-
Floridas,	-	-	-	-	1,059,293	10,339,019	177,200
Europe, (generally)	-	-	-	-	771,860	1,922,232	860,993
Fayal and the other Azores,	-	-	-	-	6,139,263	4,294,091	-
Average price,		22 cts.	21 cts.	20 cts.	15 cts.	15 cts.	14 cts.

CHAPTER V.

EXPORTS OF FOREIGN PRODUCE.

Neutral trade of the United States increased by the wars in Europe—Their trade in foreign produce greater, than in domestic, in 1805, 1806, and 1807 —Quantity of sugar, coffee, cocoa, pepper, and goods paying ad valorem duties exported, in each year, from 1791 to 1814—Quantity of sugar and coffee, and goods subject to ad valorem duties imported from different countries in 1807—Quantity of sugar and coffee exported to different countries, in different years—Average quantity of wines, spirits, teas, cocoa, and pepper, exported in the years 1805, 1806, and 1807.

The war between England and France, which began in 1793, soon after the establishment of the present national government, and between England and Spain in 1796, and which continued, with but a short interval, until it involved all the nations of Europe, threw into the hands of the American merchant, no small proportion of the trade of the world.

The vast superiority of the naval force of England, rendered the intercourse between the European powers at war with that nation, and their Colonies, extremely difficult.

They were, therefore, obliged to depend, in a great measure, upon neutrals to carry on the trade between them, and their distant possessions. The valuable productions of the French, Spanish, and Dutch East and West-Indies, had no other mode of finding their way to Europe, without great risque and expense, but by the aid of a neutral flag. The local situation of the United States, in relation to the West-India Islands, and their long accustomed habits of intercourse with them, naturally threw a great proportion of this trade into the hands of the

Americans; and the great increase of the tonnage of the United States, and the spirit and enterprise of the citizens, led them, also, to engage in the more distant trade of the East-Indies, and every other part of the world. The valuable articles of colonial produce, such as sugar, coffee, spirits, cocoa, pimento, indigo, pepper and spices of all kinds, were carried, either directly to Europe, or were first brought to the United States, and from thence exported in American vessels. These and other articles imported were allowed, under certain regulations, to be exported from the United States, with a drawback of the duties, paid or secured to be paid upon them, on their importation. The manufactures of Europe, and particularly of Great-Britain, as well as the manufactures and produce of the East-Indies and China, have also been imported, and again exported, in large quantities, to the West-Indies, to the Spanish Colonies in South-America, and elsewhere. This trade, which has been called the carrying trade, has, in some years, exceeded in value the trade of the United States, in articles of domestic produce; it has been the means, not only of increasing our commercial tonnage, but of enriching the public treasury, as well as filling the coffers of individuals. The value of the exports of domestic and foreign articles from 1803 to 1814, is stated in Chapter III.

From this it appears, that in the years 1805, 1806, and 1807, being years of trade unshakled by commercial restrictions, the value of exports of domestic produce and manufacture, was $134,590,552, being on an average $44,863,517 a year, and of exports of foreign produce and manufacture, $173,105,813, on an average $57,701,937 a year, making a difference of $38,515,261 or $12,838,420 per year. During the late war between the United States and Great-Britain, this trade has been annihilated. We were unable to procure supplies of foreign articles, for our own consumption, much less for exportation.

The progress of this trade from 1791 to 1814, may be seen from the following account of the quantities of the principal articles of foreign produce or manufacture, exported from the United States in each year, viz. sugar, coffee, pepper, cocoa, and goods principally paying duties ad valorem :—

	Sugar. lbs.	Coffee. lbs.	Pepper. lbs.	Cocoa. lbs.	Goods paying ad val. duties. dolls.
1791	74,504	962,977	492	8,322	2,840,310
1792	1,176,156	2,134,742	5,046	6,000	3,560,119
1793	4,539,809	17,580,049	14,361	234,875	4,110,240
1794	20,721,761	33,720,983	23,884	1,188,302	4,976,120
1795	21,377,747	47,443,179	301,692	525,432.	5,670,260
1796	34,848,644	62,385,117	491,330	928,107	6,794,346
1797	38,366,262	44,521,887	1,901,130	875,334	7,835,456
1798	51,703,963	49,580,927	501,982	3,146,445	8,967,828
1799	78,821,751	31,987,088	441,312	5,970,590	18,718,477
1800	56,432,516	38,597,479	635,849	4,925,518	16,076,848
1801	97,565,732	45,106,494	3,153,139	7,012,155	17,159,016
1802	61,061,820	36,501,998	5,422,144	3,878,526	14,906,081
1803	23,223,849	10,294,693	2,991,430	367,177	5,351,524
1804	74,964,366	48,312,713	5,703,646	695,135	9,377,805
1805	123,031,272	46,760,294	7,559,224	2,425,680	15,201,483
1806	145,839,320	47,001,662	4,111,983	6,846,758	19,016,909
1807	143,136,905	42,122,573	4,207,166	8,540,524	18,971,539
1808	28,974,927	7,325,448	1,709,978	1,896,990	4,765,737
1809	45,248,128	24,364,099	4,722,098	2,029,336	5,889,669
1810	47,038,125	31,423,477	5,946,336	1,286,010	8,438,349
1811	18,381,673	10,261,442	3,057,456	2,221,462	8,815,291
1812	13,927,277	10,073,722	2,521,003	752,148	3,591,755
1813	7,347,038	6,568,527	99,660	108,188	368,603
1814	762	220,594	none.	27,386	41,409

It will be perceived that during the peace concluded at Amiens in the fall of 1801, and which continued about eighteen months, the exports of foreign produce were much less than in the years succeeding. —Most of the foreign articles, which were not then in the United States, went directly to the places of their destination, without first coming to this country.

On the renewal of the war, however, in 1803, and until the commencement of our commercial prohibitions, our trade in articles of foreign produce and manufacture again increased, and exceeded that of any former years. In each of the years 1806 and 1807, more than one hundred and forty-three millions of pounds of sugar, were exported from the United States, making at one thousand pounds a hogshead, one hundred and forty-three thousand hogsheads. Nearly the whole of this was imported, and again exported in American vessels, and must have employed about seventy thousand tons of shipping. The freight of these cargoes, in the two different voyages, could not be less than between three and four millions of dollars.

The whole quantity of sugar imported into the United States in the same years, were as follows, viz.—

		Pounds.
In 1806	- - - - -	200,737,940
1807	- - - - -	215,836,202

In 1807, the following quantities of sugar were imported from the different quarters of the world, and from places in each belonging to particular nations, in American and foreign bottoms :—

From	Sugar imported in American vessels.		Sugar imported in foreign vessels.	
	Brown.	Clayed.	Brown.	Clayed.
Europe, - - -	1,414	- -	- -	-
Africa, - -	2,239,396	- -	126,962	-
Asia, - -	10,598,278	40,892	1,249,072	-
West India Islands and American Colonies,	148,095,225	43,453,979	12,639,362	1,902,699
From particular places.				
Bourbon & Mauritius	2,040,697	- -	- -	-
Danish East-Indies,	1,161,786	- -	- -	-
Dutch East-Indies,	2,467,226	- -	1,021,860	-
British East-Indies,	6,303,510	- -	227,212	-
Manilla and other Phillippine Islands, -	664,133	- -	- -	-
Swedish West-Indies,	2,437,559	- -	308,440	-

From particular places.	Sugar imported in American vessels.		Sugar imported in foreign vessels.	
	Brown.	Clayed.	Brown.	Clayed.
Danish West-Indies,	17,828,282	- -	2,122,744	79,257
Dutch West-Indies, & American Colonies, -	5,307,864	- -	968,860	-
British West-Indies,	7,660,992	- -	3,556,715	34,338
French W. Indies, & American Colonies, -	72,669,603	1,893,786	2,147,679	-
Spanish W. Indies, & American Colonies. -	41,933,784	40,729,222	3,319,946	1,779,877

Tables Nos. I. and II. shew the countries and places to which sugar was exported from 1800 to 1811.

From these it will be seen, that previous to 1808, it was principally shipped to France, Holland, Hamburg, and Bremen, Spain and Italy, and that subsequent to that period, it was generally shipped to Denmark and Norway, Sweden and Russia.

In 1807, it was shipped to the following countries, viz.

	Brown. lbs.			Clayed. lbs.
To Russia, - -	52,852	-	-	297,844
Sweden, - -	179,587	-	-	33,949
Denmark and Norway,	2,286,608	-	-	1,267,227
Holland, - -	48,012,198	-	-	8,719,529
Great-Britain, -	2,015,765	-	-	640,231
Hamburg, Bremen, &c.	2,192,991	-	-	1,066,943
France, - -	27,831,968	-	-	7,029,202
Spain, - -	6,906,740	-	-	5,524,852
Portugal, - -	178,643	-	-	188,356
Italy, - -	14,074,935	-	-	9,476,602
Europe generally, -	184,798	..	..	159,479

COFFEE.

The quantity of coffee exported, on an average of the years 1804, 1805, 1806, and 1807, exceeded forty-five millions of pounds.

The whole quantity imported in 1807, was fifty-eight million eight hundred twenty-four thousand eight hundred and twenty-one pounds, and principally from the following places, viz.—

	Pounds.
Bourbon and Mauritius, - - -	4,470,846
Dutch East-Indies, - - - -	8,842,832
Mocha, Aden, and other ports on the Red-Sea,	1,709,533
Danish West-Indies, - - - -	10,966,411
Dutch West-Indies and American Colonies,	1,404,659
British West-Indies, - - - -	2,423,611
Swedish West-Indies, - - -	1,705,670
French West-Indies and American Colonies,	16,461,478
Spanish West-Indies and American Colonies,	9,753,976

Table No. III. shews the places to which coffee was shipped from 1800 to 1811. Previous to 1808, it was shipped principally to Holland, France, Great-Britain, Hamburg and Bremen, and Italy. Subsequent to this period, it was cleared out for the northern ports in Europe.

In 1806, 1807, and 1810, the greatest part was shipped to the following places, viz.—

	1806. Pounds.	1807. Pounds.	1810. Pounds.
Russia, - - - - -		149,271	4,048,909
Prussia, - -	222,351	- - -	1,098,211
Sweden, - - - - -			7,120,496
Denmark and Norway,	606,621	756,511	14,120,990
Holland, - -	21,833,438	19,900,965	44,618
Great-Britain, -	2,543,370	1,052,075	- -

	1806.	1807.	1810.
	Pounds.	Pounds.	Pounds.
Hamburg, Bremen, &c.	5,306,950	2,644,511	1,206,389
France, - -	8,282,965	11,088,529	- -
Spain, - - -	236,113	456,428	- -
Portugal, - -	687,006	44,801	- -
Italy, - - -	4,948,814	3,490,495	784,423
Europe generally, -	- -	- - -	246,540

While we were thus carrying to Europe these valuable articles of colonial produce, we imported from them, and particularly from England, great quantities of manufactured goods, and other articles, which were again exported, and principally to the West-Indies, and Spanish American Colonies.

In 1806, goods free of duty and subject to duties ad valorem to the value of $18,571,477, and in 1807 to the value of $18,564,507 were exported from the United States. Of these in 1806 $2,383,910 and in 1807 $2,080,114 were free of duty.

The whole amount of goods paying ad valorem duties, imported in the years 1806 and 1807, was as follows, viz.—

In 1806 - - - - -	$54,461,957
1807 - - - -	58,655,917

Between one third and one quarter, therefore, of all the goods paying duties ad valorem, imported during these years, were again exported. These goods were imported from the different quarters of the world in 1807, in the following proportions, viz.—

From Europe, - - - - - -	$50,915,135
Africa, - - - - - - -	108,607
Asia, - - - - - - -	6,392,592
West-India Islands and American Colonies,	1,239,583
	$58,655,917

And principally from the following countries and places in each quarter, viz.—

	Dolls.
From the United Kingdom of G. Britain and Ireland,	38,901,838
Russia, - - - - - -	1,804,860
Sweden, - - - - - -	423,304
Denmark and Norway, - - - -	864,474
Holland, - - - - - -	1,882,583
Hamburg, Bremen, and other parts of Germany,	2,190,732
French European ports on the Atlantic, -	3,371,489
do. do. on the Mediterranean,	347,571
Spanish ports on the Atlantic, - - -	67,138
do. do. on the Mediterranean, - -	112,273
Portugal, - - - - - - -	91,088
Fayal and the other Azores, - - - -	1,188
Italy, - - - - - - -	636,432
Trieste and other Austrian ports on the Adriatic,	203,461
Danish East-Indies, - - - - -	262,685
Dutch do. - - - - -	112,508
British do. - - - - - -	4,073,910
Manilla and other Phillippine Islands, - -	12,316
Turkey, Levant, and Egypt, - - - -	60,741
Mocha, Aden, and other ports on the Red Sea, -	49,447
China, - - - - - - -	1,820,067
British West-Indies, - - - - -	276,565
British American Colonies, - - -	269,198
Spanish West-Indies and American Colonies -	457,523
French do. do. - -	93,005

Of these goods, it appears, that $43,525,320 were imported from the United Kingdom of Great-Britain and Ireland and their dependencies, $3,812,065 from France and its dependencies, and the residue, being $11,318,532 from other parts of the world.

The other articles of foreign produce and manufacture of considerable value exported from the United States, when their trade was free, before the late war between the United States and Great-Britain, were wines, spirits, teas of various kinds, spices of all kinds, paints, lead.

and manufactures of lead, iron, fish, and many others of minor importance.

On an average of the years 1805, 1806, and 1807, the annual quantity of wines, spirits, teas, cocoa, and pepper, exported, was as follows, viz.—

Wines,	-	gallons	-	-	3,423,485
Spirits,	-	do.	-	-	1,600,301
Teas,	-	- pounds	-	-	2,151,385
Cocoa,	-	do.	-	-	5,937,654
Pepper,	-	do.	-	-	5,292,791

That this trade in foreign articles, or the carrying trade, as it has been called, added much to our national wealth cannot be doubted. While it has increased our commercial tonnage, it has enriched the public treasury, as well as individuals. Many of the goods and other articles exported were not entitled to a drawback, in consequence of the owners not having complied with the law on that subject. The duties collected and secured on articles exported, without the benefit of drawback, and which, of course, were not paid by consumers in the United States, during the years 1805, 1806, and 1807, amounted to the following sums, viz.—

In 1805	-	-	-	-	$1,531,618
1806	-	-	-	-	1,297,535
1807	-	-	-	-	1,393,877
Making,		-	-	-	$4,223,030

Add to this the amount of the three and a half per cent. retained on the drawbacks, and which for the same years, was as follows, viz.—

1805	-	-	-	-	$328,144 79
1806	-	-	-	-	334,247 39
1807	-	-	-	-	368,275 50
					$1,030,667 68

and the whole amount received into the public treasury, for these three years, from duties, in consequence of this trade, and which was not paid by the people of the United States, will be $5,253,697 68 being about one ninth of all the duties, collected or secured, during that period.

The amount, which this trade has added to the wealth of individuals, and of course to the nation, it is impossible to ascertain with any degree of precision. Some light, however, may be thrown on this subject, in the subsequent chapter.

TABLE No. I.

BROWN SUGAR—pounds.

Whither exported.	1800.	1801.	1802	1803.	1804.	1805.
Russia,	-	-	61,048	-	-	-
Prussia,	-	-	-	434,840	1,545,203	177,976
Sweden,	157,283	134,311	-	-	-	210,587
Denmark and Norway,	1,062,847	110,515	88,506	-	290,613	-
Holland,	7,542,160	2,103,237	1,734,811	1,459,257	3,401,802	4,543,398
Great-Britain,	9,970,336	14,560,993	15,436,179	8,894,432	27,294,509	47,544,197
Hamburg, Bremen, &c.	13,113,504	28,587,121	5,354,807	1,886,859	752,470	1,183,833
France,	149,300	27,219,888	1,507,108	1,390,842	2,009,031	3,283,796
Spain,	12,588,765	9,645,521	12,540,795	2,913,585	13,136,673	26,079,381
Spanish West-Indies,	268,557	5,593,426	4,479,714	384,479	1,290,837	4,577,113
Portugal,	767,061	896,399	526,190	214,560	407,165	1,023,745
Madeira,	-	-	-	-	-	-
Italy,	8,319,028	6,771,831	8,120,897	1,299,878	2,293,251	3,777,164
Europe, (generally)	-	1,121,969	78,170	716,570	832,267	1,964,189

TABLE No. I.—CONTINUED.

BROWN SUGAR—pounds.

Whither exported.	1806.	1807.	1808.	1809.	1810.	1811.
Russia, - - - - - -		52,852		1,271,180	6,139,529	4,408,289
Prussia, - - - - -	347,212				654,100	-
Sweden, - - - - -	228,324	179,587		4,299,991	8,175,527	126,947
Denmark and Norway, -	3,940,175	2,286,608	486,248	8,517,927	11,069,575	-
Holland, - - - -	56,008,790	48,012,198	8,215,969	3,167,202	88,590	-
Great-Britain, - - -	3,776,064	2,015,765		513,237		-
Hamburg, Bremen, &c. -	8,079,450	2,192,991	403,138	2,010,322	181,867	-
France, - - - -	22,137,266	27,831,968	6,022,546			256,092
Spain, - - - -	2,101,418	6,906,740	2,636,906	2,128,124	818,045	-
Spanish West-Indies, -						-
Portugal, - - - -	771,902	178,643		106,176		-
Madeira, - - - -	187,208					-
Italy, - - - -	5,989,468	14,074,935	2,360,585	2,587,567	859,120	62,494
Europe, (generally) -	463,024	184,798		1,387,400	200,585	175,465

147

TABLE No. II.

WHITE SUGAR, CLAYED OR POWDERED—pounds.

Whither exported.	1800	1801	1802	1803.	1804.	1805.	1806.	1807.	1808.	1809.	1810.	1811.
Russia,	-	-	-	-	-	44,476	-	297,844	-	922,077	5,257,366	10,200,139
Prussia,	-	-	-	-	244,859	228,002	-	-	-	-	78,505	-
Sweden,	-	-	-	-	93,610	87,051	-	33,949	-	-	-	158,888
Denmark and Norway,	-	-	-	137,133	795,690	2,241,154	1,656,261	1,267,227	85,122	1,932,357	3,818,782	178,620
Holland,	-	-	-	1,057,806	7,663,882	8,455,435	10,105,151	8,719,529	1,824,479	2,853,640	6,400,747	-
Great-Britain,	-	-	-	213,313	660,263	1,248,494	2,389,899	640,231	-	836,459	76,674	-
Hamburg, Bremen, &c.	-	-	-	38,231	698,115	1,417,418	4,543,582	1,066,943	213,009	644,644	80,000	63,700
France,	-	-	-	990,614	5,966,262	5,088,082	7,505,277	7,029,202	2,387,682	1,589,980	133,584	-
Spain,	-	-	-	-	530,342	3,126,975	1,805,812	5,524,852	1,251,124	2,112,729	1,250,097	1,843,047
Portugal,	-	-	-	-	203,153	767,210	615,695	188,356	-	53,000	136,523	-
Italy,	-	-	-	872,999	2,571,341	3,357,346	8,060,191	9,476,602	1,729,020	2,306,831	708,826	187,514
Europe, (generally)	-	-	-	29,000	343,036	46,821	483,581	159,478	-	2,076,960	192,407	36,047

TABLE No. III.

COFFEE—pounds.

Whither exported.	1800.	1801.	1802.	1803.	1804.	1805.
Russia,	-	-	101,126	-	-	129,577
Prussia,	31,462	51,723	-	-	1,954,985	491,747
Sweden,	51,142	-	-	-	51,011	62,013
Denmark and Norway,	457,583	829,354	588,736	240,839	1,811,020	1,690,910
Holland,	11,618,970	13,125,837	9,320,939	2,323,902	26,082,432	23,694,991
Great-Britain,	6,790,756	9,491,133	4,386,344	647,273	861,770	585,201
Hamburg, Bremen, &c.	14,428,586	17,008,877	10,308,316	3,565,295	8,312,925	4,440,353
France,	71,280	2,403,511	7,426,859	1,598,599	6,266,326	11,301,142
Spain,	1,116,827	512,211	468,423	-	128,821	63,391
Portugal,	-	76,407	196,135	294,064	185,116	734,340
Italy,	2,094,642	1,288,125	3,286,825	1,405,150	1,439,779	1,759,206
Europe, (generally)	48,069	103,004	79,156	30,118	1,011,119	870,278

TABLE No. III.—CONTINUED.

COFFEE—pounds.

Whither exported.	1806.	1807.	1808.	1809.	1810.	1811.
Russia,	-	149,271	-	1,283,100	4,048,909	5,113,891
Prussia,	222,351	-	-	-	1,098,211	-
Sweden,	-	-	-	-	-	-
Denmark and Norway,	606,621	756,511	169,869	1,624,886	7,120,496	285,429
Holland,	21,833,438	19,900,965	3,487,872	7,953,461	14,120,990	94,989
Great-Britain,	2,543,370	1,052,075	153,308	957,122	44,618	-
Hamburg, Bremen, &c.	5,306,950	2,644,511	219,582	1,700,023	-	175,423
France,	8,282,965	11,088,529	1,632,351	3,286,263	1,206,389	-
Spain,	236,113	456,428	907,867	502,970	-	1,602,745
Portugal,	687,006	44,801	-	237,617	-	54,754
Italy,	4,948,814	3,490,495	1,133,643	986,074	784,423	188,707
Europe, (generally)	346,690	-	-	2,761,600	246,540	449,780

CHAPTER VI.

IMPORTS into the United States—Their trade with different parts of the world at different periods—Particular account of the trade with Great-Britain, France, and other countries—A comparative view of exports and imports in different years—Value of the principal articles imported at different periods—Amount of cotton and woollen goods imported from Great-Britain in 1806 and 1807, and wines and brandies from France—Origin of their trade with China and the East-Indies—Quantity of teas imported in different years from 1790 to 1812.

HAVING, in the preceding chapters, given an account of the exports of the United States, we shall now, according to the plan proposed, present a view of the imports, together with an account of our trade with the different parts of the world, and its increase since the establishment of the present government. We would here remark, that no returns are made to the treasury department, of the *value* of the various articles imported, by the collectors of the customs, except those, which pay duties ad valorem ; the value of which, at the place of importation, is ascertained by law as follows, viz.—" by adding twenty per cent. to the actual cost thereof, if imported from the Cape of Good Hope, or from any place beyond the same, and ten per cent. on the actual cost thereof, if imported from any other place or country, including all charges, commissions, outside packages, and insurance only excepted."

The goods or merchandize, thus paying ad valorem duties, embrace, as has been heretofore noticed, with few exceptions, all the woollen, cotton, linen, silk, metal, earthern, and paper manufactures imported. The *value* of these goods, ascertained in the manner before stated, and not the *quantity* is returned to the treasury department. Of all the other various articles imported, the *quantity* and not the *value* is returned to the treasury by the collectors. The treasury books, therefore, do not shew the value of the imports, as they do that of the exports of the United States. This can only be ascertained by a long and tedious calculation from the prices of the various articles (except those paying ad valorem duties) at the places of importation. To do this, with accuracy, for each year, from the commencement of the government, would require more time and labour than any one would be willing to bestow on so dry a subject. At different times, however, since the establishment of the government, at the request of the national legislature, official returns have been made to Congress, of the value of our imports for short periods. From these returns and the documents accompanying them, and from other calculations, we shall be able, we trust, to present a satisfactory view of the value of our imports and trade with different parts of the world, for the greatest part of the time from the commencement of the government. By a report of the Secretary of State, of the 16th of December 1793, having reference to the year 1792, it appears, that the countries, with which the United States at that time had their chief commercial intercourse, were Spain, Portugal, France, Great-Britain, the United Netherlands, Denmark and Sweden, and their American possessions; and that the articles of export, constituting the basis of that commerce, with their respective amount, was as follows, viz.—

	Dolls.
Bread stuffs, that is to say, bread grain, meal, and bread, to the annual amount of	7,649,887
Tobacco, - - - - - -	4,349,567
Rice, - - - - - -	1,753,796
Wood, - - - - - -	1,263,534
Salted fish, - - - - -	941,696
Pot and pearl ashes, - - - -	839,093
Salted meats, - - - - - -	599,130
Indigo, - - - - - -	537,379
Horses and mules, - - - -	339,753
Whale oil, - - - - - -	252,591
Flax seed, - - - - -	236,072
Tar, pitch, and turpentine, - - - -	217,177
Live provisions, - - - - -	137,743
Foreign goods, - - - - -	620,274
	19,737,692

The proportion of these exports which went to each of the nations before mentioned, and their dominions, the Secretary states as follows :—

			Dolls.
To Spain and its dominions,	-	-	2,005,907
Portugal and do.	-	-	1,283,462
France and do.	-	-	4,698,735
Great-Britain and do.	-	-	9,363,416
United Netherlands & do.	-	-	1,963,880
Denmark and do.	-	-	224,415
Sweden and do.	-	-	47,240

Our imports, from the same countries, are also stated to be—from

			Dolls.
Spain and its dominions,	-	-	335,110
Portugal and do.	-	-	595,763
France and do.	-	-	2,068,348
Great-Britain and do.	-	-	15,285,428
United Netherlands & do.	-	-	1,172,692
Denmark and do.	-	-	351,364
Sweden and do.	-	-	14,325
			$19,823,030*

The above account does not include the whole amount of our exports at that period, as many articles of smaller value, than those mentioned, are not included.

Tables No. I. and II. annexed to this chapter, give a view of the commercial intercourse of the United States, with foreign countries and their dependencies, from 1795 to 1801 inclusive, exhibiting the value of the exports to each nation, and its dependencies, and the value of the imports from the same, during that period. The exports were taken from the custom-house books, and the value of the imports was made out, with great care and labour, from the prices of the va-

* See printed Report of the Secretary of State

rious articles imported, (except those paying ad valorem duties) at
the places of importation.*

From these tables, the following is the amount of the exports and
imports of the United States from the year 1795 to 1801 :—

			Exports. Dolls.			Imports. Dolls.
1795	-	-	47,855,556	-	-	69,756,258
1796	-	-	67,064,097	-	-	81,436,164
1797	-	-	56,850,206	-	-	75,379,406
1798	-	-	61,527,097	-	-	68,551,700
1799	-	-	78,665,522	-	-	79,069,148
1800	-	-	70,971,780	-	-	91,252,708
1801	-	-	93,020,573	-	-	111,363,511

During the session of Congress in the winter of 1806, the Secretary
of the Treasury furnished the house of representatives with several valuable statements and documents, relative to the trade of the United
States with different parts of the world, in the years 1802, 1803, and
1804.

These statements were called for by the house, while various propositions were under their consideration, as to a total, or partial non-
intercourse with Great-Britain and her dependencies, for the purpose
of ascertaining the amount of our trade with that kingdom, in comparison with the other parts of the world, and to enable the house to see
to what extent our commerce and revenue might be affected, by a non-
intercourse with the British dominions. From these statements, the
annual value of our imports from all parts of the world, on an average
of the years 1802, 1803, and 1804, amounted to $75,316,937, and the
average value of our exports, for the same period, was $68,461,000.
The value of the imports was calculated upon the same principles, as
the value of goods paying the ad valorem duties, that is to say, by

* For these valuable Tables we are indebted to the politeness of a gentleman, who has long been one of the principal clerks in the Treasury Department, who has been much conversant with the subjects to which they relate.

adding from ten to twenty per cent. to the prime cost and charges at the places from which the articles were imported; the value of the exports was taken from the custom-house books.

The value of the principal articles imported, was estimated as follows :—

		Dolls.
Merchandize paying 12 1-2 per cent. ad valorem,		30,732,069
do. do. 15	do. -	8,303,770
do. do. 20	do. -	453,751
Nails and spikes,	-	479,041
Lead and manufactures of lead,	-	227,002
Steel,	-	147,957
Beer, ale and porter,	-	76,020
Cheese,	-	77,150
Boots and shoes,	-	101,300
Coal,	-	36,407
Salt,	-	771,996
Rum,	-	3,881,089
Geneva,	-	675,430
Brandy,	-	2,077,601
Wines,	-	2,962,039
Teas,	-	2,360,507
Coffee,	-	8,372,712
Sugar,	-	7,794,254
Molasses,	-	1,930,592
Cotton,	-	804,125
Pepper,	-	633,041
Indigo,	-	436,941
Cocoa,	-	310,773
Pimento,	-	71,927
Hemp,	-	919,443
All other articles,	-	680,000

$75,316,937

By the same statements, the amount of our commerce with the different parts of the world, on an average of the same period, was estimated as follows :—

I. WITH THE DOMINIONS OF GREAT-BRITAIN IN EUROPE (GIBRALTAR EXCEPTED.)

The annual exports are estimated at about $15,690,000, viz.—

Domestic produce.	Dolls.
Cotton,	5,640,000
Tobacco,	3,220,000
Provisions,	2,160,000
Lumber, naval stores, and pot ashes,	1,510,000
All other articles of domestic produce,	900,000
	$13,430,000
Foreign merchandize,	2,260,000
	$15,690,000

The annual imports at $27,400,000, viz.—

In merchandize paying duties on its value, embracing, with inconsiderable exceptions, all the woollen, cotton, linen, silk, metal, glass, and paper manufactures,	$26,060,000
All the articles paying specific duties, and consisting principally of salt, steel, lead, nails and porter,	1,340,000
	$27,400,000

II. WITH THE BRITISH EAST-INDIES.

Annual exports $130,000.

Domestic produce,	$47,000
Foreign do.	83,000
	$130,000

Imports $3,530,000 viz.—

In merchandize paying ad valorem duties and consisting principally of white cottons, - - - - -	$2,950,000
In all other articles, consisting principally of sugar, pepper and cotton, - -	580,000
	$3,530,000

III. WITH THE NORTHERN BRITISH COLONIES IN AMERICA.

The annual exports amount to $1,000,000, and consist of the following articles, viz.—

Domestic produce.	Dolls.
Provisions and live stock, - - -	530,000
Lumber, naval stores and, pot ashes, - -	90,000
Skins and furs, - - - -	160,000
All other articles, - - -	60,000
	$840,000
Foreign merchandize, - - -	160,000
	$1,000,000

The annual imports amount to $540,000 viz.—

In goods paying ad valorem duties, and consisting principally of merchandize for the Indian trade, and of fish, - -	$480,000
All articles paying specific duties, -	60,000
	$540,000*

* Plaister of Paris, is not included in the above sum.

IV. WITH THE BRITISH WEST-INDIES.

The exports consist of the following articles, viz.—

Provisions and live stock. - -	$4,720,000
Lumber, - - - -	990,000
All other articles, - - - -	340,000
	$6,050,000

And the imports as follows, viz.—

Spirits, - - - -	$2,460,000
Sugar and coffee, - - -	1,480,000
All other articles, - - - -	650,000
	$4,590,000

IMPORTATIONS FROM ALL PARTS OF THE WORLD.

The annual value of imports from all parts of the world, calculated on the average of three years, - - - - $75,316,000

Of which the value imported from the dominions of Great-Britain, amounts to - $35,970,000

And that imported from all other countries as follows, viz.—

From the northern powers, Prussia and Germany, - -	$7,094,000
From the dominions of Holland, France, Spain and Italy, -	25,475,000
From the dominions of Portugal,	1,083,000
From China, and other native powers of Asia, - - -	4,856,000
From all other countries, including some articles not particularly discriminated, - -	838,000
	$39,346,000
	$75,316,000

The value of the several species of merchandize, thus imported, may be arranged as followeth, viz.—

1st. Articles, principally imported from the dominions of Great-Britain, viz.—

Merchandize paying duties on its value, -	$39,489,000
Salt, nails, lead, steel, beer, cheese, shoes & boots,	1,917,000
Rum, - - - - -	3,881,000
	$45,287,000

Of which are imported from the dominions, of Great-Britain,	$33,461,000
And from all other countries,	11,826,000
	$45,287,000

2d. Articles, principally imported from other countries, viz.—

Coffee, - - - - -	$8,373,000
Sugar, - - - - -	7,794,000
Molasses, - - - -	1,930,000
Cotton, cocoa, indigo, pepper, and pimento,	2,257,000
Hemp, soap, candles, and all other articles, (wines, teas, gin and brandy excepted,)	1,600,000
	$21,954,000

Of which are imported from the dominions of Great-Britain,	$2,476,000
And from all other countries,	19,478,000
	$21,954,000

3d. Articles only incidentally imported from Great-Britain, viz.—

Brandy and Geneva, - - -	$2,753,000
Wines, - - - - -	2,962,000
Teas, - - - - - -	2,360,000
	$8,075,000

Of which are imported from the
dominions of Great-Britain, $33,000
From all other countries,   -   8,042,000

                          $8,075,000

EXPORTS TO ALL PARTS OF THE WORLD.

I. DOMESTIC PRODUCE.

The annual value of the articles of domestic produce, exported to all parts of the world, calculated on the average of the same three years, is computed at   - $39,928,000

Of which the amount exported to
the British Dominions is   - $20,653,000

And that to all other parts of the world, viz.—

To the northern powers, Prussia and
    Germany,   -   -   - $2,918,000
To the dominions of Holland,
    France, Spain, and Italy,   -   12,183,000
To the dominions of Portugal,   -   1,925,000
To all other countries, including, also,
    some articles not particularly dis-
    criminated,   -   -   2,249,000

                         $19,275,000

Considered in relation to the several quarters of the globe, and without reference to the dominions of any particular power, those exports are distributed in the following manner, viz.—

Exported to Europe, - - - $22,957,000
    to the West-Indies and other American
      Colonies, - - - 15,607,000
    to Asia, Africa, and the South Seas, - 1,364,000

                    $39,928,000

And the several articles, of which these exports consist, are respectively valued as follows, viz.—

Provisions, flour, wheat, corn, rice, and every other
    species of vegetable food, - - $13,040,000
Dried and pickled fish, - - - 2,848,000
Beef, pork, butter, cheese, and every species of ani-
    mal food, - - - - 3,728,000

                    $19,616,000

Cotton, - - - - 6,940,000
Tobacco, - - - - 6,143,000
Lumber, naval stores, and pot-ashes, - 4,387,000
All other articles, - - - - 2,842,000

                    $39,928,000

II. FOREIGN PRODUCE.

The annual value of foreign produce, re-exported to all parts of the world, calculated on the average of the same three years, is estimated at - - $28,533,000

of which the amount exported to the dominions of Great-Britain, is - - - - $3,054,000

And to all other parts of the world, is, viz.—

To the northern powers, Prussia and
  Germany,   -   - $5,051,000
To the dominions of Holland, France,
  Spain, and Italy,   -   -   18,495,000
To the dominions of Portugal,   -   396,000
To all other countries, including, also,
  some articles not particularly discri-
  minated,   -   -   1,537,000
                           ——— 25,497,000

                             $28,533,000

Considered in relation to the several quarters of the globe, and without reference to the dominions of any particular power, these exports are distributed in the following manner, viz.—

Exported to Europe,   -   -   - $20,648,000
    to the W. Indies and American Colonies,   6,688,000
    to Asia, Africa, and the South Sea,   -   1,197,000

                             $28,533,000

The several articles, of which these exports consist, are respectively valued as follows, viz.—

Merchandize, paying ad valorem duties,   - $9,772,000
Coffee,   -   -   -   -   7,302,000
Sugar,   -   -   -   -   -   5,775,000
Cotton, cocoa, indigo, pimento, and pepper,   -   2,490,000
Teas,   -   -   -   -   1,304,000
Wines,   -   -   -   -   -   1,108,000
Spirits of every description,   -   -   642,000
All other articles,   -   -   -   140,000

                             $28,533,000

GENERAL BALANCE.

Annual value of importations being stated at $75,316,000
And that of exports of domestic produce $39,928,000
    of foreign do. 28,533,000
             ————$68,461,000

               $6,855,000

Leaves an apparent balance, according to the statement of the Secretary, against the United States, of near seven millions of dollars.*

During the years 1805, 1806, and 1807, the imports, as well as the exports of the United States, were greater than in any former years.

Table No. III. shews the *quantity* and *value* of all the articles imported into the United States, from October 1st, 1806, to September 30th, 1807. The value of the articles (except those paying ad valorem duties) was ascertained from the prices, at which the same articles were valued at the Treasury, during the same period, on their exportation. The value of the imports for this year, thus ascertained, amounted to $138,574,876.

The value of the principal articles was as follows, viz :—

Goods paying ad valorem duties, - $58,655,917
Malmsey and Madeira wine, - - 1,023,321
Burgundy   do. - - - 59,279
Sherry   do. - - - 353,672
All other   do. - - - 3,051,397
Foreign spirits from grain, - - 1,477,679
Do. do. from other materials, - 9,221,175
Molasses, - - - - 3,064,044
Bohea tea, - - - 493,946
Souchong do. - - - 1,250,029
Hyson do. - - - 1,251,367
Other green do. -   - 2,117,362
Coffee, - - - - 16,470,947

* See report of the Secretary of the Treasury in 1806.

Cocoa,	$2,297,961
Sugar, brown,	17,511,061
Do. clayed,	5,901,804
Raisins in jars and boxes,	138,307
All other,	291,807
Candles, tallow,	98,538
Cheese,	288,299
Soap,	376,222
Tallow,	262,541
Pepper,	804,869
Pimento,	263,172
Indigo,	1,849,529
Cotton,	1,007,139
Gun-powder,	97,406
Iron, anchors and sheet,	70,368
Do. slit and hoop,	77,301
Do. nails and spikes,	544,328
White and red lead,	420,613
Lead, and manufactures of lead,	270,147
Steel,	205,595
Hemp,	2,116,605
Coal,	132,511
Salt, (weighing more than 56 lbs. per bushel)	1,387,903
Do. (weighing 56 lbs. or less per bushel)	288,791
Glass, black quart bottles,	184,455
Window-glass, not above 8 by 10 inches,	261,268
Do. not above 10 by 12 do.	46,335
Do. all above 10 by 12 do.	73,202
Segars,	256,240

The amount of exports, for the same year, was—

Domestic produce,	$48,699,592
Foreign do.	59,643,558
Making,	$108,343,150

Leaving a difference between the value of exports and imports, for that year, of $30,231,726

This difference, or apparent balance, against the United States, arises from the mode of calculating the value of our exports and imports ; and instead of being against the United States, is, in fact, in their favour, as will be explained, in a subsequent chapter, on the subject of what is called the balance of trade.

Having thus given a general view of our exports and imports, we shall, in the next place, as far as possible, present a view of our trade with each country, from the commencement of the government ; distinguishing the trade of the parent country, from that of her Colonies and dependencies ; together with a general account of the trade of the United States, with each quarter of the world.

I. GREAT-BRITAIN AND IRELAND.

The principal articles, exported to Great-Britain and Ireland, are cotton, tobacco, rice, occasionally wheat and flour, flax-seed, naval stores, such as pitch, tar, and turpentine, timber and plank, staves and heading, pot and pearl ashes, whale and spermaceti oil. Our imports are principally manufactured goods of various descriptions.

By the treaty of peace in 1783, the United States were, of course, subject to the navigation laws and alien duties of Great-Britain. She, however, considered it for her interest, in some degree, to relax these laws, in their favour. By an act of parliament, passed in April, 1783, (23 Geo. III. chap. 39) the king and council were authorised to regulate the trade between the two countries. This act was at first limited to a short period, but was continued in force, by subsequent acts. By an order in council, of the 26th of December, 1783, made in pursuance of this act, and which was, in substance, renewed for many years, it is declared " that any unmanufactured goods and merchandizes, the importation of which into this kingdom is not prohibited by law, (except oil), and any pitch, tar, turpentine, indigo, masts, yards, bowsprits, being the growth or produce of any of the United States of America, may (until further order) be imported directly from thence, into any of the ports of this kingdom, either in British or American ships, by British subjects, or by any of the people inhabiting in, and belonging to, the said United States, or any of them, and may be entered and landed in any port in this kingdom, upon payment of the *same duties*, as the like sort of goods or merchandize are or may be subject and liable to if imported by British subjects, in British ships, from any British island or plantation in America, and no other, notwithstanding such goods or merchandize, or the ships, in which the same may be brought, may not be accompanied with the certificate or other documents, heretofore required by law." By this order, also, the same drawbacks, exemptions, and bounties are allowed on goods exported to the United States, as on those exported to the British Islands or Colonies in America. The intercourse between the United States, and the British West-Indies, was regulated by the same order, and which will be noticed hereafter.

In consequence of this order, many articles from the United States, such as pot and pearl ashes, iron, wood, and lumber of all kinds, indigo, and flax-seed, were imported duty free, while most of the same articles, imported from other countries, were subject to heavy duties, and others, as tobacco, rice, pitch, tar, &c. paid only the same duties as when imported from British Colonies.

The importation of grain, as we have before stated, was regulated by a general law, and except in times of scarcity, was liable to so high a duty, as to amount to a prohibition.

By the 14th article of the treaty of amity, commerce, &c. of the 19th of November, 1794, liberty of commerce and navigation is established between the British dominions in Europe and the United States, subject however to the laws of the two countries ; and by the 15th article, no higher duties are to be paid by either, than are paid by all other nations ; the British government reserving to itself, the right of imposing on American vessels, entering into the British ports in Europe, a tonnage duty equal to that which shall be payable by British vessels in the ports of America ; and also such duty as may be adequate to countervail the difference of duty then payable on the importation of goods, when imported into the United States, in British or American bottoms. The treaty of 1794 expired in 1803, except the first ten articles, which were permanent.

By the treaty negociated by our commissioners in 1806, there was to have been an equalization of the tonnage and other duties in the trade between the two countries. It is understood that in the commercial treaty, lately negociated with Great-Britain, and which has not yet been ratified or made public, the same tonnage duties, and the same export and import duties are to be paid, whether such importation or exportation be in American or British vessels.

Whether such a measure would be favourable to the navigating interest of the United States has, heretofore, been doubted by many, and experience alone, perhaps, can decide the question.

The amount of the trade between the two countries, in each year, from 1784 to 1790, taken from English accounts, we have before stated in Chapter I.

In 1792, according to the foregoing estimate of the Secretary of State, our exports to Great-Britain, and her dominions, amounted to $9,363,416, and our imports to $15,285,428. Much the greatest part of the imports was from Great-Britain, exclusive of her dependencies. From 1795 to 1801, the value of our exports to Great-Britain and Ireland, and our imports from the same, was as follows, viz.* :—

	Exports. Dolls.	Imports. Dolls.
1795	6,324,066	23,313,121
1796	17,143,313	31,928,685
1797	6,637,423	27,303,067
1798	11,978,870	17,330,770
1799	19,930,428	29,133,219
1800	19,085,603	32,877,059
1801	30,931,121	39,519,218

Our exports to Great-Britain and Ireland, on the average of the years 1802, 1803, and 1804, as appears, by the foregoing statement of the Secretary of the Treasury, were in value—

Domestic produce,	$13,430,000
Foreign merchandize,	2,260,000
	$15,690,000

Our imports on the average of the same years were in value, $27,400,000

* See Tables No. I. & II. annexed to this chapter.

From 1805 to 1812, the value of the exports to Great-Britain and Ireland, was as follows :—

	Domestic produce. Value in Dolls.		Foreign produce. Value in Dolls.
1805	13,939,663		1,472,600
1806	12,737,913		2,855,583
1807	21,122,332		2,027,650
1808	3,093,978		106,327
1809	5,326,194		239,405
1810	11,388,438		892,435
1811	13,184,553		554,757
1812	4,662,296		37,187

The importations from Great-Britain and Ireland consist principally of the various manufactures of wool, cotton, silk, and flax ; manufactures of brass and copper, glass and earthern ware, haberdashery, manufactures of iron and steel, lead, and manufactures of lead, hats, salt, tin and pewter, coal, beer, ale and porter.

Much the greatest proportion of the above articles, on their importation, are subject to duties, on their value. By ascertaining therefore the amount of goods imported from Great-Britain and Ireland, paying these duties, the value of imports from that kingdom may be pretty accurately estimated. The following is the amount of goods of this description, imported for a number of years, subsequent to 1804, viz.—

				Value in Dolls.
1805				31,556,159
1806				35,779,245
1807				38,901,838
1808				18,818,882
1809				17,647,542
1810				29,123,605
1811				25,338,044
1812				7,663,179
1813				11,298,285

In 1807, the amount of goods, paying duties ad valorem, was nearly thirty-nine millions of dollars; when we add the goods imported, in the same year, duty free, and those subject to specific duties, the whole amount, imported from Great-Britain, in 1807, would not, it is believed, fall much short of fifty millions of dollars.

The British accounts of exports to, and imports from the United States, will serve, also, to shew the amount of the trade between the two countries. Tables No. IV. and V. contain the British official accounts of exports and imports, (exclusive of Scotland) for the years 1806, 1807 and 1808, ending on the 10th of October in each year, furnished the House of Commons, by the inspector general of imports and exports, containing their *real*, as well as *official* value.

By these accounts, the *real* value of British produce and manufactures, and of foreign merchandize, exported to the United States, in those years, was as follows, viz.—

	1806.	1807.	1808.
British produce and manufactures,	£11,716,620	£11,119,048	£5,718,615
Foreign merchandize,	458,875	253,822	65,788
Total exports,	£12,175,495	£11,372,870	£5,784,403

And the *real* value of the imports from the United States, into Great-Britain, was—

In 1806.	1807.	1808.
£3,508,480	£5,201,909	£2,804,707

To enable us to see, what proportion of all the exports of British produce and manufacture, was shipped to the United States, during those years, we add table No. VI. shewing the *real*, as well as *official* value of all the exports from Great-Britain, (exclusive of Scotland) to all parts of the world, for each of those years. This shews the *real* value of British produce and manufacture, exported to all

parts of the world, on an average, of the years 1806 and 1807 to
have been - - - £39,205,036, sterling,
or about $176,000,000.

And the *real* value of the same produce
and manufacture, exported to the United
States, on an average of the same two
years was · - - £11,417,834 or about
$50,500,000, making between one quarter, and one third of all the
exports of British produce and manufacture, during these two years.
Much the greatest part of our imports from Great-Britain, consist of
woollen and cotton goods. As these, with many others, on their importation into the United States, are subject to duties ad valorem,
neither their quantity, or value is separately ascertained by our custom-house books. By the English accounts contained in tables No.
V. and VI. the *real* value of cotton goods exported to the United
States, from Great-Britain (exclusive of Scotland) on an average of
the same two years, was - - £4,393,449
and of woollen goods, - - - 4,591,437
_____

Making, - - - £8,984,886 sterling,
or about $39,500,000, as valued in England, being more than nine-
teen millions of cotton goods, and about twenty millions of woollens,
in each of these years.

We would here remark, that the imports and exports of the United
States, for the years 1806 and 1807, were greater, than in any former year, and far exceed those of any subsequent year ; and that,
probably, about one third of the goods imported from Great-Britain.
especially those imported in 1806, were again exported to the West-
Indies, to South America, and elsewhere. The value of the exports
of woollens from Great-Britain has been nearly stationary for many
years, while the exports of cotton goods has increased beyond example. The United States have taken a large proportion of English
woollens. Table No. VII. contains an amount of the value of the
woollen manufactures exported from Great-Britain from 1790 to 1799,
agreeable to the estimate of the inspector general, together with the
countries, to which the same were exported.* From this, it will be

_____

* Macpherson's Annals of Commerce.

seen, that during that period, from one quarter to one third, and in some years nearly one half, of all the woollens was exported to the United States, greatly exceeding the amount exported to any other country.* We have added Table No. VIII. containing the *official* value of all the exports from Great-Britain, during the years ending on the 5th day of January, 1809, 1810, and 1811 ; also the imports into the same, during the same years ; with an appendix shewing the value of the particular articles exported and imported, for the same period. These will furnish some data from which we may judge what proportion of raw materials are received by the British manufacturer, from the United States, as well as the proportion of their manufactures received by us.

The value of our imports from Great-Britain has always exceeded that of our exports, even in those years, when we have consumed the whole of the imports. This difference, however, is less than appears from our custom-house books, as the value of our exports is ascertained from the prices of the articles, at the place of exportation. Most of the articles exported are bulky, and have been carried in our own ships.† The expense of transportation, therefore, as well as a reasonable profit to the shipper, which cannot be less than about twenty per cent. must be added to the estimated value of our exports. The balance is paid by our trade with the West-Indies, and other parts of the world.

* The manufacture of wool, as well as cotton, is rapidly advancing in the United States. Experience has proved that merino sheep will endure our climate, and this valuable breed, with their mixtures, is now spread in almost every part of the United States, and the number of sheep is increasing in every state in the union. It is believed there are now not less than from twelve to fifteen millions of sheep in the United States. If Great-Britain, with her limited extent of territory, can maintain about thirty millions of sheep, how much more easily can the United States, with their extended territory and increasing improvements, maintain not only thirty millions, but double that number ?

† The number of American ships cleared from Liverpool, in 1807, was four hundred and eighty-nine, and their tonnage one hundred twenty-three thousand five hundred and forty-five.

II. TRADE WITH THE BRITISH EAST-INDIES.

The trade of the United States with the British East-Indies commenced not long after the peace of 1783. In 1788, or 1789, Earl Cornwallis, then governour and commander in India, gave orders that American vessels should be treated at the company's settlements, in all respects, as the most favoured foreigners : and the ship Chesapeake, one of the first vessels that displayed the American colours in the Ganges, was favoured by the supreme council of Bengal, with an exemption from the government customs which all foreign vessels were bound to pay.*

This trade was negotiated by our treaty with Great-Britain of the 19th of November, 1794. The thirteenth article, relating to this subject, was as follows, viz.—

ARTICLE XIII.

" His Majesty consents, that the vessels belonging to the citizens of the United States of America, shall be admitted and hospitably received in all the sea ports and harbours of the British territories in the East-Indies. And that the citizens of the said United States may freely carry on a trade between the said territories and the said United States, in all articles of which the importation or exportation respectively, to or from the said territories, shall not be entirely prohibited. Provided only, that it shall not be lawful for them, in any time of war between the British government and any other power or state whatever, to export from the said territories, without the special permission of the British government there, any military stores, or naval stores, or rice. The citizens of the United States shall pay for their vessels when admitted into the said ports no other or higher tonnage duty, than shall be payable on British vessels, when admitted into the ports of the United States, And they shall pay no other or higher duties or charges, on the importation or exportation of the cargoes of the said vessels, than shall be payable on the same articles when imported or exported in British vessels. But it is ex-

* Macpherson's Annals of Commerce.

pressly agreed, that the vessels of the United States shall not carry any of the articles exported by them from the said British territories, to any port or place, except to some port or place in America, where the same shall be unladen ; and such regulations shall be adopted by both parties, as shall from time to time be found necessary to enforce the due and faithful observance of this stipulation. It is also understood, that the permission granted by this article, is not to extend to allow the vessels of the United States to carry on any part of the coasting trade of the said British territories ; but vessels going with their original cargoes, or part thereof, from any port of discharge to another, are not to be considered as carrying on the coasting trade. Neither is this article to be construed to allow the citizens of the States to settle or reside within the said territories, or to go into the interior parts thereof, without the permission of the British government established there, and if any transgression should be attempted against the regulations of the British government in this respect, the observance of the same shall and may be enforced against the citizens of America, in the same manner as against the British subjects or others transgressing the same rule. And the citizens of the United States, whenever they arrive in any port or harbour in the said territories, or if they should be permitted, in manner aforesaid, to go to any other place therein, shall always be subject to the laws, government, and jurisdiction of what nature established in such harbour, port, or place according as the same may be. The citizens of the United States may also touch for refreshment at the island of St. Helena, but subject in all respects to such regulations as the British government may from time to time establish there."

This article expressly provides that the goods exported should not be carried to any port or place, " except to some port or place in America." It is, however, less explicit as to the outward cargo ; and under this article, American vessels with their cargoes went directly to the East-Indies, from Europe and other places. The commercial part of thistreaty, as before stated, expired in 1803. Subsequent to its expiration, and until lately, our trade with the British East-Indies was suffered to continue on the same footing, as under the treaty. In the treaty, however, agreed to by Messrs. Monroe and Pinkney, December 31st, 1806, our commissioners found it im-

possible to obtain stipulations relative to this trade, equally favourable
to the United States as those in the former treaty. By the third article of this treaty, our trade was limited to vessels " sailing *direct*
from the United States ;" in other respects, the article was the same
as the thirteenth article of Mr. Jay's treaty. The British commissioners urged, that this limitation was really no more than was intended by the treaty of 1794 ; and as it was insisted upon, by the
East-India company, our commissioners were obliged to acquiesce in it.

Although this treaty was rejected by the President, without even
submitting it to the Senate, for their advice, yet our East-India trade
was suffered to continue as before, until April 30th, 1811, when, in
pursuance of powers vested in them, by an act of parliament passed
the 37th year of George III. chap. 107, the East-India Company established the following regulations " for the conduct of the trade of
foreign nations, to the ports and settlements of the British nation in
the East-Indies, and also for defining the duties to which such trade
shall be subject," &c.

" I. Foreign European ships, belonging to any nation having a
settlement of its own in the East-Indies, and being in amity with his
Majesty, may freely enter the British sea-ports and harbours in that
country, whether they come directly from their own country, or from
any of the ports and places in the East-Indies ; they shall be hospitably received ; and shall have liberty of trade there in imports and exports conformably to the regulations established in such places. The
ships may also be cleared out for any port or place in the East-Indies ;
but if cleared out for Europe, shall be cleared out direct for the country, to which the ships respectively belong.

" II. First. Foreign European ships, belonging to countries having no establishment in the East-Indies, and ships belonging *to the
United States* of America, may (when those countries and states respectively are in amity with his Majesty) in like manner freely enter the British sea-ports and harbours in the East-Indies ; they shall
be hospitably received there ; and have free liberty to trade in imports and exports conformably to the regulations of the place ; provided always, that they proceed from their *own ports direct* to the
said British territories, without touching at any port or place whatever in the voyage out ; except from necessity, and merely to pro-

cure refreshments, or repairs in case of distress or accident in the course of such voyage, the burthen of which necessity to rest on the parties.

" Second. The vessels of the said European powers last aforesaid, and of the United States, shall not carry any of the said articles exported by them from said British territories, to any port or place, except to some port or place in their own countries respectively, where the same shall be unladen. The said ships shall not be cleared out to carry on the coasting or country trade in India ; but vessels going with their *original cargoes*, or part thereof, from one British port of discharge to another British port, are not to be considered as carrying on the coasting trade.

" Third. The said vessels shall not be allowed to proceed, either with or without return cargo, from the said British territories to the settlements or territories of any European nation in India, or to the territory of any Indian or Chinese potentate or power, except from the like necessity as is before described, of which the proof shall rest with them. Nor shall the said vessels be allowed to enter the river in that part of the British territory situated in Bengal, for any other purpose, than that of proceeding to the port of Calcutta, for trade, refreshment, or repairs.

" Fourth. In clearing out for their respective countries, the clearance shall be *a direct one* to the country, European or American, to which the vessel belongs, and to no other whatever ; they are to *give bond*, with the security of a resident in the country, that they will deliver the cargo at the port for which the clearance is made, and such bond is to be cancelled, when a certificate from a British consul, or two known British merchants resident at such port is produced of the bona fide delivery of the cargo there."

The regulations with respect to duties were—

" First. Goods imported or exported in foreign bottoms, shall be subject to double the amount of the duties payable on goods imported or exported in British bottoms.

" Second. On that principle, goods liable to duty on importation by sea, will be chargeable with duty on their importation in British or foreign bottoms respectively, agreeable to the schedule annexed to this regulation No. I.

" Third. Pursuant to the same principle of subjecting the trade of foreigners to double duties, they will be precluded from the benefit of drawback receivable by British subjects, in cases, in which such drawback may be equal to a moiety of the duty paid on importation; and in cases in which the drawback receivable by British subjects may exceed a moiety of the import duty, the drawback receivable by foreigners will be adjusted on a consideration of the ultimate duty payable by British subjects agreeably to the schedule No. II.

" Fourth. In cases in which the drawback receivable by British subjects amounts to less than a moiety of the import duty, the foreign exporter will be subject to the payment of an additional export duty, agreeably to the detailed schedule No. III.

" Goods imported for re-exportation shall on re-exportation be allowed a drawback of two thirds of the amount of the duty paid on their importation, if exported in British bottoms, and of one third of the duty paid on their importation, if exported in foreign bottoms.

" In cases in which goods shall have paid double duty on importation, that is, the enhanced duty ordered to be levied from foreigners, a drawback shall be allowed to the exporter of two thirds of such duty, whether the goods be exported in foreign or British bottoms ; with the exceptions, however, of those goods on the exportation of which, a specific rate of drawback is established by the Table annexed to this regulation."

By these regulations, American vessels must proceed from their own ports direct, to the British East-Indies, without touching at any other port in the outward voyage, except from necessity, &c. When there, they cannot carry on the coasting trade, nor can they, either with or without a cargo, proceed to the settlements of any other European nation in India, or to any part of India or to China, nor can they go to any place on the River Ganges, except Calcutta. They must return direct to some port in the United States, and they are to give bond, to deliver their cargo at the port for which their clearance is made, and they are likewise subjected to double the duties paid by British bottoms. In consequence of these regulations, the owners of some American vessels, employed in the East-India trade, were placed in a most unfortunate situation. They had given bond in India, to land their cargo in some port in the United States; on their arrival here, the non-intercourse law prohibited the landing of the cargo, because it came from a British port; if landed in the United States, the vessel and cargo were forfeited under the laws of their own country, if carried to any other place, the bond given in India was forfeited. Thus situated, the owners were obliged to apply to Congress for relief; who granted them permission to land their goods, and finally to dispose of them, for their own use.

The exports from the United States to the British East-Indies, have been inconsiderable, except in money. The value of the imports for each year, from 1795 to 1801, will be seen in Table No. II. before mentioned. In the last of these years, the imports amounted to $5,134,456. The articles usually imported, are cotton goods of various kinds, indigo, sugar, spices, &c. In 1807, the value of goods paying duties ad valorem, consisting principally of cottons, amounted to $4,073,910.

The charter of the East-India company has lately been renewed and extended to the 10th of April, 1834. The trade, however, to India has been laid open to British subjects generally, under certain regulations, from the 10th day of April, 1814. These regulations, or the most important of them, are stated by professor Hamilton, in his enquiry concerning the national debt of Great-Britain, to be as follows: " That no vessel shall proceed on private trade to India, without a license from the directors, which shall be granted, on application, of course, to the principal settlements of Fort William, Fort George, Bombay, or Prince of Wales Island ; but no vessel may fit out to other places, unless specially authorized ; and in case the directors refuse to grant such special license, the board of controul shall ultimately determine in regard to the same. That no vessel under one hundred and fifty tons shall be employed. That goods imported in private trade, shall be brought to some port in the United Kingdom, which shall have been declared fit for that purpose by order in council. That the importation of articles of silk and cotton manufacture, for home consumption, shall be confined to the port of London, and the goods deposited in the company's ware-houses there. And the importation of tea, in private trade, is prohibted without license from the company. The company retain, till 10th of April, 1834, the government and revenue of their territorial acquisitions subject to the regulation of the board of controul, and the exclusive trade to China, and may trade as a corporation to India, in common with his Majesty's other subjects."

The commercial treaty lately agreed upon, contains, it is said, regulations relative to the American trade with British India, but what these regulations are is not yet known. The intercourse is probably limited, to a direct one, between the two countries.

III. TRADE WITH THE BRITISH WEST-INDIES.

The American trade with the British West-India islands, both before and since the war of the revolution, has been very great.

Large quantities of our lumber, fish, flour, beef, pork, horses, live cattle, indian corn and meal, peas, beans, &c. &c. have found a market in these islands.

Since the peace of 1783, the United States and Great-Britain have not formed any conventional arrangement, relative to this trade. By the provisions of the bill introduced into Parliament, in the winter of 1783, for the temporary regulation of the commerce, between the two countries, American vessels were to be admitted into the ports of the British West-Indies, with the produce of the United States, with liberty to export to the United States, any merchandize, or goods whatsoever, subject only to the same duties, as they would be subject to, in British bottoms.

This bill, from the opposition made to it, was lost, and the power of regulating this trade was left with the King and Council, as we have before stated ; and by the order in council of the 26th of December, 1783, before mentioned, American vessels were excluded from the British West-Indies.

British vessels were permitted to import into the islands, from the United States, pitch, tar, turpentine, hemp and flax, masts, yards and bowsprits, staves, heading, boards, timber, shingles, and all other species of lumber ; horses, neat cattle, sheep, hogs, poultry, and all other species of live stock and live provisions ; peas, beans, potatoes, wheat, flour, bread, biscuit, rice, oats, barley, and all other species of grain, the same being the growth, or production of the United States ; and to export to the United States, rum, sugar, molasses, coffee, cocoanuts, ginger, and pimento, upon payment of the same duties, and under the same restrictions, as though exported to any British Colony or Plantation in America.

By the 12th article of Mr. Jay's treaty, American vessels " not being above the burthen of seventy tons" were placed on the same footing with British vessels, in respect to the trade of the United States with the British West-Indies, with a proviso, that they were not to carry molasses, sugar, coffee, cocoa, or cotton to any part of the world, except the United States, either from the islands, or from the United States. This article was not agreed to, on the part of the United States, and the treaty was ratified by both governments without it. In 1806, the plenipotentiaries of the United States negotiated a commercial treaty with Great-Britain, but were unable to make any arrangement, relative to the West-India trade.

The difficulty, however, of supplying the West-India Islands, during the late wars in Europe, has rendered it necessary for the British government to open their ports to American vessels, almost every year, for certain limited periods. This was done by proclamation directly from the Governours of the islands, until 1807, when an act of Parliament was passed on the subject, called the American intercourse bill; since that period, proclamations for opening the ports have originated with the King and Council; but beef, pork, and fish, have been excluded, since that time, either in American or British bottoms.

It is understood, that the commercial treaty lately negotiated, is silent on the subject of the West-India trade, and the British have lately again shut their West-India ports against American vessels.

The value of the exports and imports from 1795 to 1801 was as follows :—

	Exports. Value—Dolls.		Imports. Value—Dolls.
1795	-	2,634,664	-	6,426,091
1796	-	5,446,559	-	6,301,534
1797	-	2,147,025	-	3,045,045
1798	-	4,283,940	-	2,925,739
1799	-	6,285,254	-	6,083,372
1800	-	6,404,785	-	5,774,411
1801	-	9,699,722	-	6,968,032

During the years 1802, 1803, and 1804, the value of the exports and imports, as appears by the foregoing statements of the Secretary of the Treasury, was as follows, viz.—

	Exports. Value—Dolls.		Imports. Value—Dolls.
1802	6,228,464	-	4,486,890
1803	5,624,647	-	4,492,861
1804	6,315,667	-	4,739,186

The quantity, as well as the value of the principal articles, exported and imported, for each of the said years, are ascertained in Tables Nos. IX. and X. taken from the same statements of the Secretary of the Treasury, together with the amount of duties paid on the imports.

During the years 1805, 1806, and 1807, the value of the exports and imports was nearly the same, as in the preceding years. The value of our exports to the British West-Indies, has generally exceeded our imports ; and as the value of the former is estimated at the place of exportation, and of the latter, at the place of importation, the real difference is much greater than appears, by our custom-house books. Most of the articles exported are bulky, and the amount of freight and insurance for some of them, particularly lumber and live stock, is equal to the first cost. The freight and charges, also, of the articles imported make no inconsiderable part of their value, in this country,

As our own ships were principally employed in this trade, the profits and advantages, arising from these sources, were chiefly confined to the American merchant.

The American tonnage, employed in this trade, on an average of the years 1799, 1800, and 1801, was one hundred and thirty-one thousand one hundred and twenty-three.

A great proportion of our lumber has gone to these islands. The average quantity of staves and heading sent there in the years 1805, 1806, and 1807, was seventeen millions six hundred and fourteen thousand, being nearly one half of the whole quantity exported, during these years. The quantity of boards and plank, for the same years, on an average, was about forty millions. In 1803, two

hundred sixty thousand five hundred and fifty-five, and in 1807, two
hundred fifty-one thousand seven hundred and six barrels of flour
were exported to these islands.

The value of flour, bread, and biscuit exported, on an average of
the years 1802, 1803, and 1804, was about two millions of dollars;
of lumber of all kinds about one million; of beef, pork, bacon, and
lard about eight hundred thousand dollars; and of indian corn, rye,
and indian meal about six hundred thousand. The quantity of
rum imported, during the same period, was about four millions of
gallons annually, and was valued at about two and a half millions of
dollars. The quantity imported, in the years 1805, 1806, and 1807,
was about four millions six hundred and fourteen thousand gallons annually.

Opinions have been advanced, with no small share of confidence,
by some British writers, that their West-India Islands could be supplied with lumber and provisions from their North-American Colonies. Experience, however, has not confirmed these opinions. Until the adoption of commercial restrictions by the United States, a
small part only of the lumber and provision, imported into the British
West-Indies, came from the British North-American Colonies. The
amount of the principal articles of provisions and lumber, imported
from different parts of the world, on an average of the years
1804, 1805, and 1806, was as follows :—*

	From the U. States.	British provinces.	G. Britain & Ireland.	Other countries.
Flour, meal and bread, cwt.	463,505	2,789	34,495	7,667
Corn, viz. indian corn, oats, peas, beans, &c. } bshls.	406,189	3,276	183,168	4,432
Rice, - bbls. -	11,740	6	50	139
Pork and beef, - do. -	54,114	1,642	54,571	385
Fish, dry cod, &c. cwt. -	138,484	101,692	3,302	3,298
Do. salt or pickled, bbls. -	38,171	27,800	57,698	991
Butter, - firkins.	8,050	204	49,818	80

* See a view of the importance of the British American Colonies, by Da-
vid Anderson, printed in 1814.

		From the U. States.	British provinces.	G.Britain & Ireland.	Other countries.
Cows and oxen,	- -	4,145	3	8	1,123
Sheep and hogs,	- -	3,484	44	- -	314
Oak and pine boards and timber,	feet,	39,022,997	942,122	- -	101,330
Staves,	pieces,	17,605,687	525,026	- -	264,500
Shingles,	-	43,051,704	332,925	- -	13,000

While the United States furnished more than four hundred sixty-three thousand hundred weight of flour, meal, and biscuit, the British provinces furnished only two thousand seven hundred and eighty-nine hundred weight; and of indian corn, oats, &c. the British provinces furnished only three thousand two hundred and seventy-six bushels, and of beef and pork, but one thousand six hundred and forty-two barrels, and of lumber not a million feet of boards and timber. Indeed, from this account, given by a late British writer, who is very far from being friendly to the United States, it appears, that, during the years 1804, 1805, and 1806, the United States supplied the British West-India Islands with more than nine tenths of their flour, meal, and bread, about two thirds of their indian corn, oats, peas, and beans, about one half of their beef and pork, more than one half of their dried fish, and nearly the whole of their live stock and lumber.

During the continuance of American commercial restrictions, the trade of the British Provinces increased, particularly in the article of lumber. It is stated, by Mr. Anderson, that the total value of exports from Quebec, in 1806, was £551,570 6s. 3d. sterling, and that in 1810, the exports amounted to £1,079,474 11s. 6d. making a difference of £527,904 5s. 3d. The value of lumber exported in 1806, is stated at £110,740 11s. 6d. and in 1810, at £505,689 15s. 6d. a difference of £394,949 4s. 0d.

There was, also, in 1810, an increase, in the exports of grain, provisions, and pot and pearl ashes, and a diminution, in the exports of furs and skins. There is no doubt, that many of the articles exported in 1810, found their way into Canada from the United States, notwithstanding the prohibition of all intercouse, between the two countries. And it is well known, that many American citizens, particularly those who had been engaged in the lumber trade, deprived of employment, at home, went to Canada and New-Brunswick, and were employed in procuring lumber, in those provinces : and it will be fortunate, for the United States, if their own citizens have not taught their neighbours, how to become their rivals in this trade.*

TRADE WITH FRANCE AND DEPENDENCIES.

I. WITH FRANCE.

The trade of the United States with France and her dependencies in 1787, is stated by Monsieur Peuchet, in his statistics of France, to have been as follows :—

Exports to the United States from France and dependencies, in

	Livres.
Coffee, sugar, rum, syrup, salt, olive oil, fruits, brandy, wine, and liqueurs, amounted to -	10,675,000
Cotton, drugs, &c. to - - -	694,000
Stuffs, laces, silk, hosiery, linen, cambrick, soap, gloves, gun-powder, glass-ware, and hard-ware, to	1,238,000
Livres,	12,607,000

or about $2,500,000.

* Mr. Anderson is obliged to admit, that the Canadians have had the as-sistance of the Americans, in procuring lumber. "The American embargo (says he) and the continental system have, ever since 1807, produced an ex-traordinary demand, in Canada, both for lumber and flour. This great de-mand, for fish and lumber, has been completely answered." For the British American forests producing timber in abundance, and "the population of these provinces being sufficiently numerous to bring it to market, (at least with the *assistance of the Americans*) the greatest demand for that article, therefore, which has ever occurred in the British colonies, has been abun-dantly answered." And he adds, "the late prohibitory laws of the United States have done a very essential service to the British American provinces, in putting an end to the absurd practice of alternately shutting and opening the ports of our West-Indian Islands to the Americans."

Imports into France and dependencies, in

	Livres.
Grain, fish, and bread stuffs, amounted to -	4,483,000
Boards, timber, staves, live stock, fish oil, peltry, pitch and tar, pot-ash, linseed, and tobacco, to	19,283,000
Manufactures introduced into the colonies, to -	547,000
Negroes, - - - - -	226,000

Livres, 24,539,000

or about $5,000,000.

Livres.

For three years preceding the French revolution, the average amount of imports from the United States, into France, alone, was estimated at - 9,600,000

or about $1,520,000.

And the exports from France to the United States, at, - - - - - 1,800,000

or about $360,000.*

The small amount of this trade, particularly of exports, disappointed the expectations of the French government, and Monsieur Arnould,† referring to this balance, against France, says—

" Voila donc pour France le *ne plus ultra* d'un commerce, dont l'espoir a pú contribuer, à faire sacrifier quelques centaines de millions, et plusieurs générations d'hommes."‡

In 1792, according to the foregoing estimate of the Secretary of State, our exports to France, and her dependencies, amounted to $4,698,735, and our imports to $2,068,348. What proportion of this trade was with France, or with her dependencies, does not appear, probably more than one half with the latter.

* Arthur Young's Travels in France.   † De la balance du commerce, 1791.

‡ Such was the utmost extent of a commerce, to secure which France sacrificed hundreds of millons of livres and vast numbers of men.

The articles of domestic produce, usually exported to France, are cotton, tobacco, rice, dried fish, whale and spermaceti oil, pot and pearl ashes, naval stores, &c. and those of foreign produce, during the war in Europe, have consisted principally of sugar and coffee, with some teas, cocoa, pepper, and other spices.

The principal articles imported were wines, brandies, silks, olive oil, and jewellery of all kinds.

The exports and imports, from 1795 to 1801, were as follows, viz. :—

	Exports. Dolls.	Imports. Dolls.
1795	7,698,683	3,671,331
1796	3,171,759	1,835,066
1797	3,825,231	3,045,796
1798	1,476,588	1,371,727
1799	- -	901,018
1800	40,400	74,228
1801	3,985,292	1,013,690

And the value of domestic and foreign produce, exported from 1804 to 1813, was—

	Domestic produce. Dolls.	Foreign produce. Dolls.
1804	3,219,112	5,604,942
1805	3,079,862	9,885,602
1806	3,226,698	8,197,694
1807	2,715,141	10,315,678
1808	708,670	2,126,396
1809	- -	- -
1810	16,782	1,672
1811	673,708	1,119,302
1812	402,803	2,435,218
1813	1,780,291	2,296,453

The quantity of wines and brandies, imported from France in 1802, 1803, 1804, and 1807, was as follows, viz. :—

		Wines. gallons.		Brandies. gallons.
1802	-	1,084,640	-	478,579
1803	-	337,534	-	1,039,222
1804	-	2,149,344	-	2,073,809
1807	-	3,185,923	-	2,867,584

The quantity of cotton exported to France, from 1800 to 1811, is contained in the preceding chapter.

The quantity of tobacco exported during the same period, was—

					Tobacco. hhds.
1800	-	-	-	-	143
1801	-	-	-	-	5,006
1802	-	-	-	-	16,216
1803	-	-	-	-	9,815
1804	-	-	-	-	14,623
1805	-	-	-	-	12,135
1806	-	-	-	-	9,182
1807	-	-	-	-	2,876
1808	-	-	-	-	566
1809	-	-	-	-	- -
1810	-	-	-	-	- -
1811	-	-	-	-	569

In some years before the commencement of our commercial restrictions, the value of exports of foreign produce to France was much greater than that of our domestic produce, and was principally in sugar and coffee. The quantity of each of these articles, shipped to France in 1807, is contained in the preceding chapter, and the quantity for each year, from 1800 to 1811, may be seen in the foregoing Tables.

TRADE WITH THE FRENCH WEST-INDIA ISLANDS.

France formerly possessed some of the most valuable islands in the West-Indies. The French part of St. Domingo is extremely fertile, and, before the troubles among the blacks, produced vast quantities of sugar and coffee. In 1786, the imports into France, from all her West-India Colonies, amounted to 174,831,000 livres, or about thirty-five millions of dollars; of this, the imports from St. Domingo alone amounted to 131,481,000 livres, or about twenty-six millions of dollars. No less than one hundred seventy-four million two hundred and twenty thousand pounds of sugar, and sixty-six million two hundred and thirty-one thousand pounds of coffee were imported into France from her West-India possessions in 1786; and this trade employed five hundred and sixty-nine ships of one hundred sixty-two thousand three hundred and eleven tons. On the 30th of August, 1784, the intercourse between the United States and the French West-Indies, was regulated by an arret of the French government.

American vessels, *of at least sixty tons*, were admitted into certain ports in the French West-India Islands, loaded with timber of all kinds, dye-woods, live stock, salt beef, (but not salt pork) salt fish, rice, legumes, raw or untanned hides, peltry, rosin, pitch and tar, and to dispose of their cargoes; and were allowed to bring away only rum and molasses, and goods brought from France, on paying the local duties, and one per cent. ad valorem, on all imports and exports. A further duty, however, of three livres was imposed upon every quintal (of 100 weight) of salt beef, cod, or other dried fish, in order to form a fund for premiums, to be given on cod and other fish from the French fisheries; but salt meat, from France, was not subject to this duty. The colonial legislatures, however, were authorized, in times of scarcity, to suspend the operation of this law. During the late wars in Europe, and the unsettled state of France, the French West-India Islands have been, generally, open to Americans for most articles either of export or import.

Before the French revolution, the national policy of France and Great-Britain was manifest, in their different regulations with respect to the trade between the United States and their West-India possessions; and whenever Europe, after her long and disastrous wars and revolutions, shall again find repose, and France shall regain (if ever she does regain) her West India Islands, both nations will, probably, return to the same system of measures. Great-Britain has already set the example.

With respect to exports from the United States, both nations admitted lumber of all kinds, live provisions, vegetables, rice, pitch, and tar, because neither could easily supply their islands with these articles. Great-Britain excluded American beef, pork, and dried fish. France admitted American beef and dried cod-fish, but subject to an additional duty of three livres on every quintal of each, to encourage her own fisheries. Great-Britain admitted flour, bread, biscuit, and all kinds of grain, while France excluded, by a general law, flour, and all kinds of grain, except indian corn.

With respect to imports from the islands, France allowed only rum and molasses, to be carried to the United States; while Great-Britain allowed not only rum and molasses to be carried, but sugar, coffee, cocoa nuts, ginger, and pimento ; the latter, however, confined the carriage both of the exports and imports to her own vessels, as a means of increasing her naval power, and the former, having few ships of her own, permitted the exports and imports in American vessels. The policy of Britain was to monopolize the *carriage* of the articles, that of France to monopolize the articles themselves.

Great-Britain was willing the United States should have their sugar and coffee, on condition that British ships might be the carriers; France, on the other hand, was willing American vessels should supply her sugar and coffee plantations, with certain productions which she was unable to furnish herself, but would not allow them to receive in return the most valuable productions of those plantations ; these she reserved for her own consumption at home, and to augment her own national wealth.

During the late wars between England and France, the latter was stripped of all her West-India Islands. The first restoration, however, of the Bourbons to the throne of France, was accompanied with the restoration of all the British conquests in this quarter of the world, with the exception of the small islands of Tobago and St. Lucie. What will be the future fate of the French West-Indies is now uncertain. The trade between the United States and the French islands was, for many years extensive, as well as profitable.

About the year 1786, the whole imports into these islands, from all foreign countries, amounted to 20,878,000 livres, and the exports to the same countries, to 14,132,000 livres; of the imports 13,065,000 were from the United States, which received in return 7,263,000 of the exports. The American tonnage employed in this trade, in the same year, was one hundred five thousand and ninety-five.

Since the French revolution in 1789, and since the late wars in Europe, and until the capture of these islands by the English, the American trade with them has increased.

The value of exports and imports of all kinds to and from these islands, from 1795 to 1801, was as follows, viz. :—

		Exports. Dolls.		Imports. Dolls.
1795	-	4,954,952	-	15,751,758
1796	-	8,408,946	-	15,743,774
1797	-	8,565,053	-	14,030,337
1798	-	5,344,690	-	15,380,091
1799	-	2,776,604	-	2,022,929
1800	-	5,123,433	-	9,385,111
1801	-	7,147,972	-	13,593,255

The value of the exports to the French West-Indies and American Colonies, from 1804 to 1807, was as follows, viz. :—

		Domestic produce. Dolls.		Foreign produce. Dolls.
1804	-	1,742,368	-	1,867,522
1805	-	2,876,384	-	4,455,599
1806	-	2,770,372	-	3,975,112
1807	-	2,901,516	-	2,968,816

About the year 1807, the whole of the French West-India Islands, (except St. Domingo, in the possession of the blacks) were in the possession of the English.

TRADE WITH SPAIN AND PORTUGAL AND THEIR DEPENDENCIES.

I. WITH SPAIN.

The exports of domestic produce to Spain have consisted, principally, of fish, flour, whale oil, rice, tobacco, &c. ; those of foreign produce, while she was engaged in the late wars in Europe, consisted of cocoa, coffee, sugar, pepper, and other spices. Our imports are principally brandies, wines, fruits of various kinds, salt, and of late years, sheep.

The exports and imports, from 1795 to 1801, were as follows, viz :—

		Exports. Value—dolls.		Imports. Value—dolls.
1795	-	2,252,754	-	1,232,844
1796	-	1,324,060	-	1,521,081
1797	-	1,612,558	-	1,333,056
1798	-	2,274,223	-	984,057
1799	-	4,237,954	-	2,576,988
1800	-	4,743,678	-	3,360,582
1801	-	2,865,101	-	2,876,974

From 1804 to 1813, the exports were—

		Domestic produce. Value—dolls.		Foreign produce. Value—dolls.
1804	-	2,304,193	-	597,143
1805	-	2,327,155	-	1,656,312
1806	-	1,363,273	-	1,758,954
1807	-	1,181,231	-	3,547,907
1808	-	541,378	-	901,003
1809	-	1,289,220	-	1,290,003
1810	-	3,488,951	-	1,218,601
1811	-	3,963,263	-	297,454
1812	-	4,567,754	-	140,711
1813	-	6,532,101	-	40,905

The quantity of wines and brandies imported, in 1802, 1803, 1804, and in 1807, was as follows :—

		Wines.		Brandies.
		Gallons.		Gallons.
1802	-	955,557	•	518,918
1803	-	790,561	•	681,851
1804	-	786,005	•	850,654
1807	-	693,056	•	548,934

The great increase of our exports of domestic produce to Spain, since 1809, was occasioned, as we have before stated, by the invasion of that country by Bonaparte, and the great demand for our grain and provisions, to support the allied armies.

II. WITH THE SPANISH WEST-INDIES AND AMERICAN COLONIES.

During the late European wars, our trade with the Spanish West-Indies and American Colonies greatly increased. We were the carriers of the rich products of the Spanish islands, and we also supplied them, to a great extent, with the manufactures of Europe. The amount and increase of this trade, from 1795 to 1801, will appear from the following amount of exports and imports during that period :—

		Exports.		Imports.
		Value—dolls.		Value—dolls.
1795	-	1,389,219	•	1,739,138
1796	-	1,821,347	-	1,718,026
1797	•	3,595,519	-	4,123,362
1798	-	5,082,127	•	8,139,169
1799	-	8,993,401	-	10,974,295
1800	-	8,270,400	-	10,587,566
1801	•	8,437,659	-	12,799,878

The exports of domestic and foreign produce to the Spanish West-Indies and American Colonies, from 1804 to 1813, were as follows :*—

	Domestic produce. Value—dolls.		Foreign produce. Value—dolls.
1804	1,725,662	-	1,176,998
1805	2,806,112	-	4,884,776
1806	2,391,172	-	8,476,061
1807	2,470,472	-	9,870,753
1808	631,086	-	3,545,967
1809	3,352,271	-	3,333,346
1810	3,182,318	-	3,604,791
1811	3,606,510	-	3,973,099
1812	2,640,502	-	1,331,636
1813	2,809,705	-	183,549

What will hereafter be our commercial situation with Spain and her Colonies, it is difficult at present to determine.

We have disputes with that country, yet unsettled, particularly with respect to former spoliations on our commerce, and with respect to the Floridas, and the western boundaries of Louisiana. It is of no small importance to the United States, that those disputes should be adjusted, and that a good understanding and free commercial intercourse should subsist between them and the Spanish West-Indies and American possessions. It is from this quarter that the United States obtain large quantities of the precious metals, by which they are enabled to carry on a trade with China and the East-Indies, as well as to pay the balances due, in Europe and elsewhere. The jealousy of the Spanish government has hitherto excluded foreigners, from much

* We would here remark, that the accounts of our trade with the West-India Islands belonging to Spain, as well as to the other European nations, are taken from the custom-house books, which shew the destination of the articles exported, from the clearance of the vessels : as, however, vessels often go to other ports, or islands, than those for which they have cleared, and as some vessels take clearances for the West-Indies, generally, the accounts cannot be considered perfectly accurate.

intercourse with their South-American Colonies, and prevented them from obtaining much information, relative to the interior of that part of the world. The late travels, however, of Baron Humboldt, through the different parts of South-America, and of New-Spain, afford much valuable information as to the population, wealth, and resources of those extensive countries ; and it is hoped, that, whether these Provinces continue dependent on old Spain, or become independent, a more liberal and enlightened policy will be pursued by them, in their intercourse with foreign nations ; and that the United States will not fail to pursue their true interest in cultivating a good understanding with them.

II. PORTUGAL.

To Portugal and the Island of Madeira, we usually export wheat, flour, corn, rice, dried fish, some whale oil, soap, and staves and heading ; and we import from thence, principally, wines, fruit, and salt. Since the invasion of Portugal by the French, our exports of flour to that country have been very great, as we have before stated.

The value of the exports and imports from 1795 to 1801, was as follows :—

		Exports. Dolls.		Imports. Dolls.
1795	-	594,801	-	1,032,339
1796	-	142,567	-	1,298,832
1797	-	229,750	-	1,338,877
1798	-	286,781	-	918,443
1799	-	538,662	-	962,909
1800	-	448,548	-	787,037
1801	-	1,139,377	-	645,111

The following is the value of the exports to and imports from the. Island of Madeira, for the same period :—

		Exports.		Imports.
		Dolls.		Dolls.
1795	-	133,476	-	917,260
1796	-	213,785	-	562,682
1797	-	191,627	-	662,248
1798	-	333,425	-	334,122
1799	-	203,185	-	163,870
1800	-	522,728	-	375,219
1801	-	528,344	-	514,791

The exports to Portugal from 1804 to 1813, were—

		Domestic produce.		Foreign produce.
		Value—dolls.		Value—dolls.
1804	-	1,282,169	-	190,716
1805	-	508,284	-	851,647
1806	-	920,841	-	857,050
1807	-	829,313	-	159,173
1808	-	342,277	-	-
1809	-	1,629,709	-	151,426
1810	-	2,664,121	-	121,578
1811	-	8,445,827	-	130,726
1812	-	7,729,997	-	45,043
1813	-	9,992,012	-	7,275

During the continuance of the American non-intercourse acts, there were shipped to Madeira, Fayal, and the other Azores, various articles ultimately destined to Great-Britain, and other parts of Europe. In 1809, the value of domestic produce, principally cotton, shipped to Madeira, was $2,336,656, and to Fayal and the other Azores, $2,926,482.

Since the removal of the Portuguese government to the Brazils, our trade with Portuguese America has increased. In 1807, we exported to the Brazils, and the other Portuguese American Colonies, to the value of about five thousand dollars.

From 1809 to 1812, the value of exports to those countries was as follows :—

		Domestic produce. Value—dolls.		Foreign produce. Value—dolls.
1809	-	540,653	-	343,082
1810	-	721,899	-	889,839
1811	-	621,417	-	1,027,931
1812	-	426,982	-	319,641

TRADE WITH RUSSIA, SWEDEN, DENMARK, HAMBURGH, AND THE NORTH OF EUROPE.

With Russia, the trade of the United States has been increasing for some years, and the importance of that country, in a commercial as well as political point of view, has lately induced the government of the United States to send a minister plenipotentiary to the Russian court, and to receive from them a minister of equal grade. Until lately, the amount of our exports to Russia has been very small, though our imports were considerable.

From 1795 to 1801, the value of exports and imports has been thus estimated :—

		Exports. Value—dolls.		Imports. Value—dolls.
1795	-	69,221	-	1,168,715
1796	-	47,381	-	1,382,978
1797	-	3,450	-	1,418,418
1798	-	60,030	-	1,067,152
1799	-	46,030	-	1,274,913
1800	-	-	-	1,524,995
1801	-	9,136	-	1,672,059

From 1805 to 1813, the value of domestic and foreign articles exported to Russia, was as follows :—

		Domestic. Dolls.		Foreign. Dolls.
1805	-	12,044	-	59,328
1806	-	3,580	-	8,827
1807	-	78,850	-	366,367
1808	-	-	-	-
1809	-	146,462	-	737,799
1810	-	1,048,762	-	2,926,936
1811	-	1,630,499	-	4,507,158
1812	-	156,980	-	1,586,617
1813	-	50,400	-	750

The principal article of domestic produce exported to this country in 1809, 1810, and 1811, was cotton ; very little, if any, of which was, prior to this period, ever exported to that country. In 1809, six hundred twenty-five thousand one hundred and twelve pounds, in 1810, three million seven hundred sixty-nine thousand one hundred and thirty-seven pounds, and in 1811, no less than nine millions three hundred sixty-eight thousand eight hundred and thirty-nine pounds of cotton, were shipped to Russia. In 1810, there were also shipped to Russia, from the United States, five thousand two hundred and seventy pounds of rice, one thousand four hundred and sixty-two hogsheads of tobacco, four thousand five hundred and thirty-six gallons of spirits from grain, and one hundred twenty-four thousand one hundred and forty-eight gallons of spirits from molasses. The principal articles of foreign produce exported to Russia have been sugar and coffee, with some pepper, tea, and cocoa.

The following is the quantity of those articles, shipped in the years 1809, 1810, and 1811.

	Coffee.	Sugar brown.	Sugar claved, and white.	Pepper.	Cocoa.	Teas.
	lbs.	lbs.	lbs.	lbs.	lbs.	lbs.
1809 -	1,283,100 -	1,271,180 -	922,077 -	138,333 -	-	- 40,216
1810 -	4,048,909 -	6,139,529 -	5,257,366 -	1,252,085 -	80,005 -	17,011
1811 -	5,113,891 -	4,408,289 -	10,200,139 -	369,409 -	446,734 -	254,570

The articles usually imported from Russia are iron, hemp, cordage, duck, and various kinds of cloth made of hemp and flax, such as drillings, diapers, broad and narrow tickings, sheetings, &c. Table No. XI. taken from Russian accounts,* contains the quantity of the various articles exported from St. Petersburgh, to the United States, from the year 1783 to 1805, together with the number of American ships employed in the trade with that port in each year, and shews the progressive increase of the American trade with that country during that period.

The average amount of goods, paying duties according to their value, and which included iron, and all goods made of hemp, or flax, during the years 1802, 1803, and 1804, was $1,302,217. In 1807, 1810, and 1811, the amount of goods paying the same duties, was as follows :—

					Dolls.
1807	-	-	-	-	1,804,860
1810	-	-	-	-	1,587,784
1811	-	-	-	-	3,049,033

The average quantity of hemp exported from Russia, in the years 1802, 1803, and 1804, was eighty-eight thousand eight hundred and thirty hundred weight, the average value of which was $779,473. The quantity of hemp, cordage tarred and untarred, and cables, imported during the years 1807, 1810, and 1811, was as follows, viz. :—

		Hemp.		Cordage tar'd.	Cordage untar'd.		Cables.
		cwt.		lbs.	lbs.		lbs.
1807	-	135,775	-	1,007,780	6,843	-	57,579
1810	-	53,148	-	137,304	-	-	30,469
1811	-	205,853	-	589,944	34,806	-	108,685

Our trade with Russia, in the year 1811, was much greater than in any preceding year; the ships which carried out large quantities

* See Oddy's European Commerce, page 125, vol. 1.

of cotton and colonial produce, during that and the preceding year, returned largely freighted with iron, hemp, and cordage.

In the articles of iron and hemp, particularly the latter, the United States may soon be independent of Russia, and all other countries. The culture of hemp has succeeded in many parts of the United States, and particularly in the state of Kentucky. In 1810, that state alone produced one hundred fifteen thousand and one hundred hundred weight of hemp, valued at $690,600, and made also, in the same year, thirty-nine thousand eight hundred and seventy hundred weight of cordage, valued at $398,400, making more than a million of dollars for those two articles.

SWEDEN.

With Sweden, the ordinary trade of the United States has been inconsiderable. The average amount of exports to that country, from 1795 to 1801, was about sixty thousand dollars, and the average value of the imports, during the same period, did not exceed eighty thousand.

Tobacco, and some other articles of domestic and foreign produce, are shipped to Sweden, for which iron is the principal article received in return. While all intercourse with Great-Britain and France was prohibited, the nominal trade with that country was far from being inconsiderable. In 1809, the value of domestic produce, principally cotton and tobacco, shipped or rather cleared for Swedish ports, was $4,030,395, and the value of foreign produce, $1,409,303; and in 1810, the value of the former, cleared for the same ports, was $1,563,336, and the value of the latter, $4,294,397. The cotton was probably destined to Great-Britain, and the colonial produce, principally to the northern parts of Europe.

SWEDISH WEST-INDIES.

With the Swedish West-Indies, our trade has been considerable. From 1795 to 1801, the annual amount of our exports to these islands was about $685,000, and the value of the imports, during the same period, was about $500,000. Some proportion of the exports was probably destined to the other West-India islands. In 1807, domestic produce shipped to the Swedish West-Indies amounted to $416,509, and foreign produce, to $911,155; and the same year, there were imported from these islands into the United States, ninety-two thousand eight hundred and fifty-eight gallons of rum, thirty thousand seven hundred and sixty-four gallons of molasses, two millions seven hundred and fifty-two thousand four hundred and twelve pounds of sugar, and one million seven hundred and five thousand six hundred and seventy pounds of coffee.

In 1809, 1810, 1811, and 1812, the exports to these islands, was—

	Domestic produce. Value—dolls.		Foreign produce. Value—dolls.
1809	-	2,757,859	-	887,960
1810	-	1,619,442	-	424,826
1811	-	884,417	-	151,926
1812	-	1,060,500	-	126,274

The quantity of rum, molasses, sugar, and coffee, imported from the same, according to our custom-house books, in 1810 and 1811, was as follows :—

	Rum. Gallons.	Molasses. Gallons.	Coffee. Pounds.	Sugar. Pounds.
1810	1,504,938	1,581,210	2,425,216	4,098,961
1811	1,156,789	1,384,297	1,315,180	6,054,032

The greatest part of the rum and molasses, no doubt, came from the British West-India islands during these years, through these Swedish neutral ports.

DENMARK AND NORWAY.

With Denmark and Norway, the American trade has been greater than with Sweden. The average value of exports to those countries, from 1795 to 1801, was about $600,000, and the average value of imports, for the same period, about $400,000.

During the years 1805, 1806, and 1807, the exports were—

		Domestic produce. Value—dolls.		Foreign produce. Value—dolls.
1805	-	435,926	-	1,481,767
1806	-	356,595	-	1,052,954
1807	-	572,150	-	836,468

In the years 1809 and 1810, in consequence of commercial restrictions with England and France, and the possession of Hamburgh by the French, great quantities of cotton and tobacco, and of colonial produce, were cleared from the United States for the ports of Denmark and Norway, though destined to other places. Indeed our customhouse books furnish but little evidence of the amount of our trade with particular countries, during these two years, as the following account of our exports to Denmark and Norway, taken from the clearances of the vessels, will shew—

		Domestic produce. Value—dolls.		Foreign produce. Value—dolls.
1809	-	958,584	-	3,327,766
1810	-	3,962,739	-	6,548,051

The following quantities of cotton, tobacco, sugar, and coffee, were cleared for these countries, in these two years.

	Cotton. lbs.	Tobacco. Hhds.	Sugar. lbs.	Coffee. lbs.
1809	2,298,827	5,950	11,371,567	7,953,461
1810	14,594,124	18,797	17,470,322	14,120,990

DANISH WEST-INDIES.

The extent of American trade with the Danish West-India Islands has been much greater, than with Denmark itself.

The following is the amount of exports and imports from 1795 to 1801 :—

	Exports. Dolls.		Imports. Dolls.
1795	-	1,659,306	-	2,329,273
1796	-	2,553,810	-	2,818,746
1797	-	2,453,606	-	2,416,088
1798	-	1,513,104	-	1,117,321
1799	-	3,397,262	-	2,139,870
1800	-	1,757,589	-	999,770
1801	-	1,049,361	-	3,035,511

From 1804 to 1807, the value of the exports to those islands was—

	Domestic produce. Dolls.		Foreign produce. Dolls.
1804	-	1,081,618	-	642,388
1805	-	1,523,106	-	575,149
1806	-	1,410,029	-	1,380,380
1807	-	1,614,711	-	1,505,988

HAMBURG AND BREMEN.

The trade of the United States with Hamburg and Bremen, during the late wars in Europe, and until those cities were occupied by the French armies, and became a prey to French rapacity, was very great, especially with the former, in articles of Colonial produce. The imperial city of Hamburg has long been the great depot of the extensive commerce of Germany, and the North of Europe. By means of the rivers Elbe and Weser, and other waters connected with them, the manufactures of Germany, particularly her linens, are brought to Hamburg, and from thence exported to the United States, and other parts of the world. Through this city, also, the rich products of the East and West-Indies have been introduced into Germany, and the interior of the continent of Europe. The principal articles of domestic produce, usually shipped to Hamburg and Bremen from the United States, are tobacco, rice, cotton, spirits from molasses, some whale oil, and pot and pearl ashes. And the articles of foreign produce have been sugar, coffee, teas, cocoa, pepper, and other spices.

The extent and value of American trade with these cities, in domestic and foreign articles, from 1795 to 1801, may be seen, from the following estimate of exports and imports, during that period.—

		Exports. Value—dolls.		Imports. Value—dolls.
1795	-	9,218,540	-	1,584,524
1796	-	9,471,498	-	2,167,390
1797	-	11,953,017	-	2,755,677
1798	-	14,534,339	-	3,738,763
1799	-	17,144,400	-	6,919,425
1800	-	8,012,846	-	4,996,886
1801	-	10,463,738	-	4,585,256

The exports to Hamburg, Bremen, other Hanse towns, and ports of Germany, but principally to Hamburg, from 1802 to 1810, were as follows :—

		Domestic produce. Value—dolls.		Foreign produce. Value—dolls.
1802	-	1,157,272	-	5,072,220
1803	-	1,368,295	-	1,911,437
1804	-	949,454	-	3,525,553
1805	-	893,591	-	2,338,917
1806	-	1,672,455	-	4,751,769
1807	-	912,225	-	2,248,057
1808	-	24,963	-	204,852
1809	-	709,981	-	1,682,662
1810	-	834,564	-	291,818

HOLLAND AND DEPENDENCIES.

The United States had great commercial intercourse with Holland, until the commencement of their restrictive measures. Although Bonaparte had given the Hollanders his brother Louis, for a king, that he might have them more completely under his control, and compel them to enforce his continental system, yet so strong were the commercial habits of the people of Holland, that means were found to evade the imperial mandates ; and the continental system, during the reign of Louis, was never carried into complete effect in that country. And notwithstanding the many vexations and spoliations, which American commerce experienced from the belligerent powers, yet it was extensive and profitable, not only with Holland, but with the rest of the world, until interrupted by commercial prohibitions.

The extent of our trade with Holland will appear from the following statement of exports and imports at different periods.—

The exports and imports from 1795 to 1801, were as follows :—

	Exports. Value—dolls.	Imports. Value—dolls
1795	1,917,336	1,329,952
1796	6,083,491	943,227
1797	7,713,976	2,404,828
1798	4,713,976	1,757,371
1799	696,968	662,590
1800	4,372,964	775,541
1801	6,234,450	2,529,128

And from 1804 to 1813, the following were the exports of domestic and foreign produce :—

	Domestic. Value—dolls.	Foreign. Value—dolls,
1804	2,064,158	11,757,002
1805	1,783,503	14,959,380
1806	3,609,964	15,051,665
1807	3,098,234	13,086,160
1808	382,121	2,227,722
1809	421,294	697,070
1810	74,194	28,992
1811	- -	- -
1812	30,747	- -
1813	29,160	- -

The articles of domestic produce usually exported to Holland, are tobacco, rice, cotton, some whale oil, pot and pearl ashes, and spirits from molasses. The principal articles have been tobacco, rice, and cotton.

The following is an account of the quantities shipped to this country in the years 1806 and 1807, together with their value, as estimated at the place of exportation :—

	Tobacco.	Value.	Rice.	Value.	Cotton.	Value.
	hhds.	dolls.	tierces.	dolls.	lbs.	dolls.
1806 -	29,851 -	2,358,229 -	17,137 -	457,993 -	3,129,146 -	688,412
1807 -	20,444 -	1,799,072 -	21,163 -	529,075 -	3,146,209 -	660,703

The articles of foreign produce have been, principally, coffee, sugar, tea, and pepper.

The following quantities of sugar and coffee were shipped to Holland, according to the custom-house books, from 1800 to 1810 :—

	Sugar, brown.	Sugar, white & clayed.	Coffee.
	pounds.	pounds.	pounds.
1800 -	7,542,160 -	- - -	11,618,970
1801 -	14,560,993 -	- - -	13,125,837
1802 -	15,436,179 -	- - -	9,320,937
1803 -	8,894,432 -	1,057,806 -	2,323,902
1804 -	27,294,509 -	7,663,882 -	26,082,432
1805 -	47,544,197 -	8,455,435 -	23,694,991
1806 -	56,008,790 -	10,105,151 -	21,833,438
1807 -	48,012,198 -	8,719,529 -	19,900,965
1808 -	8,215,969 -	1,824,479 -	3,487,872
1809 -	3,167,202 -	836,459 -	957,122
1810 -	88,590 -	76,674 -	44,618

The imports have usually consisted of woollen, linen, and other goods paying duties according to their value, spirits from grain, some nails and spikes, lead, and manufactures of lead, paints, steel, cheese, glass, anchors, shot, slit and hoop iron. The average amount of goods paying duties ad valorem for the years 1802, 1803 and 1804, was $1,110,354, and in 1807, was $1,881,741. The average quantity of gin imported, during the same three years, was one million fifty-nine thousand five hundred and forty gallons, and in 1807, was one million four hundred sixty-six thousand gallons. In our trade with Holland, the exports have generally far exceeded the imports ; the balance has been usually paid, in bills of exchange on England, and other parts of Europe.

DUTCH WEST-INDIES AND AMERICAN COLONIES, AND DUTCH EAST-INDIES.

The extent and value of the commercial intercourse of the United States with the Dutch West-Indies and American Colonies, may be estimated from the following account of exports and imports.

From 1795 to 1801, the exports and imports were—

		Exports. Value—dolls.		Imports. Value—dolls
1795	-	962,705	-	2,342,957
1796	-	1,758,548	-	3,703,787
1797	-	1,903,638	-	2,178,426
1798	-	2,720,969	-	2,475,494
1799	-	5,154,535	-	3,929,101
1800	-	1,296,052	-	2,800,766
1801	-	625,791	-	1,987,612

Exports to the same countries, from 1804 to 1810, were—

		Domestic produce. Value—dolls.		Foreign produce. Value—dolls.
1804	-	1,600,667	-	848,365
1805	-	454,645	-	138,785
1806	-	570,545	-	466,485
1807	-	496,010	-	307,366

		Domestic produce. Value—dolls.		Foreign produce. Value—dolls.
1808	-	97,734	-	14,839
1809	-	33,412	-	771
1810	-	39,724	-	31

From the Dutch East-Indies, we have imported large quantities of coffee, sugar, pepper, and other spices, and have generally paid for them, in money, or in cargoes shipped from Europe, or in bills of exchange. The late wars in Europe, in which the Dutch were unfortunately compelled to engage, threw this trade into the hands of the American merchant, and its progressive increase will appear from the following estimate of imports from 1795 to 1801—

					Imports. Value—dolls.
1795	-	-	-	-	26,706
1796	-	..	-	-	211,626
1797	-	-	-	-	1,029,995
1798	-	-	-	-	2,305,344
1799	-	-	-	-	1,446,335
1800	-	-	-	-	3,556,320
1801	-	-	-	-	4,430,733

In 1802, the quantity of coffee imported from the Dutch East-Indies, and Cape of Good Hope, was six million eight hundred twenty-five thousand two hundred and three pounds, and valued at $1,706,300, in 1804 was eight million three hundred ninety-five thousand seven hundred and eighty-three pounds, and valued at $2,098,945, and in 1807, was eight million eight hundred forty-two thousand five hundred and sixty-eight pounds. The quantity of pepper imported in 1802, was five million two hundred seventy-five thousand nine hundred and thirty-seven pounds, in 1804, four million nine hundred forty-six thousand two hundred and eighty-four pounds, and in 1807, two million five hundred eight thousand eight hundred and ninety-seven pounds. A considerable proportion of the pepper is procured by the Americans, directly from the natives of the islands.

ITALY.

The trade of the United States with Italy has consisted principally in carrying dried fish, sugar, coffee, pepper, and cocoa, and in bringing from thence, silks, wines, brandies, fruit, some lead, and cheese. The amount and increase of this commercial intercourse will be seen, from the following estimate of the exports and imports from 1795 to 1801, and of the exports from 1804 to 1813.

	Exports. Value—dolls.	Imports. Value—dolls.
1795	- - 1,223,150	- - 319,653
1796	- - 1,100,522	- - 268,237
1797	- - 767,064	- - 852,408
1798	- - 1,334,036	- - 724,209
1799	- - 1,157,212	- - 753,484
1800	- - 2,689,908	- - 1,104,833
1801	- - 2,090,439	- - 902,406

Exports from 1804 to 1813.

	Domestic produce. Value—dolls.	Foreign produce. Value—dolls.
1804	- 118,441	- 1,552,708
1805	- 142,475	- 2,320,099
1806	- 185,346	- 4,587,727
1807	- 250,257	- 5,499,722
1808	- 58,085	- 1,312,173
1809	- 49,206	- 1,106,539
1810	- 71,803	- 656,691
1811	- 151,555	- 437,381
1812	- 139,928	- 134,794
1813	- 1,947	-

CHINA AND THE NORTH-WEST COAST OF AMERICA.

The trade of the United States with China commenced soon after the close of the revolutionary war. The first American vessel, that went on a trading voyage to China, sailed from the port of New-York, on the 22d day of February 1784, and returned on the 11th of May 1785. She was three hundred and sixty tons burthen, commanded by Captain John Green, and Samuel Shaw, Esq. agent for the owners. The Americans were well received by the Chinese government, and since that time, our trade with China has greatly increased.

In 1789, there were fifteen American vessels at Canton,* being a greater number, than from any other nation, except Great-Britain. For many years, we have imported more Chinese goods, than were wanted for our consumption, and which we have again exported to other countries. The principal articles imported, are teas, silks, nankeens, and China ware. Of these, tea is of the greatest value. The quantity of this article, imported and consumed within the United States, has increased with the increase of population. The following is a statement of the quantities of the several species of tea, paying duties, after deducting the exportations from the importations, for each of the years from 1790 to 1800.

It may be observed, that as some tea might have been exported without the benefit of drawback, the whole may not have been consumed in the United States, but the difference cannot be great, as it is believed, that most of the tea exported had the benefit of the drawback.

TEAS.

	Bohea.	Souchong.	Hyson.	Other green.	Total.
	lbs.	lbs.	lbs.	lbs.	lbs.
1790	2,059,684	368,075	530,613	88,870	3,047,242
1791	774,008	91,123	107,934	12,932	985,997
1792	2,332,8 2	132,355	115,263	33,498	2,614,008
1793	1,548,993	369,687	82,882	8,007	2,009,509
1794	2,095,416	298,503	29,754	37,241	2,460,914

* Macpherson's Annals.

	Bohea. lbs.	Souchong. lbs.	Hyson. lbs.	Other green. lbs.	Total. lbs.
1795	2,079,687	146,457	99,727	48,247	2,374,118
1796	1,778,007	73,578	239,102	219,572	2,310,259
1797	1,392,271	185,359	206,177	224,592	2,008,399
1798	1,079,139	333,349	194,616	283,861	1,890,965
1799	3,412,674	309,598	240,861	538,370	4,501,503
1800	1,891,434	694,802	533,613	677,785	3,797,634
Total,	20,444,145	3,002,806	2,380,542	2,172,975	28,000,548

Making in the whole for eleven years, twenty-eight million five hundred and forty-eight pounds, consumed in the United States, being on an average of these years, two million five hundred forty-five thousand five hundred and four pounds a year.

The following quantity of teas of all kinds was imported and exported from 1801 to 1812, viz. :—

		Imported. lbs.		Exported. lbs.		Consumed. lbs.
1801	-	4,086,960	-	1,409,253	-	2,677,707
1802	-	4,269,828	-	1,894,538	-	2,375,290
1803	-	6,053,529	-	3,146,492	-	2,907,037
1804	-	3,622,828	-	1,219,233	-	2,403,595
1805	-	5,119,441	-	1,788,888	-	3,330,553
1806	-	6,870,806	-	2,002,207	-	4,868,599
1807	-	8,108,774	-	2,663,061	-	5,445,713
1808	-	4,812,638	-	237,883	-	4,574,755
1809	-	1,482,990	-	1,770,616	-	- -
1810	-	7,839,457	-	1,337,732	-	6,501,725
1811	-	3,018,118	-	1,025,962	-	1,992,156
1812	-	3,056,089	-	519,262	-	2,536,827

Making an average consumption for these twelve years of three million two hundred seventy-seven thousand one hundred and ninety-four pounds a year.

The value of goods paying duties ad valorem, which includes nankeens, all silk and cotton goods, and China ware, imported in 1797, from China and the East-Indies generally, but principally from the former, amounted to $922,161. The average value of goods paying the same duties, from China and other native Asiatic powers during the years 1802, 1803, and 1804, was about two millions three hundred thousand dollars.

From 1805 to 1813, the value of the same goods was as follows, viz. :—

				Value—dollars.
1805	-	-	-	1,802,945
1806	-	-	-	2,190,454
1807	-	-	-	1,821,321
1808	-	-	-	2,663,540
1809	-	-	-	533,929
1810	-	-	-	3,374,850
1811	-	-	-	2,889,642
1812	-	-	-	1,861,013
1813	-	-	-	566,676

The balance of trade with China, as it appears on the custom-house books, is much against the United States; as few articles, either domestic or foreign, are shipped *directly* from the United States to that country. The payments for Chinese goods have been generally made in specie, the exportation of which is not entered at the custom-house, or in seal skins, taken in the South Seas, and furs procured on the North-West Coast of America, and carried from those places, directly to China, without being brought to the United States. The amount of specie exported to China, it is difficult to ascertain, with precision. From information, however, derived from well informed merchants concerned in the trade, and from the value of imports, it cannot for some years past have been less, (except during the late war) than between two and three millions annually. The amount of trade in seal skins and furs, it is much more difficult to ascertain. The great prices obtained at Canton, for furs procured on the North-

West Coast of America, by those who were with Captain Cook, in his last voyage of discovery, induced others to engage in this trade. The enterprise of the Americans led them very early to engage in these long and hazardous trading voyages. The first of the kind undertaken from the United States, was from Boston in 1788, in a ship commanded by Captain Kendrick. This trade, at first, afforded great profits, to the concerned, and it has, ever since the year 1788, been carried on from the United States, to a considerable extent, and with greater or less profit. The furs are purchased from the Indians, many hundred miles along the coast, principally with articles of foreign merchandize, suited to the wants of the natives of that country. In 1800, the value of goods shipped to the North-West Coast, and to the South Seas, was $827,748 ; a part of these were undoubtedly destined to the Spanish settlements on the Pacific Ocean. Not only has the North-West Coast been explored, by the enterprise of the Americans for furs, but every island in the South Seas, and every part of the continent of South-America, has been visited, in search of seal skins for the same market. These sealing voyages were also, at first, very profitable, and induced many others to engage in them. The business, however, was overdone—the seal, in a few years, became so scarce, as not to be worth the pursuit. The value of this trade, in furs and seal skins, has been many millions to the United States.

TABLE No. I.

Value of Imports in each year, from 1795 to 1801.

	1795.	1796.	1797.	1798.	1799.	1800.	1801.
	Dolls.	Dolls.	Dolls.	Dolls.	Dolls.	Dolls.	Dolls.
Russia,	1,168,715	1,382,978	1,418,418	1,067,152	2,274,913	1,524,995	1,672,059
Prussia,	-	-	8,732	-	39,013	355,757	57,225
Sweden,	48,982	59,852	134,983	44,496	153,445	24,089	93,205
Swedish West-Indies,	622,514	691,471	545,895	274,747	409,054	450,567	452,035
	671,496	751,323	680,878	319,243	562,499	474,656	545,035
Denmark and Norway,	285,176	465,041	343,428	225,885	802,069	376,739	400,858
Danish West-Indies,	2,329,273	2,818,746	2,416,088	1,117,321	2,139,870	999,770	3,035,511
	2,614,449	3,283,787	2,759,516	1,343,206	2,941,939	1,376,50	5,436,369
United Netherlands,	1,329,952	943,227	2,404,828	1,757,371	662,590	775,541	2,529,128
Dutch West-Indies,	2,342,957	3,703,081	2,178,426	2,475,494	3,929,101	2,800,766	1,987,612
Dutch East-Indies,	26,706	211,626	1,029,995	2,305,344	1,446,335	3,556,3	1,452,733
	3,699,615	4,857,934	5,613,249	6,538,209	6,038,026	7,132,627	8,949,473

TABLE No. I.—CONTINUED.

	1795. Dolls.	1796. Dolls.	1797. Dolls.	1798. Dolls.	1799. Dolls.	1800. Dolls.	1801. Dolls.
England, Man and Berwick,	21,108,350	28,689,939	24,464,911	15,068,012	25,870,773	29,579,426	34,326,466
Guernsey, Jersey, Sark, &c.	16,530	4,378	55,688	55,609	25,922	144,357	120,588
Scotland,	678,213	1,241,385	1,501,481	1,748,600	2,077,940	2,624,041	3,967,457
Ireland,	1,510,028	1,992,983	1,280,987	456,549	1,158,584	529,235	1,104,707
Gibraltar,	150,501	127,972	120,371	225,397	225,084	157,882	15,825
British African Ports,	36,148	54,271	37,417	29,025	10,111	-	14,140
Cape of Good-Hope,	-	-	9,441	7,676	13,293	-	18,185
British East-Indies,	742,523	2,427,717	1,764,290	2,977,324	1,521,213	3,391,027	5,134,456
British West-Indies,	6,426,091	6,301,534	3,045,045	2,925,739	6,083,372	5,774,411	6,968,321
Newfoundland and fisheries,	6,540	10,356	21,714	41,777	18,176	37,184	115,892
British American Colonies,	297,291	276,810	319,298	215,533	207,451	340,027	427,495
	30,972,215	41,127,345	32,620,643	23,753,241	37,211,919	42,577,590	52,213,522
Germany,	78,909	9,096	-	-	9,086	2,089	101,507
Hamburg, Bremen, &c.	1,584,524	2,167,390	2,755,677	3,738,763	6,919,425	4,996,886	4,585,250
France,	3,671,331	1,835,066	3,045,796	1,371,727	901,018	74,228	1,013,690
French West-Indies,	15,751,758	15,743,774	14,030,337	15,380,091	2,022,929	9,335,111	13,593,255
Bourbon and Mauritius,	804,928	1,464,174	996,794	1,116,284	262,221	234,984	-
	20,228,017	19,043,014	18,072,927	17,868,102	3,186,168	9,644,323	14,606,945

TABLE No. I.—continued.

	1795. Dolls.	1796. Dolls.	1797. Dolls.	1798. Dolls.	1799. Dolls.	1800. Dolls.	1801. Dolls.
Spain,	1,232,844	1,521,081	1,333,056	984,057	2,576,988	3,360,582	2,876,974
Teneriffe, and other Canaries,	307,369	380,713	205,817	72,962	199,225	217,048	320,288
Honduras, Campeachy, &c.	5,653	1,384	977	1,766	15,740	83,741	75,664
Manilla and Phillippines,	61,150	-	232,674	-	24,329	142,969	351,011
Spanish West-Indies,	1,739,138	1,718,026	4,123,362	8,139,169	10,974,295	10,587,566	12,799,878
Florida and Louisiana,	593,351	219,522	139,535	211,904	507,132	904,322	956,635
Other American Colonies,	2,940	22,640	26,590	37,632	182,220	775,690	859,864
	3,942,445	3,863,366	6,062,011	9,447,490	14,479,929	16,071,918	18,240,314
Portugal,	1,032,339	1,298,832	1,338,877	918,443	962,909	787,037	645,111
Madeira,	917,260	562,682	662,248	334,112	163,870	375,219	514,791
Fayal and other Azores,	117,377	52,137	40,109	56,708	79,448	45,004	78,290
Cape de Verd Islands,	156,801	206,258	97,071	112,003	108,757	88,476	177,793
Coast of Brazil,	-	8,417	-	80	-	-	2,449
	2,223,777	2,128,326	2,138,305	1,421,346	1,314,984	1,295,736	1,418,434
Italy,	319,653	268,237	852,408	726,209	753,484	1,104,833	902,406
Africa, (generally)	87	- 49,990	609	-	219	10,988	19,465
China and East-Indies, do.	1,144,103	2,459,410	2,319,964	2,309,304	3,219,262	4,613,463	4,558,356
West-Indies, do.	85,186	13,050	52,898	16,873	101,397	26,937	4,711
Europe, do.	1,023,068	30,918	23,171	2,562	16,825	20,160	34,146
N. West Coast and South Seas,	-	-	-	-	-	23,441	18,079
Total,	69,756,258	81,436,164	75,379,406	68,551,700	79,069,148	91,252,768	111,363,511

TABLE No. II.

Value of Exports in each year from 1795 to 1802.

	1795.	1796.	1797.	1798.	1799.	1800.	1801.	1802.
	Dolls.	Dolls.	Dolls.	Dolls.	Dolls.	Dolls.	Dolls.	Dolls.
Russia,	69,221	47,381	3,450	60,030	46,330	-	9,136	73,721
Prussia,	-	-	-	-	617,046	24,884	120,238	150,920
Sweden,	23,564	17,620	-	101,657	104,071	91,342	39,176	13,037
Swedish West-Indies,	871,288	1,078,787	922,673	631,805	629,526	471,343	193,032	262,219
	894,852	1,096,407	922,673	733,462	733,597	562,685	232,208	275,256
Denmark and Norway,	302,955	421,779	183,703	1,400,258	951,577	356,853	531,825	638,911
Danish West-Indies,	1,659,306	2,553,810	2,453,606	1,513,104	3,397,262	1,757,589	1,049,361	1,082,574
	1,962,261	2,675,589	2,637,309	2,913,362	4,348,839	2,114,442	1,581,186	1,721,485
United Netherlands,	1,917,336	6,083,491	7,713,976	4,713,976	696,968	4,372,964	6,234,450	5,051,480
Dutch West-Indies,	962,705	1,758,548	1,903,638	2,720,969	5,154,535	1,296,052	625,791	915,378
Dutch East-Indies,	4,376	33,325	-	-	-	-	62,131	-
	2,884,417	7,875,364	9,384,896	7,434,945	5,851,503	5,669,016	6,922,372	5,966,858

216

TABLE No. II.—continued.

	1795. Dolls.	1796. Dolls.	1797. Dolls.	1798. Dolls.	1799. Dolls.	1800. Dolls.	1801. Dolls.	1802. Dolls.
England, Man, and Berwick,	5,045,296	15,146,171	4,997,879	9,479,137	15,045,710	15,856,260	25,309,334	13,086,494
Guernsey, Jersey, Sark, &c.	-	98,289	24,689	-	74,912	22,936	38,821	91,220
Scotland,	173,786	459,118	562,611	1,550,320	2,125,534	1,688,600	3,006,599	2,063,253
Ireland,	1,104,984	1,449,735	1,052,044	949,413	1,684,372	1,517,867	2,576,367	842,583
Gibraltar,	-	85,861	1,866	225,067	528,142	865,957	204,627	383,688
Cape of Good-Hope,	-	-	-	33,823	183,569	128,977	283,918	240,286
British East-Indies,	-	66,316	21,325	39,075	7,296	130,461	71,617	83,489
British West-Indies,	2,634,664	5,446,559	2,149,025	4,283,940	6,285,254	6,404,785	9,699,722	6,689,490
Newfoundland, &c.	15,790	55,705	44,529	143,988	12,567	40,328	125,305	107,945
British American Colonies,	244,020	366,791	360,367	479,584	599,631	654,118	815,722	576,929
	9,218,540	23,164,545	9,212,335	17,184,347	26,546,987	27,310,289	42,132,032	24,165,377
Germany,		35,959	-	70,730	105,647	31,147	52,459	121,742
Hamburg and Bremen,	9,655,524	9,471,498	11,953,017	14,554,339	17,144,400	8,012,846	10,463,738	6,107,750
France,	7,698,683	3,171,759	3,825,231	1,476,588	-	40,400	3,985,292	7,611,287
French West-Indies,	4,954,952	8,408,936	8,565,050	5,344,690	2,776,604	5,123,433	7,147,972	6,710,889
Bourbon and Mauritius,	-	42,609	58,792	147,718	3,900	-	128,487	153,261
	12,653,625	11,623,514	12,449,076	6,968,996	2,780,504	5,163,833	11,261,751	14,475,437

TABLE No. II.—CONTINUED.

	1795.	1796.	1797.	1798.	1799.	1800.	1801.	1802.
	Dolls.	Dolls.	Dolls.	Dolls.	Dolls.	Dolls.	Dolls.	Dolls.
Spain,	2,253,754	1,324,060	1,812,558	2,274,223	4,237,954	4,743,678	2,865,101	2,920,115
Teneriffe and Canaries,	8,128	29,202	50,208	96,486	154,517	303,630	267,664	184,442
Honduras and Campeachy,	-	77	129,700	218,116	531,438	291,717	100,210	32,062
Manilla and Phillippines,	-	-	-	-	-	14,112	-	-
Spanish West-Indies,	1,389,219	1,821,347	3,595,519	5,082,127	8,993,401	8,270,400	8,437,659	5,777,685
Floridas and Louisiana,	1,113,763	475,992	1,044,367	1,074,947	3,504,092	2,035,789	1,408,029	2,075,614
Other American Colonies,	-	-	-	-	-	1,280	532,153	237,941
	4,764,864	3,650,678	6,632,352	8,745,899	17,421,402	15,660,606	13,610,816	11,227,859
Portugal,	549,801	142,567	229,750	286,781	538,662	448,548	1,139,377	1,541,085
Madeira,	133,476	213,785	191,627	333,425	203,185	522,728	528,344	481,053
Fayal and other Azores,	79,173	78,573	5,508	53,749	23,706	56,868	5,120	42,254
Cape de Verd Islands,	1,825	124,523	47,129	55,934	92,178	237,700	45,918	95,268
Coast of Brazil,	-	-	-	-	-	-	-	1,041
	764,285	559,448	474,014	729,889	857,731	1,265,844	1,718,759	2,160,701
Italy,	1,223,150	1,100,522	767,064	1,334,036	1,157,212	2,689,968	2,090,439	2,423,935
Morocco,	-	-	15,000	19,188	48,000	73,449	88,740	63,932
Africa, (generally)	470,027	537,355	254,292	132,883	234,596	366,618	367,705	407,053
China and East-Indies, do.	1,023,242	1,352,860	387,310	261,795	595,249	1,047,385	1,374,506	877,267
West-Indies, do.	1,543,348	3,367,942	1,534,734	248,121	92,020	115,631	372,932	1,261,122
Europe, do.	684,127	481,725	207,077	74,858	11,818	35,389	278,158	316,022
North-West Coast and South Seas,	44,063	23,607	15,607	79,515	72,941	827,748	343,338	160,707
Total,	47,855,556	67,064,097	56,850,206	61,527,097	78,665,522	70,971,780	93,020,513	71,957,144

TABLE No. III.

Amount of goods imported into the United States for the year ending 30th September, 1807.		value.	Dollars. Cts.
Value of goods paying an ad valorem duty of 15 per cent.	- - -		46,861,538
Do. do. do. 17½ do.	- - -		11,097,676
Do. do. do. 22½ do.	- - -		696,703
Malmsey and Madeira wines, gals.	395,103 a $2 59		1,023,321 95
Burgundy,	13,948	4 25	59,279
Sherry,	315,779	1 12	353,672 48
All other wines,	4,843,489	63	3,051,397 7
Foreign spirits from grain,	1,477,679	1	1,477,679
From other materials,	9,915,243	93	9,221,175 99
Molasses,	8,511,234	36	3,064,044 24
Beer, ale, and porter,	226,559	55	124,607 45
Teas, bohea, lbs.	1,511,051	33	498,946 83
Do. souchong,	2,016,177	62	1,250,029 74
Do. Hyson,	1,251,367	1	1,251,367
Do. other green,	2,823,017	75	2,117,362 75
Coffee,	58,824,811	28	16,470,947 8
Cocoa,	9,191,344	25	2,297,961
Chocolate,	3,640	40	1,456
Sugars, brown, &c.	175,110,619	10	17,511,061 90
Do. clayed, &c.	45,398,494	13	5,901,804 22
Do. candy and refined,	159,986	18	28,797 48
Almonds,	685,400	21	143,934
Currants,	436,049	13	56,686 37
Prunes and plumbs,	103,766	14	14,527 24
Figs,	283,353	15	42,502 95
Raisins, in jars and boxes,	864,419	16	138,307 4
All others,	2,918,073	10	291,807 30
Candles, tallow,	547,546	18	98,558 28
Wax and spermaceti,	4,412	60	2,647 20
Cheese,	1,029,642	28	288,299 76
Soap,	2,090,125	18	376,222 50
Tallow,	1,750,279	15	262,541 85
Spices, mace,	2,195	7 50	16,462 50
Do. nutmegs,	3,182	3 25	10,341 50
Do. cinnamon,	9,076	1 92	17,425 92
Do. cloves,	48,526	84	40,761 84
Do. pepper,	3,499,433	23	804,869 69
Do. pimento,	1,196,239	22	263,172 58
Do. cassia,	141,348	34	48,058 32
Tobacco manufactured other than snuff and cigars,	10,261	20	2,052 20
Snuff,	57,002	25	14,250 50
Indigo,	1,010,672	1 83	1,849,529 76
Cotton,	3,377,870	31	1,047,139 70

TABLE No. III.—CONTINUED.

		value.	Dollars. Cts.
Powder, hair, - - lbs.	5,099 a	$00 16	815 84
Do. gun, - - - -	211,748	46	97,404 8
Starch, - - - -	26,209	15	3,931 35
Glue, - - - -	114,732	23	26,388 36
Pewter plates and dishes, -	59,879	25	14,969 75
Iron, anchors and sheet, -	781,875	9	70,368 75
Do. slit and hoop, - -	773,017	10	77,301 70
Do. nails and spikes, - -	4,948,443	11	544,328 73
Quick-silver, - - -	17,211	69	11,875 59
Paints, yellow in oil, - -	32,590	15	4,888 50
Do. do. dry, - -	122,460	8	9,796 80
Do. Spanish brown, - -	828,368	6	49,702 8
Do. white and red lead, - -	2,804,092	15	420,613 80
Lead, and manufactures of lead,	2,455,884	11	270,147 24
Seines, - - -	10,084	50	5,042
Cordage, tarred, - - -	1,068,329	11	117,516 19
Do. untarred, - - -	57,210	10	5,721
Cables, - - - -	67,720	12	8,126 40
Steel, - - - cwt.	15,315	13	205,595
Hemp, - - - -	141,107	15	2,116,605
Twine, - - - -	4,253	30	127,590
Glauber salts, - - -	157	5	785
Salt, weighing more than 56 lbs. per bushel, - - lbs.	126,173,054	$1\frac{1}{10}$	1,387,903 59
Do. weighing 56 lbs. or less per bushel, - - bushels	418,538	69	288,791 22
Coal, - - -	456,936	29	132,511 44
Fish, foreign caught, dried, quint.	233,902	4 50	1,052,559
Do. salmon, - - barrels	7,231	14	101,234
Do. mackerel, - -	16,098	7	112,686
Do. all other, - - -	17,057	6	102,342
Glass, black quart bottles, gross	24,594	7 50	184,455
Do. window not above 8 by 10 inches for each 100 square feet boxes, - - - -	22,719	11 50	261,268 50
Do. not above 10 by 12, -	3,089	15	46,335
Do. all above 10 by 12, -	4,183	17 50	73,202 50
Segars, - - M.	25,624	10	256,240
Lime, - - - casks	385	8	3,080
Boots, - - pairs	3,554	6 50	23,101
Shoes and slippers, silk, - -	31,880	1 75	55,790
Do. morocco, &c. for men and women,	72,875	1 25	91,093 75
Do. children's, - -	24,761	75	18,570 75
Cards, wool or cotton, - doz.	4	6	24
Do. playing, - packs	6,425	35	2,248 75
Total, - - -			$ 138,574,876 84

TABLE No. IV.

Copy of a return to an Order of the House of Commons of 13th February, 1809, for an account of the official and real value of all Imports and Exports between Great-Britain and the United States of America, for three years, being exclusive of the trade of Scotland.

IMPORTS FROM THE UNITED STATES.

ARTICLES.	Official Value. Years ending 10th October.			Real Value. Years ending 10th October.		
	1806. £	1807. £	1808. £	1806. £	1807. £	1808. £
Annotto, - - - - - -	18,670	34,272	9,419	28,339	52,020	14,020
Ashes, Pearl and Pot, - - -	47,835	66,301	32,883	68,336	94,716	46,976
Cochineal, - - - -	61,459	15,925	131	76,824	19,908	184
Coffee, - - - -	29,001	48,986	138,824	25,893	43,737	123,950
Corn, grain, and meal, - -	182,069	420,768	93,074	359,981	901,613	195,257
Hides, - - - -	4,151	9,328	1,587	9,296	20,064	3,629
Indigo, - - - -	5,481	8,804	1,953	43,852	70,835	15,829
Pitch and Tar, - - -	21,114	28,854	28,755	25,884	35,266	35,148

TABLE No. IV.—CONTINUED.

	Official Value. Years ending 10th October.			ARTICLES.	Real Value. Years ending 10th October.		
	1806.	1807.	1808.		1806.	1807.	1808.
	£	£	£		£	£	£
Seeds, flax, and linseed,	1,270	1,034	927		3,387	2,757	2,473
Skins and furs,	31,980	12,653	8,564		65,464	23,855	17,187
Sugar,	39,025	2,426	80,177		53,128	3,307	109,331
Tobacco,	191,192	180,438	135,784		361,140	340,827	258,480
Wood, deals, and fir timber,	7,765	20,312	7,105		55,442	124,699	42,208
Mahogany,	7,944	26,768	7,848		19,860	66,920	19,620
Masts,	11,881	6,728	711		9,823	5,493	582
Staves,	49,290	63,247	17,438		115,978	148,818	41,030
Wool, cotton,	714,452	1,069,638	627,185		2,028,123	3,036,392	1,780,396
Turpentine,	59,470	53,663	25,044		89,205	80,194	37,566
Other articles,	45,220	80,420	43,999		68,525	130,490	62,804
Total imports,	1,529,249	2,150,365	1,261,408		3,508,480	5,201,909	2,804,707

The rates of valuation are formed on an estimate of the average prices prior to the late (1809) advance that has taken place on many articles of American produce.

TABLE No. V.

Copy of a return to an Order of the House of Commons of 13th February, 1809, for an account of the official and real value of all Imports and Exports between Great-Britain and the United States of America, for three years, being exclusive of the trade of Scotland.

EXPORTS TO THE UNITED STATES OF AMERICA.

ARTICLES.	Official Value. Years ending 10th October.			Real Value. Years ending 10th October.		
British produce and manufactures.	1806. £	1807. £	1808. £	1806. £	1807. £	1808. £
Brass and copper manufactures,	62,441	78,471	40,673	84,004	156,960	82,612
Cotton goods,	3,747,265	3,702,772	2,237,774	4,401,112	4,385,787	2,887,797
Glass and earthen ware,	55,756	47,982	13,872	163,242	155,371	43,425
Haberdashery,	20,556	19,292	3,386	299,040	295,422	46,672
Hats,	53,497	38,280	2,782	90,389	60,855	4,940
Iron and steel,	292,917	303,844	110,142	661,332	620,714	260,798
Lead,	13,483	8,77.	10,683	46,756	29,101	35,456
Salt,	93,664	93,181	36,976	93,664	93,181	36,976

TABLE No. V.—CONTINUED.

ARTICLES.	Official Value. Years ending 10th October.			Real Value. Years ending 10th October.		
British produce and manufactures.	1806. £	1807. £	1808. £	1806. £	1807. £	1806. £
Silk manufactures, - - -	140,062	123,934	3,611	447,484	423,880	13,726
- Linens, - - -	89,075	80,595	17,623	125,015	118,075	26,189
Tin and pewter, - -	50,600	57,294	30,417	68,498	79,185	42,967
Woollens, - - -	2,966,809	2,502,929	1,134,940	4,894,008	4,288,866	1,994,902
Other articles, - - -	263,939	206,862	155,458	342,076	311,671	242,155
Total British produce, &c. -	7,830,064	7,264,212	3,798,337	11,716,620	11,119,048	5,718,615
Foreign merchandize, - -	320,700	179,064	45,457	458,875	253,622	65,788
Total exports, - -	8,150,764	7,443,274	3,843,794	12,175,495	11,372,870	5,784,403

Signed,

WILLIAM IRVING,

Inspector general of imports and exports.

Custom-House, London, 16th February, 1809,

TABLE No. VI.

Copy of a return to an Order of the House òf Commons, dated 13th February, 1809, for an account of the total official value and real value of all Imports into, and Exports from Great-Britain, for three years, ending 10th October, 1808,—distinguishing each year and foreign merchandize from British produce and manufactures.

(N. B.) This account is exclusive of the value of the imports and exports of Scotland, and likewise of the importations from the East-Indies, and China, the returns of which being made up and transmitted in annual periods, ending the 5th of January, are not received for the year 1808, and therefore the amount of both of these has been omitted in each of the two preceding years, of the account, in order to shew the comparative view of one year with another.

Official Value.			Years ending 10th Oct.	Real Value.		
	EXPORTS.				EXPORTS.	
IMPORTS.	Foreign and Colonial merchandize.	British produce and manufactures.		IMPORTS.	Foreign and Colonial merchandize.	British produce and manufactures.
£	£	£		£	£	£
22,058,003	8,395,269	24,947,782	1806	38,398,645	9,005,120	39,368,218
23,493,127	9,090,918	24,550,724	1807	40,947,300	9,679,652	39,041,854
20,707,323	6,680,024	21,925,538	1808	34,448,620	7,138,282	35,233,477

Signed,　　　　　　WILLIAM IRVING,

Inspector general of imports and exports.

Custom-House, London, 16th February, 1809.

TABLE No. VII.

Account of the total value, agreeable to the estimates of the inspector general's books, of the Woollen Manufactures exported from Great-Britain, in the last ten years.

	1790. £	1791. £	1792. £	1793. £	1794. £	1795. £	1796. £	1797. £	1798. £	1799. £
Denmark and Norway, -	18,637	60,829	41,659	22,970	29,249	27,927	38,198	43,377	31,983	29,959
Russia, - - -	76,744	134,224	182,353	82,401	71,636	129,135	153,985	120,138	136,867	149,789
Sweden, - - -	2,037	3,483	17,713	2,011	8,071	2,829	2,812	15,807	218	600
Poland, - - -	911	3,695	3,511	1,881	1,091	1,228	1,094	567	1,246	1,218
Prussia, - - -	9,519	13,857	18,040	17,769	19,268	27,479	133,903	159,999	34,846	39,296
Germany, - - -	223,226	255,303	271,638	217,193	330,024	503,706	594,898	641,098	463,019	427,053
Holland, - - -	306,414	313,845	367,583	265,565	217,381	-	-	7,712	94	175
Flanders, - - -	117,779	124,239	117,151	72,703	51,585	-	126	-	-	-
France, - - -	95,827	96,840	155,134	42,855	-	-	27	631	-	-
Portugal and Madeira,	382,038	434,375	465,373	376,171	335,811	368,660	425,038	401,920	488,469	568,788
Spain and Canaries,	407,464	346,367	472,221	259,849	265,036	191,203	262,192	26	-	-
Straits and Gibraltar, -	119,494	130,336	80,774	20,607	23,586	16,696	24,144	6,910	34,860	31,774
Italy and Venice, -	446,359	517,178	386,631	165,040	181,285	274,095	295,374	2,651	26,739	47,410
Turkey, - - -	15,070	41,095	34,334	9,078	6,395	12,228	28,580	3,056	13,927	47,398
Ireland, - - -	394,720	499,793	490,271	178,071	308,759	458,938	555,963	360,600	583,964	916,190
Man, - - -	3,382	3,753	4,737	3,141	4,163	1,535	3,004	3,963	6,328	4,737
Guernsey, &c. -	8,372	4,784	9,058	2,545	1,619	2,967	1,706	2,156	1,939	3,744
American British Colonies,	156,192	132,997	183,681	147,631	186,787	196,876	224,649	232,329	232,869	324,739
United States, - -	1,481,378	1,621,796	1,361,753	1,032,954	1,391,877	1,982,318	2,294,942	1,901,986	2,399,935	2,803,490
West-Indies, British, &c.	226,921	288,722	319,329	311,546	368,261	350,595	382,260	465,990	1,482,457	552,726
East-Indies, - -	530,614	377,815	362,509	530,307	491,152	587,054	543,387	446,629	351,475	668,161
Africa, - - -	167,538	99,696	165,204	44,237	97,871	67,403	44,842	118,800	218,095	259,683
*Totals,**	5,190,637	5,505,034	5,510,668	3,806,536	4,390,920	5,172,884	6,011,133	4,936,355	6,499,339	6,876,939

* In copying this account the shillings and pence are omitted; and thence there is some difference between the particular sums and the totals, wherein the amount of them is included.

TABLE No. VIII.

An account of the value of all Imports into and of all Exports from Great-Britain, for three years, ending 5th of January, 1811, distinguishing each year, and distinguishing the value of imports from the East-Indies and China, from the value of all other imports; also distinguishing the value of British produce and manufactures exported, from the value of foreign articles exported, together with the difference between the official value and the declared value of British produce and manufactures exported in the year ending 5th of January, 1811.

Years ending 5th January.	Official Value of Imports.		Official Value of Exports.	
	From Europe, Africa, and America.	From East-Indies and China.	British produce and manufactures.	Foreign merchandize.
	£	£	£	£
1809 or 1808.	23,780,704	5,868,669	26,691,962	7,862,305
1810 or 1809.	30,409,384	3,363,025	35,104,132	15,182,768
1811 or 1810.	36,622,142	*	34,940,550	10,945,309
	See appendix (A.)		See appendix (B.)	See appendix (C.)

NOTE. The value of British produce and manufactures exported from Great-Britain, according to the average prices current, and declarations of the exporters in the year ending 5th January, 1811, amounts to £49,975,634.

WILLIAM IRVING,
Inspector general of imports and exports.

Custom-House, London, 23d March, 1811.

* The account of imports from the East-Indies and China, cannot yet be given.

TABLE No. VIII.—CONTINUED.

APPENDIX (A 1.)

Official value of Imports into Great-Britain from Europe, Africa, and America.

ARTICLES.	1809 or 1808. £	1810 or 1809. £	1811 or 1810. £
Almonds, - - -	21,380	24,209	19,196
Annotto, - - - -	8,635	23,463	48,423
Ashes, pot and pearl, -	150,524	265,827	460,433
Barilla, - - - -	120,664	188,842	175,508
Bark, oak, - - -	1,724	11,788	8,935
Berries, juniper, - - -	12,383	22,953	30,178
Brimstone, - - -	65,622	24,855	44,229
Bristles, undressed, - -	9,886	28,081	20,992
Butter and cheese, (foreign)	321,552	258,145	128,608
Cochineal, - - - -	209,415	83,396	189,828
Cocoa, - - - -	85,538	72,513	61,496
Coffee, - - - -	4,899,184	4,690,680	5,307,112
Copper, unwrought, -	97,189	41,116	92,129
Corks, - - - -	29,213	41,116	78,788
Corn, grain, meal and rice,	146,240	1,136,971	2,701,228
Cortex, peruvianus, - -	147,165	81,577	93,705
Currants, - - -	110,502	180,329	136,831
Elephant's teeth, - -	16,476	17,628	19,336
Feathers, for beds, - -	1,475	7,054	17,735
Figs, - - - - -	5,101	13,568	5,834
Fish, viz. cod and herring,	209,731	174,419	126,878
Flax, rough, - - -	403,351	967,628	945,223
Gum arabic and senega, -	24,075	35,376	59,722
Hemp, rough, - - -	218,947	721,520	752,294
Hides, raw and tanned, -	228,712	328,306	659,724
Jalap, - - - -	11,530	5,781	38,809
Indigo, (not East-India) -	63,740	79,527	138,125
Iron, bar, - - - -	205,249	239,532	196,830
Isinglass, - - -	1,534	14,085	16,569
Lemons and Oranges, - -	33,738	30,710	33,014
Linens, (foreign) - -	174,369	843,710	938,600
Madder and madder roots, -	157,959	425,230	436,475
Oil, ordinary olive, - -	83,650	125,648	80,748
—— train, - - -	326,381	285,586	329,992
Pimento, - - - -	9,199	57,802	73,866
Pitch and tar, - - -	123,479	106,762	115,610

TABLE No. VIII.—CONTINUED.

APPENDIX (A 1.) CONTINUED.

ARTICLES.	Years ending the 5th of January.		
	1809 or 1808.	1810 or 1809.	1811 or 1810.
	£	£	£
Quicksilver, - - -	13,772	17,320	26,888
Raisins, - - - -	105,744	160,471	63,601
Salt, - - - -	32,906	63,198	23,900
Seeds, clover, - - -	13,026	23,777	38,090
—— flax and linseed, - -	61,177	130,404	213,822
Shumack, - - -	15,159	22,817	20,661
Silk, raw and thrown, - -	246,057	853,706	943,613
Skins and Furs, - -	177,757	179,077	282,719
Smelts, - - - -	6,826	22,817	9,633
Spirits, brandy, - -	251,864	441,201	174,380
—— geneva, - - -	51,798	43,395	12,056
—— rum, - - -	539,624	607,083	507,602
Succus liquoritiæ, - -	19,516	20,562	41,881
Sugar, - - - -	5,046,631	5,422,066	6,493,561
Tallow, - - - -	145,860	362,974	505,496
Tobacco, - - -	77,527	275,591	498,585
Turpentine, - - -	15,021	66,828	65,271
Wax, bees, - - -	20,209	37,336	39,648
Whale fins, - - -	76,430	75,676	103,255
Wines, - - - -	1,122,020	1,173,613	1,130,332
Wood, balks and ufas, - -	878	4,230	22,583
—— deals and deal ends, -	26,665	60,362	100,612
—— fir timber, - - -	63,267	111,611	205,264
—— fustic, - - -	24,036	47,354	66,082
—— logwood, - - -	106,663	98,239	184,400
—— mahogany, - - -	66,907	104,530	187,159
—— masts, - - -	270,405	198,251	335,807
—— oak plank and timber, -	14,886	13,504	36,106
—— redwood, - -	19,112	47,943	29,040
—— staves, - - -	33,419	95,743	109,130
Wool, cotton, - - -	1,325,318	2,797,932	3,882,359
—— sheep's, - - -	127,870	350,072	564,329
Yarn, linen, raw, - -	34,605	233,635	286,757
All other articles, - -	981,656	1,114,566	1,351,061
Foreign and Colonial produce,	19,869,723	26,933,625	33,138,686
Irish produce and manufactures,	3,910,981	3,475,759	3,283,456
Total (exclusive of importations from E. Indies and China,)	23,780,704	30,409,384	36,422,142

TABLE No. VIII.—CONTINUED.

APPENDIX (A 2.)

Official value of Imports into Great-Britain from the East-Indies and China.

ARTICLES.	Years ending the 5th of January.		
	1309 or 1808.	1810 or 1809.	1811 or 1810.
	£	£	£
Borax, - - - -	7,975	2,136	- -
Cassia lignea, - - -	3,451	325	- -
Coffee, - - - -	2,961	19,911	- -
Gum Arabic, - - -	3,107	629	- -
Indigo, - - - -	717,205	293,751	- -
Pepper, - - - -	62,254	21,612	- -
Piece goods, - - -	730,413	164,614	- -
Rhubarb, - - - -	655	5,085	- -
Salt-petre, - - -	68,521	46,495	- -
Silk, raw, - - -	182,593	93,105	- -
Spices, - - - -	137,005	41,902	- -
Sugar, - - - -	81,252	29,239	- -
Tea, - - - -	3,567,812	2,164,396	- -
Wool, cotton, - - -	145,741	318,707	- ～
All other articles, - -	137,704	161,118	- -
Total Imports from East-Indies and China, - -	5,848,649	3,363,025	- -

TABLE No. VIII.—CONTINUED.

APPENDIX (B.)

Official value of British produce and manufactures Exported from Great-Britain.

ARTICLES.	Years ending the 5th of January.		
	1809 or 1808.	1810 or 1809.	1811 or 1810.
	£.	£.	£.
Apparel, - - -	250,559	259,835	239,865
Bark, tanner's, - -	50,785	45,151	41,990
Beer, - - -	65,001	65,727	72,493
Brass and copper, - -	354,607	403,429	356,577
Cabinet and upholstery ware,	64,122	78,955	93,163
Coals, - - - -	526,845	405,634	509,991
Colors for painting, -	129,285	196,968	187,047
Cordage, - - -	32,621	46,385	63,052
Corn and flour, - -	134,055	70,541	44,152
Cotton manufactures, -	12,835,803	18,634,614	18,041,633
Do. yarn, - - -	575,015	1,097,536	1,075,187
Fish, - - - -	118,843	142,593	134,296
Glass and earthern ware, -	183,643	240,123	236,314
Gun-powder, - -	33,428	32,417	31,300
Guns, - - - -	49,689	30,480	49,604
Haberdashery, - -	51,436	55,946	64,797
Hats, - - - -	261,112	335,941	327,884
Hops, - - -	124,346	97,186	52,452
Iron & steel, wrought & unwro't,	1,178,524	1,391,761	1,577,462
Lead and shot, - -	81,801	63,278	101,993
Leather, tanned and wrought,	191,474	179,945	186,573
Linens, - - -	874,460	1,157,030	1,015,240
Musical instruments, -	33,558	41,971	51,558
Oil, train, - - -	26,025	52,499	54,779
Plate, plated ware & jewellery,	122,066	140,730	164,168
Provisions, - - -	154,294	139,132	125,249
Salt, - - -	201,669	288,258	296,759
Silks, - - -	128,775	190,177	188,023
Soap and candles, - -	89,528	129,703	120,353
Stationary, - - -	145,824	169,360	212,176
Sugar, refined, - -	948,304	1,346,769	1,220,498
Tin and pewter, - -	244,142	232,838	256,581
Woollen manufactures, -	4,853,999	5,416,149	5,773,214
All other articles, - -	1,576,324	1,925,991	1,974,127
Total,	26,691,962	35,104,132	34,940,550

TABLE No. VIII.—CONTINUED.

APPENDIX (C.)

Official value of Foreign and Colonial Merchandize Exported from Great-Britain.

ARTICLES.	Years ending 5th of January.		
	1809 or 1808.	1810 or 1809.	1811 or 1810.
	£	£	£
Annotto, - - -	3,670	7,931	28,427
Ashes, - - -	17,127	21,003	184,452
Barilla, - - -	8,951	3,065	70,683
Brimstone, - -	4,065	1,840	22,619
Cassia lignea, - -	4,068	13,741	3,666
Cochineal, - -	147,930	73,341	64,097
Cocoa, - - -	57,377	144,254	38,494
Coffee, British plantations, -	1,286,200	3,038,027	712,774
Do. foreign do. -	561,720	2,807,133	741,398
Corn, grain, flour, and rice, -	51,397	35,911	272,138
Cortex peruvianus, -	44,780	92,377	127,686
Currants and raisins, -	12,581	35,217	77,594
Fish, cod and herrings, -	320,144	198,870	126,835
Flax and hemp, rough, -	9,991	60,035	201,190
Hides, tanned and raw, -	15,256	109,145	225,893
Jalap, - - -	2,469	5,319	40,315
Indigo, - - -	323,107	636,807	491,298
Iron, bar, - -	86,231	112,551	167,916
Linens, foreign, - -	118,578	604,424	737,203
Pepper, - -	55,201	190,131	126,185
Piece goods of India, -	822,345	1,179,728	1,082,115
Pimento, - - -	15,926	50,119	29,740
Quicksilver, - -	17,819	11,757	6,209
Salt, - - -	31,263	39,555	21,973
Salt petre, - -	33,673	13,200	13,627
Silk, raw and thrown, -	55,264	85,960	92,917
Skins and furs, - -	5,261	48,646	33,268
Spices, - - -	128,579	192,620	161,188
Spirits, brandy and geneva, -	252,630	271,647	251,695
Do. rum, - -	334,339	606,174	339,470
Sugar, British plantations, -	513,500	679,281	193,620
Do. foreign do. -	270,463	1,033,849	1,277,374

TABLE No. VIII.—continued.

APPENDIX (C.) continued.

ARTICLES.	Years ending 5th of January.		
	1809 or 1808.	1810 or 1809.	1811 or 1810.
	£	£	£
Tea, - - -	714,939	703,724	569,368
Tobacco, - -	123,999	202,430	164,019
Wines, - - -	455,265	626,649	555,040
Woods, for dying, -	48,840	139,752	320,115
Wool, cotton, - -	60,283	156,215	343,550
All other articles, -	382,670	448,094	574,823
Foreign and Colonial produce,	7,397,901	14,680,524	10,470,966
Irish produce and manufactures,	464,404	502,244	474,343
Total,	7,862,305	15,182,768	10,945,309

TABLE No. IX.

Exports to the dominions of Great-Britain, in the West-Indies, for each of the years ending 30th Sept. 1802, 1803, and 1804.

I. Articles of domestic produce.		QUANTITY.			VALUE IN DOLLARS.		
		1802.	1803.	1804.	1802.	1803.	1804.
Flour,	barrels	245,708	260,555	220,586 }	1,942,233	2,063,099	1,875,747
Bread and biscuit,	kegs, do.	69,438	73,673	71,776 }			
Indian corn,	bushels	630,705	815,191	446,498 }	557,419	670,983	620,812
Rye, and Indian meal,	barrels	28,130	74,071	63,542 }			
Rice,	tierces	8,008	6,525	10,566	240,240	195,750	316,980
Oats, peas, beans, and potatoes,	bushels	159,769	120,404	136,035	104,771	78,018	80,910
Beef and pork,	barrels	51,088	52,087	93,582 }	665,074	601,314	1,163,350
Bacon and lard,	pounds	784,594	782,938	1,141,748 }			
Butter and cheese,	do.	986,435	826,319	902,430	113,584	106,625	119,348
Fish, dried,	quintals	92,679	71,495	76,822 }	550,083	484,103	529,858
Do. pickled,	barrels & kegs	33,788	29,523	37,095 }			
Horned cattle, hogs, and sheep,	number	16,507	16,004	15,113	196,850	122,763	165,599
Horses and mules,	do.	4,727	2,797	3,187	230,900	139,596	156,300
Staves and heading, hoops, &c.	M.	18,074	16,553	14,392 }	1,216,107	866,225	890,786
Boards, plank, &c.	M. feet	42,831	42,206	35,499 }			
Shingles,	M.	50,283	47,231	44,340 }			
Tobacco,	hhds.	1,398	1,335	1,378	111,840	93,450	96,460
Soap and candles,	pounds	609,196	367,772	970,619	104,231	68,131	154,424
* All other articles,	value	-	-	-	195,132	134,590	145,093
Total value,		-	-	-	6,228,464	5,624,647	6,315,667

* Consisting principally of pot-ashes, apples, beer, barley, boots and shoes, cables and cordage, wool and cotton cards, pleasurable carriages, household furniture, iron castings, &c. skins and furs, saddlery; oils, spermaceti, fish and linseed, manufactured tobacco, wax, &c.

TABLE No. IX.—CONTINUED.

II. Articles of foreign produce.		QUANTITY.			VALUE IN DOLLARS.		
		1802.	1803.	1804.	1802.	1803.	1804.
Merchandize paying duties ad valorem,	value				369,298	67,724	469,307
Spirits,	gallons	20,235	6,514	89,848	20,235	6,514	89,848
Wines,	do	61,130	6,899	168,022	59,119	7,768	138,243
Teas,	pounds	7,330	4,204	7,303	8,055	4,933	9,751
*All other articles,	value	-	-	-	4,319	4,034	24,842
Total value,		-	-	-	461,026	90,973	731,991
Value of domestic produce as above,		-	-	-	6,228,464	5,624,647	6,315,667
Total,		-	-	-	6,689,490	5,715,620	7,047,658

* Consisting principally of glauber salts, medicinal drugs, shoes and slippers, copper and brass, spices, &c.

TABLE No. X.

Importations into the United States, from British West-Indies, for each of the years ending on the 30th of September, 1802, 1803, and 1804.

Goods paying duties ad val.	QUANTITY			VALUE			Rate of Duty.	AMOUNT OF DUTY.		
	1802.	1803.	1804.	1802.	1803.	1804.	Cents.	1802.	1803.	1804.
At 12½ p. ct. val.	- - -	- - -	- - -	79,564	42,613	43,292	- -	9,945 50	5,326 62	5,411 50
15 do. do.	- - -	- - -	- - -	73,543	73,614	66,653	- -	11,031 45	11,042 10	9,997 95
20 do. do.	- - -	- - -	- - -	532	136	1,384	- -	106 40	27 20	276 80
Spirits, - gls.	4,212,792	3,627,838	4,356,190	2,527,675 20	2,176,702 80	2,613,714	25 a 46	1,248,611 67	1,063,537 57	1,295,999 72
Salt, - bush.	801,803	758,422	801,249	200,450 75	189,605 50	200,312 25	20	160,360 60	151,684 40	160,249 80
Sugar, - lbs.	10,783,925	14,900,910	11,961,375	862,714	1,192,072 80	956,910	3	271,465 92	372,948 25	300,369 83
Coffee, - do.	1,764,391	1,909,734	1,997,162	441,097 75	477,433 50	499,290 50	2¾	88,219 55	95,486 70	99,858 10
Molasses, gls.	569,823	598,799	626,360	170,946 90	179,639 70	187,908	5	28,491 15	29,939 95	31,318
Pimento, - lbs.	219,647	721,094	518,498	26,357 64	86,531 28	62,219 76	4	8,785 88	28,843 76	20,739 92
Cotton, - do.	65,193	59,436	11,534	16,298 25	14,859	2,883 50	3	1,955 79	1,783 8	346 2
*All other art. v.	- - -	- - -	- - -	87,711 37	59,654 39	104,619 1	-	15,467 78	10,031 18	15,291 48
Total,	- - -	- - -	- - -	4,486,890 86	4,492,861 97	4,739,186 2	-	1,844,441 69	1,770,650 81	1,939,859 12

* Principally consisting of wines, teas, cheese, segars, nails, lead, cordage, coal, boots and shoes, cocoa, indigo, &c.

TABLE No. XI.

Principal exports from Petersburgh to America only, from its Independence to 1805.

Denomination of Goods.		1783.	1784.	1785.	1786.	1787.	1788.	1789.	1790.	1791.	1792.	1793.
	Ships.	2.	1.	7.	10.	11.	10.	17.	22.	20.	24.	30.
Iron, - -	poods,*	6,615	6,612	33,618	31,858	10,833	17,054	24,981	78,160	48,136	132,380	177,826
nail rod, -	do.	-	-	} 15	2,322	1,260	846	1,259	} 2,526	2,621	1,132	1,071
hoop, -	do.	-	-			61	378	411		757	1,830	3,576
Hemp, clean, -	do.	7,784	8,113	21,332	52,981	44,190	41,063	60,860	137,232	78,935	112,430	160,276
outshot, -	do.	159	668	-	2,964	9,742	6,520	-	1,861	-	-	-
half clean,	do.	-	-	-	-	6,024	775	-	1,008	-	-	-
Flax, 12 head,	do.	-	1,044	8	167	410	103	-	1,071	-	2,909	634
Feathers, -	do.	-	215	-	-	58	-	-	-	-	-	-
Bristles, -	do.	-	-	-	-	3	-	-	1,803	-	145	292
Cordage, -	do.	9,614	1,761	17,168	1,626	11,705	2,122	4,550	-	578	212	2,180
Tallow, -	do.	-	-	-	-	2,423	-	-	-	-	1,700	140
candles,	do.	568	127	3,091	211	63	19	-	2,463	-	-	-
Linseed oil, -	do.	-	-	130	64	-	-	-	-	-	-	-
Ravenducks, -	pieces,	570	-	312	1,464	2,769	1,752	1,635	856	3,354	5,993	5,062
Flems, -	do.	437	-	2,709	601	1,688	1,877	565	9,804	533	2,711	5,844
Sail cloth, -	do.	500	370	4,074	6,850	9,164	7,771	11,667	5	5,184	15,577	13,391
Drillings, -	do.	4,248	-	12,510	90	372	4,884	150	2,468	-	260	760

* Sixty-three poods make one ton English.

TABLE No. XI.—CONTINUED.

Denomination of Goods.		1794.	1795.	1796.	1797.	1798.	1799.	1800.	1801.	1802.	1803.	1804.
Ships.		43.	42.	59.	26.	39.	62.	23.	61.	65.	84.	65.
Iron,	poods*	256,635	206,039	296,691	112,260	142,654	239,835	112,568	269,709	309,425	413,822	278,264
nail rod,	do.	694	504	6,405	560	1,259	126	314	426	21	-	-
hoop,	do.	1,959	1,284	2,019	1,002	631	503	1,260	427	-	253	-
Hemp, clean,	do.	249,625	137,633	182,487	90,424	172,244	241,826	16,314	169,995	205,386	315,452	187,495
outshot,	do.	-	-	1,370	-	-	15,181	18,862	51,709	33,791	45,976	87,694
half clean,	do.	-	-	3,808	-	-	-	-	1,702	2,466	639	3,340
Flax, 12 head,	do.	4,448	842	1,660	-	206	-	-	889	-	303	3,214
Feathers,	do.	194	692	2,164	621	168	278	178	2,263	2,119	1,484	419
Bristles,	do.	250	173	226	107	474	455	612	1,639	1,535	1,487	1,569
Cordage,	do.	4,986	22,404	28,603	13,120	11,059	22,309	17,349	49,606	23,074	12,415	13,618
Tallow,	do.	7,447	33,615	16,821	2,396	479	2,937	6,104	7,583	464	416	1,828
candles,	do.	2,747	10,518	5,094	194	1,192	1,433	1,651	4,532	1,490	172	319
Linseed oil,	do.	-	-	1,390	3,602	-	19	247	2,002	1,579	313	-
Ravenducks,	pieces,	14,143	10,768	10,225	7,853	14,238	19,952	9,013	33,820	10,365	10,651	23,044
Flems,	do.	11,455	6,682	5,743	10,785	18,702	20,979	14,774	34,224	7,717	13,161	19,648
Sail cloth,	do.	25,787	11,828	9,328	7,926	35,340	22,057	6,624	32,997	10,977	32,653	32,190
Drillings,	do.	606	780	118	120	100	60	30	860	2,150	1,051	1,090

* Sixty-three poods make one ton English.

TABLE No. XI.—CONTINUED.

Denomination of Goods.	Ships.	1783. 2.	1784. 1.	1785. 7.	1786. 10.	1787. 11.	1788. 10.	1789. 17.	1790. 22.	1791. 20.	1792. 24.	1793. 30.
Broad diaper,	arsheens,*	26,110	19,597	2,080	7,112	-	2,755	1,876	1,429	16,376	35,104	5,338
Narrow do.	do.	1,194	-	-	1,000	-	-	901	1,024	800	4,077	7,889
Broad linen,	do.	2,953	481	-	-	-	{7,580	250	211	-	-	-
Narrow do.	do.	13,073	-	-	1,600	-	-	-	1,340	-	1,300	-
Printed do.	do.	-	-	-	1,224	-	830	-	-	-	90	200
Crash,	do.	30,680	4,645	-	-	-	174	2,000	355	-	-	3,020
Ticken,	pieces,	-	-	-	-	-	-	-	-	-	-	900
Table cloths,	do.	-	-	-	-	-	-	-	-	-	-	-
Napkins,	do.	-	-	14	-	-	108	-	-	-	-	-
Leather,	poods,	-	-	-	-	-	-	-	-	-	-	-
Calf leather,	do.	-	-	-	-	-	-	-	-	-	-	-
Horse hair,	pieces,	-	-	-	-	138	-	-	-	-	-	-
Horse skins,	do.	-	-	48	-	-	-	-	-	-	-	-
Squirrel skins,	do.	-	-	-	-	243	-	-	-	-	-	-
Hempseed oil,	poods,	-	-	-	-	-	-	-	-	-	-	-
Soap,	do.	-	-	-	-	-	-	-	-	-	-	-
Oil,	do.	-	-	-	-	315	-	-	-	-	-	-
Glue,	do.	-	-	-	-	-	-	-	-	-	-	-

* Nine arsheens are equal to seven yards English

TABLE No. XI.—CONTINUED.

Denomination of Goods.	Ships.	1794.	1795.	1796.	1797.	1798.	1799.	1800.	1801.	1802.	1803.	1804.
		43.	42.	59.	26.	39.	62.	23.	61.	65.	84.	65.
Broad diaper,	arsheens*	9,920	68,139	78,714	20,777	26,539	83,080	53,416	98,665	92,669	239,365	83,686
Narrow do.	do.	1,325	82,290	45,805	23,683	3,752	14,093	22,668	70,178	39,824	79,278	10,546
Broad linen,	do.	-	1,200	-	-	686	6,443	4,508	2,064	11,300	28,395	949
Narrow do.	do.	100	1,110	100	-	194	5,499	10,495	1,100	25,265	7,400	-
Printed do.	do.	120	450	387	-	400	1,200	-	-	-	113,600	-
Crash,	do.	5,525	71,500	27,000	7,100	12,055	35,912	-	51,000	146,350	-	3,298
Ticken,	pieces	-	4,735	1,202	38	121	136	43	37	-	-	-
Table cloths,	do.	-	-	-	60	227	282	14	157	95	13	-
Napkins,	do.	-	-	-	261	186	126	-	591	96	26	-
Leather,	poods	3,030	11,155	-	5,500	2,700	332	1,100	2,730	1,600	320	-
Calf leather	do.	-	-	-	-	1,077	2,472	-	-	-	-	1,100
Horse hair,	pieces	-	-	355	39	45	108	60	136	495	71	5
Horse skins,	do.	-	1,206	30	-	472	3,558	110	-	12,000	870	84,044
Squirrel skins,	do.	569	660	111	-	-	189	2,050	2,101	20	-	-
Hempseed oil,	poods	-	-	-	-	-	9	-	-	656	245	-
Soap,	do.	-	4,487	3,661	-	263	762	49	-	30	13	-
Oil,	do.	459	-	-	-	-	-	-	23	-	-	-
Glue,	do.	-	-	-	-	-	-	567	829	413	56	-

* Nine arsheens are equal to seven yards English.

CHAPTER VII.

Amount of trade with the different quarters of the world—Balance of trade —Estimate of the quantity of certain imported articles consumed in the United States, at different periods.

HAVING presented an estimate of the amount of the trade of the United States with the different nations, with which they have any considerable commercial intercourse, we now give a general view of exports to each quarter of the world, from 1801 to 1812, accompanied with some remarks relative to the balance of trade, between the United States and the rest of the world, with an estimate of the quantity of certain imported articles, annually consumed, at different periods.

The following statement exhibits the value of merchandize, domestic and foreign, exported from the United States, to each quarter of the world, from 1801 to 1812 :—

	EUROPE.		ASIA.	
	Domestic.	Foreign.	Domestic.	Foreign.
Years.	Dolls.	Dolls.	Dolls.	Dolls.
1801	27,569,699	31,380,558	371,737	1,136,517
1802	19,904,389	23,575,108	547,386	820,423
1803	25,939,111	8,561,834	292,593	149,600
1804	23,094,946	27,468,725	546,278	830,223
1805	23,640,776	36,341,320	612,683	2,156,229
1806	24,384,020	40,267,711	514,621	1,968,860
1807	31,012,947	38,882,633	497,769	1,598,445
1808	5,185,720	7,202,232	26,649	267,542
1809	17,838,502	13,072,045	703,900	1,218,228
1810	27,202,534	17,786,614	377,795	406,646
1811	29,552,442	8,727,011	581,815	812,950
1812	20,626,488	5,644,433	308,510	588,299

	AFRICA.		W. INDIES, AMERICAN CONTINENT, &C.	
	Domestic.	Foreign.	Domestic.	Foreign.
Years.	Dolls.	Dolls.	Dolls.	Dolls.
1801	934,331	756,445	17,482,025	13,369,201
1802	747,544	411,855	14,982,854	10,967,585
1803	636,106	148,004	15,338,151	4,734,634
1804	1,264,737	681,499	16,561,516	7,251,150
1805	1,359,518	1,726,987	16,774,025	12,954,483
1806	1,371,475	901,916	14,983,611	17,144,759
1807	1,296,375	1,627,177	15,892,501	17,535,303
1808	278,544	218,950	3,939,633	5,308,690
1809	3,132,687	1,472,819	9,732,613	5,034,439
1810	2,549,744	722,777	12,236,602	5,475,258
1811	1,804,998	622,445	13,354,788	5,860,384
1812	1,235,457	197,587	7,861,655	2,064,808

It will be seen from this statement, taken from the custom-house books, that, in the most prosperous period of our commerce, when our exports amounted annually to more than one hundred millions of dollars, we exported to Europe, domestic produce of the value of more than twenty-six millions of dollars, and of foreign produce, more than thirty-eight millions of dollars ; to Asia, domestic produce of the value of about five hundred and forty thousand dollars, and foreign produce about one million and nine hundred thousand dollars ; to Africa, domestic produce of the value of about one million three hundred thousand dollars, and foreign produce, about one million four hundred thousand dollars ; and to the West-Indies and American continent, domestic produce, about fifteen million eight hundred and eighty thousand dollars, and foreign produce, about fifteen million eight hundred and seventy thousand dollars. The average amount of exports of domestic produce during the years, 1805, 1806, and 1807, was $44,863,198 and of foreign produce, $57,701,937. Of the whole value of domestic produce, exported during this period, about six tenths went to Europe, about four elevenths to the West-Indies and American continent, and less than one twentieth to Asia and Africa.

In the preceding chapter, we have, as far as practicable, given an account of the value of our imports, at different periods, with the countries from whence derived. It would have been fortunate, had the custom-house books furnished us with the annual value of our imports, as well as exports.

This would have enabled us, with much more certainty, to ascertain the balance of trade, between the United States and other countries.

On the subject of the balance of trade, as it has been called, writers on political economy have very widely differed. Assuming different data as the basis of their calculations, they have come to different results. Some have considered the rate of exchange between two countries, as the best evidence of the balance of trade between them; others have considered the value of exports and imports as the surest criterion, by which to judge of the increase or decrease of the wealth of a country, while some have maintained, that the rate of the interest of money is to be taken into the account. A late celebrated French writer, in his able and learned inquiry into the various systems of political economy, speaking of the " necessity of endeavouring to find out a way to know the balance of annual income, and annual consumption," asks this question,—" Is there any such way, that can be relied upon, as *certain and positive ?*" And answers it by saying " there is none." " We must, as yet," says he, " be contented with mere conjecture, built upon an augmented population, and particularly upon the increase of the industrious classes and towns, upon the good condition of agricultural buildings, upon the number of acres cleared, or enclosed, and upon the facility with which the public contributions are collected. To these conjectures, some add, those resulting from the rate of interest of money; but this conjecture is, in my opinion, erroneous and delusive.

" A high rate of interest is not always a proof of the declining wealth of a country; on the contrary, it is a proof of its prosperity, when this prosperity is progressive. The interest of money must always be very high in countries whose prosperity is progressive, because its agriculture and manufactures, increasing with its population, are always requiring fresh capitals, the demand for which necessarily keeps the rate of interest very high."

It is not, however, our intention to enter into a consideration of the various theories respecting the balance of trade. Whatever.

doubts may have perplexed writers on political economy, on the subject of the increase or decrease of wealth, or the balance of trade, among the old nations of Europe, there can be none with respect to this country.

That the United States, since the establishment of the present government, and particularly until the commencement of commercial prohibitions, and the war between them and Great-Britain, have increased in wealth, as well as population, does not rest on conjecture. It is proved by the great increase of their exports and imports, by the increase of the duties on imports and tonnage, by the unexampled increase of their commercial tonnage, by the accumulation of wealth in all their cities, towns, and villages, by the establishment of various monied institutions, and of manufactures, by the great rise in the value of lands, and by various internal improvements. If we are to form an opinion of the increase of our national wealth, by a comparative view of our exports and imports *alone*, we shall be equally certain, that this opinion does not rest on conjecture.

It is true with nations, as with individuals, if their annual consumption exceeds their annual income; if the actual value of the articles imported into any country, and *there* CONSUMED, annually exceeds the actual value of the articles exported in payment for them, that country must become indebted to the amount of the difference, and if this difference be great, and continues for a number of years, that country must be proportionably impoverished. In determining, however, the increase or decrease of national wealth, by a comparison of imports and exports, we are in the first place to inquire how, or in what manner, this value has been ascertained : a second question may also arise, whether the imports are all annually consumed in the country, or whether a part of them go to form an addition to the productive capital. The modes of valuing exports and imports are different in different countries.

In England, the rates at which the exports and imports are valued, were settled in 1696. The value of all articles at that period, exported or imported, was fixed, and the value of all the exports and imports of that country has ever since been stated in their custom-house books at the rates then established. This is called the *official value* in the English accounts of exports and imports. In consequence of the great rise in most if not all the articles of trade, for more than a century past, this official value is much less than the *real* or *actual* value. The difference in some articles is very great, in most it amounts to forty, fifty, and sixty per cent. In 1807, the *official* value of the exports of British produce and manufacture was £24,550,724, but the *real* or declared value, as ascertained by the inspector-general of imports and exports and laid before parliament, was £39,041,854.

In the United States, as we have before observed, the value of exports is stated according to the average prices of the articles, at the places of exportation. In 1807, the average price of tobacco, for instance, at the places from whence it was exported was eighty-eight dollars per hogshead, and the value of all the tobacco exported during that year was calculated at that price. The value of the imports, so far as they are ascertained at the custom-house, (and they are ascertained only on goods subject to the payment of duties ad valorem) is determined by law, as follows, viz.—" by adding twenty per cent. to the actual cost thereof, if imported from the Cape of Good Hope, or from any place beyond the same, and ten per cent. on the actual cost thereof, if imported from any other place or country, including all charges, commissions, outside packages and insurance only excepted." From this, it will readily be perceived that the value of imports of the United States, as estimated in their custom-house books, must, generally, if not always, exceed that of their exports. In the preceding Tables, containing the exports and imports from 1795 to 1801, it will be perceived that the value of the latter exceeds that of the former in each year. In 1801, the value of imports (as estimated at the place of importation) was $111,363,511, and the value of exports only $93,020,573, making a difference of $18,343,938. In 1807, our exports were valued at $108,343,150, and the imports at $138,574,876 84 cents, making a difference of $30,231,726. The value of the imports in 1807, it will be remembered, was estimated from the prices at which the same articles when exported in the same year were valued at the custom-house.

Indeed, from this mode of calculating their value, and from the circumstance that American merchants have been, for many years, principally their own carriers, however paradoxical it may appear, it is nevertheless true that the real gain of the United States has been nearly in proportion as their imports have exceeded their exports. This will be evident from a simple statement in respect to a single voyage. A vessel carries a cargo of flour to Spain or Portugal, say five thousand barrels. This was valued in 1811, at $9 50 cents per barrel, making the value of the cargo, at the place of exportation, $47,500. This flour would bring the shipper in Spain, say fifteen dollars per barrel, making the value of the cargo at a foreign port, $75,000, the difference being $27,500. This difference arises from the necessary charges on the voyage, including freight, insurance, commissions, &c. and perhaps, also, a profit more or less, according to the state of the market. If the avails of this cargo should be brought home directly in money, the value of the imports arising from it would of course be $75,000, exceeding the value of the original cargo before its exportation, $27,500. If this cargo were shipped in an American vessel, and entirely on account of the American merchant, this difference would be a gain to the United States. It is obvious, indeed, that unless the avails of the cargo, when sold in a foreign port, are sufficient to cover the expense of shipment in addition to the first cost at the place of exportation, it must be a losing voyage.

Returns, however, are not often made in money alone; the avails of an outward cargo are generally vested in some foreign articles and imported into the United States in our own vessels. The freight and other expenses on the return cargo, with a reasonable profit, are included in the value of the articles, and go to increase the difference between the estimated value of the imported and exported cargo. As most of our exports consist of bulky articles, and are carried in our own ships, the profit from freight alone has been very great. In 1811, one million four hundred and forty-five thousand and twelve barrels of flour were shipped from the United States, the average freight could not be less than two dollars per barrel, making for the whole quantity $2,890,024. When we add to this the freight on tobacco, rice, cotton, lumber, beef, pork, fish, &c. &c. &c. the whole must amount to many millions.

The imports are partly again exported, and the rest consumed in the United States. The quantity and estimated value of those exported are contained in our custom-house books, and are annually reported to congress from the treasury department, and Tables Nos. I. II. and III. shew the amount of goods paying duties ad valorem, together with the quantities of spirits, molasses, wines, teas, coffee, sugar, and salt, imported and exported at different periods.

From these it will be seen, that the value of merchandize paying duties ad valorem, and the quantities of foreign spirits, molasses, wines, teas, coffee, sugar, and salt, annually consumed in the United States at different periods, were as follows, viz. :—

	Merchandize paying duties ad valorem.
Average annual amount.	Dolls.
3 years, 1790 to 1792 - -	19,310,801
6 years, 1793 to 1798 - - -	27,051,440
3 years, 1805 to 1807 - -	38,549,966

	Spirits—foreign.
	Gallons.
3 years, 1790 to 1792 - - -	4,108,802
6 years, 1793 to 1798 - -	5,176,810
12 years, 1801 to 1812 - - -	6,834,878

	Molasses.
	Gallons.
3 years, 1790 to 1792 - -	5,423,122
6 years, 1793 to 1798 - - -	3,822,351
12 years, 1801 to 1812 - -	7,207,589

	Wines paying specific duties.	Wines paying duties ad valorem.
	Gallons.	Gallons.
3 years, 1790 to 1792 -	1,091,478 -	- -
6 years, 1793 to 1798 -	1,502,403 -	661,943
12 years, 1801 to 1812 -	1,715,892 -	- -

	Teas. pounds.
Average annual amount.	
3 years, 1790 to 1792	2,215,749
6 years, 1793 to 1798	2,175,694
12 years, 1801 to 1812	3,277,194

	Coffee. pounds.
3 years, 1790 to 1792	3,836,391
6 years, 1793 to 1798	7,351,665
12 years, 1801 to 1812	11,107,380

	Sugar. pounds.
3 years, 1790 to 1792	22,397,370
6 years, 1793 to 1798	36,149,664
12 years, 1801 to 1812	50,279,249

	Salt. pounds.
3 years, 1790 to 1792	1,475,033
6 years, 1793 to 1798	2,210,942
7 years, 1801 to 1807	3,856,543

The consumption of foreign articles has increased, with the increase of population, and in the articles of coffee and sugar particularly, the ratio of increase has been in proportion to the wealth, as well as the population of the country.

The increase of American population, it is believed, has been, without example, in the annals of the world. From 1749 to 1790, a period of forty-one years, the increase was, from little more than a million, to nearly four millions. By the first enumeration under the present constitution, in 1790, the number of inhabitants was—   3,929,326

By the second, in 1800,   5,309,758

By the third, in 1810,   7,239,903

being an increase, in twenty years, of   3,310,577

The numbers in each state, in each of these years, may be seen in tables No. IV. V. and VI.

The whole quantity of sugar consumed in the United States, for some years past, must have been about seventy millions of pounds. In 1810, about ten millions were made, in the territory of Orleans, now state of Louisiana ; and in the same year, according to the returns of the marshals, more than nine millions and a half of sugar were made from the maple tree, in the United States.

Sugar plantations have been, and still are increasing in Louisiana ; and it is stated, by those well acquainted with the subject, that, in 1814, not less than fifteen millions were made in that state ; though but a small proportion of the lands there, suitable for sugar, have yet been planted with cane.

The culture of the sugar cane has lately been introduced into the state of Georgia ; and the experiments already made have been attended with the most flattering success. In 1805, Thomas Spalding, Esq. a gentleman of wealth and enterprise, in that state, procured one hundred cane plants from the West-Indies, for the purpose of trying them on his plantation, on an island near the sea coast of Georgia. After repeated trials, in which he was guided, principally, by his own judgment and experience, he completely succeeded. About three years since, he made a small quantity of sugar of a good quality ; and in 1814, he had one hundred acres in cane, which produced seventy-five thousand weight of prime sugar, and four thousand gallons of molasses ; and but, for the want of boilers, which, on account of the war, could not be brought to his plantation, would have produced one hundred thousand weight. The culture of the cane is found not to be more laborious than cotton, and is not liable to so many accidents. One thousand pounds per acre is not considered a great crop. This at ten cents, would be one hundred dollars. Almost every planter, along the sea coast of Georgia, is now turning his attention, more or less, to the culture of the sugar cane ; and from experiments already made, the cane is found to grow luxuriantly, as far north as the city of Charleston, in South-Carolina.

There can, perhaps, be little doubt, that, at a period not very far distant, a sufficient quantity of sugar may be made, within the limits of the United States, for the consumption of the inhabitants.

TABLE No. 1.

A Statement of the value and quantities respectively of Merchandise (paying duties ad valorem,) spirits, molasses, wines, teas, coffee, sugar, and salt, on which duties actually accrued for each of the calendar years 1790 to 1800, consisting of the value or quantities remaining in the United States at the end of each year, after deducting the value and quantities exported each year, and which became entitled to draw-backs, bounties, or allowances, from the value and quantities imported during the same year, and on which duties were either paid or secured.

YEARS.	Merchandise paying duties ad va.	Foreign spirits.	Molasses.	WINES, PAYING		Teas.	Coffee.	Sugar.	Salt.
				Specific duties.	Ad valorem.				
	dolls.	glls.	glls.	glls.	glls.	lbs.	lbs.	lbs.	bushels.
			(a)		(b)				(c)
1790	16,331,986	4,143,385	5,664,345	1,088,455	-	3,047,242	4,150,754	22,719,457	1,734,053
1791	20,093,364	3,603,861	6,354,148	916,256	-	985,997	2,588,970	21,919,066	1,359,461
1792	21,507,053	4,579,160	4,250,874	1,269,723	-	2,614,008	4,769,450	22,499,588	1,331,586
1793	21,284,130	3,428,391	4,236,222	1,194,969	312,514	2,009,509	11,237,717	37,291,988	1,424,974
1794	22,624,413	5,545,681	3,144,225	1,559,773	934,579	2,460,914	6,033,618	33,645,772	2,236,718

(a) From the annual importations are deducted the annual exportations, both of molasses and of domestic spirits distilled from molasses.

(b) The non-enumerated wines paid forty per cent. ad valorem, but not exceeding thirty cents nor less than ten cents per gallon. The quantities which by that regulation paid precisely either ten or thirty cents are ascertained. The quantities which paid the duty ad valorem, viz. from ten to thirty cents per gallon, are estimated as having paid on average, twenty cents per gallon. This column shows, from the year 1793, those three kinds distinctly from wines paying specific duties, viz. Madeira, Sherry and St. Lucar, Burgundy and Champaign, Lisbon and Oporto, Teneriffe, Fayal, and Malaga.

(c) From the annual importations are deducted not only the exportations of salt, but also the quantities which did not pay duties on account of the bounties upon the exportation of salted fish and provisions, and of the allowances to fisheries; the quantities thus deducted being calculated as if the bounties and allowances had been during the whole period at the same rate as established by the now existing laws.

TABLE No. 1.—CONTINUED.

YEARS.	Merchandise paying duties ad va. dolls.	Foreign spirits. gills.	Molasses. gills.	WINES, PAYING		Teas. lbs.	Coffee. lbs.	Sugar. lbs.	Salt. bushels.
				Specific duties. gills.	Ad valorem. gills.				
1795	29,886,973	5,018,562	3,853,905	1,880,619	1,477,341	2,374,118	14,674,726	37,582,507	2,281,343
1796	36,496,589	5,599,760	3,896,241	1,896,672	321,233	2,310,259	(d)5,526,269	25,403,581	3,012,049
1797	28,044,276	6,819,728	3,724,369	1,528,458	512,955	2,008,399	13,511,877	49,767,745	2,288,172
1798	23,972,260	4,648,743	4,079,145	951,927	413,036	1,890,965	4,178,321	33,206,395	2,022,397
1799	33,093,831	7,302,297	3,889,084	1,009,799	197,702	4,501,503	10,800,182	57,079,636	1,662,511
1800	34,393,617	4,785,937	3,717,359	1,241,553	437,362	3,797,634	7,408,196	50,537,637	2,734,243
Total,	287,728,492	55,475,505	46,809,917	15,140,204	4,606,722	28,000,548	73,827,542	391,653,372	22,087,507
Total amount of the 3 yrs. 1790–1792, -	57,932,403	12,326,406	16,269,367	3,274,434	-	6,647.247	11,509,174	67,138,111	4,425,100
Average ann. amount of the 3 yrs. 1790–1792,	19,310,801	4,108,802	5,423,122 $\frac{1}{3}$	1,091,478	-	2,215,749	3,836,391 $\frac{1}{3}$	22,379,370	1,475,033
Total amount of the 6 yrs. 1793–1798, -	162,308,641	31,060,865	22,934,107	9,014,418	3,971,658	13,054,164	44,109,990	216,897,988	13,265,653
Average ann. amount of the 6 yrs. 1793–1798,	27,051,440	5,176,810 $\frac{5}{6}$	3,822,351 $\frac{1}{6}$	1,502,403	661,943	2,175,694	7,351,665	36,149,664 $\frac{4}{6}$	2,210,942

(d) Excess of exportation beyond importation for that year.

TREASURY DEPARTMENT,

Register's Office, December 12th, 1801.

JOSEPH NOURSE, Register.

TABLE No. II.

Statement exhibiting the amount or value of goods paying duties ad valorem imported into the United States, together with the duties accruing thereon—also the amount or value of the same goods exported; distinguishing those entitled to drawback and those not entitled to drawback.

YEARS.	Value of goods imported paying duties ad valorem.	Duties.	Value of goods exported paying duties ad valorem entitled to drawback.	Value of goods exported paying duties ad val. not entitled to drawback.
1801 - -	55,569,255	7,070,430	- -	- -
1802 - -	37,546,051	4,960,123	- -	- -
1803 - -	36,842,865	4,850,630	- -	- -
1804 - -	43,481,363	5,664,797	- -	- -
1805 - -	49,148,064	6,410,440	7,861,744	5,617,889
1806 - -	54,832,896	7,162,099	10,121,468	6,066,099
1807 - -	57,820,532	7,560,929	11,047,359	5,437,034
1808 - -	21,216,935	2,739,375	2, 50,192	1,443,198
1809 - -	28,549,588	3,806,263	3,587,209	1,759,216
1810 - -	52,476,125	6,814,255	3,791,835	2,837,076
1811 - -	21,874,953	2,820,166	3,535,318	3,120,884
1812 - -	24,729,282	5,782,144	1,630,122	888,900

The *importations* in these statements are from 1st January, 1801, to the 31st December, 1812, and the *exports* from the 1st of October, 1801, to the 30th September, 1812.

TABLE No. III.

Statement exhibiting the quantity of spirits, wines, teas, coffee, sugars, and salt, imported into the United States—also, the quantity of the same articles exported and consumed from the year 1801 to 1812.

YEARS.	SPIRITS.			MOLASSES.		
	Imported.	Exported.	Consumed.	Imported.	Exported.	Consumed.
	gls.	gls.	gls.	gls.	gls.	gls.
1801 - -	8,234,090	520,205	7,713,885	6,062,379	421,628	5,640,751
1802 - -	8,287,263	507,256	7,780,007	7,004,872	56,959	6,947,913
1803 - -	9,352,315	299,182	9,053,133	5,998,535	38,552	5,959,983
1804 - -	11,718,710	1,119,059	10,599,651	6,668,920	55,259	6,613,661
1805 - -	9,242,573	1,812,216	7,430,357	9,251,720	48,474	9,203,246
1806 - -	11,673,650	1,366,560	10,307,090	8,563,061	53,798	8,509,263
1807 - -	10,700,474	1,622,127	9,078,347	8,358,591	40,947	8,317,644
1808 - -	4,677,697	229,992	4,447,705	6,456,916	7,337	6,449,579
1809 - -	4,899,368	266,423	4,632,945	5,378,503	33,943	5,344,560
1810 - -	3,607,200	123,000	3,484,200	7,671,765	40,245	7,631,520
1811 - -	3,526,305	116,788	3,409,517	8,519,211	18,737	8,500,474
1812 - -	4,119,591	37,895	4,081,696	7,380,475	8,001	7,372,474
Average consumption,	- -	- -	6,834,878	- -	- -	7,207,589

TABLE No. III.—CONTINUED.

YEARS.	WINES.			TEAS.			COFFEE.		
	Imported. gls.	Exported. gls.	Consumed. gls.	Imported. lbs.	Exported. lbs.	Consumed. lbs.	Imported. lbs.	Exported. lbs.	Consumed. lbs.
1801	3,304,340	1,531,752	1,772,588	4,086,960	1,409,253	2,677,707	59,318,888	45,106,494	14,212,394
1802	2,548,459	1,327,109	1,221,350	4,269,828	1,894,538	2,375,290	33,412,853	36,501,998	-
1803	2,290,980	306,017	1,984,963	6,053,529	3,146,492	2,907,037	18,842,440	10,294,693	8,547,747
1804	5,092,311	1,585,392	3,506,919	3,622,828	1,219,233	2,403,595	60,118,793	48,312,713	11,806,080
1805	6,265,114	3,519,776	2,745,338	5,119,441	1,788,888	3,330,553	46,121,600	46,760,294	-
1806	4,468,494	3,570,209	898,285	6,370,806	2,002,207	4,868,599	64,179,613	47,001,662	17,177,951
1807	6,249,823	3,180,475	3,069,348	8,108,774	2,663,061	5,445,713	55,768,027	42,122,573	13,645,454
1808	1,536,456	1,187,081	349,375	4,812,638	237,883	4,574,755	31,479,240	7,325,448	24,153,792
1809	1,476,530	621,603	854,927	1,482,990	1,770,616	-	37,329,024	24,364,099	12,964,925
1810	1,425,573	238,923	1,186,650	7,839,457	1,337,732	6,501,725	30,862,909	31,423,477	-
1811	1,979,409	344,521	1,634,888	3,018,118	1,025,962	1,992,156	28,879,942	10,261,136	18,618,806
1812	1,669,770	303,694	1,366,076	3,056,089	519,262	2,536,827	26,523,543	10,073,722	16,449,821
Average consumption,	-	-	1,715,392	-	-	3,277,194	-	-	11,107,380

TABLE No. III.—CONTINUED.

YEARS.	SUGARS.			SALT.		
	Imported. lbs.	Exported. lbs.	Consumed. lbs.	Imported. bushels.	Exported. bushels.	Consumed. bushels.
1801 -	143,611,596	97,734,209	45,877,387	3,608,947	70,067	3,538,880
1802 -	78,476,165	61,180,208	17,295,957	3,921,774	42,832	3,878,942
1803 -	85,740,537	23,323,482	62,417,055	3,568,708	25,548	3,543,160
1804 -	129,969,997	75,096,401	54,873,596	3,483,544	28,427	3,455,117
1805 -	205,792,755	122,808,993	82,983,762	3,782,328	15,358	3,766,970
1806 -	200,737,940	145,630,841	55,107,099	4,262,705	64,949	4,197,756
1807 -	215,836,202	143,119,605	72,716,597	4,707,824	92,850	4,614,974
1808 -	86,694,229	28,962,527	57,731,702	49,345	18,524	30,821
1809 -	64,081,840	45,297,338	18,784,502	360	597	-
1810 -	68,368,792	47,024,002	21,344,790	3,297	7,657	-
1811 -	73,976,609	18,268,347	55,708,262	-	898	-
1812 -	72,437,561	13,927,277	58,510,284	-	1	-
Average consumption,	-	-	50,279,249 (for 7 yrs.)	-	-	3,856,543

TABLE No. IV.

Census of the Inhabitants of the United States in August, 1790.

	Free white males of 16 years & upwards.	Free white males under sixteen years.	Free white females.	All other freepersons.	Slaves.	Total.
Vermont,	22,435	22,328	40,505	255	16	85,539
New-Hampshire,	36,086	34,851	70,160	630	158	141,885
Maine,	24,384	24,748	46,870	538	none	96,540
Massachusetts,	95,453	87,289	190,582	5,463	none	378,787
Rhode-Island,	16,019	15,799	32,652	3,407	948	68,825
Connecticut,	60,523	54,403	117,448	2,808	2,764	237,946
New-York,	83,700	78,122	152,320	4,654	21,324	340,120
New-Jersey,	45,251	41,416	83,287	2,762	11,423	184,139
Pennsylvania,	110,788	106,948	206,363	6,537	3,737	434,373
Delaware,	11,783	12,143	22,384	3,899	8,887	59,094
Maryland,	55,915	51,339	101,395	8,043	103,036	319,728
Virginia,	110,936	116,135	215,046	12,866	292,627	747,610
North-Carolina,	69,988	77,506	140,710	4,975	100,571	393,951
South-Carolina,	35,576	37,722	66,880	1,801	107,094	249,073
Georgia,	13,103	14,044	25,739	398	29,264	82,548
Kentucky,	15,154	17,057	28,922	114	12,430	73,677
Territory of the United States North-West of River Ohio,	6,271	10,277	15,365	·361	3,417	35,691
					697,696	3,929,326

TABLE No. V.

Enumeration of persons in the several Districts of the United States in August, 1800.

Names of Districts.	FREE WHITE MALES.					FREE WHITE FEMALES.					All other free persons except Indians not taxed.	Slaves.	Total.
	Under 10 years of age	Of 10 and under 16	Of 16 and under 26, including heads of families	Of 26 and under 45, including heads of families	Of 45 and upwards, including heads of families	Under 10 years of age	Of 10 and under 16	Of 16 and under 26, including heads of families	Of 26 and under 45, including heads of families	Of 45 and upwards, including heads of families			
New-Hampshire,	30,694	14,881	16,379	17,589	11,715	29,871	14,193	17,153	18,381	12,142	852	8	183,858
Massachusetts,	63,646	32,507	37,905	39,729	31,348	60,920	30,674	40,491	43,833	35,340	6,452	-	422,845
Maine,	27,970	12,305	12,900	15,318	8,339	26,899	11,338	13,295	14,496	8,041	818	-	151,719
Connecticut,	37,946	19,408	21,683	23,180	18,976	35,736	18,218	23,561	25,186	20,827	5,330	951	251,002
Vermont,	29,420	12,046	13,242	16,544	8,076	28,272	11,366	12,606	15,287	7,049	557	-	154,465
Rhode-Island,	9,945	5,352	5,889	5,785	4,887	9,524	5,026	6,463	6,919	5,648	3,304	380	69,122
New-York,	33,161	36,953	40,045	52,454	25,497	79,154	32,822	39,086	47,710	23,161	8,573	15,602	484,065
Supplemental return for New-York state,	16,936	7,320	9,230	9,140	6,358	16,319	6,649	9,030	8,701	5,490	1,801	5,011	101,985
New-Jersey,	33,900	15,859	16,301	19,956	12,629	32,622	14,827	17,018	19,533	11,600	4,402	12,422	211,149
Eastern district of Pennsylvania,	52,767	24,438	29,393	33,864	20,824	51,176	23,427	29,879	30,892	19,329	11,253	557	327,979
Western district of Pennsylvania,	50,459	21,623	24,869	25,469	17,761	48,448	20,362	24,095	22,954	14,066	3,311	1,149	274,566
Delaware,	8,250	4,437	5,121	5,012	2,213	7,628	4,277	5,543	4,981	2,390	8,268	6,153	64,273

TABLE No. V.—CONTINUED.

Names of Districts.	FREE WHITE MALES.					FREE WHITE FEMALES.					All other free persons except Indians not taxed.	Slaves.	Total.
	Under 10 years of age	Of 10 and under 16.	Of 16 and under 26, including heads of families.	Of 26 and under 45, including heads of families.	Of 45 and upwards, including heads of families.	Under 10 years of age	Of 10 and under 16.	Of 16 and under 26, including heads of families.	Of 26 and under 45, including heads of families.	Of 45 and upwards, including heads of families.			
Maryland, inclusive of Washington county, in Columbia,	36,751	17,743	21,929	23,553	13,712	34,703	16,787	22,915	21,725	12,180	19,987	107,707	349,692
Additional return for Baltimore county,	567	226	318	343	249	571	222	375	318	199	41	847	4,276
Eastern district of Virginia,	57,837	25,998	32,444	34,588	19,087	54,597	25,469	34,807	32,641	18,821	18,194	322,199	676,682
District of Columbia, in Virginia,	889	320	483	557	221	670	313	479	473	189	383	1,172	5,949
Western district of Virginia,	34,601	14,502	16,264	15,674	11,134	32,726	13,366	15,923	8,632	15,169	1,930	23,597	203,518
North-Carolina,	63,118	27,073	31,560	31,209	18,688	59,074	25,874	32,989	30,665	17,514	7,043	133,296	478,103
South-Carolina,	37,411	16,156	17,761	19,344	10,244	34,664	15,857	18,145	17,236	9,437	3,185	146,157	345,591
Georgia,	19,841	8,469	9,787	10,914	4,957	18,407	7,914	9,243	8,835	3,894	1,919	59,699	162,686
Kentucky,	37,274	14,045	15,705	17,699	9,238	34,949	13,433	15,524	14,934	7,075	741	40,343	220,959
Territory N. W. river Ohio,	9,362	3,647	4,636	4,833	1,955	8,644	3,353	3,861	3,342	1,395	337	- -	45,365
Indiana territory,	854	347	466	645	262	791	280	424	393	115	163	135	5,641
Mississippi territory,	999	356	482	780	290	953	376	352	426	165	182	3,489	8,850
Tennessee,	19,227	7,194	8,282	8,352	4,125	18,450	7,042	8,554	6,992	3,491	309	13,584	105,602

Grand Total, 5,309,758

TABLE No. VI.

Aggregate amount of each description of Persons within the United States of America, and the Territories thereof, agreeably to actual enumeration made according to law, in the year 1810.

Names of the Districts and Territories.	FREE WHITE MALES.					FREE WHITE FEMALES.					All other free persons except Indians not taxed.	Slaves.	Totals in each district.
	Under ten years of age.	Of ten and under sixteen.	Of sixteen and under twenty-six, including heads of families.	Of twenty-six & under forty-five, including heads of families.	Of forty-five and upwards, including heads of families.	Under ten years of age.	Of ten and under sixteen.	Of sixteen and under twenty-six, including heads of families.	Of twenty-six & under forty-five, including heads of families.	Of forty-five and upwards, including heads of families.			
Dist. of Maine, -	41,273	18,463	20,403	22,079	13,291	39,131	17,827	21,290	21,464	12,515	969	-	228,705
Massachusetts,	68,930	34,964	45,018	45,854	34,776	66,881	33,391	46,366	49,229	39,894	6,737	-	472,040
N. Hampshire,	34,284	17,840	18,865	20,531	14,462	32,313	17,259	20,792	21,940	15,204	970	-	214,460
Vermont, -	38,082	18,347	19,678	20,791	13,053	36,621	17,341	20,983	20,792	11,457	750	-	217,895
Rhode-Island,	10,735	5,554	7,250	6,765	5,439	10,555	5,389	7,520	7,635	6,372	3,609	108	76,931
Connecticut, -	37,812	20,498	23,880	23,699	20,484	35,913	18,931	24,973	26,293	22,696	6,453	310	261,942
New-York, -	165,933	73,702	85,779	94,882	53,985	157,945	68,811	85,139	85,805	46,718	25,333	15,017	959,049
New-Jersey, -	37,814	18,914	21,231	21,394	16,004	36,062	17,787	21,194	21,359	15,109	7,843	10,851	245,562
Pennsylvania, -	138,464	62,606	74,203	74,193	52,100	131,769	60,943	75,960	70,826	45,740	22,492	795	810,091
Delaware, -	9,632	4,480	5,150	5,866	2,878	9,041	4,370	5,541	5,527	2,876	13,136	4,177	72,674
Maryland,	38,613	18,489	22,688	25,255	15,165	36,137	17,833	23,875	22,908	14,154	33,927	111,502	380,546
Virginia, -	97,777	42,919	51,473	52,567	35,302	90,715	42,207	54,899	51,163	32,512	30,570	392,518	974,622
Ohio, -	46,623	18,119	20,189	22,761	11,965	44,192	16,869	19,990	19,436	8,717	1,899	-	230,760
Kentucky, -	65,134	26,804	29,772	29,553	17,542	60,776	25,743	29,511	25,920	13,482	1,713	80,561	406,511

{ 700,745

TABLE No. VI.—CONTINUED.

Names of the Districts and Territories.	FREE WHITE MALES. Under ten years of age.	Of ten and under sixteen.	Of sixteen & under twenty-six, including heads of families.	Of twenty-six & under forty-five, including heads of families.	Of forty-five and upwards, including heads of families.	FREE WHITE FEMALES. Under ten years of age.	Of ten and under sixteen.	Of sixteen and under twenty-six, including heads of families.	Of twenty-six & under forty-five, including heads of families.	Of forty-five and upwards, including heads of families.	All other free persons, except Indians not taxed.	Slaves.	Totals in each district.	Total in the U. States, Total in the territories.
Dist. of N. Carolina,	68,036	30,321	34,630	34,456	21,189	65,421	30,053	37,933	33,944	20,427	10,266	168,824	555,500	
East Tennessee	18,392	7,618	8,266	7,539	4,998	17,416	7,216	8,559	7,348	4,129	510	9,376	101,367	} 261,727
West Tennessee	26,102	9,552	11,220	12,418	5,658	24,394	9,113	11,305	10,276	4,356	807	35,159	160,360	
South-Carolina	39,669	17,193	20,933	20,488	11,304	37,497	16,629	20,583	18,974	10,926	4,554	196,365	415,115	Total in the U. States,
Georgia, -	28,602	11,951	14,085	14,372	7,435	26,283	11,237	13,461	12,350	6,238	1,801	105,218	252,433	7,036,363
Ter. of Orleans,	5,848	2,491	2,963	5,130	2,508	5,384	2,588	2,874	3,026	1,499	7,585	34,660	76,556	
Mississippi,	4,217	1,637	2,692	3,160	1,144	4,015	1,544	2,187	1,753	675	240	17,088	40,352	
Louisiana, -	3,438	1,345	1,568	2,069	967	3,213	1,265	1,431	1,369	562	607	3,011	20,845	
Indiana, -	4,923	1,922	2,284	2,316	1,125	4,555	1,863	2,228	1,880	794	393	237	24,520	
Illinois, -	2,266	945	1,274	1,339	556	2,019	791	1,053	894	364	613	168	12,282	
Michigan, -	800	351	583	763	340	406	332	368	311	130	120	24	4,762	Total in the territories,
Dist. of Columbia,	2,479	1,158	1,520	2,107	866	2,538	1,192	1,653	1,734	832	2,549	5,395	24,023	203,340
	1,035,278	468,183	547,597	572,347	364,736	981,426	448,324	561,668	544,156	338,378	186,446	1,191,364	7,239,903	

Grand Total, 7,239,903

CHAPTER VIII.

We have before stated, that in April, 1783, the debt of the United States (exclusive of the State debts) was estimated at $42,000,375 and that from that time, to. the commencement of the present government, a small part only of the interest of this sum was paid. The attention of the first Congress was early called to the subject of supporting public credit, and of making provision for the payment of the public debt. The first House of Representatives, under the constitution, directed the Secretary of the Treasury, to prepare and report a plan for the support of public credit. The Secretary, in pursuance of such direction, made a report on the subject, the 9th of January, 1790, which afterwards became the basis of the various laws passed by congress for funding and paying the public debt. By this report, the whole debt of the United States, foreign and domestic, liquidated and unliquidated, was estimated at $54,124,464 and 56 cents.

The principal of the foreign debt, was   - $10,070,307
Arrears of interest to the last day of December,
1789,   -   -   -   -   -   1,640,071 62

$11,710,378 62

The foreign debt consisted of loans from governments and individuals in Europe, as follows, viz.—

CAPITAL SUMS BORROWED.

	Livres.	Dolls.	Cts.
Of the royal French treasury, on interest at five per cent. - - - 24,000,000			
In Holland, guaranteed by the French court, at four per cent. - - 10,000,000			

Livres 34,000,000 6,296,296

Of the royal Spanish treasury, at five per cent. - - - - - 174,011

Lenders in Holland,	Florins.
first loan, five per cent. - - 5,000,000	
second loan, four per cent. - 2,000,000	
third loan, five per cent. - - 1,000,000	
fourth loan, five per cent. - 1,000,000	

9,000,000 3,600,000

$10,070,307

ARREARAGES OF INTEREST TO 31ST DECEMBER, 1789.

ON THE FRENCH LOAN.

	Livres.	Dolls. Cts.
1789, Jan. 1, 5 yrs. interest on the 6,000,000 at five per cent. - -		277,777 77
Sept. 3, six years interest on the 18,000,000 at five per cent. - -		999,999 96
Nov. 5, four years interest on the 10,000,000 at four per cent. - -		296,296

ON THE SPANISH LOAN.

	Dolls. Cts.	
Arrearages on the Spanish loan of $174,011 to 21st March 1782, at 5 per ct. -	5,093 27	
March 21, seven years interest on do.	60,904 62	
		1,640,071 62
		$11,710,378 62

The principal of the liquidated domestic debt was	$27,383,917 74
The arrears of interest to the end of 1790, amount to - - - -	13,030,168 20
	$40,414,085 94
The unliquidated debt was estimated at -	2,000,000
Making together, - - -	$54,124,464 56

The state debts, including interest, were estimated at $25,000,000. In this report, the Secretary recommends to Congress an assumption of the state debts, with like provision for payment as the debts of the union, as " a measure of sound policy and substantial justice." If the United States should assume the state debts, the whole debt, to be provided for by the general government, would amount to about seventy-nine millions of dollars, and the annual interest to $4,587,444 and 81 cents, as estimated in the report.

It was doubted by the Secretary, whether, in addition to the other expenses of the government, it was in the power of the United States " to make a secure and effectual provision for so large a sum, on the terms of the original contracts." On this subject he says " the interesting problem now occurs: Is it in the power of the United States, consistently with those prudential considerations, which ought not to be overlooked, to make provision equal to the purpose of funding the whole debt, at the rates of interest which it now bears, in addition to the sum which will be necessary for the current service of the government ?

" The Secretary will not say that such a provision would exceed the abilities of this country; but he is clearly of opinion, that to make it, would require the extension of taxation to a degree, and to objects, which the true interest of the public forbids. It is therefore to be hoped, and even to be expected, that they will cheerfully concur in such modifications of their claims, on fair and equitable principles, as will facilitate to the government an arrangement substantial, durable, and satisfactory to the community. It will not be forgotten, that exigencies may, ere long, arise, which would call for resources, greatly beyond what is now deemed sufficient for the current service; and that, should the faculties of the country be exhausted or even strained to provide for the public debt, there could be less reliance on the sacredness of the provision.

" But while the Secretary yields to the force of these considerations, he does not lose sight of those fundamental principles of good faith, which dictate, that every practicable exertion ought to be made, scrupulously to fulfil the engagements of the government; that no change in the rights of its citizens ought to be attempted without their voluntary consent; and that this consent ought to be voluntary in fact, as well as in name. Consequently, that every proposal of a change ought to be in the shape of an appeal to their reason and to their interest; not to their necessities. To this end it is requisite, that a *fair equivalent* should be offered for what may be asked to be given up, and unquestionable *security* for the remainder. Without this, an alteration, consistently with the credit and honour of the nation, would be impracticable."

With these views, he submits to the consideration of Congress, various plans and propositions for the modification, security, and payment of the domestic debt. The main object of all his propositions was either to lower the rate of interest, or to postpone the payment of the interest, or a part of the sum, to a distant day, with the consent of the creditors themselves. On the 14th of August, 1790, Congress passed " an act making provision for the debt of the United States." This act proposed a loan of the whole of the domestic debt. The terms of the loan were, that two thirds of the principal of the debt subscribed should draw an interest of six per cent. per annum, from and after the first day of January, 1791, and the remaining third of the principal, to draw the same interest, from and after the year 1800 ; the interest on both to be payable quarter yearly ; and that so much of the debt subscribed, as consisted of arrears of interest, should, from and after the first day of January, 1791, bear an interest of three per cent.

By the same act, Congress assumed twenty-one and a half millions of the debts of the several states ; and the sums assumed were apportioned to each state. This sum was also to be loaned to the Unit_ ed States, by the individuals who held certain evidences of state debts, on the following terms. viz. Each subscriber to be entitled to one certificate for the sum equal to four ninths of the sum subscribed, bearing an interest of six per cent. per annum, commencing the first day of January, 1792 ; to another certificate for a sum equal to two ninths of the sum subscribed, bearing an interest of six per cent. after the year 1800 ; and to a third certificate, for a sum equal to three ninths of the sum subscribed, bearing an interest of three per cent. from the first day of January, 1792. This act was, at first, limited to one year, but was afterwards extended until the whole of the assumed debt was subscribed, and nearly the whole of the domestic debt of the United States. On the 31st day of December, 1794, the amount of the domestic or original debt of the United States, which was subscribed and *funded* according to the provisions of law, (including the debt standing to the credit of individual states, being balances found due to them on a final settlement of accounts between them and the United States, and including also, that which, previous to that time, had been purchased by the commissioners of the sinking fund,) was as follows, viz.

Six per cent. stock,	-	-	-	$20,925,894 39
Deferred stock,	-	-	-	10,462,947 61
Three per cent. stock,	-	-	-	13,394,280 01

The amount of funded assumed debt, (including that purchased or redeemed by the commissioners of the sinking fund,) on the last day of December, 1794, was as follows, viz.—

Six per cent. stock, - - -	$8,120,836	23
Deferred stock, - - - -	4,060,417	84
Three per cent. stock, - - -	6,090,560	67
Making in the whole six per cent. stock, -	$29,046,730	62
Deferred stock, - -	14,523,365	45
Three per cent. stock, -	19,484,840	68
	$63,054,936	75
Redeemed by purchase, - -	2,265,022	57
Total due, December 31st, 1794,* -	$60,789,914	18

The total amount of the *unredeemed* debt of the United States, both foreign and domestie, and the particulars of which it consisted, on the 31st day of December, 1794, was as follows, viz.—

Foreign debt, - - $14,599,129 35
Deduct instalments of foreign debt in the year 1795, to be paid out of proceeds of foreign loans, - - 853,750
———————— 13,745,379 35

Funded domestic debt, viz.
1. Arising from original domestic debt, subscribed to loan proposed by funding act,
    Stock bearing present interest of six per cent. - $17,912,138 01
    Stock bearing a future interest of six per cent. - 8,538,228 97
    Stock bearing interest of three per cent. - 12,275,347 55

* See Report of the Secretary of the Treasury, 1795.

2. Arising from state debts assumed,
  Stock bearing present interest of six per cent. - $7,908,374 19
  Stock bearing a future interest of six per cent. - 3,940,608 96
  Stock bearing an interest of three per cent. - 5,994,115 70

3. Arising from balances to creditor states,
  Stock bearing present interest of six per cent. - 2,345,056
  Stock bearing a future interest of six per cent. - 1,172,528
  Stock bearing an interest of three per cent. - 703,516 80
  ————————— 60,789,914 18

Unsubscribed debt, viz.
  Principal, exclusive of loan office certificates, bearing interest, on nominal value, - $1,072,583 40
  Interest thereupon, including indents, - - 452,826 74
  Principal of loan office certificates, bearing interest on nominal sum, - - 27,937
  Interest thereupon, - 7,830
  ————————— 1,561,175 14

Total of unredeemed debt, - - $76,096,468 67

This is exclusive of a sum of $1,400,000 due to the bank of the United States, on account of the loan of $2,000,000 had of that institution, pursuant to the eleventh section of the act by which it is incorporated, and which is not included in the mass of the debt, because it is more than counter-balanced, by a greater value in stock.

It is also exclusive of those loans, which are temporary anticipations of the revenue.

The United States, by the terms of the loan, reserved to themselves the right of paying the six per cent. and deferred stock, in any sum, not exceeding eight per cent. per annum, both on account of principal and interest ; and the three per cents. were redeemable at the pleasure of the United States.

The Secretary of the Treasury, in his report of January, 1790, on the subject of funding the debt, proposes not only that funds be appropriated for the punctual payment of the interest, but that *permanent funds*, be also provided for the ultimate extinguishment of the debt itself.

On this subject he says, " Persuaded as the Secretary is, that the proper funding of the present debt will render it a national blessing ; yet he is so far from acceding to the position, in the latitude, it is sometimes laid down, that ' public debts are public blessings,' a position inviting to prodigality and liable to danger and abuse, that he ardently wishes to see incorporated, *as a fundamental maxim*, in the system of public credit of the United States, that the creation of a debt should always be accompanied with the means of extinguishment. This he regards as the true secret for rendering public credit immortal—and he presumes that it is difficult to conceive a situation in which there may not be an adherence to the maxim. At least, he feels an unfeigned solicitude, that this may be attempted by the United States, and that they may commence their measures for the establishment of credit, with the observance of it."

In pursuance of these views of the Secretary, provision was made by law first for the punctual payment of the interest of this debt, and afterwards for the reimbursement and redemption of the principal ; and funds were appropriated and pledged for those purposes.

Prior to the year 1795, the permanent duties on imported articles, the tonnage duties, the duties on spirits distilled within the United States, and on stills, after reserving out of the same, $600,000 per annum, for the support of the government of the United States, and their common defence, were appropriated and pledged—

1st. For the payment of the interest on foreign loans.

2d. For the payment of the interest on stock created by the loan of the domestic or original debt of the United States.

3d. For the payment of the interest of the assumed debt.

4th. For the payment of the interest on the balances due to the creditor states.

These appropriations had priorities according to the order in which they are enumerated.

A fund was also created, previous to the year 1795, for the redemption of the debt, which was called " the sinking fund," and was placed under the management of the President of the Senate, the Chief Justice, the Secretary of State, the Secretary of the Treasury, and the Attorney-General for the time being, who were called Commissioners of " the sinking fund." This fund consisted—

1st. Of the surplus of the duties on imports and tonnage to the end of the year 1790.

2d. The proceeds of loans, not exceeding $2,000,000, authorized to be borrowed for that purpose.

3d. The interest on the public debt, purchased, redeemed, or paid into the treasury, together with the surplusses, if any, of monies appropriated for interest.

4th. The avails of the public lands.

This fund was to be applied by the Commissioners, with the approbation of the President of the United States, as follows, viz. :—

1st. To purchases of the debt, till the fund is equal to two per cent. of the outstanding stock, then bearing an interest of six per cent.

2d. To the redemption of that stock ; and lastly, to purchases of any unredeemed residue of the public debt.

There was reserved, however, out of this fund, a sum not exceeding eight per cent. per annum, towards the payment of interest, and reimbursing of the principal of the loans made for purchases of the debt. The amount of the debt purchased by the Commissioners of the sinking fund up to December 31st, 1794, was $2,265,022 and 56 cents.

On the 19th of November, 1794, President Washington, in his speech to Congress, at the opening of their session, recommended that further provision be made for the security of public credit, and the ultimate redemption of the public debt, in the following words.—

" The time which has elapsed since the commencement of our fiscal measures, has developed our pecuniary resources, so as to open the way for a definitive plan for the redemption of the public debt. It is believed, that the result is such, as to encourage Congress to consummate this work without delay. Nothing can more promote the permanent welfare of the nation, and nothing would be more grateful to our constituents. Indeed, whatsoever is unfinished of our system of public credit, cannot be benefitted by procrastination ; and as far as may be practicable, we ought to place that credit on grounds which cannot be disturbed, and to prevent that progressive accumulation of debt, which must ultimately endanger all governments."

The Secretary of the Treasury, according with the views of the President on this subject, on the 16th of January, 1795, submitted to Congress, a plan for the further support of public credit. This plan, drawn up with great ability, recommended the adoption of a permanent system for the ultimate extinguishment of the whole debt of the United States. For this purpose, he proposed an increase of the sinking fund, by adding thereto duties on imports and tonnage, on spirits distilled within the United States, and on stills, the avails of the sales of public lands, the dividends on bank stock belonging to the United States, and the interest of the money which should be redeemed, and that there should be appropriated to the same fund, all monies, which should be received from debts due to the United States, antecedent to the present constitution, and all surplusses of the amount of revenue of the United States, which should remain at the end of any calendar year, beyond the amount of the appropriations charged upon them, and which, during the session of Congress commencing next thereafter, should not be specially appropriated. That this fund be applied to the payment and redemption of the six per cent. and deferred stock, (excluding that standing to the credit of the Commissioners of the sinking fund, and also that standing to the credit of particular states, on account of the balances reported in their favour, by the Commissioners for settling accounts between the United

States and individual states,) according to the right reserved to the United States ; that is, to the payment annually, of eight per cent. on account of the principal and interest, and to continue until the whole of the same should be paid and redeemed, and after such redemption, the same fund to continue appropriated, until the residue of the debt of the United States, foreign and domestic, funded and unfunded, should be redeemed and discharged.

The Secretary also proposed, that the faith of the United States should be firmly pledged to the creditors, that this fund should be inviolably applied to the redemption, payment, and purchase of the whole debt of the United States, until the same was fully completed; and that for this purpose, the said fund should be vested in the Commissioners of the sinking fund, " *as property in trust.*" He also proposed, that all priorities before established, in the appropriations for the funded debt, as between different parts of it after the year 1796, should cease unless dissented to, by the creditors ; and that the revenue thus appropriated, should constitute a common or consolidated fund, chargeable indiscriminately and without priority.

The remarks of the Secretary, on the danger of a great accumulation of public debt, and on the necessary means to prevent it, are too important not to merit a place here.—" There is no sentiment," he says in his report, " which can better deserve the serious attention of the Legislature of a country, than the one expressed in the speech of the President ; which indicates the danger to every government, from the progressive accumulation of debt. A tendency to it is perhaps *the natural disease* of all governments ; and it is not easy to conceive any thing more likely than this to lead to great and convulsive revolutions of empires. On the one hand, the exigencies of a nation creating new causes of expenditure, as well from its own, as from the ambition, rapacity, injustice, intemperance and folly of other nations, proceed in unceasing and rapid succession. On the other, there is a general propensity in those, who administer the affairs of government, founded in the constitution of man, to shift off the burden from the present to a future day ; a propensity which may be expected to be strong in proportion as the form of the state is popular.

" To extinguish a debt, which exists, and to avoid contracting more, are ideas almost always favoured by public feeling and opinion ; but to pay taxes for the one or other purpose, which are the only means to avoid the evil, is always more or less unpopular. These contradictions are in human nature. And the lot of a country would be enviable indeed, in which there were not always men ready to turn them to the account of their own popularity, or to some other sinister account. Hence it is no uncommon spectacle to see the same men clamouring for occasions of expense, when they happen to be in unison with the present humour of the community, well or ill directed, declaiming against a public debt, and for the reduction of it, as an *abstract thesis;* yet, vehement against every plan of taxation which is proposed to discharge old debts, or to avoid new, by defraying the expenses of exigencies as they emerge.

" These unhandsome acts throw artificial embarrassments in the way of the administrators of governments ; and cooperating with the desire, which they themselves are too apt to feel, to conciliate public favour by declining to lay unnecessary burdens, or with the fear of losing it, by imposing them with firmness, serve to promote the accumulation of debt ; by leaving that, which at any time exists, without adequate provision for its reimbursement, and by preventing the laying with energy new taxes, where new occasions of expense occur. The consequence is, that the public debt swells, till its magnitude becomes enormous, and the burthens of the people gradually increase, till their weight becomes intolerable. Of such a state of things great disorder in the whole political economy, convulsions and revolutions of governments are a natural offspring.

" There can be no more sacred obligation, then, on the public agents of a nation, than to guard, with provident foresight and inflexible perseverance, against so mischievous a result. True patriotism and genuine policy cannot, it is respectfully observed, be better demonstrated by those of the United States at the present juncture, than by improving efficiently the very favourable situation in which they stand, for extinguishing, with reasonable celerity, the actual debt of the country, and for laying the foundations of a system which may shield posterity from the consequences of the usual improvidence and selfishness of its ancestors ; and which, if possible, may give *immortality* to public credit."

On the policy of establishing a sinking fund, and of rendering its application to any other object, than that for which it is appropriated, inviolable, the Secretary, in the same Report, says " The intent is to secure, by all the sanctions of which the subject is susceptible, an inviolable application of the fund according to its destination. No expedients more powerful can be devised for this purpose, than to clothe it with the character of *private property*, and to engage absolutely the faith of the government, by making the application of it to the object, a part of the contract with the creditors. But is this necessary ?

" Its necessity rests upon these cogent reasons. The inviolable application of an adequate sinking fund is the only practicable security against an excessive accumulation of debt, and the essential basis of a permanent national credit.

" Experience has shewn, in countries the most attentive to the principles of public credit, that a simple appropriation of the sinking fund is not a complete barrier against its being diverted when immediate exigencies press. The causes which have been stated, with another view, tempt the administrators of government to lay hold of this resource, rather than impose new taxes.

" This indicates the utility of endeavouring to give, by additional sanctions, inviolability to the fund.

" But will those proposed answer the end ? They are the most efficacious that can be imagined ; and they are likely to be entirely efficacious.

" They cannot be disregarded without a breach of faith and contract, destroying credit, and that at a juncture, when it is most indispensable ; the emergencies which induce a diversion of the fund are those in which loans, and consequently credit, are most needed."

In pursuance of the plan suggested by the Secretary, an act was passed by Congress, on the 3d day of March 1795, " making further provision for the support of public credit, and for the redemption of the public debt."

By this act the following additional appropriations are made to the sinking fund, viz.—

" First. So much of the proceeds of the duties on goods, wares, and merchandize, on the tonnage of ships or vessels, and on spirits distilled within the United States, and on stills, as together with the monies, which now constitute the said fund, and shall accrue to it, by virtue of the provisions herein before made, and by the interest upon each instalment, or part of principal, which shall be reimbursed, will be sufficient, yearly and every year, commencing the 1st day of January next, to reimburse and pay so much as may rightfully be reimbursed and paid of the principal of that part of the debt or stock, which on the said first day of January next, shall bear an interest of six per cent. redeemable on account, both of principal and interest, not exceeding in one year eight per centum, excluding that which shall stand to the credit of the Commissioners of the sinking fund, and that which shall stand to the credit of certain states, in consequence of the balances reported in their favour by the Commissioners for settling accounts between the United States and individual states.

"Secondly. The dividends, which shall be, from time to time, declared on so much of the stock of the bank of the United States, as belongs to the United States (deducting thereout such sums as will be requisite to pay interest on any part remaining unpaid of the loan of two millions of dollars, had of the bank of the United States, pursuant to the eleventh section of the act, by which the said bank is incorporated.)

"Thirdly. So much of the duties on goods, wares, and merchandize imported, on the tonnage of ships or vessels, and on spirits distilled within the United States, and on stills, as with the said dividends, after such deduction, will be sufficient, yearly and every year, to pay the remaining instalments of the principal of said loan, as they shall become due, and as together with any other monies which, by virtue of provisions in former acts, and herein before made, shall on the 1st of January, in 1802, belong to the said sinking fund, not otherwise specially appropriated; and with the interest on each instalment, or part of principal, which shall, from time to time, be reimbursed, or paid, of that part of the debt or stock, which on the first day of January, 1801, shall begin to bear an interest of six per cent. per annum, will be sufficient, yearly and every year, commencing on the 1st day of January, 1802, to reimburse and pay so much as may rightfully be reimbursed and paid, of the said principal of the said debt or stock, &c.

"Fourthly. The net proceeds of the sales of lands, belonging, or which shall hereafter belong to the United States, in the western territory thereof.

"Fifthly. All monies, which shall be received into the Treasury, on account of debts due to the United States, by reason of any matter prior to their present constitution.

"And lastly : All surplusses of revenues of the United States, which shall remain, at the end of any calendar year, beyond the amount of the appropriations charged upon the said revenues, and which, during the session of Congress next thereafter, shall not be otherwise specially appropriated, or reserved by law."

By the same act, the monies thus appropriated to the sinking fund, were placed under the direction and management of the Commissioners of that fund ; and were to continue so appropriated, until the whole debt of the United States should be reimbursed and redeemed ; and were declared to *be vested* in said Commissioners, *in trust*, to be applied to the reimbursement and redemption of the whole of said debt.

And the faith of the United States was also pledged, "that the monies or funds aforesaid shall inviolably remain and be appropriated *and vested*, to be applied to the reimbursement and redemption, in manner aforesaid, until the same shall be fully and completely effected."

The Commissioners were also authorized, if necessary, with the approbation of the President of the United States, for the purpose of paying any instalments of the debt, which might become due, to borrow the sums required. This power was entrusted with the Commissioners, in order to give complete security to the creditors, for the punctual payment of the principal, as well as the interest of the debt, according to the terms of the contracts. The reason for vesting the Commissioners with this power, is given by the Secretary in his Report : "It is proposed to authorize the Commissioners of the sinking fund to provide by new loans for the reimbursement of the instalments which from time to time accrue. This is on the ground that it is essential to the perfection of the system of redemption, that all the means of ultimate execution should be organized in it, and that there should be no need of future provision."

The Commissioners were directed, to apply this fund—

1st. To the payment of eight per cent. per annum, both on account of principal and interest, on the six per cent. stock, commencing the reimbursement on the 1st day of January, 1796.

2d. To the payment of the loan had of the bank of the United States.

3d. To the payment of eight per cent. per annum, on account of principal and interest, on the deferred stock, commencing the reimbursement on the 1st day of January, 1802, and

4th. To apply the surplus of the fund, towards the redemption of the debt, both foreign and domestic, by payment, or purchase, until the same should be fully paid or redeemed.

By an act passed the 28th of April, 1796, the Commissioners were directed to pay this eight per cent. in the manner following, viz.—On the stock then bearing an interest of six per cent. 1st. By dividends to be made on the last days of March, June, and September, in each year, from 1796 to 1818, inclusive, at the rate of one and one half per cent. upon the original capital.

2d. By dividends to be made on the last day of December, 1796, and from 1797 to 1817, inclusive, on the last day of December in each year, at the rate of three and one half per cent. upon the original capital, and by a dividend to be made on the last day of December, 1818, of such a sum, as will be then adequate, according to the contract, for the final redemption of the debt.

The dividends on the deferred stock, to be made from the year 1801 to the year 1824, in like manner and proportion.

By this permanent arrangement for the final payment of the domestic debt, the holders of six per cent. and deferred stock, were to receive an *annuity* of eight per cent. on their capital, until the whole should be paid. This annuity, it was found on calculation, would extinguish the capital of the six per cent. stock, on the last day of December, 1818, and of the deferred stock, on the last of December, 1824.

The following was the state of the public debt, on the 1st day of January, 1800 :—

	Guilders.	Dolls.	Dolls.	Cts.
Foreign debt, due in Amsterdam and Antwerp, -	26,900,000	10,760,000		
Premiums payable on the loan of 9th March, 1784,	147,500	59,000		
			10,819,000	
	27,047,500			

	Dolls.	Cts.	Dolls.	Cts.
Domestic debt, viz. six per cent. stock, - -	$30,087,650	5		
Amount passed to the credit of the sinking fund, -	1,841,607	9		
	$28,246,042	96		
Deduct instalments reimbursed to the close of the year 1799, - -	$3,215,575	37		
Amount to be reimbursed,			$25,030,467	59
Deferred stock, -	$14,649,320	21		
Amount passed to the credit of the sinking fund, -	966,376	4		
			$13,682,944	17
Three per cent. stock, -	$19,701,545	1		
Amount passed to the credit of the sinking fund, -	614,836	47		
			$19,086,708	54
Five and one half per cent. stock, - - -	$1,848,900			
Amount passed to the credit of the sinking fund, -	1,400			
			$1,847,500	

	Dolls.	
Four and one half per cent. stock, -	176,000	
Six per cent. stock per act of 31st May, 1796, - - -	80,000	
Six per cent. navy stock, issued, -	109,200	
Six per cent. navy stock, to be issued,	820,000	
Eight per cent. stock issued in 1799,	5,000,000	
		$65,832,820 30

Total amount of the unredeemed capitals of the foreign and domestic funded debt on the 1st of January, 1800,   -   -   -   -   - $76,651,820 30

TEMPORARY LOANS.

Sums obtained of the bank of the United States, in anticipation of the revenue at five per cent. - - -	$1,400,000	
Sums obtained at six per cent. -	1,840,000	
Sums due on the subscription loan for stock, - - - - -	400,000	
	$3,640,000	
Deduct the cost of two thousand two hundred and twenty shares owned by the United States, - - -	888,000	
		2,752,000

Debt of the United States, January 1st, 1800,   - $79,403,820 30

The above account of the state of the public debt was laid before a Committee of the House of Representatives, appointed on the 20th of March, 1800, " to examine the accounts of the United States relating to the public debt, and to report the amount respectively incurred and extinguished, and generally such facts as relate to the increase or diminution of the same, since the establishment of the government of the United States, under the present constitution ;" and was by them reported to the House. This Committee also reported the following as a " Statement of debts contracted under the present Government of the United States, and of debts of the late Government discharged, up to January 1st, 1800, viz. :—

DEBTS CONTRACTED.

Five and an half per cent. stock issued for an equal amount due to France, - - - -		$1,848,900
Four and an half per cent. do. do. -		176,000
Six per cent. stock per act of May 31st, 1796, -		80,000
Navy stock issued and to be issued, - -		929,200
Eight per cent. stock, - - - -		5,000,000
Temporary loans, - - -	$3,640,000	
Deduct bank shares, - - -	888,000	
		2,752,000
Amount of debts contracted, - - -		$10,786,100

DEBTS DISCHARGED.

Foreign debt, January 1st, 1791,	$12,343,437 87	
Ditto January 1st, 1800,	10,819,000	
Foreign debt, reduced, - - -		$1,524,437 87
Six per cent. stock purchased or redeemed, -		1,841,607 9
Three per cent. do. do. - -		614,836 47
Deferred stock do. do. - -		966,376 4
Five and an half per cent. stock, - - -		1,400
Reimbursement of the six per cent. stock to the close of the year 1799, - - - - -		3,215,575 37
Amount of debts discharged, - - -		$6,164,232 84

It may be observed, that the five and an half and four and an half per cent. stock, was issued for the balance due to France, on account of the former loans from the French Government, during the revolutionary war, and was made payable at the pleasure of the Government.

The ~~eighty thousand~~ six per cent. stock was obtained on loan in the United States, in 1796, in pursuance of an act of Congress of May 31st of that year. The whole loan authorized by that act, and which was to be made by the Commissioners of the sinking fund, with the approbation of the President, was five millions of dollars, to be applied to the payment of the capital, or principal of any parts of the debt of the United States then due, or to become due, in the course of that year, to the bank of the United States, or to the bank of New-York, or for any instalment of foreign debt. Books were opened for the whole sum, but eighty thousand dollars only were subscribed, and which was irredeemable, until the close of the year 1819.

The navy six per cent. stock was issued or agreed to be issued, to certain persons, who built vessels of war, for the United States, in the years 1798 and 1799, and for which they agreed to receive in payment six per cent. stock payable at pleasure; and hence it has been generally denominated, *navy* six per cent. stock.

The eight per cent. stock of five millions was issued in consequence of a loan, opened in the United States, in pursuance of an act authorizing the same, passed July 16th, 1798, and was redeemable after the year 1808.

The temporary loans were in anticipation of the revenue,* and for subscription to the bank of the United States.

The views taken by the Committee above referred to, as to the amount of public debt, at various periods, from the commencement of the Government, and as to its increase or diminution, may not be uninteresting. The Committee in their report say " The order of the House having particularly directed the attention of the Committee to the increase or diminution of debt, they have thought it their duty to bring into view the amount of debt with which the present Government commenced its operations, and to contrast the same with the balance of debt on the first of January in the present year. In discharging this duty, it will become necessary to explain the principles on which

---

* The foreign debt was due in Holland, and was payable there, in unequal annual instalments, the last of which was due in 1809

these statements rest ; which the Committee will do in as concise a manner as possible. But before they enter upon this detail, they cannot forbear to express the satisfaction which they feel in declaring, that the documents which have been obtained from the Treasury will, in their opinion, fully demonstrate the precision and ability with which the business of that department has been conducted, and that by the fiscal operations of the government, the public debt has been diminished."

" In ascertaining the amount of the old debt, two different principles have been taken by those, who have made their calculations on this subject. The first has been to include only the interest upon the debt to the close of the year 1789, as the nearest convenient period to the day, when the government commenced its operations, and after deducting from the aggregate of debt, the amount of funds then in the power of the government, to consider the balance as the amount of old debt.

" The second principle has been, to take the amount of debt, as the same has been liquidated and funded under various acts of Congress, and after deducting therefrom the funds acquired or possessed by the government at the close of the year. 1790, to consider the balance as constituting the true amount of old debt. The difference between these principles consists in this : by the last mode of computation, the interest, which accumulated upon the debt, subsequent to the close of the year 1789, and until the debt was funded and provided for by law, is considered as a part of the old debt, whereas by the first mode of computation that interest is totally excluded.

" In consequence of a difference in opinion, which it is understood still exists on this point, the Committee have thought proper to state the debt in both modes, that the result in both cases may be perfectly understood.

" The nominal amount of debt on the 1st of January, 1790, as appears by statement No. 9, amounted to   -   -   -   - $72,237,301 97

" The funds then in possession of the government, and to be deducted, were—

" Cash in the Treasury, January 1st,
   1790, - - - - - $28,239 61
" Cash in the hands of Collectors,   83,127 84
" Bonds at the custom-house,   -   590,468 60
" Debts due to the United States,
   under contracts of the late government, collected at sundry times,   62,586 74
" Debts paid in specie, during the
   year 1789, - - - - 15,927 13
" Proceeds of the sales of land to the
   state of Pennsylvania, made by
   the late government,   - - 151,392 41
                                                931,742 33

" Amount of debt January 1st, 1790,   - - $71,305,559 64

" By the same document it appears, that the debt
   contracted by the late government, as the same
   has been liquidated and funded by acts of Congress, amounts to   -   -   -   - $76,781,953 14

" That the funds possessed by this government, and
   to be deducted from the debt, were as follows :—

" Cash in the Treasury, January 1st,
   1791, - - - - $570,023 88
" Cash in the hands of Collectors,   225,786 95
" Custom-house bonds uncollected, 1,052,215 13
" Money collected from the credits
   of the late government, as in the
   preceding statement,   - - 62,586 74
" Debts paid in specie, during 1789,   15,927 13
" Sale of land to Pennsylvania,   151,392 41
" Debts purchased and discharged
   during the year 1790, - - 518,424 8
                                             2,596,356 32

" True amount of debt January 1st, 1791,   - $74,185,596 82

" By the same document No. 9, it appears that the debt, exclusive of temporary loans, on the 1st of January, 1800, amounted to - - $76,651,820 30

" Temporary loans, without deducting bank shares,   3,640,000

" Nominal amount of debt January 1st, 1800, - $80,291,820 30

" Funds acquired by the government and which may be applied to face the foregoing debt—

" Cash in the Treasury, January 1st, 1800, deducting therefrom the amount of unclaimed registered debt, and debts due to foreign officers, which are to be considered as a charge on the balance in the Treasury, - - - $2,061,683 49

" Remittance to Holland, beyond the sum necessary to meet all demands on the foreign debt, to the close of the year 1799, - - 548,955 84

" Cash in the hands of Collectors and Supervisors, - - - 532,247 81

" Bonds uncollected, at the customhouses, estimated at six millions, payable on an average of six months, deducting the interest for that term leaves, - - - 5,826,214

" Two thousand two hundred and twenty bank shares, cost - - 888,000

" Advance twenty-five per cent. - - - 222,000

             ——— 1,110,000

                                 ————— 10,079,101 14

" True amount of debt January 1st, 1800,   - $70,212,718 16

" For the purpose of shewing the rapidity with which the public debt was diminishing, at the time when the hostility of France compelled the government to incur those great and extraordinary expenses, which appear in the Treasury statements, and to enter upon that extensive system of defence, which has resulted in the security of our commerce, the Committee thought it necessary, in addition to the preceding statements, to present a view of the debt on the 1st of January, 1798, remarking at the same time, that the reduction which at that time had been made, proves, in the most satisfactory manner, the ease with which the debt may be extinguished, whenever the Government shall be left unembarrassed by internal disorder, or foreign hostility.

" The nominal amount of debt on the 1st of January, 1798,   -   -   -   -   -   - $76,366,618 82

      " Funds to be deducted were—

" Cash in the Treasury January 1st,
    1798,   -   -   -   - $1,021,889   4
" Cash in the hands of Collectors,   -   265,369   3
" Cash in the hands of Supervisors,   -   32,964 39
" Value of bonds uncollected at the
    custom-houses, January 1st, 1798,
    estimated at   -   -   -   6,309,058
" Bank stock at its value   -   1,110,000
                                     8,739,280 46

" True amount of debt January 1st, 1798— $67,627,338 36

" From whence it results (the Committe say,) that if the amount of debt on the 1st of January, 1800, is contrasted with the debt on the 1st of January, 1790, it will appear, that the debt has diminished by the sum of $1,092,841 and 48 cents, or if it is compared with the debt of January 1st, 1791, the debt has diminished, by the sum of $3,972,878 and 66 cents; so that, in either mode of stating the account, it clearly appears, that the debt has in fact been diminished."

The Committee proceed to say, they incline to the opinion, that the debt, as it was liquidated and funded by the government, after deducting the amount of funds, which arose prior to the 1st of January, 1791, ought to be considered, as constituting the true amount of debt, with which the present Government has been charged by the Constitution.

There can be little doubt, that the debt as funded, ought to be considered, as the amount of the public debt, and whatever difference in opinion there may be, in estimating the amount of public debt, at any period, as to the propriety of deducting the amount of funds then in the hands of the government, from this *funded* debt, there can be no doubt, that the funds arising from revenues, and from the value of bank stock, should be offset, against temporary loans made in anticipation of that revenue, and for the payment of the bank stock.

If we take this as a rule, the debt of the United States will be less, on the 1st day of January, 1800, than when the same was *funded*, according to the various acts of Congress.

The amount of debt as liquidated and funded, according to the foregoing statement of the Committee was - - - - - - $76,781,953 14

Amount of debt, *exclusive of temporary loans*, on the 1st of January, 1800, was - - - 76,651,820 30

Making a difference of - - - - - 130,132 84

And this, notwithstanding the great expenses in the mean time incurred by Government, in the wars with the Indians, $1,250,000 expended in suppressing two insurrections in Pennsylvania, more than one million and a half in our transactions with Algiers and the other Barbary powers, and the still greater expenses occasioned by the disputes with France, in 1798 and 1799.*

---

* In 1800, a further sum of $1,482,500, was borrowed at eight per cent. in pursuance of an act passed on the 7th day of May of that year, payable after 1808.

The funds provided and appropriated for the payment of the debt, subsequent to the 3d of March, 1795, up to 1801, were as follows, viz.— By an act passed March 3d, 1797, additional duties were laid on certain articles imported into the United States, and were appropriated, first, for the payment

On a change of Administration in 1801, a new modification of the sinking fund took place. On the 29th of April, 1802, an act was passed, entitled "an Act making provision for the redemption of the whole of the public debt of the United States." This act provides, that the sum of seven millions, three hundred thousand dollars, should be appropriated annually to the *sinking fund;* which sum was to be paid, out of the duties on merchandize and tonnage, and the other monies, other than surplusses of revenue, which then constituted the sinking fund, or which might accrue to it, by virtue of any former provisions. This sum, the act declares, " to be vested in the Commissioners of the sinking fund, in the same manner, as the monies heretofore appropriated to the said fund, to be applied by the said Commissioners, to the payment of interest and charges, and to the reimbursement, or redemption of the principal of the public debt ; and shall be and continue appropriated, until the whole of the present debt of the United States, and the loans which may be made for reimbursing or redeeming any parts or instalments of the principal of the said debt, shall be reimbursed and redeemed." It was made the duty of the Secretary of the Treasury, by this act, to pay to the Commissioners of the sinking fund, this sum of $7,300,000, in each year, and at such times, as to enable them to pay the interest and principal of the debt, faithfully and punctually, according to the engagements of the United States. The Commissioners were to apply

of the principal of the then existing foreign debt ; secondly for the payment of the principal of the debt then due by the United States, to the bank of the United States.

By the act passed July 16th, 1798, authorizing a loan of five millions of dollars, and which was obtained at eight per cent. so much of the surplus of the duties on imports and tonnage, beyond the permanent appropriations before charged thereon, were pledged and appropriated, for the payment of the interest and principal of the loans, which might be made under the act, according to the terms and conditions of the same. A similar pledge and appropriation were made for the loan, obtained under the act passed 7th of May, 1800, and which loan was obtained, as before stated, at eight per cent.

On the 13th day of May, 1800, additional duties were laid on certain articles, imported into the United States, and were solely appropriated for the discharge of the interest and principal of the debts of the United States, before that time contracted, or to be contracted during the year 1800.

this sum annually, in the first place, to the payment of the interest and principal of the public debt, as the same should become due, according to the engagements of the United States, and also the interest and principal of all loans, which had been, or might be made on account of the debt; and in the next place, to apply the surplus, towards the further and final redemption, by payment, or purchase, of the debt. No purchases, however, of the debt were to be made above par. By the act of March 3d, 1795, the duties on spirits distilled within the United States and on stills, constituted a part of the sinking fund, and were pledged for the payment of the debt, but as all the internal taxes were repealed, in 1802, these duties made no part of the fund provided by the act of the 29th of April of that year.

In 1803, the nominal amount of the debt was a little more than seventy millions of dollars, of this $32,119,211 and 25 cts. was owned by foreigners, of which the English owned - $15,882,797 95

The Dutch, - - - - - -	13,693,918 30
Other foreigners, - - - - - -	2,542,495

Of the residue—

Particular States owned - - - -	$ 5,603,564
Incorporated bodies, in the United States, -	10,096,398 72
Individuals, - - - do. - -	22,330,606 36

In the purchase of Louisiana, the United States agreed to pay the government of France, fifteen millions of dollars, three millions seven hundred and fifty thousand dollars, to be paid to our own merchants, for their claims of a certain description on the French government, and the remainder, being $11,250,000, to be paid, in stock, at six per cent. To carry into effect this agreement, stock to that amount, was issued, in pursuance of an act of Congress passed November 10th, 1803, and made payable to the assignees of the French government. The interest on this stock was payable in Europe, and the principal was payable in four equal annual instalments, the first becoming due in 1818.

By the act, which created this stock, a further sum of $700,000 annually, was added to the sinking fund, for the purpose of enabling the Commissioners to pay the interest on the same; which sum was to be paid out of the duties on imports and tonnage. By this addition, the whole sum to be paid annually to the Commissioners of the sinking fund, amounted to $8,000,000, and was vested in them, for the purpose of paying the former debt, and also the Louisiana debt so called, and was to continue, so vested and appropriated, until the whole was paid. And it was made the special duty of the Commissioners, out of this fund, to pay the instalments of the Louisiana debt, as they should fall due.

On the 11th of February, 1807, the Government of the United States, by an act of that date, proposed to the holders of six per cent. deferred and three per cent. stocks, to exchange the same for six per cent. stock, redeemable at the pleasure of the Government.

For this purpose, books were opened at the Treasury, and at the several Loan Offices, for subscriptions, to the whole amount of the stock standing on the books at the Treasury, and at the Loan Offices. On such subscriptions, the old certificates were to be given up, and new ones to issue, for the unredeemed amount of the six per cent. and deferred stock, due at the date of the subscription, bearing an interest of six per cent. per annum, payable quarter yearly, and redeemable at the pleasure of the Government, with a condition " that no single certificate should issue for a greater amount than ten thousand dollars, and that no reimbursement should be made, except for the whole amount of any such new certificate, nor till after, at least, six months previous public notice of such intended reimbursement." For the subscriptions in the three per cent. stock, the subscribers were to receive a new certificate for a sum equal to sixty-five per cent. of the amount of the principal of the stock subscribed, bearing an interest of six per cent. per annum, payable quarter yearly, and subject likewise to redemption, at the pleasure of the Government; with a restriction, however, on the part of the United States, that no part of the stock thus converted, should be reimbursed, without the assent of the holder, until after the whole of the eight per cent. and four and half per cent. stock, as well as all the six per cent. and deferred stock, which might be exchanged, under that act, should be redeemed. The sinking fund was also pledged for the payment of the interest and reimbursement of this new stock. Under this act, the amount of unredeemed six per cent. and deferred stock, subscribed, and for which new certificates were issued, was $6,294,051 and 12 cents, and which was called *exchanged* six per cents. and the three per cents. subscribed, at sixty-five per cent. on the amount, produced $1,859,850 and 70 cents, drawing an interest of six per cent. per annum, and was called *converted* six per cent. stock. In 1812, in pursuance of another act of Congress passed in that year, $2,984,746 and 72 cents, of the unredeemed amount of the six per cent. and deferred stock was exchanged for other six per cent. stock redeemable after the 31st day of December, 1824.

After the United States had concluded a peace with France in 1800, the vast increase of their revenues, arising from duties on imports and tonnage, owing to a rapidly increasing population, and an unparalleled extension of their commerce, enabled them, very fortunately, while Europe was at war, to pay off a large proportion of this debt.

The amount of public debt, on the 1st day of January, 1812, according to official Treasury statements, was   - $45,154,189

and consisted of the following particulars, viz. :—

Six per cent. and deferred stock, unredeemed, - - - -		$17,067,096
Three per cent. stock,	$16,157,890	
Converted do. do.	565,318	
		16,723,208
1796 six per cent. stock, - - -		80,000
Registered debt, and debt due to foreign officers, - - - - -		33,885
		$33,904,189
Louisiana six per cent. stock, -		11,250,000
		$45,154,189

The payments made, on account of the principal of the debt from April 1st, 1801, to January 1st, 1812, according to Treasury statements, amounted to   -   -   -   -   - $46,022,810 and were as follows, viz. :—

1. Foreign debt paid in full, -	$10,075,004
2. Eight per cent. five and a half per cent. four and a half per cent. navy six per cent. stock, and temporary loans, due on the 1st of April, 1801, to the bank of the United States,	12,657,700
3. Reimbursement of six per cent. and deferred stock, - - -	14,452,123 53
4. For lands, and purchased, -	74,569 81
5. Exchanged stock paid in full, •	6,294,051 12
6. Three per cent. stock, including reimbursement of converted stock, and deducting converted stock, outstanding, - - - - - ,	2,379,269 44
7. On account of unfunded debt, -	90,092 58

$46,022,810

During the period in which the Government paid this sum, no additional taxes of any importance were imposed, except an additional duty of two and a half per cent. on goods imported, paying ad valorem duties, to defray the expenses of the war with Tripoli, and of intercourse with the other Barbary powers, and which was called " the Mediterranean fund." This duty was to cease in three months after the termination of the war with Tripoli, but was continued by various acts of Congress until 1815, when it was suffered to expire, and has been applied to the general expenses of the Government.

The sums received into the Treasury from 1801 to 1811, inclusive, and which were applicable to the payment of the interest and principal of the debt, amounted to about ninety millions of dollars.

Debt incurred during the late war between the United States and Great-Britain, as far as ascertained, up to February, 1815.

War was declared against Great-Britain, June 18th, 1812. In anticipation of this event, by an act of Congress of 14th of March preceding, a loan of eleven millions of dollars was authorized at an in-

terest not exceeding six per cent. per annum, reimbursable after the
expiration of twelve years from the 1st day of January, 1813. Under this act, there was obtained, in the course of the year 1812, the
sum of $10,184,700. Of this sum $2,150,000 was obtained of certain banks, on special contracts, and was payable as follows, viz.—
$1,350,000 in 1813, $750,000 in 1814, and $50,000 in 1817; and
the residue, being $8,034,700, was funded, and made redeemable af-
ter January 1st, 1825. About one half of this last sum was obtained
of banks, and the other half of individuals. In the year 1813, the
Commissioners of the sinking fund redeemed, by purchase, $324,200
of this stock, leaving the funded stock of this loan $7,710,500.

On the 8th of January, 1813, a further sum of sixteen millions of
dollars was authorized to be borrowed, by the President of the United States, without any limitation as to the rate of interest, or any
other limitations, except, that the United States should not be precluded from reimbursing the same, at any time, after the expiration
of twelve years, from the 1st day of January, 1814. This sum was
obtained by contract, and principally from individuals, at the rate of
eighty-eight dollars for one hundred, viz. for every eighty-eight dollars, paid in money, a certificate of stock for one hundred dollars
was to be issued, bearing an interest of six per cent. or what is the
same, for every one hundred dollars, which the United States received, they were to issue a certificate of stock for $113 63 cents and
7-11ths of a cent, bearing interest at six per cent. The amount of
stock issued for this loan was $18,109,377 and 51 cts. making a bo-
nus to the lenders, of $2,109,377.

The first offers of the Secretary of the Treasury for this loan were,
that the lender should be entitled to a certificate of stock, at six per
cent. interest, and an annuity of one per cent. for thirteen years, and
for which he was to receive a separate certificate; $531,200 were
eventually taken at par, with an annuity of one and a half per cent.
for thirteen years. The annuities on this sum amount to $7,968.
By an act of August 2d, 1813, a further loan of seven and a half millions of dollars was also authorized, and without any other limitations, than was contained, in the act relative to the sixteen million
loan. This loan was obtained, on the following terms, viz. for every
$100 received, the United States issued stock for $113 31 cents and

4-9th of a cent, bearing interest at six per cent. ; and reimbursable, at any time, within twelve years, after January 1st, 1814.

The six per cent. stock issued on this loan, amounted to $8,498,583 and 50 cents, making a premium or bonus of $998,583 and 50 cents. March 24th, 1814, a loan of twenty-five millions of dollars was also authorized, towards the expenses of the war, for that year. On the 4th of April following, the Secretary of the Treasury issued his notice, that proposals would be received by him, until the second day of May then next, for ten millions, part of the twenty-five millions : the sums offered under this notice amounted to $11,900,806, of which $2,671,750 were at rates less than eighty-eight per cent. and $1,183,400 at rates less than eighty-five per cent. leaving $9,229,056, at eighty-eight per cent. or at rates more favourable to the United States. Of this sum, however, five millions were offered, with a condition, that, if terms more favourable to the lenders, should be allowed for any part of the twenty-five millions authorized to be borrowed that year, the same terms should be extended to those holding the stock of the ten million loan. The Secretary of the Treasury thought proper to accept the loan at eighty-eight and on the condition above stated. Offers were afterwards made to this loan, of sums, amounting to $566,000, and which were accepted on the same terms ; making the sum accepted $9,795,056. Of this sum, there was paid into the Treasury, prior to the 1st of July, 1814, $6,087,011. There was, however, a failure of payment on the part of some of those, whose offers were accepted for this loan, on the days fixed by the terms of the loan, to the amount of about two millions of dollars.

On the 25th day of July, 1814, proposals were again invited, from the Treasury Department, for a loan of a further sum of six millions ; part of the twenty-five millions, to be received by the 22d day of August next succeeding. The amount offered, on this loan, was $2,823,300, of which $100,000 was at less than eighty per cent. $2,213,000 at $80, for $100, in six per cent. stock ; and $510,300, at various rates, from eighty to eighty-eight. The loan was accepted at eighty per cent. The amount accepted, on these terms, was $2,723,300, to be paid, in four equal instalments ; the 1st on the 10th of September, and the remainder on the 10th of each of the ensuing months of October, November and December. On this loan, a further sum of $207,000, was afterwards accepted, on the same terms, making the amount taken $2,930,300. Some persons, however, who had offered to take $416,000 of this loan, gave notice, that they could not carry their proposals into execution. This reduced the sum to $2,520,300. The sums actually paid into the Treasury, therefore, from the proceeds of the loans of twenty-five millions authorized by the act of March 24th, 1814, up to the 1st day of January, 1815, amounted only to about the sum of $11,400,000. As the terms of the last loan were more favourable to the lenders, than those of the preceding two million loan, the same terms were extended, according to the original contract, to those who had taken the first. These terms were, that for every $100 paid in, the United States were to issue certificates of stock, for $125, bearing an interest of six per cent. per annum, payable quarter yearly, and reimbursable at the end of twelve years, from the 1st day of January, 1815. The amount of six per cent. stock, therefore, issued or to be issued, up to the 6th of January, 1815, for the proceeds of the two loans, as far as the same had been ascertained, at the Treasury, was as follows, viz.—

On the ten million loan, six per cent. stock to the
    amount of   -   -   -   -   -   - $9,919,476 25
On the six million loan, do.   do. to the
    amount of   -   -   -   -   -   -   4,342,875

                             $14,262,351 25

Making a bonus or premium of about $2,852,000.

The terms of these loans, were so disadvantageous to the United States, and the price of stocks was so depressed, some having been sold as low as sixty-nine and seventy, for cash, that no further sums were obtained under the act authorizing the twenty-five million loan, but Treasury notes were directed to be issued to make up the deficiency.

The amount of stock issued, on these various loans, was as follows, viz.—

On the eleven million loan, - - -	$ 8,034,700
On the sixteen million loan, - - -	18,109,377 51
On the seven and a half million loan, - - -	8,498,583 50
On the ten million loan, - - - -	9,919,476 25
On the six million loan, - - - - -	4,342,875
	$48,905,012 26
The amount received for this stock, was -	42,934,700
Making a difference of - - - -	$5,970,312 26

In addition to these sums, the committee of defence of the city of Philadelphia, loaned to the Government $100,000 for the special purpose of fortifying an Island in the river Delaware, at par, for which stock has or will be issued under the act of March, 1812, and the corporation of the city of New-York have also advanced money, for the defence of that city, on the terms of the six million loan, and for which stock has, or will be issued to the amount of $1,100,009 87

Making the whole amount of funded stock issued
or to be issued on these loans   -   -   - $50,105,022 13
$500,000, part of the eleven million loan, which become due in December, 1814, was not paid on the 20th of February, 1815.

TREASURY NOTES.

On the 30th of June, 1812, the President of the United States was authorized to cause to be issued Treasury Notes, not exceeding five millions of dollars, to be reimbursed within one year, from the time of issuing the same, and bearing an interest of five and two fifths per cent. per annum. These notes were to be signed by persons to be appointed by the President, and countersigned by the Commissioner of loans for that state, where they were made payable, and were made transferable, by delivery and assignment, endorsed thereon, by the person, to whose order, the same were made payable, and were receivable, in payment of all duties and taxes, laid by the authority of the United States, and of all public lands sold. The whole sum of five millions was issued at various times under this act. By an act of February 25th, 1813, the President was authorized to issue a further sum of five millions, with the same limitation, as to rate of interest and time of payment, as the former. Five millions were also issued, at different periods, under this act. As a part of the supplies, for the year 1814, a further sum of five millions was authorized to be issued by an act of March 4th, 1814, and by the same act, the President was authorized to issue an additional sum of five millions, if he should deem it expedient, to be taken as part of the sum of twenty-five millions, authorized to be obtained on loan, during that year. On the 26th of December, 1814, a sum not exceeding $7,500,000 was authorized to be issued to make up the deficiency of the twenty-five million loan, and in lieu of the three million loan authorized November 15th, 1814. Part of the Treasury notes were paid, as they became due, others, to a large amount, were left unpaid; and the amount, which had been issued, and were unpaid, or were ordered to be issued, on the 20th of February, 1815, was as follows, viz. :—

1st. Those payable on or before the 1st of January, 1815, due and unpaid, amounted to (principal) - $2,799,200

2d. Those payable since January 1st, 1815, due and unpaid, - - - - - - - 620,000

3d. Those payable almost daily, from the 11th of March, to and including the 1st of January, 1816, - 7,227,280

4th. Those payable from 11th of January, to and including the 1st of March, 1816, - - - 7,806,320

Making - - - - - - $18,452,800

The amount of the debt incurred by the late war, so far as the same had been *ascertained* at the Treasury, on the 20th of February, may be stated as follows :—

1st. Stock issued or agreed to be issu-
    ed on permanent loans,   - $50,105,022 13
Deduct purchased by Commissioners
    ers of sinking fund,   -   -   324,200

      Leaves,   -   -   -   - $49,780,822 13

2d. Temporary loans, part of the eleven million loan,
    unpaid,   -   -   -   -   -   550,000

3d. Treasury notes issued, or ordered, as above
    stated,   -   -   -   -   18,452,800

      Makes,   -   -   -   - $68,783,622 13

To which add the old debt, or debt created before the late war, estimated on the 31st of December, 1814, at $39,905,183 66, and consisting of the following particulars :—

1st. Old six per cent.
    stock nominal a-
    mount being,   - $17,250,871 39
Reimbursed,   -   12,879,283 78

Leaving due December 31st, 1814, $4,371,587 61

2d. Deferred stock,
    nominal amount be-
    ing   -   - $9,358,320 35
Reimbursed,   -   3,971,148 36

Leaving due December 31st, 1814, $5,387,171 99

3d. Three per cent. stock,   -   16,158,177 34

4th. Exchanged six per cent. stock
    under the act of 1812,   - $2,984,746 72

5th. Six per cent. stock of 1796,   -   80,000

6th. Louisiana six per
  cent. stock,   - $11,250,000
Purchased by Commis-
  sioners of sinking fund,   326,500

    Leaves,   -   - $10,923,500

                          $39,905,183 66

Makes the debt of the United States on the 20th
  of February, 1815, as *ascertained* at the
  Treasury,   -   -   -   - $108,688,805 79

There are also claims on the Treasury, to a large amount, yet unsettled, which may go to increase the public debt. It appears by the
letter of the Secretary of the Treasury of the 24th of February, 1815,
to the Committee of way and means, that " contracts for loans"
had been made " *through the medium of the war department*, which
had been recognized at the Treasury, to be paid in six per cent.
stock, but which had not been so liquidated as to furnish a ground to
estimate their amount."

This is the first, and only account, which has been given to the
public, or even to Congress, of any loans, made " through the medium of the war department." In what *manner*, under what *authority*, and on what *terms*, these loans were obtained, is not stated by the
Secretary. It is understood, however, that commanders of divisions
of the army, probably by orders from the head of the war department, made these contracts for the purpose of either paying or supplying the men under their immediate command.

Treasury notes, to a large amount, have been issued since the 20th
of February, 1815. On the 24th day of February, 1815, the Secretary of the Treasury was authorized to issue Treasury notes, to the

amount of twenty-five millions of dollars ; those under $100, to be without interest, those over that sum, to bear an interest of five and two-fifths per cent. or to be without interest, as the Secretary, with the approbation of the President, should direct. The notes, without interest, to be funded at seven·per cent. and those bearing an interest, part of the twenty-five million, as well as those previously issued, may be funded at six per cent. reimbursable at any time, after the last day of December, 1824. The Secretary was also authorized to re-issue the notes, which might be delivered up and exchanged for funded stock, or paid in, for taxes or other demands, and to apply them to the same purposes, as when originally issued. The amount issued, under this authority, has not been made public. Probably the whole, or nearly the whole of those fundable at seven per cent. will be funded, and go to increase the amount of the funded debt.

On the 3d of March, 1815, a loan for the sum of $18,452,800, was also authorized ; this loan might be made in Treasury notes, previously issued, and which, by law, were made a charge on the sinking fund ; and the stock was reimbursable, after the expiration of twelve years, from the last day of December, 1815.

Individual states have, also, large claims upon the general government, for expenses incurred in defending themselves, during the late war.

To what amount, the national debt will be increased, from these sources, cannot yet be·ascertained.

The sinking fund, as before stated, since 1803, has consisted of a permanent annual appropriation ,of eight millions of dollars. The funds, from which this sum is paid, are—

1. The fund arising from the *interest* on the debt, redeemed by payment, or purchase, and which has
   passed to the credit of the Commissioners of the
   sinking fund, and which, in 1813, amounted to $1,932,107 92

2. The fund arising from the sales of public lands,
   which in 1813, was -   -   -   -   -   830,671 53

3. From the proceeds of the duties on goods, wares
and merchandize, imported, and on the tonnage of
vessels, sufficient to make up the balance.

If the whole of the eight millions was not expended, by the Commissioners, in any one year, the balance went into the expenditures
of the succeeding year. After paying the interest and reimbursement of the debt, and such parts of the principal as became due, by
contract, it was made the duty of the Commissioners, to apply the
balance of the eight millions, to the *purchase* of stock, whenever it
was below par. Notwithstanding this, the whole of the late loans, as
well as all the Treasury notes, issued prior to February 20th, 1815,
were made a charge on this fund, without any addition being made to
the fund itself. In consequence of this, the fund became overcharged
several millions, (even without applying any part, to the purchase of
stock, though it was much below par,) and afforded no security to
the money lender.

Sensible of this, at last, Congress declared by the act of November 15th, 1814, authorizing a loan of three millions of dollars, for
which stock was to issue reimbursable in twelve years, " that in addition to the annual sum of eight millions of dollars, heretofore appropriated to the sinking fund, adequate and permanent funds shall,
during the present session of Congress, be provided and appropriated,
for the payment of the interest and reimbursement of the principal of
said stock created by this act." And by the same act, declared
" that an adequate and permanent sinking fund, gradually to reduce,
and eventually to extinguish the public debt, *contracted,* and to be
contracted during the present war, shall also be established during the present session of Congress." And by various subsequent
acts, passed during the same session, an annual direct tax of six
millions of dollars, and all the internal taxes, including the duties on the postage of letters, were pledged " towards establishing
an adequate revenue, to provide for the payment of the expenses of
Government; for the punctual payment of the public debt, principal
and interest, contracted and to be contracted, according to the terms
of the contracts respectively; and for creating an adequate sinking
fund, gradually to reduce, and eventually to extinguish the public
debt, contracted and to be contracted," &c. " and were to remain so

pledged, until other taxes and duties, equally productive, were provided, and established by law, for the same purposes."

The plan of the sinking fund, originally adopted by the United States, was taken, substantially, from that of Great-Britain. The present British sinking fund, was established by Mr. Pitt, in 1786 ; and commenced, by a permanent annual appropriation of one million sterling, to be applied by Commissioners, called Commissioners of the sinking fund, to the redemption of the public debt by purchases of stock ; and the interest of the stock, thus purchased, was to be applied to the same purpose. A further permanent annual grant of two hundred thousand pounds, was afterwards added to this sum for the same object. Afterwards, Parliament made it a standing rule, that the creation of a new debt should be accompanied with the means of extinguishment, and on every new loan, permanent funds to the amount of one per cent. of the loan, were provided, and added to the sinking fund. Other sums were afterwards added to the sinking fund, in consequence of loans obtained on a particular plan of extinguishment, the details of which it is unnecessary to specify. The sinking fund of Great-Britain has, generally, been applied to purchases of stock ; while that of the United States has not been so applied, except in its commencement, unless a balance remained in the hands of the Commissioners, after the reimbursement of the six per cent. and deferred stock, and the payment of that part of the principal of the debt, which fell due in each year ; and not then, unless stocks were below par.

The United States stock redeemed by payment, or purchase, has, in the Treasury books, passed to the credit of the Commissioners of the sinking fund ; the interest of which, as before stated, constitutes, in their hands, a part of the sinking fund.

The amount thus passed to their credit, on the 1st day of January, 1814, was as follows :—

Foreign debt—five per cent. stock, $8,200,000
        Four and a half per
          cent. stock, -   820,000
        Four per cent. stock, 3,180,000
                 ———— $12,200,000

Domestic debt—six per cent. stock,	$1,946,026	92
Three per ct. stock,	698,555	41
Deferred six per ct. stock, - -	1,005,179	83
Eight per cent. stock,	6,182,500	
Exchanged six per cent. stock, -	6,294,051	12
Converted six per cent. stock, -	1,859,850	70
Four and a half per cent. stock, -	176,000	
Five and a half per cent. stock, -	1,848,900	
Navy six per cent. stock, - -	711,700	
Louisiana six per ct. stock, - -	326,500	
Six per cent. stock of 1812, -	324,200	
	21,373,463	98

$33,573,463 98

Those, who have a curiosity to see the increase of the national debt of Great-Britain, from the time of the revolution, in 1689, to February 1st, 1813; together with the amount of money applied to the redemption of the national debt of that country, from the commencement of the sinking fund in 1786, to February 1st, 1813, and the produce of the sinking fund, at the latter period, may consult Tables No. I. and II. taken from Hamilton's late enquiry, concerning the national debt of Great-Britain.

From these, it will be seen, that, in 1689, the British national debt, was only £1,054,921 sterling, and that on the 1st of February, 1813, the funded debt of that Kingdom amounted to £812,013,135 sterling; that of this sum £210,461,356 had been redeemed by the Commissioners of the sinking fund, £1,961,582 converted for life annuities, and that £24,378,804, had been transferred, for the purpose of the land tax, making £236,801,742 redeemed, leaving the unredeemed amount of funded debt, February 1st, 1813, £575,211,393 ; that this debt was invested in the following funds, viz.—

Bank annuities, - - - - - -	£11,686,800
Loan of 1726, - - - - - - -	1,000,000
South Sea annuities, including loan of 1751, -	16,125,684
Three per cent. consolidated, - - - -	312,894,703
Three per cent. reduced, - - - -	78,760,033
	£420,467,222
Four per cent. consolidated, - - - -	61,060,921
Five per cent. consolidated, £92,060,254	
Loyalty loan, - - - 1,622,994	
	93,683,248
	£575,211,393

The three per cents. were redeemed, at an average nearly

	at	-	$62\frac{7}{8}$
The four per cents. -	at	-	$84\frac{1}{2}$
The five per cents. -	at	-	$89\frac{3}{8}$

That the produce of the sinking fund, on the 1st of February, 1813, was £13,013,914 sterling.

Besides the *funded* debt of Great-Britain, the *floating* debt, as it is called, consisting of navy debt, and exchequer bills outstanding, amounted, on the 5th of January, 1813, to £53,155,372. (See No. VI. Appendix No. II.)

For the amount of the funded debt of Great-Britain, redeemed and unredeemed, the annual charges of the same, with the sinking fund, applicable to the reduction of the debt, for each year, from 1804 to 1813, see No. IV. in Appendix No. II.

The amount of capital *funded* in Great-Britain, has greatly exceeded the sums *raised*, as most of the loans have been taken in the three per cents. This excess, during the war of the American revolution, and from 1793 to 1812 inclusive, is stated by Mr. Hamilton, as follows.—

	Sums raised.	Capital funded.
Debt contracted during the war of		
the American revolution, -	£ 91,760,842	£115,267,993
Loans from 1793 to 1812 inclusive,	322,358,532	498,861,867
Bills funded, in that period, -	62,258,173	74,920,020
	£476,380,547	£689,049,880
Of which redeemed by the Commissioners, - - -	133,536,836	210,461,356
	£342,843,711	£478,588,524
		342,843,711
Excess of capital funded, above sums raised, -		£135,744,813

In consequence of the operation of the sinking fund in Great-Britain, the national funded debt of that Kingdom has increased but about ninety-one millions sterling, from 1804 to 1813, a period of nine years ; notwithstanding the loans, obtained in each year, were large.   In 1804, the unredeemed amount of funded debt was £484,162,622, and in 1813, was £575,211,393.   The difference is £91,048,771, or about $400,000,000, principally in the three per cents. being an annual increase, of about forty-four millions of dollars.

The British sinking fund, in 1804, was £6,282,947, being in proportion to the debt, as one to seventy-seven, and in 1813, was £13,013,914, being in proportion to the debt, at that time, as one to forty-four.   (See No. IV. in Appendix No. II.)

What will be the annual increase of the debt of the United States, in consequence of the late war, cannot yet be ascertained with precision.   Making an allowance, for the difference between the value of stock at three per cent. and six per cent. the *annual increase* of the American national debt, during the late war, cannot fall much short of the *annual increase* of the British funded debt, for the above period of nine years.

That the United States, however, while they remain at peace, will be able to pay the interest of their debt, as well as the other necessary expenses of the government, and also to extinguish the principal of the debt, within a reasonable time, with a proper application of their funds, there can be no doubt.

TABLE No. I.

The amount of the National Debt of Great-Britain, at the Revolution, and at the commencement and termination of each war, to February 1st, 1813, has been as follows :—

		£
National debt at the revolution,	1689	1,054,925
— at the peace of Ryswick,	1697	21,515,742
— at the commencement of the war,	1701	16,394,701
— at the peace of Utrecht,	1714	53,681,076
— at the commencement of the war,	1740	46,449,568
Funded debt at the peace of Aix la Chapelle,	1748	78,293,313
— at the commencement of the war,	1756	72,289,673
— at the peace of Paris,	1763	133,959,270
including what was contracted in subsequent years, to discharge arrears.		
— at the commencement of the American war,	1775	122,963,254
— at the peace of Versailles,	1783	238,231,248
— including what was funded in subsequent years, and this being reduced by purchases made by the Commissioners for the redemption of the national debt, there remained unredeemed at the commencement of the war,	1793	227,989,148
— at the peace of Amiens,	1802	
including the loan of that year, £567,008,978		
of which redeemed, 67,225,915		
		499,783,063
There was no reduction of the national debt during the short peace which followed the treaty of Amiens.		
Funded debt 1st February,	1813	
£812,013,135		
Of which redeemed or converted into life annuities, 212,422,938		
		599,590,197

In this statement the value of annuities granted for years is not included.

TABLE No. II.

The amount of money applied for the redemption of the national funded debt of Great-Britain, and of capital and interest redeemed since the commencement of the sinking fund in 1786, to 1st February, 1813, and the produce of the sinking fund, at that time, are as follows :—

	Sums expended.	Capital redeemed.	Interest redeemed.
	£	£	£
Three per cents. - -	126,822,903	202,522,956	6,075,688
Four per cents. - -	6,586,934	7,796,400	311,856
Five per cents. - -	126,998	142,000	7,100
	133,536,835	210,461,356	6,453,491
Converted for life annuities, -		1,961,582	
Transferred for purchase of land tax, -		24,378,804	
		236,801,742	
Permanent annual grant to sinking fund, - -			1,000,000
Additional permanent annual grant, - -			200,000
Amount of one per cent. sinking fund, - -			4,738,683
Sinking fund of 1807, on Lord Henry Petty's plan, -			626,255
Annuities, the term of which is expired, - -			79,880
Life annuities, of which the nominees have died, prior to July 5th, 1802, - - - - - -			21,141
Life annuities unclaimed for three years, prior to January 5th, 1813, - - - - - -			30,135
			13,149,587
Deduct life annuities granted for capital, £40,333			
Of which expired, - - - 4,660			35,673
Amount of sinking fund 1st February, 1813, -			13,013,914

The three per cents. were redeemed nearly at 62 7-8 at an average.
The four per cents. at 84 1-2.
The five per cents. at 89 3-8.

The funded debt, 1st of February, 1813, was -	£812,013,135
Redeemed by sinking fund, - - -	210,461,356
	£601,551,779
Converted for life annuities, - - - -	1,961,582
	£599,590,197
Transferred for purchase of land tax, - -	24,378,804
Unredeemed debt of Britain, 1st February, 1813, -	£575,211,393

Which debt was invested in the following funds :—

Bank annuities, - - - - -		£11,686,800
Loan of 1726, - - - - - -		1,000,000
South sea annuities, including loan of 1751, - -		16,125,684
Three per cent. consolidated, - - -		312,894,703
Three per cent. redeemed, - - - -		78,760,033
		£420,467,222
Four per cent. consolidated, - - -		61,060,921
Five per cent. consolidated, -	£92,060,254	
Loyalty loan, - - -	1,622,994	
		93,683,248
		£575,211,392

CHAPTER IX.

Revenues, derived, principally, from duties on imports and tonnage—
Amount received from the customs, from the commencement of the Government, to 1814—Gross and net amount of the customs, accruing annually, in each state and territory, from the commencement of the Government, to December 31st, 1810, with the amount of drawbacks, &c.—An account of internal duties laid prior to 1802—Amount received, prior to, and
since their repeal in that year—Various internal taxes laid since 1812—Direct taxes, which have been laid, at different periods—Amount of the valuation of lands and houses, in 1799—Comparative view of the value of
lands and houses, in 1799, and 1814, in several states—Proceeds of sales
of public lands—Estimate of the quantity of public lands yet unsold—
Post-Office establishment—Amount of postage received—Receipts and expenditures, at different periods.

Previous to the late war, between the United States and Great-
Britain, the revenues of the United States were derived from the following sources, viz.—

1. Imported articles.
2. The tonnage of ships and vessels.
3. Spirits distilled within the United States, and on stills.
4. Postage of letters.
5. Taxes on patents.
6. Dividends on bank stock.
7. Snuff manufactured, in the United States.
8. Sugar refined, in the United States.
9. Sales at auction.
10. Licenses to retail Wines and distilled spirits.
11. Carriages for the conveyance of persons.
12. Stamped paper.
13. Direct taxes.
14. Sales of public lands.

The revenues of the United States, have been principally derived from duties on imports and tonnage. Internal taxes were laid, at different periods, after the commencement of the Government, and by an act passed April, 1802, were all discontinued, from and after the 30th of June of the same year. On the 14th of July, 1798, a direct tax, of two millions of dollars, was laid upon the United States, and was the only direct tax imposed previous to the late war.

The customs, as they are called, consist of duties on imports and tonnage, and also of monies, arising from passports, clearances, light money, &c. The *gross* amount of the customs is that, which *accrues* on the importation of merchandize, the *net* amount, as it is called in the Treasury book, is that which remains, after deducting the drawbacks on the exportation of the same merchandize ; and also for drawbacks on domestic spirits exported, on which a duty has been paid, and for bounties and allowances for the fisheries, and on the exportation of salted provisions, and also, after deducting the expenses of prosecution and collection.

This amount is secured to the Government, by bonds payable at different periods, according to the term of credit, given to the importer. Owing, however, to the bankruptcy of obligors, failure of collectors, and other causes, the whole of the money thus secured, does not come into the public Treasury.

The amount of the actual *receipts* from the customs, from the commencement of the Government, to the year 1813, was as follows, viz.—

From 4th March, 1789, to

31st December,				Dolls.	Cts.
1791	-	-	-	4,399,472	99
1792	-	-	-	3,443,070	85
1793	-	-	-	4,255,306	56
1794	-	-	-	4,801,065	28
1795	-	-	-	5,588,461	26
1796	-	-	-	6,567,987	94
1797	-	-	-	7,549,649	65
1798	-	-	-	7,106,061	93
1799	-	-	-	6,610,449	31

Years.				Dolls.	Cts.
1800	-	-	-	9,080,932	73
1801	-	-	-	10,750,778	93
1802	-	-	-	12,438,235	74
1803	-	-	-	10,479,417	61
1804	-	-	-	11,098,565	33
1805	-	-	-	12,936,487	04
1806	-	-	-	14,667,698	17
1807	-	-	-	15,845,521	61
1808	-	-	-	16,363,550	58
1809	-	-	-	7,296,020	58
1810	-	-	-	8,583,309	31
1811	-	-	-	13,313,222	73
1812	-	-	-	8,958,777	53
1813	-	-	-	13,224,623	25

The amount receivable, in 1814, was estimated at about } 7,000,000

In consequence of the late peace, and the double duties, there is no doubt, that the amount of the customs, which will *accrue* in 1815, will exceed that of any former year ; estimates of the amount have varied from fifteen to thirty millions.

The *gross* and *net* annual amount of the customs, which have *accrued*, with the amount of drawbacks on merchandize, and on spirits exported, of bounties and allowances, and expenses of collection, in each state, and territory, from March 4th, 1789, to 1810, inclusive, appears from table No. I. This statement was laid before Congress, on the 27th of February, 1812, and serves to shew, not only the amount of the customs, with the drawbacks, but also the extent of trade in each state and territory.

The amount of duties, which accrued, in 1805, 1806 and 1807, was much greater, than in any preceding, or subsequent years.

The net amount accruing in 1805, being - $14,980,218 62

1806, - - 16,081,976 60

1807, - - 16,493,434 75

Making - - - - - $47,555,629 97

Of this sum, the amount which accrued, and was secured in the states of Massachusetts, New-York, Pennsylvania, Maryland, and South-Carolina, was as follows, viz.—

Massachusetts in 1805,	-	-	$3,308,046 41	
1806,	-		3,524,326 92	
1807,	-	-	3,576,674 15	
				$10,409,047 48
New-York, in 1805,	-	-	$4,882,076 56	
1806,	-		4,875,783 02	
1807,	-	-	4,826,713 42	
				$14,584,573 00
Pennsylvania, in 1805,	-	-	$2,300,563 37	
1806,	-		3,017,403 45	
1807,	-	-	3,162,733 16	
				$8,480,699 98
Maryland, in 1805,	-	-	$1,130,834 31	
1806,	-		1,446,597 73	
1807,	-	-	1,633,899 84	
				$4,211,331 88
South-Carolina, in 1805,	-	-	$843,135 47	
1806,	-		871,393 26	
1807,	-	-	735,527 84	
				2,450,056 57
Making, in these five states,	-	-	-	$40,135,708 91

The duties remained nearly the same from 1802 to 1812, except an addition of two and a half per cent. on merchandize imported, paying duties ad valorem, which constituted the Mediterranean fund; the great increase of the duties, therefore, from 1802, to the commencement of commercial restrictions, was owing, principally, to the increased population, and consumption of the country, and to the prosperous state of American commerce, during this period.

The duties on imports are laid, either upon the value of the articles imported, and which are called duties ad valorem, or a certain sum is imposed, on the articles themselves, called specific duties. Many articles, however, are imported duty free. These consist of articles in a raw state, which are necessary for our manufactures, or agriculture, such as bullion, copper, old pewter, tin, salt-petre, sulpher, dying drugs and woods, woad, wool, furs, raw hides, to which are added sea stores, wearing apparel, personal baggage and implements of trade, belonging to emigrants, and philosophical apparatus, for the use of seminaries of learning.

For some years, prior to 1804, goods imported subject to duties ad valorem, were divided into three classes, the first class paid twenty per cent. the second fifteen, and the third twelve and a half per cent on their value.*

On the 25th of March, 1804, by an act, entitled " An act further to protect the commerce and seamen of the United States against the Barbary powers," an additional duty of two and a half per cent. was laid on all the imports then paying duties ad valorem. This increased the rate of these duties to twenty-two and a half, seventeen and a half and fifteen per cent. A separate account was to be kept, of the monies arising from this additional duty, and it constituted a distinct fund, by the name of " the Mediterranean fund," and was to be applied solely " for the purpose of defraying the expenses of equipping, officering, manning, and employing such of the armed vessels of the United States, as may be deemed requisite by the President of the United States, for protecting the commerce and seamen thereof, and for carrying on warlike operations against the regency of Tripoli, or any other of the Barbary powers, which may commit hostilities against the United States, and for the purpose of defraying any other expenses incidental to the intercourse with the Barbary powers, or which are authorized by this act." This additional duty was to cease, and be discontinued at the expiration of three months, after the ratification of a treaty of peace, with the regency of Tripoli.

Peace was made with that regency, in 1805, yet this additional

* On goods imported in foreign vessels an addition of ten per cent. is made to the amount of this and other duties.

duty has been continued by various acts of Congress, until March 3d, 1815, when it ceased ; and the proceeds of it have been applied, to the general expenses of the Government. On the 1st day of July, 1812, an addition of one hundred per cent. was made to all the *permanent* duties, to continue during the war then existing between Great-Britain and the United States, and one year thereafter. As the additional duty, which constituted the Mediterranean fund, was *temporary*, this was not increased by the act. This addition of one hundred per cent. increased the rates of duties ad valorem, to forty-two and a half, thirty-two and a half, and twenty-seven and a half per cent. until March 3d, 1815, when the Mediterranean fund ceasing, they will continue at forty, thirty, and twenty-five, until the 18th day of February, 1816, being one year from the exchange of ratifications of the treaty of peace, between the United States and Great-Britain.

The articles subject to duties ad valorem, are numerous, and include all manufactures of wool, cotton, silk, hemp and flax, all manufactures of metals (except nails, spikes, steel, wool and cotton cards, which pay specific duties) all manufactures of earth, stone, and leather, (except boots and shoes) all carriages and parts of carriages, cabinet wares, paper hangings, carpets and carpeting, and many other articles.

The net amount of the ad valorem duties, from 1801 to 1812, was as follows, viz.—

				Dollars.
1801	-	-	-	7,070,430
1802	-	-	-	4,960,123
1803	-	-	-	4,850,630
1804	-	-	-	5,664,797
1805	-	-	-	6,410,440
1806	-	-	-	7,162,099
1807	-	-	-	7,560,929
1808	-	-	-	2,739,375
1809	-	-	-	3,806,263
1810	-	-	-	6,814,255
1811	-	-	-	2,820,166
1812	-	-	-	5,782,144

Imported spirits, wines, molasses, teas, coffee, sugar, and salt, have paid specific duties. In some years prior to the late war, the duty on spirits was, on an average, about twenty-nine cents per gallon, wines from fifty-eight to twenty-three cents per gallon, and molasses five cents, teas, on an average, about twenty cents per pound, coffee five cents, sugar two and a half cents, and salt twenty cents per bushel, weighing fifty-six pounds.

Table No II. shews the gross amount of duties, on each of these articles, from 1793 to 1810, inclusive, (except on salt, which ceased in 1807,) and the amount of drawbacks on the same, for the same period.

The net amount of duties accruing, on each of them, for the years 1805, 1806, and 1807, was as follows, viz. :—

			Dolls.	Dolls.
Spirits,	1805	-	2,267,389	
	1806	-	3,102,219	
	1807	-	2,683,802	
				8,053,410
Wines,	1805	-	843,319	
	1806	-	559,703	
	1807	-	868,812	
				2,271,834
Molasses,	1805	-	464,445	
	1806	-	428,883	
	1807	-	414,133	
				1,307,461
Teas,	1805	-	681,774	
	1806	-	975,053	
	1807	-	1,223,968	
				2,880,795

			Dolls.	Dolls.
Coffee,	1805	-	352,871	
	1806	-	1,005,574	
	1807	-	714,975	
				2,073,420
Sugar,	1805	-	1,922,220	
	1806	-	1,999,886	
	1807	-	1,885,473	
				5,807,579
Salt,	1805	-	763,391	
	1806	-	846,318	
	1807	-	711,819	
				2,321,528

The net amount of duties on spirits imported, from 1793 to 1810, inclusive, was $33,536,140, being about one fifth of all the duties on imports, during that period. Specific duties have also been laid, on various other articles imported, at different rates, which produced, in 1806, the net amount of $1,014,841 and 30 cents. (See Table No. III.)

INTERNAL TAXES.

Soon after the establishment of the Government, duties on spirits distilled within the United States, and on stills, were laid ; other internal taxes were afterwards, at different periods, added, and which, as before stated, were repealed in 1802. Those which were imposed, prior to that time, and, in the Treasury books, were denominated internal taxes, were—

1. Duties on spirits distilled within the United States, and on stills.
2. — on snuff manufactured in the United States.
3. — on refined sugar.
4. — on sales at auction.
5. — on licenses to retail wines, and spirituous liquors.

315

6. Duties on carriages for the conveyance of persons.
7. — on stamped paper.

The sums actually paid into the Treasury from those internal taxes, from their commencement, to September 30th, 1812, was $6,460,003 54 cents, and the annual receipts were—

				Dolls.	Cts.
1792	-	-	-	208,942	81
1793	-	-	-	237,705	70
1794	-	-	-	274,089	62
1795	-	-	-	337,755	36
1796	-	-	-	475,289	60
1797	-	-	-	575,491	45
1798	-	-	-	644,357	95
1799	-	-	-	779,136	44
1800	-	-	-	809,396	55
1801	-	-	-	1,048,033	43
1802	-	-	-	621,898	89
1803	-	-	-	215,179	69
1804	-	-	-	50,941	29
1805	-	-	•	21,747	15
1806	-	-	-	20,101	45
1807	-	-	-	13,051	40
1808	-	-	-	8,210	73
1809	-	-	-	4,044	39
1810	-	-	-	7,430	63
1811	-	-	-	2,295	95
1812	-	-	-	4,903	6

$6,460,003 54

The greatest amount of these taxes *accrued*, in 1801, being $989,533 and 29 cents, and the amount accruing in each state according to official Treasury statements, was as follows, viz. :—

			Dolls.	Cts.
New-Hampshire,	-	-	9,785	70

				Dolls.	Cts.
Massachusetts,	-	-		232,566	33
Rhode-Island,	-	-	-	32,156	99
Connecticut,	-	-		27,220	14
Vermont,	-	-	-	3,360	73
New-York,	-	-		143,757	89
New-Jersey,	-	-	-	8,043	53
Pennsylvania,	-	-		209,545	46
Delaware,	-	-	-	6,994	81
Maryland,	-	-	-	83,562	96
Virginia,	-	-	-	115,444	32
North-Carolina,	-	-		32,476	23
South-Carolina,	-	-		45,612	63
Georgia,	-	-	-	6,452	37
Kentucky,	-	-	-	-	-
Tennessee,	-	-	-	9,456	99
Ohio,	-	-	-	23,095	21

$989,533 29

And during that year, the following was the amount accruing from each object—

From spirits distilled within the United States,	$178,659	21
From stills, - - -	257,070	3
From refined sugar, - -	76,539	65
From sales at auction, - -	66,122	84
From licenses to retailers, - -	69,173	74
From carriages, - -	73,926	21
From stamped paper, - -	268,041	61

$989,041 61

Although these internal duties were repealed in 1802, their collection has never yet been completed. Considerable sums have been annually paid into the Treasury, from officers entrusted with the collection of them, since their repeal; and on the 1st day of January, 1812, the balances due from the Supervisors and other officers of the internal revenue, in the several states, as appears by the Treasury books, amounted to   -   - $254,940 64

At the first session of the thirteenth Congress, held in the summer of 1813, the following internal duties were laid, viz. :—

1. Duties on licenses for stills and boilers.
2. — on carriages, for the conveyance of persons.
3. — on licenses to retailers of foreign merchandize, wines, and spirituous liquors.
4. — on sales at auction.
5. — on refined sugar.
6. — on stamped paper of a certain description.

These taxes were to commence on the 1st day of January, 1814. And for the purpose of collecting the same, each state was divided into a certain number of collection districts, each district having a principal collector, with power to appoint deputies under him.

The amount of the tax laid, on most of these objects, was about double the former tax on the same, and on licenses to retailers, was about three times the amount of the former.

The original plan of the Treasury department, and which was adopted by Congress, contemplated a reliance on loans to carry on the war, and to pay the reimbursements of the old debt. A revenue sufficient to defray the *ordinary* expenses of the Government, to pay the *interest* of the existing public debt, and the *interest* on new loans, was to be provided.

The Secretary of the Treasury, in his letter to the Committee of ways and means, of January 10th, 1812, in answer to their enquiries relative to supplies and revenue, *in the event of war*, stated, that the sum of about nine millions of dollars, would be sufficient to defray the ordinary expenses of Government, and to pay the interest of the existing public debt ; and that this sum, with the amount of interest on new loans, must annually be provided.

Supposing ten millions to be borrowed in 1812, the sum to be raised by taxes in 1813, according to the statement of the Secretary, would amount to $9,600,000. To meet this, the Secretary calculated, that the duties on imports, if doubled, and with a duty of twenty

cents per bushel on salt, would produce— - $5,400,000
and proceeds of sales of land, - - 600,000

6,000,000
Leaving a deficiency of - - 3,600,000

9,600,000

To make up this deficiency, the Secretary proposed a direct tax of three millions of dollars, and a tax on spirits distilled and on stills, on refined sugar, on licenses to retailers, on sales at auction, on carriages, and stamp paper, sufficient to produce two millions more, both
amounting to - - - $5,000,000
Deducting the expenses of collection, assessment, and
losses, estimated at - - - 750,000

Leaving, when in full operation, in 1814, - 4,250,000
But which were estimated to produce, in 1813, only 3,600,000

These taxes, however, were not laid by Congress, until the summer of 1813, to commence from the 1st of January, succeeding.

The sums which *accrued* from these internal taxes, (exclusive of the direct tax) for the two first quarters of 1814, amounted to $2,212,491 and 73¼ cents, and the sums accruing from each, were as follows, viz. :—

Licenses on stills and boilers, -	$1,062,758 99
Carriages, - -	214,639 73¼
Licenses to retailers, - -	663,887
Sales at auction, - - -	53,695 38¾
Refined sugar, - - -	146 34
Stamped paper, - -	217,364 28¼

$2,212,491 73¼

The amount accruing in each State and Territory, was as follows, viz.:—

	Licenses for stills & boilers.		Carriages.		Licenses to retailers	Sales at auction.		Sugar refined.		Stamps.	
	Dolls.	Cts.	Dls.	Cts.	Dls.	Dls.	Cts.	Dls.	Cts.	Dolls.	Cts.
New-Hampshire,	4,817	98	6,155	8	15,154	351	29	-	-	544	5
Massachusetts,	61,217	86	33,160	78	79,220	12,285	5	120	9	14,281	18
Vermont,	19,710	52	2,532	18	12,271	7	96	-		13	35
Rhode-Island,	16,265	23	2,842	88	15,702	6,039	23	-		5,329	80
Connecticut,	42,873	36	13,092	61	28,556	79	48¼	-		7,388	37
New-York,	154,484	67	21,687	23	156,492	8,872	69¾	-		51,935	6
New-Jersey,	18,429	59	16,253	92	27,163	2,823	86	-		3,350	49
Pennsylvania,	271,780		25,707	8½	118,852	10,871	61	-		45,590	45
Delaware,	1,447		5,118	18	7,477	116	25	-		2,701	56
Maryland,	36,736		16,965	97¼	42,300	5,344	11¼	-		20,300	82
Virginia,	148,442		28,836	91	46,691	2,018	20	-		21,378	3
North-Carolina,	44,780		13,594	29	20,644	444	14	-		5,212	41
Ohio,	34,708		465	24	15,200	201	36	-		3,246	87
Kentucky,	56,082	19	2,634	69	13,684	160	8	-		4,185	38
South-Carolina,	32,215	67	15,024	72	20,343	923	52	-		10,810	16
Tennessee,	46,855	97	661	11	7,612	-		-		946	5
Georgia,	11,076	68	6,532	12	11,931	1,003	17	-		3,145	76
Louisiana,	5,485	8	840	81	7,079	1,878	30	26	25	7,119	86
Illinois Territory,	490	14	62		835	-		-		5	60
Michigan do.	-		54		1,135	28	93	-		21	94
Indiana do.	1,263	73	4		1,396	-		-		-	
Missouri do.	2,027	38	75		1,340	-		-		45	45
Mississippi do.	1,562	7	303		3,305	91	82	-		652	76
District of Columbia,	-		2,044	91	9,505	154	32	-		10,159	56
Total,	1,062,758	99	214,639	73¼	663,887	53,695	38¼	146	34	217,364	28½

It is calculated that the duties *accruing* in the two last quarters of 1814, will amount to about one million of dollars, making for that year, three millions from internal duties, of which about two millions will be received into the Treasury, in 1814.

During the session of Congress which commenced the 19th of September, 1814, a duty of twenty cents, on every gallon of spirits distilled within the United States, was laid, in addition to the duty on licenses for stills and boilers, fifty per cent. was added to the duty on licenses to retailers, an addition was also made to the duties on carriages, sales at auction, and on stamped paper.

TAX ON MANUFACTURES.

Duties were also laid during the same session, on the following goods, wares, and merchandize, manufactured within the United States, viz. :—

On pig iron per ton, one dollar.

Castings, of iron, per ton, one dollar and fifty cents.

Bar iron, per ton, one dollar.

Rolled or slit iron, per ton, one dollar.

Nails, brads, and sprigs, other than those usually denominated wrought, one cent per pound.

Candles, of white wax, or in part of white and other wax, per pound, five cents.

Mould candles, of tallow, or of wax, other than white, or in part of each, per pound, three cents.

Hats and caps, in whole, or in part of leather, wool, or fur, bonnets in whole or in part of wool or fur, if above two dollars in value, eight per centum ad valorem.

Hats, of chip or wood, covered with silk or other materials, or not covered, if above two dollars in value, eight per centum ad valorem.

Paper, three per centum ad valorem.

Umbrellas and parasols, if above the value of two dollars, eight per centum ad valorem.

Playing and visiting cards, fifty per centum ad valorem.

Saddles and bridles, six per centum ad valorem.

Boots and shoes, exceeding five dollars per pair in value, five per centum ad valorem.

Beer, ale, and porter, six per centum ad valorem.

Manufactured tobacco, snuff, and segars, twenty per centum ad valorem.

Leather, including all hides and skins, whether tanned, tawed, dressed, or otherwise made, on the original manufacture thereof, five per centum ad valorem.

Gold and silver plated ware, jewellery, and paste work, six per centum ad valorem.

These duties, as the act imposing them directs, are " to be paid by the owner or occupier of the buildings or vessels, in which, or of the machines, implements, or utensils wherewith the said goods, wares, and merchandize, shall have been manufactured, or made, or by the agent or superintendant thereof."

To insure the collection of this tax on manufactures, the law also directs, that no person, after the expiration of ninety days, from the passing of the act, owning or occupying any building, or vessel, machine, implement, or utensil, used or intended to be used, in such manufactures, shall use the same, without a license from the Collector of the district, for a term not exceeding one year, so to do ; and before such license can be obtained, such person is to give bond, with two sureties, 1st. That he will make a true and exact entry and report in writing, to the Collector, of every building, or vessel, machine, implement, or utensil owned or occupied by him, with the size thereof, the place where situate, and the manner, in which, and the time for which, not exceeding one year, he intends to employ the same.

2d. A like report of the denominations and qualities of articles manufactured, on hand, and the value thereof.

3d. That he will from day to day, as long as he may use the same, enter in a book or books, to be kept for that purpose, the denominations and qualities of articles manufactured, and an account of the denominations and quantities sold, with the price for which the same were sold, and the name of the person to whom sold, when the amount shall exceed ten dollars in value, and that he will render to the Collector, at the end of every three months, or within ten days

322

thereafter, a gener l account of the denominations and quantities of
articles manufactured, with the aggregate value thereof, for three
months preceding, also a statement in writing, taken from his books,
specifying the denominations and quantities of manufactured articles
sold on each day, stating distinctly each sale, with the name of the
purchaser, and the price, when the quantity sold shall exceed ten
dollars, and the aggregate denominations and quantities and aggregate
value of all other sales ; this account and statement to be verified by
oath or affirmation. The Collector to have a right to inspect the
books kept by the manufacturer, every day, between the rising and
setting of the sun.

4th. That he will pay the duties on the articles manufactured.

In addition to these duties on manufactures, duties were likewise
laid, the same session, on household furniture, on gold and silver
watches, and fifty per cent. was added to the rate of postage on letters, besides an annual direct tax, on houses, lands, and slaves, of six
millions of dollars.

From estimates made at the Treasury, it was calculated, that these
internal duties, for an entire year, when in full operation, would produce $10,159,000, (except the duty on gold, silver, and plated ware,
and jewellery, not laid at the time of the estimates.)

The product of each, was estimated as follows, viz.—

Stamps,	$510,000
Carriages,	300,000
Sales at auction,	300,000
Refined sugar,	150,000
Licenses to retailers,	900,000
Licenses for stills, with the duty on spirits,	4,000,000
Postage,	250,000
Furniture,	1,238,000
Gold watches,	60,000
Silver watches,	170,000
Boots,	75,000
Saddles and bridles,	66,000
Paper,	50,000

Candles,	-	-	-	-	$200,000
Playing cards,	-	-	-	-	80,000
Tobacco and snuff,	-	-	-		200,000
Hats,	-	-	-	-	400,000
Iron,	-	-	-	-	350,000
Nails,	-	-	-	-	200,000
Beer, ale, and porter,	-	-	-		60,000
Leather,	-	-	-	-	600,000

$10,159,000

Their product, however, for 1815, was estimated at only - - - - - $7,053,000

It will be observed, that most of the internal duties, and particularly those on manufactures, are laid upon the articles according to their value ; and that, not only the *value*, but the *quantity* of the articles, manufactured is made to depend, principally, on the books and oath of the manufacturer himself, or of the persons employed by him. This is a new mode of collecting duties, and whether it will ensure a faithful collection, can be best known from experience. The policy of multiplying oaths, among so many classes of the community, especially in cases, where the temptations to violation, arising from interest, are so strong, may well be questioned.

DIRECT TAXES.

On the 14th of July, 1798, the first direct tax under the Constitution, (being two millions of dollars,) was laid upon the United States, and was apportioned among the several states, according to the principles of the Constitution, as follows, viz.—

			Dolls.	Cts.	Mls.
New-Hampshire,	-	-	77,705	36	2
Massachusetts,	-	-	260,435	31	2
Rhode-Island,	-	-	37,502	8	0
Connecticut,	-	-	129,767	0	2
Vermont,	-	-	46,864	18	7

				Dolls.	Cts.	Mls.
New-York,	-	-	-	181,680	70	7
New-Jersey,	-	-	-	98,387	25	3
Pennsylvania,	-	-		237,177	72	7
Delaware,	-	-	-	30,430	79	2
Maryland,	-	-	-	152,599	95	4
Virginia,	-	-	-	345,488	66	5
Kentucky,	-	-	-	37,643	99	7
N. Carolina,	-	-		193,697	96	5
S. Carolina,	-	-	-	112,997	73	9
Georgia,	-	-	-	38,814	87	5
Tennessee,	-	-	-	18,806	38	3

This tax was laid upon all dwelling-houses, and lands, and on slaves between the ages of twelve and fifty, within the United States. The houses and lands were valued, according to the provisions of a law passed, on the 9th of July, 1798, and by the same act, all slaves above the age of twelve and under the age of fifty, except such as " from fixed infirmity or bodily disability, were incapable of labour," were also enumerated. This sum of two millions was assessed, on the dwelling-houses, lands, and slaves according to the valuations and enumerations, made by said act, in the manner following, viz.—

" Upon every dwelling-house, which, with the out-houses, appurtenant thereto, and the lot, whereon the same were erected, not exceeding two acres, shall be valued at more than one hundred dollars, and not more than five hundred dollars, a sum equal to two tenths of one per cent. on the amount of valuation—

At more than $500, and not more than $1,000, three tenths of one per ct.
At more than 1,000, and not more than 3,000, four tenths of do.
At more than 3,000, and not more than 6,000, five tenths of do.
At more than 6,000, and not more than 10,000, six tenths of do.
At more than 10,000, and not more than 15,000, seven tenths of do.
At more than 15,000, and not more than 20,000, eight tenths of do.
At more than 20,000, and not more than 30,000, nine tenths of do.
And on all dwelling-houses, valued at
more than - - - 30,000, one pr ct. on the valuation."

Upon every slave enumerated, there was assessed fifty cents.

After deducting the amount of the sums, thus assessed upon dwelling-houses and slaves, within each state, from the sum apportioned to such state, the remainder was assessed, upon the lands in such state, according to the valuation made in pursuance of said act, and at such rate per centum, as was sufficient to produce the said remainder.

The number of acres of lands in the United States, valued under the act, was - - - 163,746,688, And was valued at $479,293,263 13

The number of dwelling-houses, over one hundred dollars, was - 276,695, 140,683,984 79

Making for both, - - - - $619,977,247 92

And the number of slaves enumera- ted, was - - - - 393,219

The proportion of the two millions, assessed upon hou- ses, according to the foregoing principles, was - $471,988 96
Upon land, - - - - - - - 1,327,713 21
And upon slaves, - - - - - - 196,609 50

Table No. IV. exhibits a general view of the number of acres of land, and number of dwelling-houses, with their respective valuations, and number of slaves, in each state, with the proportion of the tax, assess- ed upon each of them.

The quantity of land valued in each state, and the amount of its valuation, was as follows, viz.—

	No. of acres.		Valuation. Dolls. Cts.
New-Hampshire,	-	3,749,061	-	19,028,108 03
Massachusetts,	-	7,831,628	-	59,445,642 64
Rhode-Island,	- -	565,844	-	8,082,355 21
Connecticut,	-	2,649,149	-	40,163,955 34
Vermont,	- -	4,918,722	-	15,165,484 02
New-York,	-	16,414,510	-	74,885,075 69
New-Jersey,	- -	2,788,282	-	27,287,981 89

	No. of acres	Valuation.
		Dolls. Cts.
Pennsylvania,	11,959,865	72,824,852 60
Delaware,	1,074,105	4,053,248 42
Maryland,	5,444,272	21,634,004 57
Virginia,	40,458,644	59,976,860 04
N. Carolina,	20,956,467	27,909,479 70
S. Carolina,	9,772,587	12,456,720 94
Georgia,	13,534,159	10,263,506 95
Kentucky,	17,674,634	20,268,325 07
Tennessee,	3,951,357	5,847,662 00
	163,746,686	$479,293,263 13

In some of the states, the valuations were not completed, until three or four years after the tax was laid. The amount of this direct tax, received into the public Treasury, to the 30th of September, 1812, was $1,757,240 84, and in the following years, viz.—

	Dolls. Cts.
In 1800	734,223 97
1801	534,343 38
1802	206,565 44
1803	71,879 20
1804	50,198 44
1805	21,882 91
1806	55,763 86
1807	34,732 56
1808	19,159 21
1809	7,517 31
1810	12,448 68
1811	7,666 66
To Sept. 30th, 1812	859 22
	$1,757,240 84

Large balances of this tax are still due, from the Supervisors, or other officers entrusted with the collection of it, in some of the states; and in the act of July 24th, 1813, establishing the office of Commissioner of the revenue, it is made the duty of the Commissioner " to superintend the collection of the residue of the former direct tax and internal duties, which may be still outstanding," &c.

The balance of this tax, due from the Supervisors and other officers, on the 1st day of January, 1812, was - - - $91,684 33

Of this balance there was due from the Supervi-

sors, &c. of Massachusetts, - - - -	$6,528 46
of Vermont, - - - -	7,226 62
of South-Carolina, - - -	24,374 62
of Georgia, - - - -	24,588 96

A second direct tax was laid, August 2d, 1813, its amount was three millions of dollars, and was apportioned among the states, according to the Constitution, on the census of 1810, as follows :—

	Dolls. Cts.
New-Hampshire,	96,793 37
Massachusetts,	316,270 98
Rhode-Island,	34,750 78
Connecticut,	118,167 71
Vermont,	98,343 71
New-York,	430,141 62
New-Jersey,	108,871 83
Pennsylvania,	365,479 16
Delaware,	32,046 25
Maryland,	151,623 94
Virginia,	369,018 44
Kentucky,	168,928 76
Ohio,	103,150 14
N. Carolina,	220,238 28
S. Carolina,	151,905 48
Tennessee,	110,086 55
Georgia,	94,936 49
Louisiana,	28,295 11

The sums, thus apportioned to each state, were, by the act laying the tax, again apportioned to each *county*, in the state. This apportionment among the several counties, was made, according to two different rules, recommended by the Secretary of the Treasury. In those states, where there was a state tax, each county's quota of the direct tax was made to bear the same proportion to the whole quota of the state, as the amount of the state tax, paid by such county, bore to the whole sum paid in the state, for the state tax.

The second rule, as stated and explained by the Secretary, was as follows, viz.—

" In those states, where there is no state tax, or if there be one, the proportions, in which it is apportioned among the counties is not known, the principle assumed for a basis is, that the comparative advancement of wealth (or rather the increase in the value of property, subject to the direct tax now to be imposed) and of population in the different districts of the same state, have been equal, since the year 1799 ; so that if a given portion of a state containing, for example, one fourth of the population of the state, and which paid in 1799, one fourth of the direct tax of that state, now contains one third of the whole population of the state, it ought now to pay one third of the whole tax to be imposed upon the state. And in respect to *population* for both epochs, although the *federal numbers*, or numbers represented in Congress, have been taken as the Constitution directs, for ascertaining the quota of each state, of the whole sum to be raised in the United States, yet, for apportioning the sum thus found as the quota of any state, among the several counties of that state, the whole numbers of the several counties, including slaves, have been taken ; because it is considered that the slaves increase the wealth, or the ability to pay, in a ratio at least, equal to the augmented quota, which this mode will give, to those parts of a state, in which slaves are possessed, over those in which there are none, or a smaller number. Maryland is the only state where there is a considerable proportion of slaves, to which this mode of apportioning the tax among the counties has been applied. The process then is, to make the quota of each county in a given state, compared with its population in 1810, bear the same proportion to the present quota of the state, compared with its whole population in 1810, as the quota of the same county, of the direct tax of 1799, compared with its population by the census of 1800, bore to the quota of the whole state of the direct tax of 1799, compared with its whole population in 1800." A difference in the value of lands and houses, in different counties, produced a great inequality in the sums paid by individuals, in the same state, though possessed of lands valued alike, and shewed the injustice of both of these modes, of apportioning each state's quota, among the several counties. In the state of Massachusetts, the inhabitants of the county of Cumberland, for every hundred dollars value of their lands and houses, paid thirty-eight cents and nine mills, while in several other counties, the sum paid on every one hundred dollars value of lands and houses, was only seventeen cents, and the average paid through the whole state, was only twenty-one cents and two mills, for every one hundred dollars. Similar inequalities, though not, in many instances, so great, took place, in all the states in which valuations were made.

This tax was laid and assessed " on the value of all lands and lots of ground, with their improvements, dwelling houses, and slaves ;" and these several articles were to be enumerated and valued by the respective assessors, at the rate each of them was worth in money. The valuations were to be made, within sixty days, after the 1st day of February, 1814. Each state had the right of assuming its proportion of this tax, with a deduction of fifteen per cent. if assumed and paid, before the 10th day of February, 1814, and if assumed and paid before the 1st day of May of the same year, with a deduction of ten per cent. The states of New-Jersey, Pennsylvania, Virginia, South-Carolina, Georgia, Kentucky, and Ohio, assumed their proportion of the tax, and were allowed a deduction of fifteen per cent. The sums paid into the Treasury by these states, was $1,159,796 and 83 cents.

In the states which assumed the tax, no valuations were made, under the act. In the other states, the valuations and enumerations were made, according to the law.

In the following states, the valuations were as follows :—

New-Hampshire,	- -	$36,957,825
Massachusetts,	- -	149,253,514

Vermont,	-	-	-	$32,747,290
Rhode-Island,		-	-	21,567,020
Connecticut,	-	-	-	86,550,033
Delaware,		-	-	14,361,469
Maryland,		-	-	122,577,572

The amount of valuations, in the state of New-York, (except the counties of Essex, Clinton, Franklin, Gennessee, Niagara, Allegany, Chautaugue, and Cattaragus,) was   -   232,494,940
North-Carolina, according to the best estimate from the returns made,   - -   92,157,487
Tennessee, exclusive of the valuations in the third district,   - - -   34,415,971

The above sums include the valuations taken of slaves, as well as of lands and houses.

A comparative view of the difference in the value of lands and houses in 1799, and in 1814, is highly interesting; and serves to shew the increasing wealth of the United States. As the valuations in many of the states were not made in 1814, and in others not completed, this view, at present, can only be a partial one, and confined principally to those states, where there are few, or no slaves.

New-Hampshire, Massachusetts, Vermont, Rhode-Island, Connecticut, and New-York, have few slaves; and the valuations in these states in 1799 and 1814, were as follows:—

		1799.	1814. Lands & houses.	Increase.
		Dolls.	Dolls. Dolls.	Dolls.
New-Hampshire,	lands,	19,028,108		
	houses,	4,146,938		
		23,175,046	36,957,825	13,782,779
Massachusetts,	lands,	59,445,642		
	houses,	24,546,826		
		83,992,468	149,253,514	65,261,046

		1799. Dolls.	1814. Dolls.	Lands & houses. Dolls.	Increase. Dolls.
Vermont,	lands,	15,165,484			
	houses,	1,558,389			
			16,723,873	32,747,290	16,023,417
Rhode-Island,	lands,	8,082,355			
	houses,	2,984,002			
			11,066,357	21,567,020	10,500,663
Connecticut,	lands,	40,163,955			
	houses,	8,149,479			
			48,313,434	86,550,033	38,236,599
New-York,	lands,	74,885,075			
	houses,	25,495,631			
			100,380,706	232,494,940	132,114,234
			$283,651,884	559,570,622	275,918,730

The increase, therefore, in these six states, in the value of lands and houses, so far as ascertained, has been, in fifteen years, nearly two hundred and seventy-six millions of dollars. Making every allowance for a difference in the judgments of the assessors, and for the depreciation of money, arising from the increase of banks and bank paper, and other causes, the increase in the *real* value, must be great beyond example. In 1799, the whole value of lands and houses, in the United States, was $619,977,247, and in 1814, in these six states, the value falls but about sixty millions short of that sum. The whole amount of the valuations, in New-York, when completed will probably be two hundred and fifty or sixty millions.

In Maryland, in 1799, the value

of lands, was	-	$21,634,004	
of houses,	- -	10,738,286	
			$32,372,290

And in 1814, the valuations made of lands, houses, and

slaves, was	-	-	-	122,577,572
Being a difference of	-	$90,205,282.		

In Delaware, in 1799, the value

  of lands, was - $4,053,248

  of houses, - - 2,180,165

           ———————— $6,234,413

and in 1814, the value of lands, houses, and *slaves*, was $14,361,469

  Being a difference of - $8,127,056.

In North-Carolina, in 1799, the

  value of lands, was - $27,909,479

  of houses, - - 2,932,893

           ———————— $30,842,372

And in 1814, the value of lands, houses, and *slaves*,

  from the best estimates, was - - 92,157,487

  Being a difference of - $61,315,115

In Tennessee, in 1799, the value

  of lands, was - $5,847,662

  of houses, - - 286,446

           ———————— $6,134,108

And in 1814, the value of lands, houses, and *slaves*,

  (with the exception of one whole district) was $34,415,971

  Being a difference of - $28,281,863

What part of the valuations, in these states, was made from slaves, we have not been able to ascertain. If we take the number of slaves in each state, from the census of 1810, and estimate the value of each slave at three hundred dollars, the increase in the value of lands and houses, will be

  In Maryland, about - $57,000,000

  Delaware, - - 7,000,000

  North-Carolina, - - 11,000,000

  Tennessee, (so far as ascertained) 15,000,000

           ————————

  Being an increase, in these states of about $90,000,000

Making the value of lands and houses, in 1814, so far as can, at present, be ascertained, and from the foregoing estimate, of the value of slaves, about seven hundred and twenty-four million five hundred and seventy thousand dollars, in ten states, being an increase, in the value of lands and houses, in those states, since 1799, of about three hundred and sixty-five millions of dollars.

The average value of lands, per acre, including all the buildings thereon, according to the valuations made in 1814, in the states of New-Hampshire, Massachusetts, Vermont, Rhode-Island, Connecticut, and New-York, was nearly as follows :—

	Per Acre.
	Dls. Cts.
New-Hampshire,	9
Massachusetts,	13 75
Vermont,	6 40
Rhode-Island,	39
Connecticut,	34
New-York,	14 50

The amount of this direct tax of three millions, received at the Treasury, from the non-assuming states, up to December 31st, 1814, was about one million two hundred and ten thousand dollars; at that time, there were in the hands of Collectors, about sixty-six thousand dollars, and the sum then remaining to be collected, was about three hundred and seventy-six thousand.

On the 9th of January, 1815, Congress passed an act laying an *annual* direct tax of six millions of dollars. This was laid, and was to be assessed in the same manner, as the direct tax of 1813. In those states, which had assumed the former direct tax, valuations and assessments are to be made under this act; and in those, which did not assume the tax, the assessments made under the act of 1813, are to remain, except, where changes of property, have rendered alterations necessary.

The quotas of each state were not again apportioned among the several counties, in this tax, as in the former, but the valuations through each state are to be equalized by the principal assessors, and the tax is to be laid and collected on the assessments thus equalized.

Each state has, also, the right of assuming and paying, every year, its quota of this tax, and if assumed and paid, before the 1st day of May, in each year, is to have an allowance of fifteen per cent. and if paid, before the 1st of October, an allowance of ten per cent. This tax was laid, as the title declares " for defraying the expenses of Government, and maintaining the public credit ;" and is to be collected every year, and the Secretary of the Treasury, is authorized to fix a day, in the month of February, in each year, when the Collectors shall proceed, and collect the same. This tax, as well as all the *internal taxes*, as before stated, are pledged and appropriated, " towards establishing an adequate revenue, to provide for the payment of the expenses of Government ; for the punctual payment of the public debt, principal and interest, contracted and to be contracted, according to the terms of the contracts respectively ; and for creating an adequate *sinking fund*, gradually to reduce and eventually to extinguish the public debt, contracted and to be contracted," &c. and remain so pledged and appropriated, until other taxes or duties, which shall be equally productive, and for the same purposes, shall be provided and substituted.

SALES OF PUBLIC LANDS.

Since the opening of the several land offices for the sale of lands belonging to the United States, the following sums have been received into the Treasury, each year from the proceeds of the sales of public lands, viz. :—

				Dolls.	Cts.
In 1796	-	-	-	4,836	13
1797	-	-	-	83,540	60
1798	-	-	-	11,963	11
1799	-	-	-	-	-
1800	-	-	-	443	75
1801	-	-	-	167,726	6
1802	-	-	-	188,628	2
1803	-	-	-	165,675	69
1804	-	-	-	487,526	79

				Dolls.	Cts.
1805	-	-	-	540,193	80
1806	-	-	-	765,245	73
1807	-	-	-	466,163	27
1808	-	-	-	647,939	6
1809	-	-	-	442,252	33
1810	-	-	-	696,548	82
1811	-	-	-	1,040,237	53
1812	-	-	-	869,219	8
1813	-	-	-	821,218	8
1814	-	-	-	1,038,173	75

$8,437,531 60

The whole number of acres sold, at the different land offices, up to September 30th, 1814, was five millions three hundred eighty-five thousand four hundred and sixty-seven acres; the whole purchase money amounted to $11,356,687 and 71 cents; and the balance, remaining due at that time, was about three millions of dollars.

In December, 1813, the Commissioner of the land office, in his report to Congress, estimated the lands then belonging to the United States, to be four hundred millions of acres, and which were situated as follows:—

In the state of Ohio.

Lands to which the Indian title has been
extinguished,   -   -   6,725,000
Lands to which the Indian title has not
been extinguished,   -   5,575,000

Total number of acres of land in Ohio,   -   12,300,000

In the Territory of Michigan.

Lands to which the Indian title has been
    extinguished,   -   -   5,100,000
Lands to which the Indian title has not
    been extinguished,   -   -   11,400,000

    Total in Michigan,   -   -   16,500,000

In the Indiana and Illinois south of the parallel of latitude passing by the south extremity of Lake Michigan.

Lands to which the Indian title has been
    extinguished,   -   -   33,000,000
Lands to which the Indian title has not
    been extinguished,   -   -   23,200,000

    Total in Indiana and Illinois,   -   -   56,200,000

In the Territory west of Lake Michigan, and north of said parallel of latitude.

Lands to which the Indian title has been
    extinguished,   -   -   5,500,000
Lands to which the Indian title has not
    been extinguished,   -   -   54,500,000

    Total west of Michigan,   -   -   60,000,000

In the Mississippi Territory.

Lands to which the Indian title has been
    extinguished,   -   -   5,900,000
Lands to which the Indian title has not
    been extinguished,   -   -   49,100,000

    Total in the Mississippi Territory,   55,000,000

In the cession made by the French Government, April 30th, 1803, and including the Territory of Missouri and State of Louisiana, and the Land east of the River Mississippi and Island of New-Orleans, as far as the River Perdido, at least,   -   200,000,000

Grand total number of acres,   -   400,000,000

Making the quantity of lands, unsold, to which the Indian title has been extinguished, east of the Mississippi river, fifty-six millions two hundred and twenty-five thousand acres. As to the quantity obtained by the cession from France, the Commissioner of the land office does not give the data on which he made his calculation. As the northern and western bounds of Louisiana are yet undetermined, the calculation, it is presumed, must rest, in no small degree, on conjecture.

The various taxes laid in 1815 were considered as war taxes, and necessary to support public credit ; and in addition to the internal duties and direct tax, the produce of the customs was estimated, at four millions a year, during the war, and the proceeds of the sales of public lands at one million, making the whole revenues of the United States, when all the taxes were in full operation, about twenty-one millions of dollars.

Internal duties by estimate, - -	$10,159,000
Direct tax, - - - - -	6,000,000
Customs, - - - - - -	4,000,000
Lands, - - - - - -	1,000,000
	$21,159,000

This is about three dollars and fifty cents for every white inhabitant, in the United States, or including slaves, about three dollars for every person.

The annual amount of the revenues of Great-Britain and Ireland, for some years past, has been about seventy millions sterling, or $310,000,000. The population of the United Kingdom of Great-

Britain and Ireland, is about fifteen millions ; making the amount of taxes for each person about twenty dollars and seventy cents a year.

The amount of the net revenue of France, in 1806, was estimated at one thousand and fifty millions of francs, or about two hundred and ten millions of dollars.*

The return of peace, and revival of commerce, will, probably, enable the United States to dispense with many of the internal duties, and so to modify those, which may be retained, as to be less oppressive and burdensome to the community.

POSTAGE.

By the Constitution, Congress have power to establish post-offices and post-roads : and soon after the commencement of the Government, laws were passed, to carry this power into effect.

The benefits arising from the post-office establishment, to individuals are immense, and in some years, the public have derived no inconsiderable revenue, from this source.

Table No. V. exhibits an account of the post-office establishment, from 1789 to October 1st, 1813, containing the number of post-offices, amount of postage, compensation to post-masters, incidental expenses, transportation of the mail, net revenue, and extent of post-roads, for each year, during that period.

From this will be seen, the increase of the establishment, at the following periods—

	No. of post-offices.		Net revenue. Dolls. Cts.		Extent in miles of post-roads.
1791	-	89	-	9,637 29	-	1,905
1801	-	1,025	-	65,291 84	-	22,309
1811	-	2,403	-	88,148 51	-	37,035

* See Mr. Walch's very able letter, on the genius and disposition of the French Government, including a view of the taxation of the French Empire—1810.

The net revenue for each year, was as follows :—

				Dolls.	Cts.
1790	-	-	-	5,794	95
1791	-	-	-	9,637	29
1792	-	-	-	12,913	06
1793	-	-	-	32,707	10
1794	-	-	-	38,974	28
1795	-	-	-	42,726	78
1796	-	-	-	63,495	42
1797	-	-	-	63,884	16
1798	-	-	-	63,892	94
1799	-	-	-	76,808	44
1800	-	-	-	66,810	81
1801	-	-	-	65,291	84
1802	-	-	-	45,120	25
1803	-	-	-	29,458	74
1804	-	-	-	51,947	40
1805	-	-	-	44,005	92
1806	-	-	-	33,872	17
1807	-	-	-	24,877	62
1808	-	-	-	-	-
1809	-	-	-	8,621	78
1810	-	-	-	55,715	02
1811	-	-	-	88,148	51
1812	-	-	-	109,042	66
to Oct. 1, 1813	-	-	-	24,178	87

The weekly transportation of the mail, in stages, on the 3d of March, 1793, was eight thousand five hundred and sixty-seven miles, in sulkies and on horseback was seven thousand six hundred and sixty-two miles, and yearly transportation, was eight hundred forty-five thousand four hundred and sixty-eight miles ; and on the 3d of March, 1811, the weekly transportation, in stages, was forty-six thousand three hundred and eighty miles ; in sulkies and on horseback, was sixty-one thousand one hundred and seventy-one, and yearly transportation was five million, five hundred ninety-two thousand, six hundred and fifty-two miles. In some of the states, the expenses of the establishment, have generally exceeded the amount of the postage ; while in others, the receipts have greatly exceeded the expenses. Table No. VI. presents a view of the amount of postage on letters and newspapers, with the expenses, in each state and territory, in 1802, by which it appears, that in Massachusetts proper, and in the states of Rhode-Island, Connecticut, New-York, New-Jersey, Pennsylvania, Delaware, Maryland and Georgia, and the District of Columbia, the amount of postage exceeded the expenses, and in New-Hampshire, Vermont, Province of Maine, Ohio, Virginia, Kentucky, North-Carolina, Tennessee, and South-Carolina, and in Indiana and Mississippi Territory, the expenses exceeded the receipts. The debt and credit account, between the states, and the post-office establishment, during, that year, was as follows, viz.—

	Cr. Dolls. Cts.	Dr. Dolls. Cts.
New-Hampshire,	- - -	558 85
Vermont,	- - -	1,836 73
Massachusetts,	12,767 84	- -
District of Maine,	- - -	421 17
Rhode-Island,	1,760 05	- -
Connecticut,	744 71	- -
New-York,	26,118 40	- -
New-Jersey,	397 35	- -
Pennsylvania,	27,810 11	- -
Ohio,	- - -	2,971 21
Indiana Territory,	- -	1,242 97
Delaware,	827 15	- -
Maryland,	12,903 49	- -
District of Columbia,	9,096 35	- -
Virginia,	- - -	3,417 83
Kentucky,	- -	3,526 62
North-Carolina,	- - -	12,122 43
Tennessee,	- - -	2,957 99
South-Carolina,	- - -	3,991 10
Georgia,	361 15	- -
Mississippi Territory,	- - -	1,664 32
	$92,786 60	$34,713 21

The revenue derived from the post-office, in Great-Britain, for the year ending the 4th of January, 1808, was £1,277,538 sterling, and in the year ending January 5th, 1812, was £1,478,505 sterling, or about $6,600,000. The net revenue from the post-office in France, in 1807, was about seven millions of francs, or one million, four hundred thousand dollars.* The receipts from fees on patents, and other sources, may be seen, in table No. VII. under the head "Miscellaneous."

RECEIPTS AND EXPENDITURES.

A general view of the annual receipts from the various sources of revenue, and of the annual expenditures of the Government, from its commencement, to 1814, and the objects of expenditure, cannot be uninteresting. Table No. VII. exhibits a statement of the annual receipts, from the customs, internal revenue, direct tax, postage, public lands, and other miscellaneous sources; and also, the annual expenditures for the military, Indian, and naval departments, foreign intercourse, Barbary powers, civil list, and miscellaneous civil, from the commencement of the Government to the 30th of September, 1812.

The aggregate amount of the receipts and of the expenditures for the objects above mentioned, for that period, were as follows :—

From 4th of March, 1789, to 31st December,	Receipts. Dolls. Cts.	Expenditures. Dolls. Cts.
1791 -	4,418,913 99 -	1,718,129 37
1792 -	3,661,932 31 -	1,766,077 15
1793 -	4,614,423 14 -	1,707,348 28
1794 -	5,128,432 87 -	3,500,348 20
1795 -	5,954,534 59 -	4,350,596 45
1796 -	7,137,529 65 -	2,531,930 40
1797 -	8,303,560 99 -	2,833,590 96
1798 -	7,820,575 80 -	4,623,223 54

* Walch's letter.

Years.	Receipts. Dolls. Cts.	Expenditures. Dolls. Cts.
1799	- 7,475,773 31	- 6,480,166 72
1800	- 10,777,709 10	- 7,411,369 97
1801	- 12,846,530 95	- 4,981,669 90
1802	- 13,668,233 95	- 3,737,079 91
1803	- 11,064,097 63	- 4,002,824 24
1804	- 11,826,307 38	- 4,452,858 91
1805	- 13,560,693 20	- 6,357,234 62
1806	- 15,559,931 7	- 6,080,209 36
1807	- 16,398,019 26	- 4,984,572 89
1808	- 17,060,661 93	- 6,504,338 85
1809	- 7,773,473 12	- 7,414,672 14
1810	- 9,384,214 28	- 5,311,082 28
1811	- 14,423,529 9	- 5,592,604 86
From January 1st, to 30th of September, 1812	- 6,927,706 56	- 11,760,292 21
	$215,786,783 27	$108,102,221 21

The receipts from the customs, during this
  period, were — — $199,524,131 78
      Internal revenue, — — 6,460,003 54
      Direct tax, — — 1,757,240 84
      Postage of letters, — — 667,348 70
      Sales of public lands, — 6,161,283 2
      Miscellaneous, — — 1,216,775 39

$215,786,783 27

The expenditures, for the pay and
  subsistence of the army, were $38,572,575 15
Fortification of ports and harbours, 3,493,758 96
Fabrication of cannon, — 263,611 54
Purchase of salt-petre, — — 150,000
Additional arms, — — 300,000

Arming and equipping the militia,	500,000	
Detachment of militia, -	170,000	
Services of militia, - -	406,800	
Services of volunteers, -	210,000	
		$44,066,745 65

Indian department—

Holding treaties, &c.	$822,838 68	
Trading houses, -	430,298 84	
		$1,253,137 52

Naval department, - -	29,889,660 78

Foreign intercourse, exclusive of Barbary powers, and which includes the sum of $6,361,000 paid under the convention with France, of 30th of April, 1803, and with Great-Britain, of 8th of

January, 1802, - - .,	10,311,145 33
Barbary powers, - - -	2,328,810 40
Civil list, - - - -	12,686,493 36
Miscellaneous civil, - - -	7,566,228 17
	$108,102,221 21

In addition to the above sum of -	$215,786,783 27

received, from various sources of revenue, from March 4th, 1789, to September 30th, 1812, there was received into the Treasury, during the same period, for

Sales of bank stock, - -	2,671,860
Dividends on do. - -	1,101,720
Interest on stock remitted to Europe, -	136,400
Gain on exchange, - -	805,127 59

And from foreign and domestic loans, (of which $5,847,212 50 cents, was part of

the eleven million loan, in 1812,) -	35,141,512 61

Making the total amount of receipts to the 30th of September, 1812, .. -	$255,643,403 27

Besides the sum of expended for the above objects; the expenditures, during the same period, for the payment of the interest, charges on the foreign loans, and principal of the foreign and domestic debts, at the Treasury of the United States, and by Commissioners abroad, were	$108,102,221 21
	$144,862,260 67
And the expenditures, on account of the revolutionary Government, were	316,268 70
Making the whole expenditures of the United States, to 30th September, 1812,	$253,280,750 58
Leaving a balance, in the Treasury, at that time, of	2,362,652 69
	$255,643,403 27

It will be observed, that the foregoing account of receipts and expenditures, includes those of nine months of the year 1812, when the United States were preparing for, or were engaged in war, and the expenditures were much greater than in any former year.

The receipts from the whole revenue of the United States, from March 4th, 1789, to December 31st, 1811, were $208,859,076 71; and the expenditures, (exclusive of the public debt) for the same period, were $96,341,929. The receipts, for a little more than the first half of this period, that is, from March 4th, 1789, to 1801, inclusive, were $78,139,915 80

And from 1802 to 1811, inclusive, were 130,719,160 91

Being a difference of $52,579,245 11

The expenditures, from March 4th, 1789, to 1801, inclusive, were $41,904,450 94

And from 1802 to 1811, inclusive, were 54,437,478 6

A difference of $12,533,027 12

The increase of expenditures, in the latter period, was principally in the naval department, foreign intercourse, civil list, and miscellaneous civil.

Since the 1st of January, 1812, the whole amount of the expenses of the United States, has not yet been ascertained.

The expenditures from January 1st, 1812, to September 30th, 1812, as far as they have been ascertained, were—

1. For civil list, foreign inter- course, &c. -	$1,556,864 46	
2. For the military department,	7,464,814 80	
3. For the naval department,	2,638,612 95	
		$11,660,292 21

From September 30th, 1812, to September, 30th, 1813, the money paid from the Treasury :—

1. For civil list, foreign intercourse, &c. amounted to -	$1,705,016 35	
2. For the military department,	18,404,650 49	
3. For the naval department,	6,317,411 15	
		$26,427,077 99

And from September 30th, 1813, to December 31st, 1813, being the last quarter of 1813, the amount paid :—

1. For civil list, foreign inter- course, &c. was -	$400,000	
2. For the military department,	5,887,747	
3. For the naval department,	1,248,145 10	
		$7,535,892 10
Making an aggregate, for the years 1812 and 1813, of -	-	$45,623,262 30

The sums authorized to be expended in 1814, and for which appropriations were made, were—

1. For civil list, foreign intercourse, &c. -	$2,445,355 59	
2. For the military department,	24,502,906	
3. For the naval department,	8,169,910 87	
		$35,118,172 46

It is well known, that the expenses of 1814 exceeded the appropriations, by some millions, and that there are claims upon the Treasury, to the amount of many millions, yet unsettled, some of which are mentioned, in the preceding Chapter, on the subject of the public debt. What will be the amount of the expenses, on a final adjustment of these various claims, is yet uncertain. The whole amount of expenses incurred in the years 1812, 1813, and 1814, for the civil list, foreign intercourse, &c. and for the military and naval departments, will probably equal, if not exceed, the whole expenses, for the same objects, from the commencement of the Government, to the 1st of January, 1812. As the army was not disbanded, until the summer of 1815, and the naval establishment remained nearly the same, the expenditures of 1815 cannot fall greatly short, of those of the preceding year.

The receipts into the Treasury, for the years 1812, 1813, and 1814, from the various sources of revenue, and other incidental receipts, (exclusive of loans and Treasury notes) were as follows :—

1812 - - -	$9,801,132 76	
1813 - - -	14,340,409 95	
1814 (on estimate) about	12,000,000	

TABLE No. I.

Statement exhibiting the gross and net amount of the Customs, together with the amount of drawbacks, &c. and Expenses of Collection, in each State and Territory, from the commencement of the present Government, annually, to the 31st day of December, 1810.

STATES.	Gross amount of Duties on merchandize, tonnage, fines, penalties and forfeitures.	Payments for		Expenses of prosecutions and collections.	Net Revenue.
		Drawbacks on merchandize.	Bounties on salted fish.		
New-Hampshire,	60,005 26	344 19	855 44	5,772 48	53,033 15
Vermont,	- -	-	-	-	- -
Massachusetts,	1,081,372 19	19,130 19	25,046 59	59,279 17	977,916 24
Rhode-Island,	156,607 87	521 87	1,928 13	7,619 45	146,538 42
Connecticut,	223,355 27	- -	1,273 37	15,395 27	206,681 63
New-York,	1,415,449 33	22,289 20	382 79	28,267	1,364,510 34
New-Jersey,	16,448 88	-	7	1,537 89	14,903 99
Pennsylvania,	1,535,970 66	8,976 17	-	35,970 88	1,491,023 61
Delaware,	43,546 56	138 32	-	2,482 48	40,925 76
Maryland,	680,292 48	13,584 94	14 50	25,672 99	641,020 5
Virginia,	878,909 51	904 68	27 90	26,059 41	851,917 52
North-Carolina,	122,025 37	29 45	141 60	6,843 57	115,010 75
South-Carolina,	560,874 24	3,684 78	-	18,405 86	538,783 60
Georgia,	98,926 4	202 6	-	6,725 21	91,998 77
Total,	6,873,783 66	69,805 85	29,682 32	240,031 66	6,534,263 83

From the commencement of the present Government to the 31st of December, 1791.

TABLE No. I.—CONTINUED.

From the 1st of January to the 31st of December, 1792.

STATES.	Gross amount of Duties on merchandize, tonnage, fines, penalties and forfeitures.	Payments for Drawbacks on Merchandize.	Drawbacks on domestic spirits bounties on fish and provisions.	Expenses of prosecutions and collection.	Net Revenue.
New-Hampshire,	47,149 39	383 21	1,872 85	3,771 26	41,422 7
Vermont,	1,038 19	-	-	295 18	743 1
Massachusetts,	835,263 93	12,009 71	111,652 29	33,360 27	678,246 66
Rhode-Island,	104,079 12	12,714 91	39,087 91	6,263 50	46,012 80
Connecticut,	152,391 6	32 67	2,907 36	7,362 46	142,088 57
New-York,	1,256,738 99	45,592 24	16,769 78	24,567 44	1,169,809 53
New-Jersey,	5,769 1	-	18 20	987 48	4,763 33
Pennsylvania,	1,156,901 33	37,752 66	830 99	21,489 58	1,096,828 10
Delaware,	21,832 41	-	-	2,755 13	19,077 28
Maryland,	494,569 29	24,039 54	3,931 79	17,305 98	449,291 98
Virginia,	494,441 15	1,736 22	1,252 64	16,957	474,495 29
North-Carolina,	85,648 60	160 98	383 80	7,040 97	78,062 85
South-Carolina,	380,051 49	3,360 33	2,492 77	13,289 16	360,909 23
Georgia,	59,740 57	79 12	-	6,487 54	53,173 91
Total,	5,095,919 53	137,861 59	181,200 38	161,923 95	4,614,924 61

TABLE No. I.—CONTINUED.

From the 1st of January to the 31st of December, 1793.

STATES.	Gross amount of Duties on merchandize, tonnage, fines, penalties and forfeitures.	Payments for Drawbacks on merchandize.	Payments for Drawbacks on domestic spirits bounties and allowances.	Expenses of prosecutions and collection.	Net Revenue.
New-Hampshire,	52,637 21	183 41	2,515 57	5,032 59	44,905 64
Vermont,	585 81	-	-	417 14	168 67
Massachusetts,	1,142,453 42	37,138 28	119,378 93	35,775 95	950,160 26
Rhode-Island,	182,910·93	2,886 1	38,483 32	7,669 93	133,871 67
Connecticut,	172,834 72	1,197 71	6,556 53	10,216 83	154,863 65
New-York,	1,267,300 32	42,560 70	3,715 23	25,288 24	1,195,736 15
New-Jersey,	17,242 77	-	114 47	1,255 19	15,873 11
Pennsylvania,	1,940,609 90	102,659 26	1,282 23	32,349 98	1,804,318 43
Delaware,	61,017 60	32 86	61 43	3,455 31	57,468
Maryland,	948,853 59	54,642 83	2,006 86	22,522 36	869,681 54
Virginia,	408,927 39	2,857 39	1,442 42	16,436 59	388,190 99
North-Carolina,	70,570 80	80 74	184 50	6,538 64	63,766 92
South-Carolina,	412,300 33	35,412 94	3,006 79	15,396 70	359,113 90
Georgia,	42,110 83	157 70	-	6,559 57	35,393 56
Total,	6,720,985 62	279,809 83	178,748 28	188,915 2	6,073,512 49

350

TABLE No. I.—CONTINUED.

From the 1st of January to the 31st of December, 1794.

STATES.	Gross amount of Duties on merchandize, tonnage, fines, penalties and forfeitures.	Payments for Drawbacks on merchandize.	Payments for Drawbacks on domestic spirits bounties and allowances.	Expenses of prosecutions and collection.	Net Revenue.
New-Hampshire,	52,404 46	4,482 30	3,202 42	5,921 41	38,798 33
Vermont,	2,051 50	-	-	630 53	1,420 97
Massachusetts,	1,485,185 30	327,594 15	110,001 20	42,705 53	1,0J4,884 42
Rhode-Island,	147,185 29	25,019 72	23,683 81	9,057 71	89,424 5
Connecticut,	188,499 34	376 16	5,740 57	10,553 56	171,829 5
New-York,	2,161,208 7	266,302 51	3,575 73	31,045 65	1,860,284 18
New-Jersey,	16,007 38	158 45	23 1	1,135 4	14,690 88
Pennsylvania,	2,012,334 6	502,446 87	381 75	35,509 12	1,473,996 32
Delaware,	28,908 50	498 27	-	3,819 82	24,590 41
Maryland,	1,232,153 85	407,668 30	1,629 11	27,687 70	795,173 24
Virginia,	429,958 14	23,076 36	248 86	16,936 42	389,696 50
North-Carolina,	87,521 5	-	305 72	8,419 1	78,796 32
South-Carolina,	729,183 97	56,037 90	1,386 55	19,843 48	651,916 4
Georgia,	98,589 72	1,912 95	-	8,863 62	87,813 15
Total,	8,671,195 63	1,615,574 44	150,178 73	222,128 60	6,683,313 86

TABLE No. I.—CONTINUED.

From the 1st of January to the 31st of December, 1795.

STATES.	Gross amount of Duties on merchandize; tonnage, fines and forfeitures.	Payments for		Expenses of prosecutions and collection.	Net Revenue.
		Drawbacks on merchandize.	Drawbacks on domestic spirits sugar, bounties and allowances.		
New-Hampshire,	60,338 81	8,097 28	1,961 83	5,977 31	44,302 39
Vermont,	1,226 55	-	-	502 92	723 63
Massachusetts,	2,018,296 77	457,424 78	90,716 89	54,985 91	1,415,169 19
Rhode-Island,	349,695 74	63,788 60	29,757 86	11,498 59	244,650 69
Connecticut,	172,026 5	1,795 61	3,170 53	11,892 82	155,167 9
New-York,	2,735,204 17	688,172 19	5,669 78	40,672 58	2,000,689 62
New-Jersey,	21,104 96	2,562 67	44 10	1,638 72	16,859 47
Pennsylvania,	3,067,739 1	752,550 17	865 82	42,699 64	2,271,623 38
Delaware,	32,537 31	4,194 29	49 35	3,790 82	24,502 85
Maryland,	1,348,503 85	789,167 1	1,895 46	33,794 45	523,646 93
Virginia,	462,950 73	49,280 77	102 20	16,686 96	396,880 80
North-Carolina,	109,845 96	1,032 14	211 50	8,725 58	99,876 74
South-Carolina,	791,616 26	60,650 48	266 63	20,246 61	710,452 54
Georgia,	82,646 86	20,049 80	-	7,732 68	54,864 38
Total,	11,253,733 3	2,898,765 79	134,711 95	260,845 59	7,959,409 70

TABLE No. I.—CONTINUED.

From the 1st of January to the 31st of December, 1796.

STATES.	Gross amount of Duties on merchandize, tonnage, passports and clearances, &c.	Payments for Drawbacks on merchandize.	Drawbacks on domestic spirits, sugar, snuff, bounties, &c.	Expenses of prosecutions and collection.	Net Revenue.
New-Hampshire,	96,938 76	33,877 39	2,103 94	7,437 24	53,520 19
Vermont,	2,132 70	-	-	452 75	1,679 95
Massachusetts,	2,377,456 98	814,373 84	161,470 73	66,847 74	1,334,764 67
Rhode-Island,	342,637 87	150,695 26	39,760 46	14,477 14	137,705 1
Connecticut,	193,370 36	33,685 33	4,002 91	14,279 19	141,402 93
New-York,	3,078,002 37	865,877 43	9,996 13	43,706 28	2,158,422 53
New-Jersey,	1,848 43	932 60	-	1,765 27	-
Pennsylvania,	3,661,329 88	1,586,064 78	15,892 65	46,627 74	2,012,744 71
Delaware,	47,042 36	29,871	-	4,849 34	12,322 2
Maryland,	1,642,635 69	842,803 44	2,806 40	35,207 64	761,818 21
Virginia,	662,686 88	43,707 28	273 60	20,429 5	598,276 95
North-Carolina,	89,774 44	10,421 32	681 76	9,922 21	68,749 15
South-Carolina,	420,043 59	346,447 80	210 25	17,381 4	56,004 50
Georgia,	65,966 9	25,292 65	18	9,095 88	31,559 56
Total,	12,681,866 40	4,784,050 12	237,216 83	292,478 51	7,368,970 38

The net amount of revenue exhibited in the above statement, is - - - 7,368,970 38

From which, deduct excess of expenditure beyond the duty in the state of New-Jersey, 849 44

True net amount of duties, &c. - - - $7,368,120 94

TABLE No. I.—CONTINUED.

From the 1st of January to the 31st of December, 1797.

STATES.	Gross amount of Duties on merchandize, tonnage, passports and clearances, &c.	Payments for			Net Revenue.
		Drawbacks on merchandize.	Drawbacks on domestic spirits, sugar, snuff, bounties, &c.	Expenses of prosecutions and collection.	
New-Hampshire,	45,817 1	8,827 68	2,197 30	7,065 28	27,726 75
Vermont,	-	-	-	-	-
Massachusetts,	2,201,101 26	636,721 57	126,626 22	65,444 85	1,372,308 62
Rhode-Island,	403,211 72	95,985 93	14,258 75	16,578 27	276,388 77
Connecticut,	163,396 71	30,398 48	2,588 53	15,367 10	115,042 60
New-York,	2,977,663 32	862,013 71	9,251 90	46,810 53	2,059,587 18
New-Jersey,	11,028 60	-	-	2,054 12	8,974 48
Pennsylvania,	2,925,016 26	1,086,839 11	28,536 57	66,369 10	1,743,271 48
Delaware,	55,912 93	14,088 19	221 4	5,838 54	35,765 16
Maryland,	2,021,042 51	834,089 92	3,495 51	38,324 55	1,145,132 53
Virginia,	703,819 33	70,251 62	337 18	27,085 17	606,145 36
North-Carolina,	119,857 23	1,254 20	224 43	13,071 43	105,307 17
South-Carolina,	1,297,387 16	564,203 44	1,770 86	31,175 58	700,237 28
Georgia,	75,615 97	3,054 58	-	10,473 87	62,087 52
Tennessee,	235 74	-	-	99 21	136 53
Total,	13,001,105 75	4,207,728 43	189,508 29	345,757 60	8,258,111 43

TABLE No. I.—CONTINUED.

From the 1st of January to the 31st of December, 1798.

STATES.	Gross amount of Duties on merchandize, tonnage, passports, & clearances, &c.	Drawbacks on merchandize.	Payments for Drawbacks on domestic spirits, sugar, snuff, bounties, &c.	Expenses of prosecutions and collection.	Net Revenue.
New-Hampshire,	106,777 52	9,618 59	2,270 45	22,616 4	72,272 44
Vermont,	2,437 98	-	-	1,281 18	1,156 80
Massachusetts,	2,159,549 88	800,094 32	118,995 81	72,373 47	1,168,086 28
Rhode-Island,	252,882 77	112,874 74	20,243 11	14,813 63	104,951 29
Connecticut,	184,962 27	37,819 15	5,086 58	14,976 33	127,080 21
New-York,	2,729,963 20	916,281 63	5,327 18	54,765 75	1,753,588 64
New-Jersey,	18,296 15	10,589 13	-	4,210 13	3,496 89
Pennsylvania,	2,098,921 69	1,018,127 13	3,767 79	47,449 5	1,029,577 72
Delaware,	85,016 76	18,709 50	-	8,583 62	57,723 64
Maryland,	2,412,074 11	1,483,322 33	809 83	42,928 38	885,013 57
Virginia,	690,495 66	25,837 99	256 20	34,989 43	629,412 4
North-Carolina,	142,030 21	5,804 12	521 59	14,715 33	120,989 17
South-Carolina,	643,688 58	360,419 64	2,803 54	40,942 94	239,522 46
Georgia,	428 67	-	-	1,261 45	-
Tennessee,	565 55	-	-	156 70	408 85
Total,	11,528,091	4,799,498 27	160,082 8	376,063 43	6,193,280

The net amount of revenue exhibited in the above statement, is - - 6,193,280

From which, deduct excess of expenditure beyond the duty in the state of Georgia, - 832 78

True net amount of duties, &c. - - - $ 6,192,447 22

TABLE No. I.—CONTINUED.

From the 1st of January to the 31st of December, 1799.

STATES AND TERRITORY	Gross amount of Duties on merchandize, tonnage, passports and clearances, &c.	Drawbacks on merchandize.	Payments for Drawbacks on domestic spirits, sugar, bounties, &c.	Expenses of prosecutions & collection.	Net Revenue.
New-Hampshire,	120,943 57	11,170 52	3,550 56	7,094 1	99,128 48
Vermont,	4,432 41	-	-	1,591 39	2,841 2
Massachusetts,	2,865,539 76	1,019,029 69	159,553 29	79,885 44	1,607,071 34
Rhode-Island,	370,466 91	72,517 57	23,159 73	14,668 45	260,121 16
Connecticut,	338,432 92	21,021 70	7,119 20	20,659 75	289,632 27
New-York,	3,598,325 64	1,157,589 39	7,809 87	59,384 6	2,373,542 32
New-Jersey,	2,180 40	2,340 89	84 6	1,739 83	-
Pennsylvania,	2,236,626 71	935,264 10	1,447 47	40,516 12	1,259,399 2
Delaware,	104,424 18	20,510 10	71 20	9,708 78	74,134 10
Maryland,	2,565,299 60	1,357,230 9	3,758 63	42,615 16	1,161,695 72
Virginia,	1,026,985 31	89,500 57	170 16	41,182 18	896,132 40
North-Carolina,	178,072 30	2,524 71	720 15	20,403 43	154,424 1
South-Carolina,	2,025,251 84	1,091,963 39	3,315 46	71,431 48	858,541 51
Georgia,	1,550 64	-	-	1,655 28	-
Tennessee,	1,036 82	-	-	263 14	773 68
Michigan Territory,	-	-	-	-	-
Total,	15,439,569 1	5,780,662 72	210,759 78	412,798 50	9,037,437 3

The net amount of revenue, exhibited in the above statement, is - - 9,037,437 3
From which, deduct excess of expenditure beyond the duty in the state of New-Jersey, 1,984 38
Ditto ditto in the state of Georgia, - - 104 64
2,089 2
True net amount of duty, &c. - - - $9,035,348 1

TABLE No. I.—CONTINUED.

From the 1st of January to the 31st of December, 1800.

STATES AND TERRITORY.	Gross amount of Duties on merchandize, tonnage, passports and clearances, &c.	Payments for		Expenses of prosecutions & collection.	Net Revenue.
		Drawbacks on merchandize.	Drawbacks on domestic spirits, sugar, bounties, &c.		
New-Hampshire,	164,799 12	7,044 39	3,289 72	11,785 60	142,679 41
Vermont,	3,698 20	-	35	1,327 36	2,335 84
Massachusetts,	3,196,260 44	1,008,234 12	127,557 82	85,471 80	1,974,996 70
Rhode-Island,	561,274 76	109,348 88	41,284 32	17,000 27	393,641 29
Connecticut,	208,856 16	15,748 38	3,412 63	20,003 19	169,691 96
New-York,	3,671,906	869,402 55	5,709 24	54,993 59	2,741,800 62
New-Jersey,	1,172 66	-	-	2,400 83	-
Pennsylvania,	3,197,450 25	1,785,108 61	3,412 63	58,603 2	1,350,325 99
Delaware,	59,184 49	33,388 14	301 83	9,262 51	16,232 1
Maryland,	1,933,772 80	1,263,406 83	2,043 16	44,753 98	623,568 83
Virginia,	780,308 62	90,704 77	21	44,988 71	644,594 14
North-Carolina,	159,502 51	4,555 8	993 60	27,492 56	126,461 27
South-Carolina,	2,233,312 71	1,006,783 77	3,977 58	63,265 56	1,159,285 80
Georgia,	1,162 12	-	-	1,949 78	-
Tennessee,	1,288 92	-	-	552 6	736 86
Michigan Territory,	7,475 57	-	-	463 50	7,012 7
Total,	16,181,425 33	6,193,725 52	192,038 53	444,314 32	9,353,362 79

The net amount of revenue, exhibited in the above statement, is - - - 9,353,362 79

From which, deduct excess of expenditure beyond the duty in the state of New-Jersey, 1,228 17

Ditto   ditto   in the state of Georgia, -   787 66

2,015 83

True net amount of duty, &c. - - - $9,351,346 96

TABLE No. I.—CONTINUED.

From the 1st of January to the 31st of December, 1801.

STATES AND TERRITORIES.	Gross amount of Duties on merchandize, tonnage, passports and clearances, &c.	Payments for			Net Revenue.
		Drawbacks on merchandize.	Drawbacks on domestic spirits, sugar, bounties, &c.	Expenses of prosecutions & collection.	
New-Hampshire,	167,006 88	16,844 63	4,457 18	12,055 21	133,649 86
Vermont,	2,198 72	-	52 50	1,364 58	781 64
Massachusetts,	4,479,827 34	1,347,475 9	106,102 60	96,496 50	2,929,753 15
Rhode-Island,	526,748 99	211,346 92	10,063 62	20,700 50	284,637 95
Connecticut,	371,774 69	15,721 15	5,571 61	22,422 29	328,059 64
New-York,	5,047,418 8	1,172,407 76	7,164 81	57,069 10	3,810,776 41
New-Jersey,	9,538 3	-	51 75	2,661 79	6,824 49
Pennsylvania,	3,728,041 24	1,540,700 62	9,693 27	54,458 87	2,123,188 48
Delaware,	156,419 63	56,188 56	205 16	8,698 79	91,327 12
Maryland,	2,176,894 30	1,135,717 36	3,469 47	35,855 2	1,001,854 45
District of Columbia,	104,901 39	4,922 98	-	5,303 52	94,674 89
Virginia,	843,033 29	59,139 6	259 65	37,380 45	746,254 13
North-Carolina,	147,847 28	1,507 95	1,712 90	19,498 22	125,128 21
South-Carolina,	2,280,061 16	1,221,253 24	1,380 89	55,284 67	1,002,142 36
Georgia,	764,617 4	49,173 95	-	51,944 2	663,499 7
Tennessee,	659 91	-	-	147 42	512 49
Kentucky,	1,224 91	-	53 80	363 52	807 59
Ohio,	-	-	-	-	-
Michigan Territory,	4,635 63	-	-	357 52	4,278 11
Indiana do.	-	-	-	-	-
Mississippi do.	15,392 13	-	-	839 77	14,552 36
Total,	20,828,240 64	6,832,399 27	150,239 21	482,899 76	13,362,702 40

TABLE No. I.—CONTINUED.

From the 1st of January to the 31st of December, 1802.

STATES AND TERRITORIES	Gross amount of Duties on merchandize, tonnage, passports and clearances, &c.	Payments for			Net Revenue.
		Drawbacks on merchandize.	Drawbacks on domestic spirits, bounties and allowances.	Expenses of prosecutions and collection.	
New-Hampshire,	157,689 26	26,461 75	5,293 53	6,248 5	119,686 3
Vermont,	1,483 7	-	89 75	1,222 5	171 27
Massachusetts,	3,503,792 68	1,712,580 18	161,830 75	103,471 89	1,525,909 86
Rhode-Island,	481,277 10	243,785 56	35,982 12	23,492 96	178,016 46
Connecticut,	350,010 20	53,522 58	6,185 55	27,441 89	262,860 18
New-York,	3,599,015 55	1,033,315 74	6,413 91	68,430 73	2,490,855 17
New-Jersey,	6,890 92	-	-	2,925 85	3,965 7
Pennsylvania,	2,770,302 82	1,297,662 11	13,263 62	49,014 22	1,410,362 87
Delaware,	159,392 39	64,576 50	242 10	11,607 30	82,966 49
Maryland,	1,426,556 84	754,479 10	8,513 20	29,430 8	634,134 46
District of Columbia,	144,627 38	5,056 7	265	5,972 81	133,333 50
Virginia,	751,317 52	29,884 8	749 44	31,261 52	689,422 48
North-Carolina,	287,068 64	2,742 38	3,033 69	28,895 25	252,397 32
South-Carolina,	1,228,410 38	863,399 37	934 90	83,941 29	280,134 82
Georgia,	228,452 22	-	-	16,525 22	211,927
Tennessee,	139 37	-	-	64 63	74 74
Kentucky,	1,605 38	-	-	383 7	1,222 31
Ohio,	-	-	-	75	-
Michigan Territory,	26,087 81	-	-	1,665 16	24,422 65
Indiana do.	2,526 76	-	-	191 20	2,335 56
Mississippi do.	23,782 25	-	-	645 46	23,136 79
Total,	15,150,428 54	6,087,465 42	242,797 46	492,905 63	8,327,335 3

The net amount of revenue, exhibited in the above statement, is - - 8,327,335 3

From which, deduct excess of expenditure beyond the duty in the state of Ohio, - 75

True net amount of duty, &c. - - - $8,327,260

TABLE No. I.—CONTINUED.

From the 1st of January to the 31st of December, 1803.

STATES AND TERRITORIES.	Gross amount of Duties on merchandize, tonnage, passports and clearances, &c.	Drawbacks on merchandize.	Payments for Drawbacks on domestic spirits, sugar, bounties, &c.	Expenses of prosecutions & collection.	Net Revenue.
New-Hampshire,	167,350 9	25,517 52	6,581 28	12,734 36	122,516 93
Vermont,	2,901 62	-	10 25	1,170 61	1,720 76
Massachusetts,	3,470,753 24	757,667 12	132,430 89	90,124 55	2,490,530 68
Rhode-Island,	550,435 40	151,849 91	11,606 53	20,298 46	366,680 50
Connecticut,	355,619 26	21,401 63	8,658 76	23,758 4	301,800 83
New-York,	4,138,251 17	545,010 64	7,646 49	60,759 60	3,524,834 44
New-Jersey,	6,128 38	-	-	2,974 79	3,153 59
Pennsylvania,	2,267,949 5	561,040 68	6,906 26	44,279 31	1,655,722 80
Delaware,	77,497 40	40,016 50	248	8,592 69	28,640 21
Maryland,	1,216,084 87	249,318 82	4,522 49	25,787 53	936,461 3
District of Columbia,	154,375 95	3,041 84	97 22	7,806 60	143,430 29
Virginia,	778,394 70	25,553 6	792 94	38,206 59	713,842 11
North-Carolina,	192,207 91	1,785 97	2,184 37	28,272 38	159,965 19
South-Carolina,	889,577	217,328 93	1,631 4	24,490 93	646,126 10
Georgia,	207,390 23	11,133 44	433 13	13,360 97	182,462 69
Kentucky,	1,673 96	-	-	257 39	1,416 57
Ohio,	26 67	-	-	150 80	-
Michigan Territory,	25,333 78	-	-	1,909 50	23,424 28
Indiana do.	3,001 19	-	-	346 19	2,655
Mississippi do.	18,701 12	-	-	1,533 60	17,167 52
Total,	14,523,652 99	2,610,661 6	183,749 65	406,814 89	11,322,551 52

The net amount of revenue, exhibited in the above statement, is - - 11,322,551 52
From which, deduct excess of expenditure beyond the duty in the state of Ohio, - 124 13
True net amount of duty, &c. - - - $11,322,427 39

TABLE No. 1.—CONTINUED.

From the 1st of January to the 31st of December, 1804.

STATES AND TERRITORIES.	Gross amount of Duties on merchandise, meditterra-nean fund, tonnage, light money,&c.	Payments for		Expenses of prose-cutions & collection.	Net Revenue.
		Drawbacks on merchandize.	Drawbacks on domestic spirits, sugar, bounties, &c.		
New-Hampshire,	213,047 14	85,071 2	7,965 1	11,271 62	108,739 49
Vermont,	2,752 5		579 25	1,373 43	799 37
Massachusetts,	5,468,388 29	1,572,074 3	146,172 49	119,210 63	3,630,931 24
Rhode-Island,	650,083 78	199,895 83	5,388 69	23,707 80	421,091 46
Connecticut,	434,205 9	47,150 29	12,411 84	26,589 61	348,053 35
New-York,	5,240,652 53	1,283,604	8,364 97	76,327 64	3,872,355 92
New-Jersey,	6,294 67			2,936 65	3,358 2
Pennsylvania,	3,540,936 62	872,237 94	5,850 23	52,917 17	2,609,931 28
Delaware,	56,027 67	23,209 45	165 50	6,542 50	26,110 22
Maryland,	2,200,767 32	614,852 84	2,874 85	44,316 26	1,538,723 37
District of Columbia,	171,261 69	33,600 2	694 5	8,542 73	128,424 89
Virginia,	969,363 45	33,723 46	1,174 97	31,793 99	902,671 3
North-Carolina,	216,172 75	3,754 68	2,353 33	23,424 78	186,639 96
South-Carolina,	1,090,399 51	335,841 18	66	35,973 57	718,518 76
Georgia,	200,767 93	6,689 79		13,657 84	180,420 30
Kentucky,					-
Ohio,	30 59			150 92	-
Michigan Territory,	39,296 52			2,712 60	36,583 92
Indiana do.	714 43			435 53	278 90
Mississippi do.	5,406 24			1,224 67	4,181 57
Orleans do.	293,066 87	1,820 19		11,974 37	279,272 31
Total,	20,799,635 24	5,113,524 72	194,061 18	495,084 31	14,997,085 36

The net amount of revenue, exhibited in the above statement, is - - 14,997,085 36

From which, deduct excess of expenditure beyond the duty in the state of Ohio, 120 33

True net amount of duty, &c. - - - $14,996,965 3

TABLE No. I.—CONTINUED.

From the 1st of January to the 31st of December, 1805.

STATES AND TERRITORIES.	Gross amount of Duties on merchandize, mediterranean fund, tonnage, light money, &c.	Payments for			Net Revenue.
		Drawbacks on merchandize.	Bounties and allowances.	Expenses of prosecutions and collection.	
New-Hampshire,	172,582 58	43,553 45	8,373 89	11,099 63	109,555 61
Vermont,	2,414 76	-	193 50	1,441 71	779 55
Massachusetts,	6,046,344 41	2,449,040 57	149,704 37	139,553 6	3,308,046 41
Rhode-Island,	655,330 19	274,910 3	4,333 73	26,459 10	349,627 33
Connecticut,	471,448 11	80,488 40	11,727 82	24,514 94	354,716 95
New-York,	7,046,104 18	2,062,509 46	5,964 87	95,553 29	4,882,076 56
New-Jersey,	20,861 95	-	-	2,452 15	18,409 80
Pennsylvania,	3,679,122 31	1,319,869 65	3,146 87	55,542 42	2,300,563 37
Delaware,	171,968 9	56,179 16	177	10,022 59	105,589 34
Maryland,	2,316,948 44	1,142,355 97	3,525 85	40,232 31	1,130,834 31
District of Columbia,	150,414 57	23,799 21	872 35	6,731 78	119,011 23
Virginia,	980,047 24	135,107 71	788 67	38,920 28	805,230 58
North-Carolina,	200,935 97	10,646 93	1,473 22	23,547 78	165,268 4
South-Carolina,	1,330,775 72	448,812 88	29 40	38,797 97	843,135 47
Georgia,	113,561 27	6,037 21	-	11,575 27	95,948 79

TABLE No. I.—CONTINUED.

From the 1st of January to the 31st of December, 1805.

STATES AND TERRITORIES.	Gross amount of Duties on merchandize, mediterranean fund, tonnage, light money, &c.	Payments for			Net Revenue.
		Drawbacks on merchandize.	Bounties and allowances.	Expenses of prosecutions and collection.	
Kentucky,	-	-	-	64 43	-
Tennessee,	-	-	-	12 59	-
Ohio,	5,333 69	-	-	512 39	4,821 30
Michigan Territory,	44,902 88	-	-	1,110 11	43,792 77
Indiana do.	-	-	-	261 11	-
Mississippi do.	1,318 83	-	-	603 33	715 50
Orleans do.	469,249 60	97,110 66	362 50	29,680 73	342,095 71
Total,	23,879,664 79	8,150,421 29	190,674 4	558,688 97	14,980,218 62

The net amount of revenue, exhibited in the above statement, is   14,980,218 62

From which, deduct excess of expenditure beyond the duty in the state of Kentucky, 64 43

Ditto   ditto   in the state of Tennessee,   12 59

Ditto   ditto   Indiana Territory,   261 11

    338 13

True net amount of duty, &c. $14,979,880 49

TABLE No. I.—CONTINUED.

STATES AND TERRITORIES.	From the 1st of January to the 31st of December, 1806.				
	Gross amount of Duties on merchandize, mediterranean fund, tonnage, light money, &c.	Payments for		Expenses of prosecutions and collection.	Net Revenue.
		Drawbacks on merchandize.	Drawbacks on domestic spirits sugar, bounties and allowances.		
New-Hampshire,	224,615 89	86,345 51	9,134 31	11,753 94	117,382 13
Vermont,	2,599 8	-	142 75	1,457 6	909 27
Massachusetts,	6,295,470 61	2,479,025 63	151,854 43	140,263 63	3,524,326 92
Rhode-Island,	682,326 58	289,365 29	5,033 58	26,246 19	361,681 52
Connecticut,	484,579 98	114,715 48	17,489 26	27,257 64	325,117 60
New-York,	7,392,103 8	2,406,462 99	6,400 82	103,456 25	4,875,783 2
New-Jersey,	17,029 51	5,581 60	217 25	3,374 59	7,856 7
Pennsylvania,	5,136,050 90	2,052,551 31	3,203 21	62,892 93	3,017,403 45
Delaware,	36,000 54	88,680 12	158	13,571 36	-
Maryland,	2,935,560 33	1,442,461 35	3,300 70	43,200 55	1,446,597 73
District of Columbia,	161,969 88	17,023 64	610 90	7,256 15	137,079 19
Virginia,	788,309 50	109,876 14	384 35	58,032 25	620,016 76
North-Carolina,	230,385 45	2,011 56	1,232 77	25,085 89	202,055 23
South-Carolina,	1,365,665 18	449,380	125	44,766 92	871,393 26
Georgia,	190,156 54	-	-	6,821 37	183,335 17

TABLE No. I.—CONTINUED.

From the 1st of January to the 31st of December, 1806.

STATES AND TERRITORIES.	Gross amount of Duties on merchandize, mediterranean fund, tonnage, light money, &c.	Payments for			Net Revenue.
		Drawbacks on merchandize.	Drawbacks on domestic spirits, sugar, bounties and allowances.	Expenses of prosecutions and collection.	
Kentucky,	-	-	-	-	-
Tennessee,	-	-	-	-	-
Ohio,	1,743 3	-	-	859 94	883 9
Michigan Territory,	30,650 75	-	-	3,217 10	27,433 65
Indiana do.	-	-	-	250	-
Mississippi do.	1,805 72	-	-	653 61	1,152 11
Orleans do.	561,964 86	166,069 27	283 75	34,131 41	361,480 43
Total,	26,538,987 41	9,709,549 8	199,571 8	614,548 78	16,081,976 60

The net amount of revenue, exhibited in the above statement, is   16,081,976 60

From which, deduct excess of expenditure beyond the duty in the state of Delaware, £6,408 94

Ditto   ditto   Indiana Territory,   250

                    66,658 94

True net amount of duty, &c.   -   -   - $16,015,317 66

TABLE No. I.—CONTINUED.

From the 1st of January to the 31st of December, 1807.

STATES AND TERRITORIES.	Gross amount of Duties on merchandize, mediterranean fund, tonnage, light money, &c.	Drawbacks on merchandize.	Payments for		Net Revenue.
			Bounties and allowances.	Expenses of prosecutions and collection.	
New-Hampshire,	179,465 36	60,967 65	8,324 99	10,491 27	99,681 45
Vermont,	2,197 71	-	184 50	1,517 50	495 71
Massachusetts,	6,453,638 86	2,580,623 40	149,904 54	146,436 77	3,576,674 15
Rhode-Island,	444,129 26	292,736 65	5,371 27	22,270 96	123,750 38
Connecticut,	470,190 99	114,896 6	15,522 37	25,338 72	314,433 84
New-York,	7,711,466 32	2,669,334 85	3,881 59	111,536 46	4,926,713 42
New-Jersey,	20,289 86	2,408 16	-	3,265 16	14,616 54
Pennsylvania,	5,241,324 65	2,012,542 80	1,498 67	64,550 2	3,162,733 16
Delaware,	156,837 24	56,530 23	35 50	14,123 81	86,147 70
Maryland,	3,033,026 63	1,337,128 65	2,124 25	59,873 89	1,633,899 84
District of Columbia,	148,723 83	16,827 96	410 60	7,603 54	123,881 73
Virginia,	641,314 58	104,409 94	329 10	29,990 3	506,585 51
North-Carolina,	218,964 88	5,921 78	938	15,712 13	196,392 97
South-Carolina,	1,378,185 78	594,386	19 52	48,252 42	735,527 84

366

TABLE No. I.—CONTINUED.

From the 1st of January to the 31st of December, 1807.

STATES AND TERRITORIES.	Gross amount of Duties on merchandize, mediterranean fund, tonnage, light money, &c.	Payments for			Net Revenue.
		Drawbacks on merchandize.	Bounties and allowances.	Expenses of prosecutions and collection.	
Georgia,	528,230 60	16,542 46	33 30	22,164 79	489,490 5
Ohio,	516 40	-	-	929 87	-
Michigan Territory,	25,116 21	-	-	3,565 55	21,550 66
Indiana do.	-	-	-	132 21	-
Mississippi do.	1,057 6	-	-	473 10	583 96
Orleans do.	668,550 97	130,302 56	90	57,882 57	480,275 84
Total,	27,323,227 19	9,995,559 15	188,668 20	646,110 77	16,493,434 75

The net amount of revenue, exhibited in the above statement, is - 16,493,434 75

From which, deduct excess of expenditure beyond the duty in the state
of Ohio, - - - 413 47

Ditto ditto Indiana Territory, - - 132 21

545 62

True net amount of duty, &c. - - $16,492,889 7

TABLE No. I.—CONTINUED.

From the 1st of January to the 31st of December, 1808.

STATES AND TERRITORIES.	Gross amount of Duties on merchandize, mediterranean fund, tonnage, light money, &c.	Payments for		Expenses of prosecutions and collections.	Net Revenue.
		Drawbacks on merchandize.	Bounties and allowances.		
New-Hampshire,	62,234 55	23,289 95	7,025 58	12,270 82	19,648 20
Vermont,	1,082 51	-	-	4,805 16	-
Massachusetts,	2,335,281 51	895,243 17	129,298 11	125,818 28	1,184,921 95
Rhode-Island,	333,598 79	37,323 35	5,098 50	20,745 13	270,431 81
Connecticut,	259,196 5	24,314 11	11,495 7	26,262 87	197,124
New-York,	3,651,179 63	799,796 33	2,948 19	83,892 57	2,764,542 54
New-Jersey,	12,807 32	5,587 28	-	5,286 10	1,933 94
Pennsylvania,	2,621,267 73	928,567 49	1,095 50	44,535 34	1,647,068 90
Delaware,	54,484 40	15,344 99	226 55	25,121 78	13,791 58
Maryland,	1,081,584 38	449,852 57	2,291 80	41,294 87	588,145 14
District of Columbia,	27,151 15	1,076 75	128 10	5,639 53	20,306 77
Virginia,	141,675 15	6,259 35	79	25,004 15	110,332 65
North-Carolina,	51,894 5	2,390 22	291 15	32,294 19	16,918 49
South-Carolina,	461,991 43	171,228 7	-	65,325 17	225,438 19

TABLE No. I.—CONTINUED.

STATES AND TERRITORIES.	Gross amount of Duties on merchandize, mediterranean fund, tonnage, light money, &c.	From the 1st of January to the 31st of December, 1808. Payments for			Net Revenue.
		Drawbacks on merchandize.	Bounties and allowances.	Expenses of prosecutions and collection.	
Georgia, - - -	60,117 63	7,692 95	-	17,339 30	35,085 38
Ohio, - - -	97 54	-	-	670 10	-
Michigan Territory, -	12,417 19	-	-	3,606 20	8,810 99
Indiana do. -	-	-	-	-	-
Mississippi do. -	140 67	-	-	575 29	-
Orleans do. -	180,492 44	75,297 14	175	27,805 86	77,214 44
Total,	11,348,694 12	3,443,263 72	160,152 55	568,292 71	7,181,714 97

The net amount of revenue, exhibited in the above statement, is - - - 7,181,714 97

From which, deduct excess of expenditure beyond the duty in the
state of Vermont, - - - 3,722 65
Ditto   ditto   in the state of Ohio. - - 572 56
Ditto   ditto   Mississippi Territory, - - 434 62

    4,729 83

True net amount of duty, &c. - - - $7,176,985 14

TABLE No. I.—CONTINUED.

STATES AND TERRITORIES.	From the 1st of January to the 31st of December, 1809.				
	Gross amount of Duties on merchandize, mediterranean fund, tonnage, light money, &c.	Payments for			Net Revenue.
		Drawbacks on merchandize.	Bounties and allowances.	Expenses of prosecutions and collection.	
New-Hampshire,	57,832	7,800 30	2,453 89	8,431 2	39,146 79
Vermont,	12,939 81	-	-	2,970 99	9,968 82
Massachusetts,	2,717,391 72	1,158,105 26	41,450 55	133,086 63	1,384,749 28
Rhode-Island,	274,376 12	211,808 27	1,081 45	25,503 67	35,982 73
Connecticut,	170,372 49	16,729 72	3,198 42	21,191 84	129,252 51
New-York,	3,860,927 29	791,116 59	749 37	87,132 73	2,981,928 60
New-Jersey,	29,592 2	5,639 84	-	4,350 99	19,551 19
Pennsylvania,	2,340,150 47	897,451 87	131	37,443 77	1,405,123 63
Delaware,	107,085 51	24,304 37	-	18,256 11	64,525 3
Maryland,	1,046,758 92	848,237 80	525 10	42,714 36	155,281 66
District of Columbia,	71,551 52	6,148 22	-	5,259 87	60,143 43
Virginia,	320,264 1	38,431 39	-	24,113 98	257,718 64
North-Carolina,	87,297 57	-	-	22,069 82	65,227 75
South-Carolina,	551,342 33	137,600 20	-	36,048 86	377,693 27
Georgia,	17,094 58	312 43	-	10,070 73	6,711 42

TABLE No. I.—CONTINUED.

From the 1st of January to the 31st of December, 1809.

STATES AND TERRITORIES.	Gross amount of Duties on merchandize, mediterranean fund, tonnage, light money, &c.	Payments for			Net Revenue.
		Drawbacks on merchandize.	Bounties and allowances.	Expenses of prosecutions and collection.	
Kentucky,	14,400 59	-	-	3,215 1	11,185 58
Ohio,	179 83	-	-	540 66	-
Michigan Territory,	1,086 87	-	-	483 84	603 3
Mississippi do.	-	-	-	-	-
Orleans do.	162,933 23	7,668 95	-	21,020 45	134,243 83
Total,	11,843,576 88	4,151,405 21	49,589 78	503,905 33	7,139,037 39

The net amount of revenue, exhibited in the above statement, is - 7,139,037 39

From which, deduct excess of expenditure beyond the duty in the state of Ohio, - 360 83

True net amount of duty, &c. - - - $7,138,676 56

TABLE No. I.—CONTINUED.

From the 1st of January to the 31st of December, 1810.

STATES AND TERRITORIES.	Gross amount of Duties on merchandize, mediterranean fund, tonnage, light money, &c.	Payments for		Expenses of prosecutions and collection.	Net Revenue.
		Drawbacks on merchandize.	Bounties and allowances.		
New-Hampshire,	63,017 57	2,484 49	15 50	7,107 58	53,410
Vermont,	12,047 9	-	-	2,881 34	9,165 75
Massachusetts,	4,039,809 11	1,151,868 34	2,599 94	111,114 49	2,774,226 34
Rhode-Island,	557,440 75	101,664 82	-	20,289 51	435,486 42
Connecticut,	193,438 15	8,312 50	996	17,003 89	167,125 76
New-York,	5,341,670 41	842,539 55	-	80,070 40	4,419,060 46
New-Jersey,	16,509 85	8,496 62	-	2,522 73	5,490 50
Pennsylvania,	3,357,847 30	879,527 36	132 85	39,168 22	2,439,018 87
Delaware,	40,355 29	26,900 12	-	9,962 20	1,492 97
Maryland,	1,415,854 65	450,616 85	24	37,191 37	928,022 43
District of Columbia,	62,007 98	6,017 25	-	5,228 73	50,762
Virginia,	530,792 1	46,543 52	-	22,731 91	461,516 58
North-Carolina,	81,425 39	4,185 55	-	18,993 71	58,246 13
South-Carolina,	730,473 22	138,854 92	-	24,597 13	567,021 17
Georgia,	161,577 93	493 20	-	26,173 5	134,911 68

TABLE No. I.—continued.

From the 1st of January to the 31st of December, 1810.

STATES AND TERRITORIES.	Gross amount of Duties on merchandize, mediterranean fund, tonnage, light money, &c.	Payments for Drawbacks on merchandize.	Payments for Bounties and allowances.	Payments for Expenses of prosecutions and collection.	Net Revenue.
Kentucky, - - -	- -	47 95	146 50	900 56	- -
Ohio, - - -	672 74	- -	- -	502 16	170 58
Michigan Territory, -	10,147 99	- -	- -	2,920 13	7,227 86
Mississippi do. -	1,958 73	- -	- -	515 8	1,443 65
Orleans do. -	281,493 24	19,310 13	- -	17,993 97	224,189 14
Total,	16,898,539 40	3,689,863 17	3,914 79	447,868 16	12,757,988 29
	Deduct 62 5	Being for duties refunded in the state of Kentucky			62 5
	16,898,477 35				12,757,926 24

Deduct excess of expenditure beyond the duty in the state of Kentucky, -   1,095 1

True net amount of duty, &c. - - $12,756,831 23

TREASURY DEPARTMENT,

Register's Office, *February 27th,* 1812.

JOSEPH NOURSE, *Register.*

TABLE No. II.

Statement exhibiting the amount of duties collected on wines, spirits, &c. from 1793 to 1810.

	1793.	1794.	1795.	1796.	1797.	1798.	1799.	1800.	1801.
	Dolls.	Dolls.	Dolls.	Dolls.	Dolls.	Dolls.	Dolls.	Dolls.	Dolls.
On Wines, -	469,835	762,657	887,398	886,063	775,322	561,812	651,212	802,378	945,532
Spirits, for. & dom*	1,026,641	1,618,513	1,492,753	1,761,722	1,003,703	1,472,504	2,303,390	1,548,536	2,343,205
Molasses, -	148,230	104,735	127,759	145,747	145,858	177,262	167,911	194,248	299,768
Teas, - -	314,485	333,975	302,289	330,394	307,965	329,620	673,052	864,795	756,627
Coffee, - -	1,396,652	1,680,163	2,694,902	2,829,062	2,820,073	2,556,561	1,932,504	2,120,368	2,983,447
Sugar, - -	768,906	816,359	974,806	913,705	1,641,025	1,892,494	2,532,883	2,818,258	3,758,963
Salt, -	247,622	361,128	345,770	443,550	391,134	543,310	488,617	687,387	686,454
DRAWBACKS.									
On Wines, -	12,526	44,565	79,163	299,566	251,187	219,401	236,712	281,131	478,730
Spirits, foreign,	31,380	38,117	59,183	156,919	121,970	117,837	259,132	114,016	138,236
Ditto domestic, *	-	-	-	271	115	2	175	172	54
Molasses, -	228	140	156	1,122	1,631	1,194	1,277	446	15,927
Teas, - -	13,816	28,929	7,997	17,719	18,676	13,007	20,262	169,200	299,963
Coffee, - -	169,928	1,141,524	1,946,226	3,102,982	2,299,646	2,321,589	1,464,170	1,773,422	2,439,944
Sugar, - -	16,432	243,553	418,956	523,354	827,657	1,169,163	1,596,497	1,576,062	2,413,969
Salt, - -	21	574	177	3,853	12,436	32,242	20,805	5,190	13,864

* From foreign materials.

TABLE No. II.—CONTINUED.

	1802.	1803.	1804.	1805.	1806.	1807.	1808.	1809.	1810.
	Dolls.	Dolls.	Dolls.	Dolls.	Dolls.	Dolls.	Dolls.	Dolls.	Dolls.
On Wines,	856,891	749,949	1,470,952	1,727,528	1,300,699	1,707,504	461,027	584,369	487,074
Spirits, for.&dom.*	2,416,961	2,731,606	3,409,538	2,724,475	3,443,793	3,136,195	1,367,479	1,418,994	1,314,065
Molasses,	353,431	303,584	328,412	465,645	430,305	415,358	325,899	274,982	385,999
Teas,	741,970	930,251	676,684	1,028,750	1,401,854	1,626,641	975,887	332,971	1,561,814
Coffee,	1,682,439	948,672	3,001,066	2,345,853	3,265,335	2,865,818	1,606,385	1,936,508	1,563,159
Sugar,	2,028,914	2,217,223	3,290,054	5,403,172	5,227,788	5,643,565	2,291,870	1,715,162	1,823,167
Salt,	792,838	721,355	686,799	765,804	862,694	731,508	6,017	43	-

DRAWBACKS.

	1802.	1803.	1804.	1805.	1806.	1807.	1808.	1809.	1810.
On Wines,	154,262	132,659	494,885	874,209	740,996	838,692	54,358	155,315	76,823
Spirits, foreign,	122,652	123,834	333,926	457,086	341,574	452,393	15,391	70,984	33,323
Ditto domestic,*									
Molasses,	1,706	629	1,579	1,200	1,422	1,225	-	1,941	969
Teas,	337,118	406,369	184,845	346,976	426,801	402,673	2,632	363,454	235,613
Coffee,	1,284,376	499,251	2,601,646	1,992,982	2,259,761	2,150,843	26,661	1,480,297	1,206,337
Sugar,	969,379	860,663	1,839,803	3,480,952	3,227,902	3,757,092	43,354	1,351,815	1,014,979
Salt,	6,607	4,561	5,992	2,413	16,376	19,689	113	-	-

* From foreign materials.

TABLE No. III.

Amount of duties accruing on the following articles, imported in 1806, with the rates of duties on each.

	QUANTITIES.			
	Excess of importation over exportation	Excess of export. o- ver im- port.	Rate of duty. Cts.	Excess of duties over drawback.
Beer, ale, & porter, glls.	181,815	- -	8	14,545 20
Cocoa, - - lbs.	1,418,232	- -	2	28,364 64
Chocolate, - -	2,117	- -	3	63 51
Sugar candy, - -	1,573	- -	$11\frac{1}{2}$	180 89
loaf, - -	3,180	- -	9	286 20
other refined and lump,	976	- -	$6\frac{1}{2}$	63 44
Almonds, - - -	282,517	- -	2	5,650 34
Currants, - -	372,097	- -	2	7,441 94
Prunes and plumbs, -	66,479	- -	2	1,329 58
Figs, - -	408,449	- -	2	8,168 98
Raisins in jars and muscadel,	773,398	- -	2	15,467 96
all other, -	2,412,221	- -	$1\frac{1}{2}$	36,182 31
Candles, tallow, - -	175,820	- -	2	3,516 40
wax, - -	6,254	- -	6	375 24
Cheese, - -	262,846	- -	7	18,399 22
Soap, - - -	819,241	- -	2	16,384 82
Tallow - -	1,755,841	- -	$1\frac{1}{2}$	26,337 62
Mace, - - -	- -	2,620	125	- -
Nutmegs, - -	173	- -	50	86 50
Cinnamon, - - -	- -	9,149	20	- -
Cloves, - -	- -	24,318	20	- -
Pepper, - - -	1,848,617	- -	6	110,917 2
Pimento, - -	468,008	- -	4	18,720 32
Chinese cassia, - -	181,802	- -	4	7,272 8
Tobacco, manufactured other } than snuff and segars, }	6,638	- -	6	398 28
Snuff, - -	16,562	- -	10	1,656 20
Indigo, - -	264,163	- -	25	66,040 75
Cotton, - - -	785,378	- -	3	23,561 34
Powder, hair, - -	5,514	- -	4	220 56
gun, - -	204,822	- -	4	8,192 88
Starch, - -	14,565	- -	3	436 95
Glue, - - -	105,612	- -	4	4,224 48
Pewter plates and dishes,	78,200	- -	4	3,128
Anchors and sheet iron, -	582,236	- -	$1\frac{1}{2}$	8,733 54
Slit and hoop do. -	271,063	- -	1	2,710 63

	QUANTITIES.			
	Excess of importation over exportation.	Excess of exportation over importation.	Rate of duty. Cents.	Excess of duties over drawback.
Nails, - - lbs.	3,059,529	- -	2	61,190 58
Spikes, - -	407,936	- -	1	4,079 36
Quicksilver, -	51,606	- -	6	3,096 36
Ochre, yellow, in oil, -	22,079	- -	1½	331 19
dry yellow, -	119,854	- -	1	1,198 54
Spanish brown, - -	619,710	- -	1	6,197 10
White and red lead, -	2,648,981	- -	2	52,979 62
Lead & manufactures of lead,	3,513,351	- -	1	35,133 51
Seines, - -	10,651	- -	4	426 4
Cordage, tarred, -	206,096	- -	2	4,121 92
untarred, -	47,391	- -	2½	1,184 77
Cables, - -	30,542	- -	2	610 84
Steel, - - cwt.	12,228	- -	100	12,228
Hemp, - -	116,101	- -	100	116,101
Twine and pack thread, -	3,361	- -	400	13,444
Glauber salts, -	103	- -	200	206
Coal, - bushels,	311,146	- -	5	15,557 30
Fish, dried, - quintals,	219,349	- -	50	109,674 50
pickled salmon, bbls.	6,862	- -	100	6,862
mackarel, -	14,756	- -	60	8,853 60
other, -	16,271	- -	40	6,508 40
Glass, black qt. bottles, gro.	20,273	- -	60	12,163 80
window, not above 8 by 10, 100 sqr. ft.	22,546	- -	160	36,073 60
do. 10 by 12, -	3,985	- -	175	6,973 75
do. above 10 by 12,	4,243	- -	225	9,546 75
Segars, - - M.	22,969	- -	200	45,938
Foreign lime, - casks,	339	- -	50	169 50
Boots, - pairs,	3,817	- -	75	2,862 75
Shoes, silk, - -	6,913	- -	25	1,728 25
kid, Morocco, &c.	45,758	- -	15	6,863 70
all other, -	5,374	- -	10	537 40
Cards, wool & cotton, dozs.	4	- -	50	2
playing, - packs,	11,672	- -	25	2,906 75

Total excess of duties over drawback, - - -   1,024,809 70

Excess of drawback over duties on Mace, - 3,275

—   —   —   —   Cinnamon, - 1,829 80

—   —   —   —   Cloves, - - 4,863 60

                9,968 40

Total, - - - - - - - - 1,014,841 30

Treasury Department, Register's Office, 4th November, 1807.

JOSEPH NOURSE, Register.

TABLE No. IV.

A general view of the assessment and apportionment of the Direct Tax, laid by the acts of Congress, of July 9th and July 14th, 1798.

STATES.	Land.		Dwelling-Houses.		Slaves.
	No. of Acres.	Valuation.	Number.	Valuation.	Number.
New-Hampshire,	3,749,061	19,028,108 3	11,142	4,146,938 90	-
Massachusetts,	7,831,028	59,445,642 64	48,984	24,546,826 46	-
Rhode-Island,	565,844	8,082,355 21	7,034	2,984,002 87	143
Connecticut,	2,649,149	40,163,955 34	23,565	8,149,479 28	654
Vermont,	4,918,722	15,165,484 2	5,437	1,558,389 36	-
New-York,	16,414,510	74,885,075 69	33,416	25,495,631 39	9,994
New-Jersey,	2,788,282	27,287,981 89	19,624	9,149,918 84	2,433
Pennsylvania,	11,959,865	72,824,852 60	51,772	29,321,048 33	1,100
Delaware,	1,074,105	4,053,248 42	5,094	2,180,165 83	3,125
Maryland,	5,444,272	21,634,004 57	16,932	10,738,286 63	48,254
Virginia,	40,456,644	59,976,860 6	27,693	11,248,267 67	153,087
North-Carolina,	20,956,467	27,909,479 70	11,760	2,932,893 9	59,968
South-Carolina,	9,772,587	12,456,720 94	6,427	5,008,292 93	65,586
Georgia,	13,534,159	10,263,506 95	3,446	1,797,631 25	27,704
Kentucky,	17,674,634	20,268,325 7	3,339	1,139,765 13	15,820
Tennessee,	3,951,357	5,847,662	1,030	286,446 83	5,351
Total *Numbers,*	163,746,686	-	276,659	-	393,219
Total *Valuation,*	-	479,293,263 13	-	140,683,984 79	-

TABLE No. IV.—CONTINUED.

STATES.	Amount of Tax on			Total.
	Lands.	Dwelling Houses.	Slaves.	
New-Hampshire,	66,283 76	11,684 38	-	77,968 14
Massachusetts,	169,958 77	82,738 47	-	252,697 24
Rhode-Island,	28,906 15	8,415 66	71 50	37,393 31
Connecticut,	108,307 59	21,647 12	327	130,281 71
Vermont,	43,209 57	3,722 54	-	46,932 11
New-York,	77,909 31	99,335 12	4,997	182,241 43
New-Jersey,	70,417 24	26,592 36	1,216 50	98,226 10
Pennsylvania,	138,269 23	99,111 75	550	237,930 98
Delaware,	22,424 70	6,462 55	1,562 50	30,449 75
Maryland,	88,897 53	40,820 79	24,127	153,845 32
Virginia,	234,018 94	34,826 40	76,543 50	345,388 84
North-Carolina,	155,385 96	7,296 67	29,984	192,666 63
South-Carolina,	62,345 46	19,306 11	32,793	114,444 57
Georgia,	18,917 4	6,039 90	13,852	38,808 94
Kentucky,	96,980 77	3,275 68	7,910	38,166 45
Tennessee,	15,481 19	713 46	2,675 50	18,870 15
Total Tax,	1,327,713 21	471,988 96	196,609 50	1,996,311 67

TABLE No. V.

Table of the Post-Office Establishment, *from 1789, to October 1, 1813.*

Years	No. of post offices	Amount of postages	Compensation to post-masters	Incidental expenses	Transportation of the Mail	Net Revenue	Ext. in miles of Post-roads
1789	75	-	-	-	-	-	-
1790	75	37,934 92	8,197 80	1,861 19	22,081 8	5,794 95	1,875
1791	89	46,294 43	10,312 28	3,091 79	23,293 10	9,637 29	1,905
1792	195	67,443 86	16,517 98	5,281 50	32,731 32	12,913 6	5,642
1793	209	104,746 67	21,645 96	5,659 73	44,733 88	32,707 10	5,642
1794	450	128,947 19	27,155 65	9,812 48	53,004 88	38,974 28	11,984
1795	453	160,629 97	30,272 1	12,261 96	75,359 22	42,726 78	13,207
1796	468	195,066 88	35,729 59	14,353 21	81,488 66	63,495 42	13,207
1797	554	213,998 50	47,109 39	13,622 68	89,382 27	63,884 16	13,207
1798	639	232,977 45	56,035 6	16,035	107,014 45	63,892 94	16,180
1799	677	264,846 17	63,957 75	14,605 22	109,474 76	76,808 44	16,180
1800	903	280,804 31	69,242 52	16,106 76	128,644 32	66,810 81	16,180
1801	1,025	320,442 40	79,337 74	23,362 81	152,450 1	65,291 84	20,817
1802	1,114	327,044 58	85,586 94	21,657 78	174,670 61	45,129 25	22,309
1803	1,258	351,822 66	93,169 51	24,084 8	205,110 33	29,458 74	25,315
1804	1,405	389,449 64	107,715 71	24,231 29	205,555 24	51,947 40	25,315
1805	1,558	421,373 23	111,551 97	26,179 88	239,635 52	44,005 92	29,556
1806	1,710	446,105 79	119,784 39	23,416 11	269,033 12	33,872 17	31,076
1807	1,848	478,762 71	129,041 16	32,092 64	292,751 29	24,877 62	33,431
1808	1,944	460,564 18	128,653 12	28,676 18	305,499 49	-	33,755
1809	2,012	506,633 85	141,579 9	23,516 22	332,916 77	8,621 78	34,035
1810	2,300	551,683 97	149,438 16	18,564 57	327,966 23	55,715 2	34,035
1811	2,403	587,246 73	159,243 72	20,688 93	319,165 57	88,148 51	37,035
1812	2,610	649,207 71	177,422 12	22,116 71	340,626 22	109,042 66	-
to Oct. 1, 1813	2,977	703,154 52	199,170 54	41,246 13	438,556 13	24,178 87	-

TABLE No. VI.

An account of the Post-Office Establishment, in each State and Territory, in the year 1802.

STATES AND TERRITORIES.	Postage on Letters.	Postage on Newspapers.	Amount.	Free Letters	Commission on Letters.	Commission on Newspapers.	Amt. of commission to Post-masters.
New-Hampshire,	4,495 64	468 44	4,964 8	75 86	1,572 80	334 5	1,882 71
Vermont,	2,316 97	356 96	2,673 93	49 57	1,039 30	178 37	1,267 24
Massachusetts,	30,712 41	1,659 48	32,371 89	203 78	6,454 81	830 36	7,487 95
District of Maine,	7,455 66	778 18	8,233 84	116 46	2,560 87	388 83	3,067 16
Rhode-Island,	5,145 13	391 88	5,537 1	82 20	1,570 40	195 89	1,848 49
Connecticut,	10,914 60	1,334 55	12,249 15	165 46	3,956 66	667 32	4,789 44
New-York,	52,724 75	2,567 50	55,292 25	200 15	8,827 59	1,282 71	10,310 45
New-Jersey,	7,263 7	1,164 22	8,427 29	88 90	2,495 81	582 2	3,166 73
Pennsylvania,	53,478 46	1,871 76	55,350 22	119 8	8,297 31	935 49	9,351 88
Ohio,	2,495 85	184 78	2,680 63	30 94	775 9	92 37	898 40
Indiana Territory,	370 58	43 7	413 65	3 78	111 10	21 54	136 42
Delaware,	3,468 15	541 72	4,009 87	47 14	1,308 86	270 80	1,626 80
Maryland,	29,428 52	2,572 42	32,000 94	85 82	5,331 85	1,280	6,703 67
District of Columbia,	15,498 56	540 75	16,039 31	683 32	4,205 65	270 34	5,159 31
Virginia,	36,735 87	5,125 6	41,860 93	398 1	9,849 8	2,561 86	12,808 95
Kenucky,	3,570 9	457 34	4,027 43	82 27	1,304 27	228 5	1,615 9
North-Carolina,	7,799 52	1,311 10	9,110 62	195 74	2,652 73	655 23	3,503 70
Tennessee,	1,787 22	137 73	1,924 95	72 33	560 1	68 73	701 7
South-Carolina,	17,102 98	1,160 46	18,263 44	69 87	3,769 34	580 25	4,419 46
Georgia,	10,382 87	996 11	11,378 98	46 10	2,711 60	498 3	3,255 73
Mississippi Territory,	1,054 77	74 66	1,129 43	4 76	285 9	37 35	327 20
Total,	304,201 67	23,738 17	327,939 84	2,821 54	69,640 22	11,866 9	84,327 85

TABLE No. VI.—CONTINUED.

STATES AND TERRITORIES.	Ship Letters.	Way-Letters.	Contingent expenses.	Balance due General-Post Office.	Amt. paid for transportation of the Mails.	Cr.	Dr.
New-Hampshire,	24 52	4 5	223 9	2,829 71	3,338 56	-	558 85
Vermont,	912	7 55	123 92	1,275 22	3,113 95	-	1,838 73
Massachusetts,	85 88	35 4	693 56	23,243 2	10,475 18	12,767 84	-
District of Maine,	191 95	10 95	365 70	4,704 15	5,125 32	-	421 17
Rhode-Island,	96 92	2 3	119 14	3,375 37	1,615 32	1,760 5	-
Connecticut,	2,209 12	39 1	381 90	6,941 88	6,197 17	744 71	-
New-York,	1 16	31 97	1,511 45	41,229 26	15,110 86	26,118 40	-
New-Jersey,	1,208 58	4 16	137 45	5,117 79	4,720 44	397 35	-
Pennsylvania,	-	6 69	1,810 12	42,972 95	15,162 84	27,810 11	-
Ohio,	-	1 26	139 62	1,641 35	4,612 56	-	2,971 21
Indiana Territory,	107 38	20	20	257 3	1,500	-	1,242 97
Delaware,	507 98	1 72	165 97	2,108	1,280 85	827 15	-
Maryland,	28 44	10 87	722 40	24,056 2	11,152 53	12,903 49	-
District of Columbia,	211 26	23	431 46	10,419 87	1,323 52	9,096 35	-
Virginia,	-	21 13	1,172 37	27,647 22	31,065 5	-	3,417 83
Kentucky,	50 24	68	219 33	2,192 33	5,718 95	-	3,526 62
North-Carolina,	679 34	3 6	406 40	5,147 22	17,269 64	-	12,122 42
Tennessee,	197 60	40	191 98	1,031 50	3,989 49	-	2,957 99
South-Carolina,	-	3 26	679 2	12,482 36	16,473 46	-	3,991 10
Georgia,	-	13 14	450 68	7,461 83	7,100 68	361 15	-
Mississippi Territory,	-	19	43 96	758 8	2,422 40	-	1,664 32
Total,	6,512 72	197 59	10,009 52	226,892 16	168,818 77	92,786 60	34,713 21

TABLE No. VII.

A Statement of the Annual Revenue of the United States, from the commencement of the Federal Government, until the 30th of September, 1812, comprising the net amount derived from the Customs, Internal Taxes, Direct Taxes, Sale of Lands, and all other sources ; also, an account within the same period of the Annual Expenditures, on account of the Army, Indian Department, the Navy, Foreign Intercourse, Barbary Powers, Civil List, Miscellaneous Civil, formed in pursuance of a resolution of the House of Representatives of the United States, of the 24th December, 1812.

RECEIPTS.

YEARS. From 4th March, 1789, to 31st Dec.	Customs.	Internal revenue.	Direct tax.	Postage.	Public lands.	Miscellaneous	Aggregate.
1791 -	4,399,472 99	-	-	-	-	19,440 10	4,418,913 9
1792 -	3,443,070 65	208,942 81	-	-	-	9,918 65	3,661,932 31
1793 -	4,255,306 56	337,705 70	-	-	-	10,390 37	4,614,423 14
1794 -	4,801,065 28	274,089 62	-	11,020 51	-	23,799 48	5,128,432 87
1795 -	5,588,461 26	337,755 36	-	29,478 49	-	5,917 97	5,954,534 59
1796 -	6,567,987 94	475,289 60	-	22,400	-	16,506 14	7,137,529 65
1797 -	7,549,649 65	575,491 45	-	72,909 84	4,836 13	30,379 29	8,303,560 99
1798 -	7,106,061 93	644,357 95	-	64,500	83,540 60	18,692 81	7,820,575 80
1799 -	6,610,449 31	779,136 44	-	39,500	11,963 11	45,187 56	7,475,773 31
1800 -	9,080,932 73	809,396 55	734,223 97	78,000	443 75	74,712 10	10,777,709 10
1801 -	10,750,778 93	1,048,033 43	534,343 38	79,500	167,726	266,149 15	12,846,530 95

TABLE No. VII.—CONTINUED.

YEARS.	Customs.	Internal revenue.	Direct tax.	Postage.	Public lands.	Miscellaneous.	Aggregate.
1802 -	12,438,235 74	621,898 89	206,565 44	35,000	188,628 2	177,905 86	13,668,233 95
1803 -	10,479,417 61	215,179 69	71,879 20	16,427 26	165,675 69	115,518 18	11,064,097 63
1804 -	11,098,565 33	50,941 29	50,198 44	26,500	487,526 79	112,575 53	11,826,307 38
1805 -	12,936,487 4	21,747 15	21,882 91	21,342 50	540,193 80	19,039 80	13,560,693 20
1806 -	14,667,698 17	20,101 45	55,763 86	41,117 67	765,245 73	10,004 19	15,559,931 7
1807 -	15,845,521 61	13,051 40	34,732 56	3,614 73	466,163 27	34,935 69	16,398,019 26
1808 -	16,363,550 58	8,210 73	19,159 21	-	647,939 6	21,802 35	17,060,661 93
1809 -	7,296,020 58	4,044 39	7,517 31	-	442,252 33	23,638 51	7,773,473 12
1810 -	8,583,309 31	7,430 63	12,448 68	-	696,548 82	84,476 84	9,384,214 28
1811 -	13,313,222 73	2,295 95	7,666 66	37 70	1,040,237 53	60,068 52	14,423,529 9
From 1st January to 30th September, 1812 -	6,348,865 65	4,903 6	859 22	85,000	452,362 33	35,716 30	6,927,706 56
Total,	199,524,131 78	6,460,003 54	1,757,240 84	667,348 70	16,161,283 21	1,216,775 39	215,786,783 27

TABLE No. VII.—CONTINUED.

EXPENDITURES.

MILITARY DEPARTMENT.

YEARS.	Pay and subsistence, &c. of the army.	Fortifications of ports and harbors.	Fabrication of cannon.	Purchase of salt-petre, &c.	Additional arms.	Arming & equipping militia.	Detachment of militia.	Services of militia.	Services of volunteers.	Total.
From 4th March, 1789, to 31st Dec. 1791	632,804 3									632,804 3
1792,	1,100,702 9									1,100,702 9
1793,	1,130,249 8									1,130,249 8
1794,	2,597,047 93	42,049 66								2,639,097 59
1795,	2,399,136 63	81,773 50								2,480,910 13
1796,	1,234,502 58	25,761 26								1,260,263 84
1797,	999,311 88	40,090 78								1,039,402 66
1798,	1,823,565 96	185,956 34								2,009,522 30
1799,	2,295,819 56	171,127 42								2,466,946 98
1800,	2,444,878 77	116,000								2,560,878 77
1801,	1,587,944 8	85,000								1,672,944 8
1802,	1,048,135 75	18,000	155,012 50							1,221,148 25
1803,	773,456 81		108,599 4							882,055 85
1804,	938,923 93									938,923 93
1805,	768,281 28									768,281 28
1806,	1,383,555 38									1,383,555 38
1807,	1,094,285 91	225,000					70,000			1,389,285 91
1808,	1,766,434 40	1,075,000				100,000	100,000			3,041,434 40
1809,	2,365,772 17	655,000		150,000	300,000					3,470,772 17
From 1810,	1,851,923 94	428,000				110,000				2,389,923 94
1st Jan. to 1811,	1,837,828 19	95,000				190,000				2,122,828 19
30th Sept. 1812,	6,498,014 80	250,000				100,000		406,800	210,000	7,464,814 80
Total,	38,572,575 15	3,493,758 96	263,611 54	150,000	300,000	500,000	170,000	406,800	210,000	44,066,745 65

TABLE No. VII.—CONTINUED.

YEARS.	INDIAN DEPARTMENT.		Naval department.	Foreign intercourse.	Barbary powers.	Civil list.	Miscellaneous civil.	Aggregate.
From 4th March,1789 to 31st December,	Treaties.	Trading houses.						
1791 -	27,000	-	570	1,733 33	13,000	757,134 45	285,887 56	1,718,129 37
1792 -	13,648 85	-	53 2	78,766 67	-	380,917 58	191,988 94	1,766,077 15
1793 -	27,282 83	-	-	89,500	-	358,241 8	102,075 29	1,707,348 28
1794 -	13,042 46	-	61,408 97	146,403 51	-	440,946 58	199,449	3,500,348 20
1795 -	21,475 68	2,000	410,562 3	912,685 12	-	361,633 36	161,330 13	4,350,596 45
1796 -	55,563 98	58,000	274,784 4	109,739 64	75,120	447,139 5	251,319 85	2,531,930 40
1797 -	32,396 38	30,000	382,631 89	172,504 23	497,284 31	483,233 70	196,137 79	2,833,590 96
1798 -	16,470 9	-	1,381,347 76	242,711 22	214,717 52	504,605 17	253,849 48	4,623,223 54
1799 -	20,302 19	-	2,858,081 84	199,374 11	72,000	592,905 76	270,555 84	6,480,166 72
1800 -	31 22	-	3,448,716 3	185,145 33	210,142 85	748,688 45	257,767 32	7,411,369 97
1801 -	9,000	-	2,111,424	139,851 73	155,825	549,288 31	343,336 78	4,981,669 90
1802 -	20,000	32,000	915,561 87	416,253 62	134,672 31	596,981 11	400,462 75	3,737,079 91
1803 -	-	-	1,215,230 53	1,001,968 34	108,866 43	526,583 12	268,119 97	4,002,824 24
1804 -	53,000	-	1,189,832 75	1,129,591 62	57,063 95	624,795 63	459,651 3	4,452,858 91
1805 -	41,000	100,000	1,597,500	2,655,769 62	142,259 15	585,849 79	466,574 78	6,357,234 62

TABLE No. VII.—CONTINUED.

Years.	INDIAN DEPARTMENT.		Naval department.	Foreign intercourse.	Barbary powers.	Civil list.	Miscellaneous civil.	Aggregate.
	Treaties.	Trading houses.						
1806	-	75,000	1,649,641 44	1,613,922 9	146,499 21	684,230 53	527,360 71	6,080,209 36
1807	60,825	44,000	1,722,064 47	419,845 61	157,980 73	655,524 65	535,046 52	4,984,572 89
1808	70,725	2,250	1,884,067 80	214,233 26	90,759 57	691,167 80	509,701 2	6,504,338 85
1809	169,150	43,353 84	2,427,758 80	74,918 12	91,387 92	712,465 13	424,866 16	7,414,672 14
1810	58,225	23,800	1,654,244 20	48,795 60	32,571 88	703,994 3	399,527 63	5,311,082 28
1811	57,725	4,150	1,965,566 39	181,746 15	83,158 32	644,467 27	532,963 54	5,592,604 86
From 1st Jan. to 30th Sept. 1812	55,973	15,745	2,738,612 95	275,686 41	45,501 25	635,700 81	528,255 99	11,760,292 21
Total,	822,838 68	430,298 84	29,889,660 78	10,311,145 33	2,328,810 40	12,686,493 36	7,566,228 17	108,102,221 21

Stated from the annual accounts of receipts and expenditures of the United States.

TREASURY DEPARTMENT,

REGISTER'S OFFICE, *January 10,* 1813.

JOSEPH NOURSE, *Register.*

CHAPTER X.

The increase of the tonnage of the United States has been without example, in the history of the commercial world. This has been owing to the increased quantity of bulky articles of domestic produce exported, to the increase of their population, and to the extent of their carrying trade.

The actual tonnage was not ascertained, at the Treasury Department, until the year 1793. Previous to that time, the only account of the tonnage kept at the Treasury was that, on which duties were collected, and which included the repeated voyages made by the same vessels in the course of the year.

The following is the amount of tonnage on which duties were collected from 1789 to 1792 inclusive, with its employment, in the foreign trade, coasting trade, and fisheries :—

	Foreign trade.	Coasting trade.	Fisheries.
1789	123,893	68,607	9,062
1790	346,254	103,775	28,348
1791	363,110	106,494	32,542
1792	411,438	120,957	32,062

In consequence of acts of Congress passed in 1792 and 1793, no vessel can be employed, in foreign trade, unless duly *registered* by the Collector of the district, where such vessel belongs, and the owner obtains from the Collector a certificate of such registry ; and no vessel can obtain a register, unless she was built in the United States, or has been taken and condemned as lawful prize, and is owned by an American citizen.

No vessel can be employed in the coasting trade, unless duly *enrolled* or *licensed* by the Collectors of the districts. This register, enrollment, or license, specifies the tonnage of each vessel, and an account of each vessel so registered, enrolled, or licensed, is annually transmitted by the Collectors, to the Treasury Department.

There are also other vessels employed in foreign trade, owned by citizens of the United States, but which, on account of being foreign built, or some other cause, are not entitled to a register, or to be considered as American vessels. These vessels have however papers called sea letters, and are therefore denominated *sea letter* vessels. In 1806, the tonnage of vessels having sea letters, and employed in foreign trade, was eighty-seven thousand tons.

To give an American character to a vessel, it is not necessary that any part of the crew, except the captain, should be citizens of the United States. If the captain be an American citizen, all the rest of the crew may be foreigners.

The following duties on tonnage are paid in the United States, by *permanent acts.*

American registered vessels, pay 6 cents per ton upon entry,
            Coasting vessels, - 6   do.   do.   per annum,
            Fishing vessels, - 6   do.   do.   do.
American vessels not registered (having sea letters) 50 cents per ton upon entry.
American built vessels, owned by foreigners, 30 cents per ton, and 50 cents light money.
Foreign built vessels, owned by Americans, 50 cents per ton.
Vessels entirely foreign, 50 cents per ton and 50 cents light money.

By an act passed July 1st, 1812, and which is to continue during the war, vessels belonging wholly, or in part, to the subjects of foreign powers, pay an *additional duty* of one dollar and fifty cents per ton.

With respect to merchandize imported, American registered vessels pay American rates of duties, and merchandize imported in all other vessels, whether having sea letters, or being American built, are owned by foreigners, or foreign built, are owned by Americans, or are entirely foreign, pay foreign duties.

By an act of the 27th of March, 1804, an American registered vessel loses its American character, " if owned by a person *naturalized* in the United States, and residing for more than one year in the country from which he originated, or for more than two years in any foreign country—unlesss such person be in the capacity of Consul, or other public agent."

It is understood, that the late Commercial Treaty between the United States and Great-Britain places the tonnage duties of the vessels of both nations on the same footing in their respective ports. Whether this will eventually benefit American navigation, indeed, whether it will not be injurious to it, remains yet to be decided ; and experience alone must determine. Were the British West-India ports open to American vessels, there would, perhaps, be less room to doubt on the subject. The American trade with the British West-Indies always has been, and will, probably, continue to be great ; and can now only be carried on in British vessels, navigated according to British laws. Should this policy continue, there can be little doubt, that, in this trade, American capital, to a certain extent, will be employed in navigating British vessels, and in supporting British seamen. And it is, perhaps, yet doubtful, whether in the circuitous trade between Great-Britain and her West-India Islands, by the way of the United States, British vessels will not be able to carry, on freight, between the United States and Great-Britain, cheaper than American vessels.

The amount of registered tonnage, employed in foreign trade, from 1793, to 1813, was as follows, viz.—

			Tons.	95ths.
1793	-	-	367,734	23
1794	-	-	438,862	71

			Tons.	95ths.
1795	-	-	529,470	63
1796	-	-	576,733	25
1797	-	-	597,777	43
1798	-	-	603,376	37
1799	-	-	669,197	19
1800	-	-	669,921	35
1801	-	-	718,549	60
1802	-	-	560,380	63
1803	-	-	597,157	05
1804	-	-	672,530	18
1805	-	-	749,341	22
1806	-	-	808,284	68
1807	-	-	848,306	85
1808	-	-	769,053	54
1809	-	-	910,059	23
1810	-	-	984,269	05
1811	-	-	768,852	21
1812	-	-	760,624	40
1813	-	-	674,853	44

And the following tonnage was employed in the coasting trade, from 1793 to 1812.

		Enrolled.			Licensed. Under 20 tons.	
		Tons.	95ths.		Tons.	95ths.
1793	-	114,853	10	-	7,217	53
1794	-	167,227	42	-	16,977	36
1795	-	164,795	91	-	19,601	59
1796	-	195,423	64	-	22,416	66
1797	-	214,077	5	-	23,325	66
1798	-	227,343	79	-	24,099	43
1799	-	220,904	46	-	25,736	8
1800	-	245,295	4	-	27,196	91
1801	-	246,255	34	-	28,296	91
1802	-	260,543	16	-	29,079	58

		Enrolled.			Licensed. Under 20 tons.	
		Tons.	95ths.		Tons.	95ths.
1803	-	268,676	12	-	30,384	34
1804	-	286,840	1	-	30,696	56
1805	-	301,366	38	-	31,296	73
1806	-	309,977	5	-	30,562	54
1807	-	318,189	93	-	30,838	39
1808	-	387,684	43	-	33,135	33
1809	-	371,500	56	-	33,661	75
1810	-	371,114	12	-	34,232	57
1811	-	Enrolled and licensed,	-	420,362		
1812	-	do.	do.	-	477,971	

The increase of the registered tonnage, or that employed in foreign trade, from 1793 to 1801, was three hundred and fifty thousand eight hundred and fifteen tons and thirty-seven ninety-fifths, having nearly doubled, in that short period. From 1793 to 1810, a period of seventeen years, the increase of tonnage, employed in foreign trade, was six hundred sixteen thousand five hundred and thirty-five tons and eighty-two ninety-fifths. In 1793, the tonnage employed in the coasting trade, was one hundred twenty-two thousand and seventy tons and sixty-three ninety-fifths, and in 1801, amounted to two hundred seventy-four thousand five hundred and fifty-one tons, making a difference of one hundred fifty-two thousand four hundred and eighty-one tons; and from 1793 to 1810, the increase was two hundred eighty-three thousand two hundred and seventy-six tons. We have before stated the amount of tonnage employed in the fisheries; the increase from 1793 to 1807, was about forty thousand tons. Tables No. I. and II. contain the amount of tonnage, annually employed, in *foreign* trade, and in the *coasting* trade, owned in each state, from 1793 to 1810.

The whole amount of tonnage, in the United States, in 1810, was one million four hundred twenty-four thousand seven hundred and eighty-one tons, according to Treasury statements.—Of this,

	Tons.
New-Hampshire owned	28,817

					Tons.
Massachusetts,	-	-	-	-	495,203
Rhode-Island,	-	-	-	-	36,155
Connecticut,	-	-	-	-	45,108
New-York,	-	-	-	-	276,557
New-Jersey,	-	-	-	-	43,803
Pennsylvania,	-	-	-	-	125,430
Delaware,	-	-	-	-	8,190
Maryland,	-	-	-	-	143,785
Virginia,	-	-	-	-	84,923
North-Carolina,	-	-	-	-	39,954
South-Carolina,	-	-	-	-	53,926
Georgia,	-	-	-	-	15,619
Ohio,	-	-	-	-	none
New-Orleans,	-	-	-	-	13,240

The state of Massachusetts has many hundred miles of sea-coast, with numerous inlets and harbours ; and many of her inhabitants have always been engaged in navigation. The amount of tonnage owned in that state, in 1810, was more than one third of the whole tonnage in the United States.

The amount of tonnage owned in the ports of Boston, New-York, Philadelphia, Baltimore, and Charleston, in 1810, was as follows :—

				Tons.	95ths.
Boston,	-	-	-	149,121	85
New-York,	-	-	-	268,548	1
Philadelphia,	-	-	125,258	15
Baltimore,	-	-	-	103,444	69
Charleston,	-	-	-	52,888	16

It is believed, that the shipping, belonging to the port of New-York, is equal to, if it does not exceed, that of any port, in the world, except the port of London.

The tonnage of vessels built in the United States, from 1804 to
1813, was as follows :—

				Tons.	95ths.
1804	-	-	-	103,753	91
1805	-	-	-	128,507	3
1806	-	-	-	126,093	29
1807	-	-	-	99,783	92
1808	-	-	-	31,755	34
1809	-	-	-	91,397	55
1810	-	-	-	127,575	86
1811	-	-	-	146,691	82
1812	-	-	-	84,691	42
1813	-	-	-	31,153	40

The number of vessels built and registered, during the same period,
in all the ports of the British empire (except Ireland) with the amount
of their tonnage, is contained in No. XIII. of Appendix No. II. ; the
greatest amount built in any one year was one hundred thirty-five
thousand three hundred and forty-nine.

The amount of American tonnage for 1810, as stated above, taken
from Treasury documents, is greater than the actual amount. It was
made from the abstracts, furnished by the Collectors of the several
districts, in which a deduction for vessels worn out, lost at sea, or taken and condemned in foreign countries, was not always made.

The true amount for 1810 may be stated at about one million and
a quarter. The amount of American registered tonnage, employed
in foreign trade, in 1807, and on which duties were paid (including
the repeated voyages) was one million eighty-nine thousand eight
hundred and seventy-six. The amount of tonnage of vessels which
entered inwards, at the several ports of Great-Britain, from all parts
of the world, (including their repeated voyages) was, for the same
year, one million four hundred eighty-two thousand four hundred and
twelve. This amount of British tonnage includes those vessels, which
entered inwards from Ireland, the islands of Jersey, Guernsey, and
Man, and the whale fisheries.—(See No. XV. Appendix No. II.) The
amount of *British tonnage*, which cleared outwards, from all the ports

of Ireland, to all parts of the world, in 1807, was five hundred seventy-four thousand six hundred and eighty-eight.—(See No. XXI. Appendix No. II.) Mr. Anderson, in his view of the importance of Canada, &c. states the amount of British tonnage, entered inwards, into the ports of Great-Britain, from Ireland, Jersey, Guernsey, and Man, and the whale fisheries, on an average, from 1804 to 1813, to be about seven hundred thousand. This would leave the amount of British tonnage, employed in trade with all other parts of the world, in 1807, about eight hundred thousand.—(See Anderson, Appendix Nos. XVI. and XVII.)

That the increase of American tonnage has been without example, at least in modern times, will appear, on comparing it with the increase of the tonnage of other commercial nations, and particularly Great-Britain.

In 1581, in the reign of Elizabeth, a period so much celebrated in history, the tonnage of England was only seventy-two thousand four hundred and fifty ; an amount far less, than is now owned, in either of the ports of Boston, New-York, Philadelphia, or Baltimore. In 1700, the commercial tonnage of England was estimated at two hundred seventy-three thousand six hundred and ninety three, in 1750, at six hundred nine thousand, seven hundred and ninety-eight, and in 1800, at one million two hundred sixty-nine thousand, three hundred and twenty-nine ;* having little more than doubled, in each half century, from 1700 to 1800. On the 5th of January, 1813, the British tonnage amounted to one million five hundred seventy-nine thousand, seven hundred and fifteen.—(See No. XV. Appendix No. II.) The state of New-York now owns as great, and the state of Massachusetts a much greater amount of shipping, than was owned by England, a little more than a century ago.

For many years past, the United States have owned a much greater amount of tonnage, than any other nation, except Great-Britain.

About the year 1787, the amount of tonnage, employed in the foreign trade of France, was a little more than one million ; of this France owned about three hundred thousand ; the rest was foreign tonnage. The navigation of France has decreased since that period.

* See Chalmer's Estimate, 234.

395

In 1800, the number of vessels employed in the foreign commerce of France, that entered inwards, was seven thousand five hundred and eighty-one ; their tonnage two hundred seventy-three thousand, four hundred and eighty-six—Of this ninety-eight thousand three hundred and four tons was French, and one hundred seventy-four thousand eight hundred and thirty-three foreign. The number of vessels, that cleared outwards, the same year, was eight thousand six hundred and thirty-six, their tonnage three hundred twelve thousand nine hundred and sixty-seven ; the French owned one hundred four thousand, six hundred and eighty-seven of this, and the residue was owned by foreigners.*

In 1804, the number of trading vessels, belonging to the states and nations around the Baltic, including those of Norway and Holstein, was four thousand one hundred and thirty-four, and their tonnage about four hundred ninety-three thousand, four hundred and seventeen British.† The shipping of the Baltic has not, probably, increased since that period. The American tonnage, therefore, is more than double that of all the maritime nations of the north of Europe.

The rapid increase of American tonnage, after the commencement of the present government, in a few years, almost excluded foreign tonnage from the trade of the United States. Table No. III. contains a statement of American and foreign tonnage employed in the foreign trade of the United States, for each year, from 1790 to 1799. In 1790, the proportion of foreign tonnage, to the whole amount of tonnage, employed in the foreign American trade was as 41. 4 to 100, and in 1799 was as 14. 9 to 100. In 1807, the proportion was as 7. 3 to 100. Table No. IV. presents a statement of the tonnage of vessels, entered in the United States, from 1790 to 1796, and the nations to which the same belonged. In 1790, the amount of foreign tonnage employed in the foreign trade of the United States was two hundred fifty-one thousand and fifty-eight tons, in 1796, was forty-nine thousand, nine hundred and sixty, in 1802, (a year of peace in Europe) was one hundred forty-six thousand, seven hundred and seventy-nine, and in 1807 was eighty-six thousand three

* See Macpherson's Annals of Commerce, 4th vol. p. 521.   † Oddy.

hundred and twenty-two. In the years 1790, 1796, and 1802, it was owned by foreign nations, as follows :—

	1790.	1796.	1802.
	Tons.	Tons.	Tons.
Great-Britain, -	216,914	- 19,669	- 104,262
France, - -	12,059	- 2,055	- 7,659
Spain, - - -	7,381	- 2,449	- 8,582
Portugal, - -	3,777	- 637	- 1,111
Italy, - - -	- -	- 758	- - -
United Netherlands, -	6,136	- 301	- 102
Imperial, - -	459	- - -	- - -
Hanse Towns, -	1,978	- 4,987	- 12,980
Denmark, - -	1,113	- 10,430	- 6,492
Sweden, - - -	535	- 5,560	- 1,127
Prussia, - -	394	- - -	- - -
Russia, - -	- - -	- - -	- 2,994
American built owned by Great-Britain, - }	- - -	- - -	519
British built owned by Americans, - }	- - -	- - -	951

The extensive coasting trade of the United States, as well as the fisheries, will tend to increase the American navigation, and will always be an excellent nursery for seamen, from whence the American navy in case of emergency can be supplied with hands. Fortunately for the country, the American navy, formerly considered by many a mere gangrene upon the nation, seems now to be the favourite of all parties. Its brilliant success, during the late war, and in its late excursion to the Mediterranean, has raised its own fame, as well as that of the American character, and justly entitles it to public patronage, both in peace and war. The American navy, in the summer of 1815, consisted of about seventy ships, brigs, and schooners, besides some small sloops, and gun-boats. Not having in our possession an official list, we are unable to state the exact number of vessels, or the number of guns. Among this number, however, there are, it is believed, five, carrying seventy-four guns, six, forty-four guns, one thirty-eight guns, two, thirty-six guns, two, thirty-two guns, and twenty-three from twenty-eight to sixteen guns.

TABLE No. I.

Registered Tonnage employed in Foreign Trade in each State, from 1793 to 1810.

STATES.	1793. Tons.	95.	1794. Tons.	95.	1795. Tons.	95.	1796. Tons.	95.	1797. Tons.	95.	1798. Tons.	95.
New-Hampshire,	12,521	25	12,952	25	13,463	46	15,579	46	15,970	50	16,589	48
Massachusetts,	135,599	68	143,783	61	171,748	12	186,199	59	187,447	47	178,798	41
Rhode-Island,	18,604	42	17,933		20,327	27	20,159	36	19,686	13	19,802	84
Connecticut,	18,015	85	20,511	59	23,549	91	26,045	39	19,634	25	23,549	44
New-York,	45,355	89	71,693	17	93,421	67	103,945	53	110,983	57	111,488	72
New-Jersey,	260	27	484	4	637	85	901	27	762	72	1,344	28
Pennsylvania,	60,924	57	67,895	30	83,623	92	90,568	94	83,400	72	85,476	49
Delaware,	927	45	1,064	11	1,290	37	1,574	28	2,724	24	2,357	89
Maryland,	26,792	74	38,007	77	48,007	53	46,314	82	55,964	46	63,480	92
Virginia,	23,997	72	26,130	13	31,767	28	36,278	26	40,936	41	43,657	58
North-Carolina,	10,167	49	14,438	76	12,601	19	15,515	4	19,645	61	18,603	33
South-Carolina,	12,998	15	21,369	35	25,483	75	29,994	17	31,360	57	33,753	22
Georgia,	1,568	40	2,599	43	3,548	1	3,556	84	4,260	48	4,473	42
Total,	367,734	23	438,862	71	529,470	63	576,733	25	597,777	43	603,376	37

TABLE No. I.—CONTINUED.

STATES.	1799. Tons.	95.	1800. Tons.	95.	1801. Tons.	95.	1802. Tons.	95.	1803. Tons.	95.	1804. Tons.	95.
New-Hampshire,	19,875	14	14,120	18	18,379	10	18,799	59	18,718	59	18,167	28
Massachusetts,	191,067	31	213,197	28	241,319	5	209,704	40	222,024	81	250,638	47
Vermont,	-		186	91	179	24	-		-		223	52
Rhode-Island,	18,562	39	18,841	20	23,747	29	23,603	1	23,890	66	26,123	36
Connecticut,	31,632	63	31,260	39	34,465	58	24,940	5	26,770	54	23,683	67
New-York,	120,253	6	97,791	6	106,023	18	79,152	85	89,382	17	105,610	54
New-Jersey,	1,271	34	860	15	1,046	8	1,551	9	1,708	35	1,445	88
Pennsylvania,	90,944	30	95,631	74	109,036	45	64,637	26	67,629	10	71,198	67
Delaware,	2,217	16	2,066	62	2,752	2	1,957	82	1,793	81	2,512	55
Maryland,	81,446	81	81,508	36	55,986	30	43,295	72	46,487	49	53,842	13
District of Columbia,	-		-		-		-		-		9,915	43
Virginia,	46,858	68	41,838	47	44,850	92	31,943	87	37,832	24	33,614	11
Kentucky,	-		-		-		388	83	675	52	675	52
North-Carolina,	19,214	52	20,949	47	21,812	63	21,399	71	21,063	13	18,908	82
South-Carolina,	38,567	42	43,731	70	51,192	21	31,353	75	30,993	34	41,868	75
Georgia,	286	18	7,937	52	7,759	35	7,652	33	7,742	30	8,125	54
Ohio,	-		-		-		-		444	65	509	
Orleans Territory,	-		-		-		-		-		5,466	49
Total,	669,197	19	669,921	35	718,549	60	560,380	63	597,157		672,530	18

TABLE No. I.—CONTINUED.

STATES.	1805. Tons.	95.	1806. Tons.	95.	1807. Tons.	95.	1808. Tons.	95.	1809. Tons.	95.	1810. Tons.	95.
New-Hampshire,	19,719	36	20,606	29	22,367	64	20,101	51	23,010	47	24,534	
Massachusetts,	285,689	32	306,075	87	310,309	69	266,519	91	324,690	8	352,806	82
Vermont,	301	27	301	27	301	27	301	27	476	11	494	51
Rhode-Island,	28,531	33	28,617	19	28,492	24	23,282	93	28,403	55	28,574	93
Connecticut,	29,563	31	26,026	37	27,071	11	22,297	87	21,306	46	22,671	35
New-York,	121,614	9	141,186	14	149,061	61	146,682	61	169,535	39	188,556	73
New-Jersey,	1,293	5	891	84	952	13	525	29	15,596	67	17,338	51
Pennsylvania,	77,238	52	86,728	35	93,993	16	94,658	69	106,621	90	109,628	57
Delaware,	1,715	21	1,073	29	1,105		755	49	1,461	83	1,242	88
Maryland,	62,004	93	71,819	92	79,782	49	74,699	43	88,188	55	90,045	16
District of Columbia,	8,512	81	7,797	93	8,643	87	6,556	49	7,482	41	9,416	26
Virginia,	37,674	19	34,015	29	33,503	5	29,485	28	36,699	29	45,339	78
Kentucky,	675	52										
North-Carolina,	22,576	69	22,180	70	21,394	58	16,623	24	23,161	64	26,472	47
South-Carolina,	35,107	60	40,158	61	45,222	85	41,628	11	42,675	74	43,354	77
Georgia,	8,592	77	10,909	89	12,827	18	11,305	46	10,942	83	12,405	41
Ohio,	169	73	160									
Orleans Territory,	8,361	12	9,735	33	12,778	68	13,629	56	9,805	86	11,386	45
Total,	749,341	22	808,284	68	848,306	85	769,053	54	910,059	23	984,269	5

TABLE No. II.

Enrolled Tonnage employed in the Coasting Trade in each State, from 1793 to 1810.

STATES.	1793.		1794.		1795.		1796.		1797.		1798.	
	Tons.	95.	Tons.	95.	Tons.	95.	Tons.	95.	Tons.	95.	Tons.	95.
New-Hampshire,	1,254	84	1,428	31	962	65	1,086	42	1,321	84	1,571	30
Massachusetts,	51,402	87	72,478	46	52,297	69	61,837		65,195	62	70,555	33
Rhode-Island,	4,502	20	6,195	52	6,049	5	5,761		5,700	55	5,234	49
Connecticut,	7,255	44	9,628		9,761	58	11,527	47	12,918	49	12,802	80
New-York,	13,986	81	22,470	25	34,806	40	42,454	70	46,053	63	47,365	62
New-Jersey,	4,577	13	6,069	73	7,107	15	9,115	58	11,484	87	13,279	75
Pennsylvania,	4,579	83	6,074	12	7,074	59	7,402	71	7,738		7,854	8
Delaware,	577	9	1,155	85	2,521		3,281	46	3,900	54	4,110	82
Maryland,	9,512	59	15,544	13	18,392	56	22,073	76	24,249	18	26,438	53
Virginia,	12,098	8	15,731	62	17,215	36	18,915	90	21,626	64	23,469	47
North-Carolina,	2,764	3	4,398	51	3,500	28	4,531		5,651	23	5,700	14
South-Carolina,	2,058	55	4,464	34	4,369	30	6,615	81	7,458	8	7,783	78
Georgia,	283	34	1,588	33	738	10	820	53	778	8	1,177	38
Total,	114,853	10	167,227	42	164,795	91	195,423	64	214,077		227,343	79

TABLE No. II.—CONTINUED.

STATES.	1799. Tons.	95.	1800. Tons.	95.	1801. Tons.	95.	1802. Tons.	95.	1803. Tons.	95.	1804. Tons.	95.
New-Hampshire,	1,293	44	1,698	25	1,355	75	1,069	34	1,041	16	2,069	8
Massachusetts,	64,723	52	75,080	46	67,949	8	74,747	51	73,123	26	79,096	65
Rhode-Island,	5,268	93	5,764	42	5,291	74	4,780	23	5,531	11	6,331	52
Connecticut,	11,046	54	12,488	1	13,129	59	12,783	35	13,638	51	14,890	20
New-York,	49,118	17	51,553	47	55,666	71	61,509	36	63,049	9	65,411	1
New-Jersey,	14,297	41	15,222	10	15,598	68	15,301	37	16,893	67	18,950	57
Pennsylvania,	7,230	86	7,380	61	6,798	68	8,318	54	8,997	18	9,134	78
Delaware,	4,032	32	4,140	40	4,198	32	4,438	47	4,743	50	4,995	49
Maryland,	28,179	14	30,973	61	33,183	93	33,548	12	36,198	31	36,674	62
District of Columbia,	-		-		-		-		-		3,514	26
Virginia,	22,736	23	26,224	52	27,114	73	26,594	8	26,068	37	25,833	60
North-Carolina,	5,147	6	5,823	13	6,081	53	7,200	61	8,139	71	9,073	25
South-Carolina,	7,606	32	7,114	13	8,340	58	8,288	94	8,716	58	8,410	92
Georgia,	224	27	1,831	68	1,545	62	1,962	94	2,535	39	2,072	79
Orleans Territory,	-		-		-		-		-		380	87
Total,	220,904	46	245,295		246,255	34	260,543	16	268,676	12	286,840	1

TABLE No. II.—CONTINUED.

STATES.	1805.		1806.		1807.		1808.		1809.		1810.	
	Tons.	95.	Tons.	95.	Tons.	95.	Tons.	95.	Tons.	95.	Tons.	95.
New-Hampshire,	1,639	65	1,560	16	3,602	41	3,866	56	3,066	61	2,863	87
Massachusetts,	86,413	36	89,892	16	89,982	78	127,893	79	113,325	63	107,260	72
Rhode-Island,	6,182	24	5,766	47	6,279	53	8,981	54	8,265	83	6,899	11
Connecticut,	15,555	51	15,236	26	15,884	93	21,947	27	19,477	70	19,346	83
New-York,	67,812	61	70,225	68	72,567	43	77,522	10	78,252	61	83,536	60
New-Jersey,	19,323	49	19,654	37	20,535	85	22,539	65	23,268	84	23,927	60
Pennsylvania,	10,016	19	9,252	66	10,355	29	13,455	6	13,497	49	14,255	76
Delaware,	5,228	67	5,587	72	5,878	2	6,292	56	6,371	94	6,261	74
Maryland,	38,080	87	38,879	88	40,400	18	46,916	38	47,715	69	46,247	92
District of Columbia,	3,976	12	3,968	31	4,073	58	4,772	70	5,125	32	4,783	1
Virginia,	26,464	76	28,244	45	27,360	80	29,378	62	29,052	39	31,284	35
North-Carolina,	9,086	60	9,091	26	9,602	2	11,377	44	10,640	94	10,562	56
South-Carolina,	8,779	29	8,972	29	7,773	18	8,858	71	8,043	58	9,449	54
Georgia,	2,249	77	2,915	49	3,351	38	3,178	44	3,237	78	3,107	37
Orleans Territory,	556	85	729	54	542	25	703	26	2,057	71	1,326	69
Total,	301,366	38	309,977		318,189	93	387,684	43	371,500	56	371,114	12

TABLE No. II.—CONTINUED.

Licensed Vessels, under twenty Tons, employed in the Coasting Trade in each State, from 1793 to 1810.

STATES.	1793. Tons. 95.	1794. Tons. 95.	1795. Tons. 95.	1796. Tons. 95.	1797. Tons. 95.	1798. Tons. 95.	1799. Tons. 95.	1800. Tons. 95.	1801. Tons. 95.
New-Hampshire,	35 43	45 9	123 14	177 15	87 56	58 22	82 59	102 16	152 61
Massachusetts,	877 31	2,902 79	3,115 53	3,253 56	3,172 51	3,374 6	3,481 44	3,590 45	3,688 57
Rhode-Island,	499 70	580 18	617 64	638 45	652 16	679 12	638 87	661 8?	552 58
Connecticut,	383 16	988 92	1,429 20	1,348 82	1,373 66	1,297 14	1,213 24	1,365 4	1,319 65
New-York,	412 25	843 55	1,043 44	1,537 47	1,839 55	1,913 43	2,086 2	2,240 85	2,487 34
New-Jersey,	499 69	790 72	1,203 94	1,507 64	1,795 78	1,913 53	2,039 13	2,222 5?	2,496 84
Pennsylvania,	45 3	199 16	250 18	265 77	440 36	493 67	626 16	650 89	644 82
Delaware,	-	80 22	193 65	229 45	260 81	322 72	509 57	539 38	553 20
Maryland,	1,333 74	4,832 18	6,078 89	7,110 93	6,971 28	7,278 41	7,638 42	8,063 86	8,174 84
Virginia,	2,015 9	3,844 58	3,653 24	3,947 90	4,494 91	4,459 39	4,963 26	5,341 49	5,824 61
North-Carolina,	1,115 93	1,737 15	1,778 32	1,980 4	1,914 86	1,913 82	2,011 15	1,947 83	1,983 42
South-Carolina,	-	85 1	96 26	375 59	303 94	339 44	350 43	366 42	346 93
Georgia,	-	47 56	17 86	23 54	17 86	56 23	95 55	103 88	76 38
Total,	7,217 53	16,977 36	19,601 59	22,416 66	23,325 64	24,099 43	25,736 43	27,196 91	28,296 19

404

TABLE No. II.—CONTINUED.

STATES.	1802. Tons. 95.	1803. Tons. 95.	1804. Tons. 95.	1805. Tons. 95.	1806. Tons. 95.	1807. Tons. 95.	1808. Tons. 95.	1809. Tons. 95.	1810. Tons. 95.
New-Hampshire,	96 65	60 94	85 27	53 84	72 68	78 16	86 47	117 23	133 56
Massachusetts,	3,356 3	3,680 93	3,435 63	3,479 35	3,285 13	3,452 36	4,047 88	3,759 67	3,739 60
Rhode-Island,	492 90	550 80	515 63	419 80	419 13	475 2	322 59	361 22	329 42
Connecticut,	1,442 45	1,378 48	1,315 44	1,217 89	1,160 11	1,264 67	1,339 24	1,433 8	1,387 88
New-York,	2,752 50	3,071 30	3,303 77	3,373 28	3,501 5	3,695 35	3,822 36	3,978 63	4,051 82
New-Jersey,	2,612 89	2,490 48	2,433 66	2,341 67	2,342 35	2,242 29	2,885 90	2,549 93	2,538 19
Pennsylvania,	631 79	858 25	859 94	984 45	1,043 73	1,085 17	1,216 34	1,424 3	1,547 49
Delaware,	585 6	608 42	604 34	637 29	615 19	624 93	644 35	634 2	687 45
Maryland,	8,240 1	8,243 85	7,973 10	7,954 9	7,163 28	7,275 67	7,511 20	7,489 78	7,493 80
District of Columbia,			868 69	942 75	1,029 76	1,090 81	1,205 93	1,206 91	1,342 25
Virginia,	6,386 33	6,699 6	6,531 5	6,674 29	6,939 11	6,512 46	6,828 20	6,965 90	7,300 51
North-Carolina,	2,004 41	2,241 54	2,239 7	2,426 79	2,471 80	2,637 55	2,860 10	2,970 66	2,920 18
South-Carolina,	364 48	384 12	403 59	364 48	15 7	15 7	30 48	100 34	123 83
Georgia,	113 78	115 82	82 45	110 42	107 60	98 49	90 38	111 69	107 33
Orleans Territory,	-	-	44 58	315 94	396 30	290 9	243 56	558 31	528 86
Total,	29,079 58	30,384 34	30,696 56	31,296 73	30,562 54	30,838 39	33,135 33	33,661 75	34,232 57

TABLE No. III.

Statement of the amount of American and Foreign Tonnage, respectively employed in Foreign Trade, for each of the years 1790 to 1799, as taken from the Records of the Treasury.

YEARS.	American tonnage in foreign trade.	Foreign tonnage.	Total amount of tonnage employed in the foreign trade of the United States.	Proportion of foreign tonnage to the whole amount of tonnage employed in the foreign trade of the United States.
1790	354,767	251,058	605,825	41.4 to 100
1791	363,662	240,740	604,402	39.8 — do.
1792	414,679	244,278	658,957	37. — do.
1793	447,754	164,676	612,430	26.8 — do.
1794	525,649	84,521	610,170	13.8 — do.
1795	580,277	62,549	642,826	9.7 — do.
1796	675,046	49,960	725,006	6.9 — do.
1797	608,078	76,693	684,771	11.2 — do.
1798	522,245	88,566	610,811	14.5 — do.
1799	626,495	109,599	736,094	14.9 — do.
Average of the three years 1790 to 1792,	377,702	245,358	623,060	39.4 to 100
Average of the six years 1793 to 1798,	559,841	87,827	647,668	13.6 to do.

TREASURY DEPARTMENT,

Register's Office, *December 12th, 1801.*

JOSEPH NOURSE, *Register.*

TABLE No. IV.

A comparative statement of the Tonnage of Vessels entered into the United States, from 1st January, 1790, to 31st December, 1796.

	UNITED STATES VESSELS.			Vessels owned in part by Americans & foreigners.	Vessels foreign built owned by Americans.	Vessels American built owned by foreigners.	Great-Britain.	France.
	In foreign trade.	In coasting trade.	In fishing trade.					
	Tons.	Tons.	Tons.	Tons.	Tons.	Tons.	Tons.	Tons.
For the year 1790 -	354,767	103,775	28,348	312	-	-	216,914	12,059
1791 -	363,662	106,494	32,542	192	-	-	210,618	8,988
1792 -	414,679	120,957	32,062	-	-	-	206,065	24,343
1793 -	447,754	141,639	38,177	-	1,497	1,110	100,180	45,287
1794 -	525,649	192,686	27,260	-	5,443	50	37,058	11,249
1795 -	580,277	171,918	34,102	-	3,114	274	27,097	7,425
1796 -	675,046	200,372	38,920	-		-	19,669	2,055

TO WHAT NATION BELONGING.

TABLE No. IV.—CONTINUED.

TO WHAT NATION BELONGING.

	Spain.	Portugal	Italy.	United Netherlands.	Imperial.	Hanse Towns.	Denmark.	Sweden.	Prussia.	Russia.
	Tons.	Tons.	Tons.	Tons.	Tons.	Tons.	Tons.	Tons.	Tons.	Tons.
For the year 1790	7,381	3,777	-	6,136	459	1,978	1,113	535	394	-
1791	4,337	4,766	-	3,751	2,326	2,989	2,092	361	-	320
1792	2,692	2,341	-	3,557	-	3,214	1,159	907	-	-
1793	3,090	3,153	458	577	4,972	1,166	2,364	2,319	-	-
1794	2,230	6,044	192	417	978	4,373	9,390	11,043	-	-
1795	1,999	738	409	1,128	1,077	4,006	8,637	4,316	-	-
1796	2,449	637	758	301	-	4,987	10,430	5,560	-	-

TREASURY DEPARTMENT,

REGISTER's OFFICE, *April 5th,* 1798.

JOSEPH NOURSE, *Register.*

APPENDIX No. I.

—◆—

THE country, or vice-royalty, of New-Spain and its dependencies, adjoins Louisiana; the following brief account of the coinage and commerce of that country, and particularly that part of the commerce carried on from the port of Vera Cruz, cannot be uninteresting to an American merchant or statesman. It was taken from accurate documents on the spot, in 1810, by a gentleman of ability, and may be therefore depended on as correct.

The country is very extensive, includes the province and city of Mexico, and contains the most valuable silver mines in the world. The city of Mexico is much more populous, than any city, either in North or South America. By the last census or enumeration, it contained upwards of one hundred and eighty thousand inhabitants; and in 1809, the number of births in the city, was 6,693, and the deaths, 6,160. Judging by this, its population is about one third of that of London or Paris. The coinage of gold and silver is carried on in the mint, which is established in the city of Mexico.

In 1809, the whole coinage was as follows, viz. :—

In Gold,	-	-	-	$1,464,818
In Silver,	-	-	-	24,708,164
Making the whole coinage for 1809,			-	$26,172,982

If we add to this, the amount coined from the first establishment of the mint in 1630, to the end of the year 1808, a space of 178 years, being - - - - - 1,496,832,112

It forms the enormous total of coinage, from the first foundation of the mint, of - $1,523,005,094

The commerce of New-Spain is carried on, principally, from the port of Vera Cruz, on the Gulph of Mexico, and Acapulco, on the Pacific Ocean.

The commerce carried on from the port of Vera Cruz, in 1809, was as follows :—

IMPORTS.

		Dolls.
From Old Spain, { National produce and manufactures,		10,252,698
Foreign, do. do.		6,914,607
		$17,167,305

From the Colonies. { Colonial industry, -	$1,643,018	
Effects from Europe,	1,620,183	
		3,263,201
Total amount of importations for 1809,	-	$20,430,506

EXPORTS.

		Dolls.
To Old Spain, - - - - -		21,825,226
To the Colonies, - - - - -		6,452,307
Total amount of exports for 1809,	-	$28,277,533

COASTING TRADE FROM THE SAME PORT.

Imports, - - - - - -	$624,012
Exports, - - - - - -	346,711

In the year 1809, there arrived from Old Spain, square	
rigged vessels, - - - - - -	119
From the Colonies, - - - - -	172
Total, - - - - - -	291

In the same period, cleared out for Old Spain, - -	62
Do. do. do. for the Colonies, -	177
Total, - - - - - -	239

The imports and exports, on Government account, are not included in the foregoing statement ; they amount to very considerable sums. Government imports principally quicksilver for the mines, playing cards, paper, &c. &c

and the exports consist, in money, gold, silver, tobacco, gun-powder, copper, tin, lead, &c. The money alone exported by Government in 1809, exceeded twenty-five millions of dollars.

		Dolls.
The gold coin exported by individuals in 1809, was	-	13,052
Silver do. do. do. was	-	21,761,188
Total amount of specie exported by individuals and contained in the above statement of exports for 1809,	-	21,774,240
To which may be added the specie exported by Government, during the same period, and which may be stated, at least to be - - - -		25,000,000
Makes the grand total of cash exported in 1809,	-	$46,774,240

Although this statement appears enormous, yet it is under-rated, for though the coinage during the year 1809, was only twenty-six millions, yet it must be recollected, that since the year 1804, in which the war broke out with Great-Britain, but a small proportion of money had been exported, and of course much had been accumulated. The exports of flour from Vera Cruz, to the Havanna, in the year 1809, was twenty-six thousand seven hundred and twenty-four bales, of two quintals each, upwards of twenty-seven thousand barrels. New-Spain is a beautiful wheat country, and could supply not only the Island of Cuba, but all Spanish America.

The articles of produce and manufacture exported from New-Spain, are cotton, indigo, sugar, cocoa, coffee, flour, horns, lard, rice, cheese, jerked beef, soap, allspice, anniseed, venilla bean, sarsaparilla, bark, jallap, dye-woods, oil or extract thereof, leather, morocco, cordovan and sole, hides and deer skins, cochineal, wool, tin, copper, lead, pearls, gold and silver, in bullion and coined, gold leaf for gilders' use, earthern ware from the manufactory of Xalapa, cloths, hats, &c. &c. &c. In the year 1809, the produce of the interiour brought down to Vera Cruz, took up fifty-three thousand seven hundred and eighteen mules.

APPENDIX No. II.

PROPOSED RESOLUTIONS ON FINANCE, TRADE, AND COMMERCE; 8th July, 1813.

No. 1.

That the supplies, voted for the service of the United Kingdom, for the several years 1803, 1804, 1805, 1806, 1807, 1808, 1809, 1810, 1811, 1812, and 1813, inclusive, may be stated as follows:—

	1803. £.	1804. £.	1805. £.	1806. £.	1807. £.	1808. £.
Army, including extraordinary	11,786,000	19,108,000	18,581,000	18,507,000	19,875,000	19,439,000
Navy, - - - -	10,211,000	12,350,000	13,967,000	15,994,000	17,399,000	8,317,000
Ordnance, - - -	920,000	3,737,000	4,457,000	4,198,000	3,321,000	3,713,000
Subsidy, - - -	-	-	-		180,000	1,400,000
Vote of credit, - -	2,000,000	2,300,000	3,500,000	3,000,000	5,000,000	2,700,000
Miscellaneous, - -	1,627,000	1,947,000	*2,179,000	†2,731,000	1,756,000	1,454,000
Total,	26,544,000	39,442,000	42,684,000	44,430,000	47,531,000	47,023,000
Proportion of Great-Britain, 15/17	23,421,000	34,802,000	37,663,000	39,203,000	41,939,000	41,491,000
Proportion of Ireland, 2/17	3,123,000	4,640,000	5,021,000	5,227,000	5,592,000	5,532,000

* Anno 1805, including £1,000,000; voted for the re-payment to the East-India Company for expenses incurred by them in India, upon the public account.

† Anno 1806, do. £1,000,000: do.

No. 1.—CONTINUED.

	1809. £.	1810. £.	1811. £.	1812. £.	1813. £.
Army, including extraordinary,	21,144,000	20,337,000	21,286,000	25,264,000	33,089,000
Navy,	19,578,000	19,829,000	20,935,000	20,362,000	21,212,000
Ordnance,	5,311,000	3,819,000	4,352,000	4,620,000	4,464,000
Subsidy,	700,000	1,380,000	2,400,000	2,400,000	3,400,000
Vote of credit,	3,300,000	3,200,000	3,200,000	3,200,000	5,200,000
Miscellaneous,	1,462,000	1,900,000	1,756,000	2,047,000	*4,185,000
Total,	51,495,000	50,465,000	53,929,000	57,893,000	71,550,000
Proportion of Great-Britain, $\frac{15}{17}$,	45,437,000	44,528,000	47,595,000	51,782,000	63,133,000
Proportion of Ireland, $\frac{2}{17}$,	6,058,000	5,937,000	6,334,000	6,811,000	8,417,000

* Anno 1813, including £2,000,000 ; voted for the re-payment to the East-India Company for expenses incurred by them in India, upon the public account.

No. 2.

That the money raised, or voted to be raised, in the same years, (1803 to 1813) in Great Britain, for the service of Great-Britain, by taxes and by borrowing, may be respectively stated as follows:—

	1803. £.	1804. £.	1805. £.	1806. £.	1807. £.	1808. £.
Actual surplus, consolidated fund,	4,561,002	2,452,857	3,559,591	3,746,077	4,476,870	3,141,827
Annual duties,	2,750,000	2,750,000	2,750,000	2,750,000	2,750,000	3,000,000
War taxes,	4,500,000	15,440,000	14,500,000	18,000,000	19,800,000	20,000,000
Lottery,	400,000	250,000	300,000	380,000	350,000	350,000
Total taxes,	12,211,002	20,892,857	21,109,591	24,876,077	27,376,870	26,491,827
MONEY BORROWED.						
Loan,	10,000,000	10,000,000	20,000,000	18,000,000	12,200,000	8,000,000
EXCHEQUER BILLS.						
Funded,	-	-	-	-	-	4,000,000
Total, money borrowed,	10,000,000	10,000,000	20,000,000	18,000,000	12,200,000	12,000,000
Total, money raised, &c.	22,211,002	30,892,857	41,109,591	42,876,077	39,576,870	38,491,827

No. 2.—CONTINUED.

	1809. £.	1810. £.	1811. £.	1812. £.	1813. £.
Actual surplus, consolidated fund, -	7,019,774	5,753,715	4,073,531	1,245,983	500,000
Annual duties, - - -	3,000,000	3,000,000	3,000,000	3,000,000	3,000,000
War taxes, - - -	19,000,000	19,500,000	20,000,000	20,400,000	21,000,000
Lottery, - - -	300,000	350,000	300,000	300,000	200,000
Total taxes,	29,319,774	28,603,715	27,373,531	24,945,983	24,700,000
MONEY BORROWED.					
Loan, - - - -	11,000,000	8,000,000	12,481,300	22,439,625	21,000,000
EXCHEQUER BILLS.					
Funded, - - -	7,932,100	8,311,000	7,018,700	5,431,700	15,755,700
Debentures, - - -	-	-	-	-	800,000
Total money borrowed,	18,932,100	16,311,000	19,500,000	27,871,325	37,555,700
Total money raised, &c.	48,251,874	44,914,715	46,873,531	50,610,950	62,255,700

(1*.) Exclusive of £3,000,000 lent by the bank, and included in the account of unfunded debt, and exclusive also of £500,000 advanced by the bank out of unclaimed dividends.

(2*.) Exclusive of £600,000 raised for Portugal.

(3*.) Exclusive of the sum of £4,500,000 appropriated for the service of Ireland, but the charge of which has hitherto been defrayed by Great-Britain.

(4*.) Exclusive of £2,500,000 raised for the East-India Company.

No. 3.

That the money raised for the service of Ireland, by taxes, and by borrowing, in the same years, (1803 to 1813) may be respectively stated as follows, (in Irish currency.)

	1803.	1804.	1805.	1806.	1807.	1808.	1809.	1810.	1811.	1812.	1813.
	£.	£.	£.	£.	£.	£.	£.	£.	£.	£.	£.
Actual produce of the ordinary revenues pd. into the exchequer,	2,823,670	3,293,372	3,399,561	3,884,968	4,448,242	4,633,449	4,335,016	3,673,714	4,241,035	4,975,000	5,200,000
Mon. raised { G.Britain, by loan, in { Ireland,	2,166,666 11,000	4,875,000 1,250,000	4,333,333 - -	2,166,666 2,000,000	3,791,666 53,000	2,708,333 2,000,000	3,250,000 1,250,000	5,850,000 6,198	*4,875,000 2,501,000	4,712,500 1,513,000	6,500,000 2,000,000
Total revenue and loans,	5,001,336	9,418,372	7,732,894	8,051,634	8,292,908	9,341,782	8,835,016	9,529,912	11,671,035	11,200,500	13,700,000

* The interest and charges of this loan have been defrayed by Great-Britain.

No. 4.

That the amount of the public funded debt of Great-Britain, redeemed and unredeemed; the annual charges of each year, together with the sinking fund applicable to the reduction of debt, may, for the years ending 1st February, 1804, 1805, 1806, 1807, 1808, 1809, 1810, 1811, 1812, and 1813, be stated as follows :—

| Years ending 1st February, | Total debt. | DEBT. | | Annual charge of unredeemed debt. | Sinking fund. | Total annual charge respecting the debt. | Proportion of sinking fund to the unredeemed debt. |
		Unredeemed.	Redeemed.				
	£.	£.	£.	£.	£.	£.	
1804	583,008,978	484,162,622	98,846,355	17,795,194	6,282,947	24,078,142	1-77th.
1805	603,925,792	493,127,726	110,798,066	18,055,154	6,834,114	24,889,269	1-72d.
1806	640,752,103	517,280,561	123,471,542	18,720,048	7,566,539	26,286,588	1-68th.
1807	669,652,846	533,076,124	136,576,722	19,157,176	8,237,288	27,394,464	1-64th.
1808	687,689,958	536,776,026	151,913,931	18,894,987	9,291,913	28,186,900	1-57th.
1809	701,229,515	535,741,052	165,488,462	19,005,325	9,843,674	28,848,999	1-54th.
1810	722,466,770	541,977,854	180,488,916	19,468,190	10,509,392	29,977,582	1-51st.
1811	742,239,101	545,662,698	196,576,403	19,763,797	11,171,949	30,935,746	1-48th.
1812	771,370,396	556,284,819	215,085,577	20,418,318	11,992,814	32,411,132	1-46th.
1813	812,013,135	575,211,393	236,801,742	21,274,650	13,013,914	34,288,564	1-44th.

No. 5.

That the amount of the public funded debt of Ireland, redeemed and unredeemed; the annual charges of each year, together with the sinking fund, applicable to the reduction of debt, may, for the years ended 5th January, 1804, 1805, 1806, 1807, 1808, 1809, 1810, 1811, 1812, and 1813, be stated as follows, (in Irish currency.)—

Years end. 5th January,	Total debt.	DEBT.		Annual charge of unredeemed debt.	Sinking fund.	Total annual charge of debt exclusive of management.	Proportion of sinking fund to the unredeemed debt.
	£.	Unredeemed. £.	Redeemed. £.	£.	£.	£.	
1804	43,019,325	40,143,149	2,876,176	1,578,111	552,133	2,130,245	1·72d.
1805	53,296,356	49,533,452	3,762,904	1,882,732	686,683	2,569,415	1·72d.
1806	58,344,690	53,504,734	4,839,955	2,085,388	781,792	2,867,180	1·68th.
1807	64,721,356	58,619,940	6,101,416	2,249,773	886,372	3,136,148	1·66th.
1808	70,647,783	63,140,826	7,506,957	2,392,939	989,384	3,282,224	1·63d.
1809	76,110,856	67,132,027	8,978,829	2,572,537	1,090,376	3,662,914	1·61st.
1810	81,510,856	70,931,541	10,579,315	2,715,068	1,205,946	3,921,017	1·58th.
1811	89,728,992	77,382,908	12,346,083	2,871,883	1,377,918	4,249,804	1·56th.
1812	92,729,992	78,274,685	14,455,307	2,901,883	1,482,971	4,384,854	1·52d.
1813	102,836,992	85,950,647	16,886,345	3,142,126	1,661,042	4,803,168	1·51st.

No. 6.

That the amount of the unfunded debt of Great-Britain, under the heads of Navy Debt, and Exchequer Bills outstanding, may, for the years 1804, 1805, 1806, 1807, 1808, 1809, 1810, 1811, 1812, and 1813, be stated as follows:—

Years ending 5th January,	Navy debt.	Exchequer bills outstanding.	Total.
	£.	£.	£.
1804 -	4,037,307	19,067,600	23,104,907
1805 -	5,001,567	25,253,500	30,255,067
1806 -	5,911,588	27,180,400	33,0:'1,988
1807 -	5,885,819	27,207,500	33,043,319
1808 -	6,561,237	31,942,900	38,504,137
1809 -	7,221,167	39,301,200	46,522,367
1810 -	8,263,175	39,164,100	47,427,275
1811 -	7,595,838	38,286,000	47,681,838
1812 -	7,883,890	41,491,800	49,375,690
1813 -	7,748,872	45,406,400	53,155,372

No. 7.

That the amount of the unfunded debt of Ireland, under the head of Treasury Bills outstanding and unprovided for, in the years ending 5th January, 1804, 1805, 1806, 1807, 1808, 1809, 1810, 1811, 1812, and 1813, may be stated as follows:—

Years ending 5th January,	Irish Currency £.
1804 -	1,999,000
1805 -	1,099,000
1806 -	299,000
1807 -	- -
1808 -	400,000
1809 -	541,666
1810 -	655,729
1811 -	114,062
1812 -	1,840,479
1813 -	2,508,940

No. 8.

That the net produce of the new, and additional duties, imposed in Great-Britain, in each year, from the 5th January, 1803, to the present year, on an average of the two years, last past, or of the last two years thereof a separate account has been laid before Parliament, was respectively as follows :—

Year ended	Permanent Taxes.	War Taxes.		Total.
5th Jan.	£	£	£	£
1804	578,188	{ Customs & excise, 7,299,056 } { Property, - - 4,891,501 }	12,190,557	12,768,745
1805	960,346	{ Customs taken at the estimated amount for this year, and which with part of the sum included in the preceding year under the head, customs and excise, makes the total actual produce of the temporary or war duty in the two last years— }	1,000,000	1,960,346
1806	1,506,877	Property, - - - - - -	1,417,886	2,924,763
1807	996,779	{ Excise, - - - 518,617 } { Property, - - 6,555,571 }	7,074,188	8,070,967
1808	- -	Excise - - - - - - -	63,681	63,681
1809	*1,222,287	- - - - - - - - - -	- -	1,222,287
1810	105,000	- - - - - - - - - -	- -	105,000
1811	- -	- - - - - - - - - -	- -	- -
1812	†466,101	Customs, - - - - - -	64,790	530,891
1813	‡646,409	Excise, - - - - - - -	15,699	662,108

* Exclusive of, £375,000, short annuities expired, and £65,000, saving on management of public debt.

† The produce of the only complete year the duties have been in existence.

‡ Actual produce from 5th July, 1812, to 5th July, 1813, including the estimated amount of linen bounties repealed.

No. 9.

That the total sum, to be provided, by Great-Britain, within the year 1813, *may be estimated as follows :—*

	£	£
Interest on the public funded debt, charges of management, and sinking fund including the addition to the sinking fund in the present session	34,939,534	
Interest on imperial loan, - - - -	496,277	35,435,811
Proportion to be defrayed by Great-Britain of the following charges viz.—Civil Government of Scotland, pensions on revenue, militia and deserters warrants, bounties for promoting fisheries, &c. for the United Kingdom, estimated to be the same as in the year ended 5th Jan. 1813,	835,000	
Charges of collection and management of the revenue of Great-Britain and Ireland, estimated to be the same as in the year ended 5th Jan. 1813,	4,099,000	
Civil list and other charges on the consolidated fund of Great-Britain, and civil list and permanent grants for Ireland, estimated to be the same as in the year ended 5th January, 1813, -	2,038,000	
15-17 of -	£6,972,000	6,152,000

SEPARATE CHARGES OF GREAT-BRITAIN.

		£
On the consolidated fund, estimated as at 5th January, 1813, - - £ 35,000		
Loyalty loan repaid, - - - - - 171,836		
Interest on exchequer bills, - - - 1,800,000		
Do. on debentures, - - - - - - 40,000		
Grant to sinking fund in respect to exchequer bills unprovided for, - - 260,000		
To discharge exchequer bills issued on account of the vote of credit, Anno. 1812, - - - - - - - 3,000,000		5,307,136

	£	
Supplies voted 1813 for Great-Britain & Ireland including a vote of credit of £5,200,000	71,550,000	
Deduct, proportion of supplies to be defrayed by Ireland, . - - - -	8,417,000	63,133,000
		£110,028,947

No. 10.

That the total sum, to be provided by Ireland within the year 1813, may be esti-mated as follows :—

			Irish Curr'y.
Interest of public funded debt, charge of management and sinking fund, including charges on the loan for present session, - - - - - - - - - -			£
			5,425,400
Proportion to be defrayed by Ireland of the following charges, viz.—			
Civil Government of Scotland (Pensions to the Hereditary revenue of G. Britain) &c. &c. (same as No. 9.) - - - - - - -		905,100	
Charges of collection and management of the revenues of Great-Britain & Ireland, &c. &c. (same as No. 9.) - - - - - -		4,441,000	
Civil list and other permanent charges on the consolidated fund of G. Britain, &c. &c. (same as No. 9.) - - - - - - -		2,207,800	
2-17 of -		£7,553,900	888,700
SEPARATE CHARGES OF IRELAND, VIZ.—			
Interest on exchequer bills, - £125,500			
Grant to sinking fund in respect to treasury bills, - - - 21,604			
		£	147,104
Supplies voted 1813 for G. B. and Ireland including a vote of credit of £5,200,000 British, -		77,512,500	
Deduct, proportion of supplies to be defrayed by Great-Britain, - - - - -		68,394,000	9,118,500
			£15,579,704

No. 11.

That the total official value of imports, into Great-Britain, in the years ended 5th January, 1804, 1805, 1806, 1807, 1808, 1809, 1810, 1811, 1812, and 1813, may be taken as follows:—

Years ended 5th January,	Foreign and colonial produce.	Irish produce.	East-India and China.	Total.
	£.	£.	£.	£.
1804 -	21,643,577 ⎱	includ.Ireland	6,348,887 ⎱	27,992,464
1805 -	23,986,869 ⎰		5,214,621 ⎰	29,201,490
1806 -	21,292,870	2,979,598	6,072,160	30,344,628
1807 -	21,841,005	3,248,131	3,746,771	28,835,907
1808 -	21,958,382	3,494,767	3,401,509	28,854,658
1809 -	19,869,723	3,910,981	5,848,649	29,629,353
1810 -	26,933,625	3,475,759	3,363,025	33,772,409
1811 -	33,146,975	3,280,747	4,708,413	41,136,135
1812 -	21,201,450	3,318,879	4,106,251	28,626,580
1813 -	19,443,574	3,551,269	Not yet made up.	

No. 12.

That the total official value of exports, from Great-Britain, in the years ended the 5th January, 1804, 1805, 1806, 1807, 1808, 1809, 1810, 1811, 1812, and 1813, may be taken as follows:—

Years ended 5th January,	British produce & manufactures.	Foreign and colonial merchandize.	Irish produce and manufactures.	Total.
	£.	£.	£.	£.
1804 -	22,252,027	9,326,468 ⎱	Includ. Irish	31,578,495 ⎱
1805 -	23,935,793	10,515,575 ⎰	produce.	34,451,367 ⎰
1806 -	25,004,337	9,552,423	398,085	34,954,845
1807 -	27,402,685	8,789,368	335,131	36,527,184
1808 -	25,171,422	9,105,827	289,322	34,566,571
1809 -	26,691,962	7,397,901	464,404	34,554,267
1810 -	35,104,132	14,680,524	502,244	50,286,900
1811 -	34,923,575	10,471,941	474,343	45,869,859
1812 -	24,131,734	7,975,396	302,541	32,409,671
1813 -	31,243,362	11,508,673	489,506	43,241,541

No. 13.

That the number of Vessels, with the amount of their Tonnage, which have been built and registered in the several ports of the British Empire, (except Ireland) may be stated as follows :—

Year ended 5th January	Ships.	Tonnage.
1804 -	1,402	135,349
1805 -	991	95,979
1806 -	1,001	89,584
1807 -	772	69,198
1808 -	770	68,000
1809 -	568	57,140
1810 -	596	61,396
1811 -	685	84,891
1812 -	870	115,630
1813 -	760	94,198

No. 14.

That the number of Vessels, with the amount of their Tonnage, and the number of Men and Boys usually employed in navigating the same, which belonged to the several ports of the British Empire, (except Ireland) on the 30th September, 1803, 1804, 1805, 1806, 1807, 1808, 1809, 1810, 1811, and 1812, may be stated as follows :—

Year ended 30th September,	Ships.	Tons.	Men.
1803 -	19,828	2,108,990	148,600
1804 -	20,713	2,210,508	148,598
1805 -	20,984	2,226,636	152,642
1806 -	21,106	2,208,169	150,940
1807 -	21,192	2,224,720	152,658
1808 -	21,542	2,265,860	151,781
1809 -	21,951	2,307,489	155,038
1810 -	22,577	2,367,394	158,779
1811 -	22,973	2,415,619	157,063
1812 -	22,996	2,421,695	159,710

No. 15.

That the number of Vessels, with the amount of their Tonnage, and the number of Men and Boys, employed in navigating the same (including their repeated voyages) which entered inwards, at the several ports of Great-Britain, from all parts of the world, in the years ended 5th January, 1804, 1805, 1806, 1807, 1808, 1809, 1810, 1811, 1812, and 1813, may be stated as follows :—

Year ended 5th January,	BRITISH.			FOREIGN.		
	Ships.	Tons.	Men.	Ships	Tons.	Men.
1804 -	11,996	1,614,365	93,004	4,252	638,034	33,660
1805 -	10,508	1,395,387	82,979	4,271	607,299	30,744
1806 -	11,409	1,494,075	87,148	4,515	691,703	34,719
1807 -	12,110	1,482,412	88,963	3,792	612,800	31,346
1808 -	11,213	1,436,667	84,997	4,087	680,144	32,488
1809 -	11,316	1,314,241	82,754	1,925	282,892	15,512
1810 -	12,656	1,539,573	95,796	4,922	759,287	38,285
1811 -	13,557	1,609,088	102,900	6,876	1,176,243	60,094
1812 -	12,908	1,522,692	94,740	3,216	687,180	34,157
1813 -	13,869	1,579,715	96,371	2,536	518,443	25,519

No. 16.

That the number of Vessels, with the amount of their Tonnage, and the number of Men and Boys, employed in navigating the same (including their repeated voyages) which cleared outwards, at the several ports of Great-Britain, to all parts of the world, in the years ended 5th January, 1804 to 1813, inclusive, may be stated as follows :—

Years ended 5th January,	BRITISH.			FOREIGN.		
	Ships.	Tons.	Men.	Ships	Tons.	Men.
1804 -	11,072	1,444,840	92,940	3,662	574,542	30,414
1805 -	11,131	1,463,286	93,748	4,093	587,849	30,507
1806 -	11,603	1,494,968	94,388	3,930	605,641	30,910
1807 -	12,239	1,485,725	94,513	3,457	567,988	29,616
1808 -	11,428	1,424,103	89,715	3,846	631,910	31,411
1809 -	11,923	1,372,810	89,632	1,892	282,145	15,671
1810 -	11,499	1,531,152	102,523	4,530	699,750	37,256
1811 -	13,092	1,624,274	107,724	6,641	1,138,527	60,870
1812 -	12,774	1,507,353	96,739	3,350	696,232	37,262
1813 -	14,328	1,665,518	105,004	2,647	540,902	27,841

No. 17.

*That the official value, in Irish currency, of all imports into, and exports from
Ireland, for ten years, ending 5th January, 1813, distinguishing each year
and the value of foreign articles exported, was as follows:—*

Years ending the 5th January,	Official value of exports.	Official value of	
		Irish produce and manufactures exported	Foreign & colonial merchandize exported.
1804 -	5,275,650	4,629,086	141,302
1805 -	5,712,802	4,903,261	171,179
1806 -	5,736,214	5,059,867	142,481
1807 -	5,605,959	5,033,354	157,666
1808 -	6,637,907	5,307,806	150,370
1809 -	7,129,507	5,696,897	234,112
1810 -	7,471,557	5,408,910	330,933
1811 -	6,564,578	5,471,012	627,472
1812 -	7,234,603	5,833,996	256,415
1813 -	8,820,359	6,463,744	404,424

No. 18.

*That the number of Vessels, with the amount of their Tonnage, that were built
and registered, in the several ports of Ireland, in the ten years, ending 5th
January, 1813, was as follows:—*

Years ended 5th January,	Vessels.	Tons.
1804 -	42	2,418
1805 -	38	1,611
1806 -	28	1,212
1807 -	41	1,687
1808 -	33	1,838
1809 -	32	1,235
1810 -	31	1,643
1811 -	21	1,331
1812 -	41	1,655
1813 -	50	1,952

No. 19.

*That the number of Vessels, with the amount of their Tonnage, and number of
Men and Boys usually employed in navigating them, which belonged to the
several ports of Ireland, in the ten years, ending 30th September, 1812, distinguishing each year, was as follows:—*

Years ending 30th September,	Ships.	Tons.	Men.
1803 - -	1,065	58,871	5,218
1804 - -	1,061	58,060	5,176
1805 - -	1,067	56,755	5,062
1806 - -	1,076	55,545	5,081
1807 - -	1,098	56,902	5,217
1808 - -	1,104	68,958	5,324
1809 - -	1,119	61,150	5,560
1810 - -	1,126	58,646	5,416
1811 -	1,133	59,154	5,484
1812 - -	1,111	57,103	5,320

No. 20.

That the number of vessels, with the amount of their tonnage, and the number of men and boys employed in navigating the same, (including their repeated voyages) and entered inwards, in the several ports of Ireland, from, or to all parts of the world: in the ten years ending 5th Jan. 1813—distinguishing each year, and the Irish, British, and foreign vessels, was as follows :—

Years ending 5th Jan.	INWARDS.								
	IRISH.			BRITISH.			FOREIGN.		
	Ships	Tons.	Men.	Ships	Tons.	Men.	Ships	Tons.	Men.
1804 -	1,315	97,946	6,529	5,996	569,704	32,286	600	94,800	6,159
1805 -	1,243	90,541	6,116	6,242	610,618	33,553	534	79,778	5,182
1806 -	1,276	91,290	6,230	6,139	580,752	33,775	545	82,420	5,539
1807 -	1,497	102,163	7,049	6,687	630,368	36,818	498	80,001	5,055
1808 -	1,503	107,733	7,231	6,836	652,946	36,539	461	78,533	4,674
1809 -	1,583	111,614	7,485	7,189	696,403	38,426	159	25,326	1,580
1810 -	1,546	103,698	7,217	5,975	535,299	30,648	343	56,946	3,525
1811 -	1,982	130,991	8,983	7,514	673,540	38,536	660	119,188	6,643
1812 -	1,956	133,748	9,125	7,404	686,255	39,504	644	129,994	6,673
1813 -	2,229	152,355	10,398	9,022	830,473	47,809	405	79,307	4,255

No. 21.

That the number of vessels, with the amount of their tonnage, and the number of men and boys employed in navigating the same, including their repeated voyages, that cleared outwards, in the several ports of Ireland, from, or to, all parts of the world: in the ten years, ending 5th January, 1813, distinguishing each year, and the Irish, British and foreign vessels, was as follows :—

Years ending 5th Jan.	OUTWARDS.								
	IRISH.			BRITISH.			FOREIGN.		
	Ships	Tons.	Men.	Ships	Tons.	Men.	Ships	Tons.	Men.
1804 -	1,211	90,254	6,324	5,160	509,387	29,368	553	93,995	5,728
1805 -	1,080	82,934	5,832	5,013	507,177	28,337	531	78,971	5,093
1806 -	1,172	90,173	6,077	5,442	535,761	30,648	521	77,783	4,910
1807 -	1,353	97,162	6,754	5,888	574,688	32,441	522	83,048	5,139
1808 -	1,320	97,856	6,797	6,294	615,702	34,631	418	72,662	4,130
1809 -	1,405	108,435	7,221	6,473	641,157	35,715	163	27,856	1,591
1810 -	1,527	109,144	7,398	5,877	538,699	30,477	333	56,267	3,225
1811 -	1,841	125,389	8,650	6,931	627,012	35,595	639	117,414	6,312
1812 -	1,853	129,031	8,651	6,865	642,767	36,051	621	126,588	6,265
1813 -	2,103	151,141	10,042	8,465	792,829	45,437	421	85,505	4,368

ERRATA.

Page 27, line 1, for " inclusive" read *exclusive*—page 33, last line, for " one" read *our*—page 35, line 1, for "those" read *these*—page 47, line 9, for "these" read *their*—page 76, Table No. VII. the *heading* inserted by mistake—page 92, line 10, strike out " in"—page 95, line 20, for " prices" read *price*—page 99, line 1, for " 1804" read 1814—page 102, Note, for " Peccohet's" read *Peuchet's*—page 105, line 15, for "parts" read *ports*—·page 110, line 26, for "1795" read 1793—page 116, line 20, for "the" before climate, read *her*—page 136, line 2, for " the" before citizens, read *their*—page 141, line 8, for " them" read *thence*—page 144, last line, for "chapter" read *chapters*—page 170, line 15, strike out the word " and" and figures VI.—page 172, line 10, for "negotiated" read *regulated*—page 196, line 21, for "pounds" read *tierces*—page 248, for " pounds" after the word " salt" read *bushels*—page 264, line 31, for " or" read *on*—page 290, line 10, strike out " and" between "lands *and* purchased"—page 301, line 12, for " 373" read 673, and for " 573" read 873—page 301, last line, for " purpose" read *purchase*—and page 306, Table No. II. line 35, for " redeemed" read *reduced*.